Design Thinking with Problem-Solving Techniques

AF660983

M.S. NARASSIMA
Assistant Professor
Great Lakes Institute of Management
Chennai

SHRIRAM K. VASUDEVAN
Technology Leader
Intel Corporation

SINI RAJ PULARI
Program Manager
Bahrain Polytechnic
Kingdom of Bahrain

PHI Learning Private Limited
Delhi-110092
2026

In fond memory of ***Shri Asoke K. Ghosh*** *(October 1942 – February 2024), Founder Chairman and Managing Director of PHI Learning, whose vision endlessly inspires.*

The Legacy Continues....

Published by Pushpita Ghosh, PHI Learning Private Limited, Rimjhim House, 111, Patparganj Industrial Estate, Delhi-110092 and Printed by Syndicate Binders, A-20, Hosiery Complex, Noida, Phase-II Extension, Noida-201305 (N.C.R. Delhi).

₹ 625.00

DESIGN THINKING WITH PROBLEM-SOLVING TECHNIQUES
M.S. Narassima, Shriram K. Vasudevan and Sini Raj Pulari

© 2026 by PHI Learning Private Limited, Delhi.

All right reserved. This publication is protected by copyright and may not be reproduced, in whole or in part, in any form or by any electronic, mechanical, or other means, now known or hereafter invented, including photocopying, recording, or any information storage and retrieval system, OR to train artificial intelligence systems without permission in writing from the publisher.

ISBN-978-93-5443-910-0 (Print Book)
ISBN-978-93-5443-905-6 (e-Book)

The export rights of this book are vested solely with the publisher.

Dedication

Parents, Wife, Mentors, Grandparents, with a special mention to Late Mr. Venkatraman (grandfather), and my students.

—Narassima

To the dearest kids Saihari, Smaran, Sailakshmi and Hasini

—Shriram

To Dr. Shriram, my Mentor and Friend, with gratitude for your invaluable guidance, support, and inspiration throughout my career.

—Sini

Contents

Preface

This book really began with a question that would not leave us alone: How can businesses and organisations consistently generate new ideas that genuinely benefit people? The business world today is a fast-moving, complicated place, and the old ways of just crunching numbers do not always cut it. Many companies struggle to keep up. So, it became pretty obvious we needed something different—something built on understanding people, thinking creatively, and trying things out over and over again. And that is where Design Thinking stepped in, offering a really solid, all-around way to tackle these tricky situations. As we wrote, we really tried to keep the language easy to get into. We aimed to break down some complex ideas and sophisticated methods so that they made sense without any fuss. We filled the pages with stories and examples from a wide range of companies worldwide, including names you would recognise. We did this to show that Design Thinking is not just a theory you read about; it is something you can use to make a big difference if you do it right. We set up the chapters so that you build up your understanding step by step. You will start with the basics and then gradually move into some of the more advanced methods for solving problems. You will also find plenty of hands-on exercises and questions that prompt you to think critically. We want you to be engaged what you are reading, try these ideas out in real life, and let them sink in. What we hope to achieve with this book is more than just sharing information. We want to give you a new way of looking at things, a particular mindset, and some real tools that help you tackle tough problems without flinching. The goal is to spark some genuine innovation and, hopefully, help you make some good, positive changes whether you are at work or in your own life. Hopefully, reading this will spark your curiosity, sharpen your problem-solving skills, and encourage you to become someone who thinks with empathy and has a knack for generating new ideas.

Narassima, M.S.
Shriram Vasudevan
Sini Raj Pulari

CHAPTER 1

Introduction to Design Thinking

LEARNING OBJECTIVES

After reading this Chapter, the readers will be able to:

- Understand the evolution and foundational concepts of Design Thinking.
- Identify the core concepts of Design Thinking: Human-centered approach.
- Understand the potential of Design Thinking through real-world examples.
- Appreciate the importance of empathy in fostering innovation.
- How to balance between various aspects of business while offering solutions.

1.1 THE BIRTH OF DESIGN THINKING

Problem-solving can be dated to the evolution of humans, a journey kick-started by our ancestors. From the inception of the Stone Age, or earlier, over time, with the emergence of discoveries, innovations, growing requirements of humans, formation of civilisations, governments, etc., survival became the most pressing problem. Earlier, humans grappled with finding appropriate shelter, food, and safety from predators. These led to the innovation of rudimentary tools, including fire, sharp-edged stones, etc. Humans intuitively developed the instinct of sharpening the tools for hunting, shaping them as required to be used for building shelters, contours that can hold food, etc. These tools underwent refinement over the ages based on the changing requirements and evolving ideas for betterment. These could be analogous to the simple algorithms developed, which form the basis of modern technology. In today's world, optimisation processes that reduce costs, increase profit and improve productivity could all be attributed to the refinement of tools at an early age. Although most human inventions happened because of some requirement, some groundbreaking innovations have accidentally happened across ages.

These were because of the ability of humans to keenly observe the surroundings and each phenomenon that took place around them. The capability to ask questions like "Why does a phenomenon take place?", "Why does it have to take place this way?", "What would happen if it occurs?", "How can these be beneficial?", "How can these be prevented if undesired?" further triggers the investigation of each happening(s) in daily life.

Pathbreaking innovations and inventions have occurred over the years as a result of understanding the requirements of humans, observing how nature works, analysing the patterns and causes of phenomena that occur around us, and others. Various thought processes have led to these innovations in India (Table 1.1) and worldwide (Table 1.2).

TABLE 1.1 Innovations as a result of Design Thinking in India

Year	*Innovation*	*Design thought Process and Expertise*	*Resulting Invention*
~3000 to 2000 BCE	Indus Valley Drainage and Urban Planning	Empathy for living as communities, sanitation, and civilisations. This gave birth to city or township layouts and collaboration among architects, engineers, and city planners.	Advanced planning for grid-structured cities and drainage systems.
~600 BCE	Ayurveda (Ancient Indian Medicine)	Compassion for holistic well-being and healthy lifestyle. This resulted from conscientious observations and trials on herbs and treatments and interdisciplinary collaboration among physicians, botanists, and scholars.	It is a natural medicinal system that still significantly impacts modern wellness practices.
3rd Century BCE	Ashokan Pillars and Edicts	Human-centric communication to educate and guide people. This arose from the iterative placement and improvement of the carvings and inscriptions by scholars, artisans, and architects.	Promotion of ethical conduct and governance principles through inscribed stone pillars with edicts.
~200 BCE	Kautilya's Arthashastra	Need to strengthen the military strategies to improve the operational effectiveness of governance and economic policies. A result of continuous monitoring of administrative systems involving collaboration between political scientists and economists.	A foundational treatise on military strategies, statecrafts, and economic policies.

Year	*Innovation*	*Design thought Process and Expertise*	*Resulting Invention*
16th Century	Step-wells	Human-centred perspective on water accessibility for societal use. This involved an iterative architectural advancement to optimise the structure, design, and stability. Engaged engineers, architects, and water management experts.	Ingeniously designed step-wells for water storage and access in arid regions.
18th Century	Mysorean Rockets by Tipu Sultan	Aimed to reinforce military capabilities. It demanded phased testing of metal casings for accuracy, capacity, and range. This fostered interdisciplinary collaboration between blacksmiths, military engineers, and metallurgists.	Advanced rockets formed the roots of the European advancements in rocketry.
18th Century	Jantar Mantar (Astronomical Observatories)	The requirement of precise astronomical measurements. This involved the careful design and manufacture of instruments with the help of astronomers, mathematicians, and architects.	Large-scale observatories for tracing celestial bodies and predicting star movements.
1853–1855	Railway System in India	Motivation to improve the transportation network across vast distances. This had exhaustive planning and development of routes and rails with the combined effort of engineers, surveyors, and British and Indian administrators.	An extensive railway network that bridged major cities and boosted trade.
1947–1951	Green Revolution Initiatives	Address the risk of food security and attain agricultural self-sufficiency. It involved testing of high-yield crops and methods with the combined expertise of agronomists, policymakers, and farmers.	Initiation of modern farming techniques and high-yielding seeds to improve production.
1980s	Jaipur Foot (Prosthetic Limb)	Human-centered approach to mobility and affordability. This underwent modifications for usability, comfort, and function. The innovation demands collaboration between orthopaedic specialists and craftsmen.	A plausible prosthetic limb to offer mobility to thousands of amputees.

(*Contd.*)

Year	Innovation	Design thought Process and Expertise	Resulting Invention
1990s	Amul Cooperative Model	Empathy to empower farmers and ensure fair pricing. This involved designing and developing a structured supply chain with intertwining between farmers, engineers, and business strategists.	A dairy cooperative society to revolutionise milk production and streamline distribution in India.
2008	Tata Nano	A human-centred approach was used to deliver an affordable car for families. Laborious engineering was employed to minimise costs while retaining safety and functions from auto-motive engineers, designers, and business planners.	The world's most affordable car for middle-income households.
2014	Mangalyaan (Mars Orbiter Mission)	The desire to explore space at a lower cost necessitated an iterative mission design with continuous budget management and collaboration between scientists, engineers, and policymakers.	India's first minimal-budget interplanetary mission that was successful at the first go.
2021	CoWIN Platform for COVID-19 Vaccination	A human-centred approach to managing mass vaccination efficiently with continuous data collection, update, and user interface improvements. It needed the efforts of IT profe-ssionals, healthcare experts, and government.	A digital platform that facilitated vaccination distribution, administration, and tracking.

TABLE 1.2 Innovations as a Result of Design Thinking Worldwide

Year	Innovation	Design Thought Process and Expertise	Resulting Invention
1440	Gutenberg Printing Press	Motivation to make written documents accessible to more people. It took iterative testing of movable mechanics involving collaboration between metalworking, ink production, and manuscript copying.	The first mechanical printing press to scale up learning and communication.
1503–1519	Leonardo da Vinci's Inventions	Keen observation of natural systems, iterative sketching and model-building. Required skills for blending art, engineering, and anatomy.	Prototypes for flying machines, hydraulic pumps, and early mechanics and robotics.

Year	*Innovation*	*Design Thought Process and Expertise*	*Resulting Invention*
1769	Watt Steam Engine	The need to improve the existing Newcomen engine's performance by experimenting with steam condensing and power output. Involved collaboration of mechanics and metalworkers.	The steam engine that fueled the Industrial Revolution.
1794	Eli Whitney's Cotton Gin	To ease the labour-intensive process of cotton separation, iterative development of comb-like mechanisms. This had collaboration between agricultural and mechanical fields.	The cotton gin reduced the processing time.
1824	Portland Cement by Joseph Aspdin	Concern to develop stronger building materials. Involved trials to refine the mixture and process that required expertise from chemistry and construction.	A stronger, more durable cement is the foundation for modern construction.
1876	Alexander Graham Bell's Telephone	Desire to push human communication over long distances. Electrical engineers and sound mechanics mandated testing with different electrical and mechanical systems.	The first practical telephone.
1879	Thomas Edison's Light Bulb	A human-centred approach to creating a safe, long-lasting light source. This needed rigorous testing of filaments and the knowledge of engineers and chemists.	The practical light bulb.
1940s	Polio Vaccine Development	Concern for public health and patient needs. Achieved through several clinical trials and collaboration among virologists and public health experts.	The first effective polio vaccine.
1969	The Apollo Guidance Computer	Need for dynamic and reinforced problem-solving with continuous testing and feedback. Demanded multidisciplinary efforts from engineers and scientists.	Computer-based guidance for Apollo 11 to the moon.
1970s	Development of the Post-it Note (3M)	Identifying the need for temporary notes. It involved testing of adhesive failures and deeper investigation within 3M.	The Post-it Note, an innovative office utility.

(*Contd.*)

Year	*Innovation*	*Design Thought Process and Expertise*	*Resulting Invention*
1984	Apple Macintosh	A human-centred approach to improving accessibility and aesthetics. This required exhaustive testing of graphical user interfaces by designers and engineers.	The first commercially successful personal computer with a GUI.
2004	Facebook's Social Network	Empathy for user connection and communication needs that demanded feature additions based on user feedback and interdisciplinary collaboration between computer science and social psychology.	A platform that redefined social networking and leveraged networking.
2008	Airbnb Platform	A human-centred approach to offer unique lodging experiences and improve the experience during platform use. It intertwined expertise between technology, design, and marketing.	A global home-sharing service that transformed the travel experience.
2015	Tesla Autopilot	Commitment to improving driving safety and convenience through constant software updates. This took cross-functional expertise from software engineers, automotive designers, and AI specialists.	The semi-autonomous driving feature in Tesla vehicles.
2020	COVID-19 Vaccine Development	Empathy for global health and safety needs. Involved rigorous clinical trials, testing, and administration, which was possible with collaboration across virology, biotechnology, and logistics.	Introduction of mRNA vaccines at unprecedented speed.

The emergence and growth of societies increased the complexity of problems faced. Forming of groups among people, migration in search of resources for survival, etc., led to the evolution of cultures and lifestyles. The former could be related to the present-day scenario of businesses' increased complexity with the size of networks. The latter could be attributed to the similarities and differences among people. Identification of resources and appropriate shelter locations transformed the nomadic lifestyles into settled agricultural communities. This solved the challenges related to finding food and shelter. However, new challenges like understanding food patterns, crop management, seasonal planning, resource allocation, etc., emerged.

From the Past: The knowledge of Rig Veda people dates back to approximately 2000 BCE, reflecting their knowledge of geography, places, rivers, cities, etc. They knew about the settlement of their allies and enemies within and beyond India (Sanyal and Rajendran, 2017).

This imitates modern-day industrial problems like selecting proper production methods, mapping resources, demand forecasting, etc. Other characteristics to be monitored are environmental conditions, resource availability, the impact of climate on the growth of crops, and other factors related to inventory management and external factors that impact business. The application of these principles helped people manage resources effectively. Later, the problem of scarcity and inadequate resources to cater for the demand led to the search for alternates in their geography and around. This led to the conglomeration of groups or the conquer of weaker groups by the stronger ones.

These led to the formation of defined cities and incepted trade of resources based on requirements. Problems like choosing trade routes, exchange of goods/currencies, risk management, etc., were handled by Merchants and early bankers. They mimic the roles performed by financial analysts and economists today in the modern world. The concepts such as trust and proper communication (directly or through indirect channels) have led to modern-day ideas like "Terms of Trade" and "Data Sharing", respectively. The former dictates the roles and responsibilities, ownership of goods/currency during transit, allocation of resources for handling shipments, etc. The latter deals with various data attributes like authenticity, accuracy, reliability, completeness, security, transparency, etc.

The origination of machines, factories, structured business networks, etc., significantly increased the complexity of problems faced during the Industrial Revolution. Concepts related to present-day businesses, like labour management, production scaling, and mechanisation, surfaced. These have led to the formation of various production methods like push and pull, production systems like mass manufacturing, job shops, batch production, etc., and automation, standardisation, generalisation, and others. The scarcity of resources also mandated optimising resource utilisation and the emergence of continuous improvement, which has driven techniques like Lean Management and Six Sigma.

In today's digital age, the problems encountered by businesses are not only physical but also virtual. Learning from experience and exploring ways to solve problems have helped organisations tackle issues in data management, logistics and supply chain management, cybersecurity, and real-time decision-making. Learning has been inoculated into machines through artificial intelligence (AI) and machine learning (ML), which have revolutionised the world. These tools can identify the patterns to make predictions, learn continuously with every bit of information, make rational recommendations, etc.

Takeaway: The problems faced have acted as catalysts for innovations, the evolution of lifestyle, the formation of civilisations, and the ultimate transformation of humans. Every problem, right from the Stone Age till today's digital age, every challenge has imparted learning and driven cognitive development. As we build modern AI and ML systems, they must be equipped with the ability to adapt, predict, and upgrade to handle similar problems in the future with ease and more complex problems with more effectiveness. Ultimately, evolution reflects the endeavour to observe, understand, explore, innovate, and overcome.

1.2 NEED FOR DESIGN AND DESIGN THINKING?

Design can be considered as an unsolved and incomplete puzzle where each piece indicates a decision or a choice based on internal and external capabilities and constraints. As is obvious, every piece cannot fit everywhere in a puzzle, similar to how businesses are bound to make a limited number of choices from the available options. Designing is an iterative process of investigating and refining ideas to solve problems. Sometimes, where the objective is clear, the designer knows what is to be achieved and is better positioned to arrange the puzzles to obtain the final image. Contrarily, when the objectives are partial, undefined, or unknown, the designers have the task of investigating more to understand the problem, requirements, data required to solve the problem, methods, constraints, etc. These have led to the formation of the idea called "Problem-Solving". It is the tool widely adopted by managers, policymakers, consultants, analysts, and others as a foundation stone for innovation and design thinking. It helps cultivate the mindset to handle complex problems methodically from multiple perspectives. Applying various problem-solving frameworks has allowed companies to effectively make decisions, enhance operational performance, and generate precise solutions. It aligns with design thinking by employing a "customer-centric approach" and creativity. This approach can foster trust and credibility and empower organisations to deliver innovative, practical solutions. It allows organisations and businesses to form effective strategies to solve complex problems and learn continuously.

To quickly understand the significance of design thinking, you can watch the lecture given by the authors at **https://youtu.be/t8K-KzsXg5w**. Alternatively, one can scan below presented QR code to watch the lecture.

Scan to watch the lecture—Why is design thinking important? What is it?

1.3 THE CORE ELEMENTS OF DESIGN THINKING

1.3.1 Human-centric Approach: The Heart of Innovation

This approach forms the foundation of design thinking as it insists on getting into the users' shoes to gain more insights and perspectives. These perspectives define the actual selling points of the business. It allows designers to experience the pains and challenges that users face while using a product or a service. The designers need to investigate deeper into the requirements, preferences, and other aspects related to the usage of the offerings before manifesting themselves as users. These augment the complete immersion of designers and innovators in the users' world, allowing them to effectively collect all required data through keen observation from multiple perspectives.

Technological advancements have levitated companies to different levels. Companies have started gathering data that is beyond what we can imagine. Devices collect data based on sleep patterns, words we utter during conversations, patterns in which a car driver controls different pedals, body positioning and movement during exercise and yoga, etc. These are possible by considering what is required in the service and what needs to be optimised to leverage the service offered. The data gathered are used to give tailored recommendations to the users, enhancing the personal connection between the users and the business, thereby increasing trust and loyalty. However, these cannot be done simultaneously; they can be performed iteratively over time through continuous evaluation, feedback, and improvement.

1.3.2 Iterative Problem-Solving: The Journey of Continuous Improvement

It originated with the belief that the perfect solutions do not come at the first attempt. Rather, they are obtained after various rounds of iterations and refinements of the initial solution. These are possible only when the evaluations are meticulous, feedback is valid, and the improvement steps are in the proper direction. These do not follow a linear pattern; they often swing around the optimal solution and reach the optimal point after several iterations, depending on the flexibility and adaptability of the business or service. Concepts like agile, which pushes the product to the customer as much as possible, are techniques organisations employ to be more responsive. Minimum Viable Product (MVP) has also become vital as it helps businesses to evidence a promising solution at a very early project stage. The MVP solution has all the functionalities and requirements and can address the users' core problems. They project themselves as the simplified versions of the complex solution that shall be presented in due course of the project. The idea of MVP also allows the designers and innovators to get user feedback and make corrections at a very nascent stage rather than postponing these changes after developing a significant proportion of the service or product.

Apart from identifying any deviation from the actual requirement, the iterative technique also allows for the testing of the model assumptions and approximations earlier to minimise errors. It is a way to release the idea faster into the market, which is key for products with shorter product life cycles, like electronic gadgets. Any delay in production, testing, or development will pave the way for the competitor products to enter the market earlier, thereby causing a downfall of the product.

1.3.3 Interdisciplinary Collaboration: Harnessing Collective Expertise

This aims at stitching the minds of people from various disciplines to get new or different perspectives on approaching a problem. Apart from this, some real-world problems necessitate the requirement of a multidisciplinary skillset to solve a problem because of the complexity involved and the requirement of expertise from various fields. We can start with an example of a production facility manufacturing automobile horns in India.

Suppose they plan to invest in the manufacture of automobile tyres. In that case, they might have to gather information from the market regarding the existing product from the sales and marketing team, gather insights on the technical requirement of the tyres from the analytics team, determine the resources or machinery required to initiate the production from the production team, investigate the design and development of the product from the Research & Development team, and finally, budget within which all of these need to be accomplished by the finance team. Though these decisions are from various functions of the organisation, none of them act in silos. Instead, they discuss and arrive at a consensus considering the overall development and profit of the business. Another variation could be gathering expertise from various businesses with different skill sets to solve a multidisciplinary problem. An example could be gathering people from epidemiology policymaking, logistics managers, healthcare practitioners, data analysts, modellers, etc., to model a vaccine distribution network based on the spread of COVID-19. These three core elements need to be integrated to stand out in innovation.

Readers are invited to watch the lecture on the core elements of design thinking by clicking the link—**https://youtu.be/Sp_e3Iz5GN8**. Alternatively, the same lecture can be accessed by scanning the QR code provided below.

SCAN ME

Scan to watch the lecture—Core Elements of Design Thinking—Traditional vs. Design Thinking Approach.

1.4 HOW DOES DESIGN THINKING FOSTER CREATIVITY AND EMPATHY?

Doug Dietz was a pleasant and emotional person. With two decades of expertise at General Electric (GE), he controls GE Healthcare's design and development of high-tech medical imaging systems. His multimillion-dollar magnetic resonance imaging (MRI) systems probe effortlessly into the human body. Doug was extremely excited seeing the installation and operation of his MRI scanner in the scanning suite of a hospital. While interacting with the technician, he mentioned that the innovation had been nominated for the "Oscard of Design", i.e., the International Design Excellence Award. He admitted abashedly, "It was a perfect example of bad interviewing technique". The technician requested Doug to leave the room as a patient entered to get scanned. Doug witnessed a frail young girl walking towards the machine with fear while she was holding the hands of her parents. As the girl continued to shed tears, the technician received a call from an anesthesiologist. Doug realised that sedation is given to pediatric patients to eliminate their fear during the long process. In the absence of an anesthesiologist, the scan is postponed, which prolongs the worries of the families.

The fear the machine instilled in the minds of the patients made Doug experience a sense of failure. His perspective of innovation and design changed thereon. Despite the efforts to develop a sleek design and technology, the fact that it sounded scary to most patients transformed his pride into sorrow. He sought suggestions from his colleagues and friends. Based on the advice offered by his boss, he flew to California for an executive workshop to get a different perspective. He explored different methods to make MRI machines less scary, especially for younger patients. The workshop inculcated the idea of a "human-centred approach" to design and innovation. His discussions with peers, patients, and experts in the industry (from different companies) made him consolidate more ideas and converge to the core requirements. The interbreeding of ideas raised his creativity and hopes when he admitted, "I started to imagine how powerful this tool could be if I brought it back and got cross-functional teams to work together." Sooner, he returned to Milwaukee, determined to provide a solution for the younger population. Given his organisation's constraints and limited resources, he could not conduct a Research and Development (R&D) project. Rather, he used a "human-centric approach" to redesign the patient experience during the process. He discussed and got ideas from volunteers from GE, child life specialists at a daycare centre, doctors and employees of two hospitals, and personnel from a children's museum. This made him understand what the pediatric patients went through and develop the "Adventure Series" scanner that was made operational at the children's hospital at the University of Pittsburgh Medical Center for a pilot program.

The machine was transformed into an adventure story with the patient undergoing the process in the lead role. Without altering the technology in the MRI scanner, the team installed decals on the surface of the MRI machine, walls, ceiling, and floor. A script was developed for the operators to steer the patients through the adventure. One of the nine different adventures developed is a pirate ship (Figure 1.1) experience that possesses a wooden captain's steer-wheel surrounding the opening of the machine. The seafaring design projects a smaller chamber opening that is less claustrophobic. The operator instructs the kids to stay still during the sea journey while inside the pirate ship. Upon completing the journey, they are asked to pick up the treasure from the other side of the room, from the pirate's chest. Yet another adventure projects the MRI as a spaceship, taking the kids into space. Moments before the machine starts producing banging noise, the operator instructs the kids to listen carefully as the craft "shifts into hyperdrive." This revamps the frightening "BOOM-BOOM-BOOM" noise to a part of the adventure.

This innovation reduced the number of pediatric patients who required sedation during the process. GE and the hospital were immensely satisfied as the availability of anesthesiologists was no longer a concern for this process, and the facility could scan more patients daily. This also improved patient satisfaction by 90 percent. Though these numbers quantify the success and augment more internal support, he felt rewarded and worthwhile when he heard a six-year-old girl asking her mom after the process. The girl uttered, "Mommy, can we come back tomorrow?". This creative confidence propelled him to become a thought leader at GE. People with a creative mindset are the ones capable of

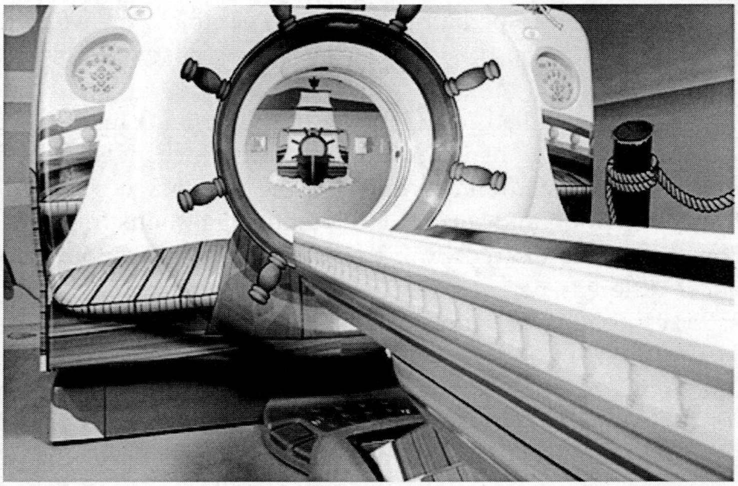

FIGURE 1.1 MRI Scanner designed as Pirate Ship as taken from IDEO (2024).

portraying the future precisely using imagination. They can optimise the happenings and ideas around them personally and professionally. Creative confidence helps us to have an optimistic view of what is possible. This innovation narrates how a "human-centric approach" can lead to pathbreaking innovations. Such innovations happen when the designers consider the empathy and experience of the audience. While the primary task is to bring modifications with respect to technical features, Doug's differentiated way gave a whole new perspective to the process and improved the patient experience (Kelley and Kelley, 2013).

These could be termed the sweet spot (Figure 1.2) with the right mix of feasibility, business, and people. The first component, feasibility, deals with the technical aspects of design and innovation. There have been revolutionising innovations like aircraft and supercar components made of carbon fibre, surgical equipment with minimal invasion, multi-touch displays, AI drones, autopilot vehicles, and others. Though all these are mind-blowing innovations, they must balance the other two components to align with the sweet spot of implementation in real-time. The second factor is business or economic viability. These innovations need to be scalable and reproducible by using an optimal amount of resources with a viable distribution mechanism. Even government or non-profit organisations' initiatives like improving sanitation in Ghana or safer domestic water in India could be possible only over the long term through sustained practices. The third factor involves the people, i.e., human factors. It is about understanding people's core needs and preferences in innovations. This is closer to the "human-centric approach" that paved the way to reinventing MRI machines for pediatric patients, which was possible by factoring in the human experience during the process. Most schools and educational programs focus on technical and economic factors that make most companies strong in these two. The third one comes from empathy for the users and viewing the problem from their perspectives. It is all about understanding what people do in the present and how it could be changed in the future for betterment. Best innovations happen when we undergo the experience

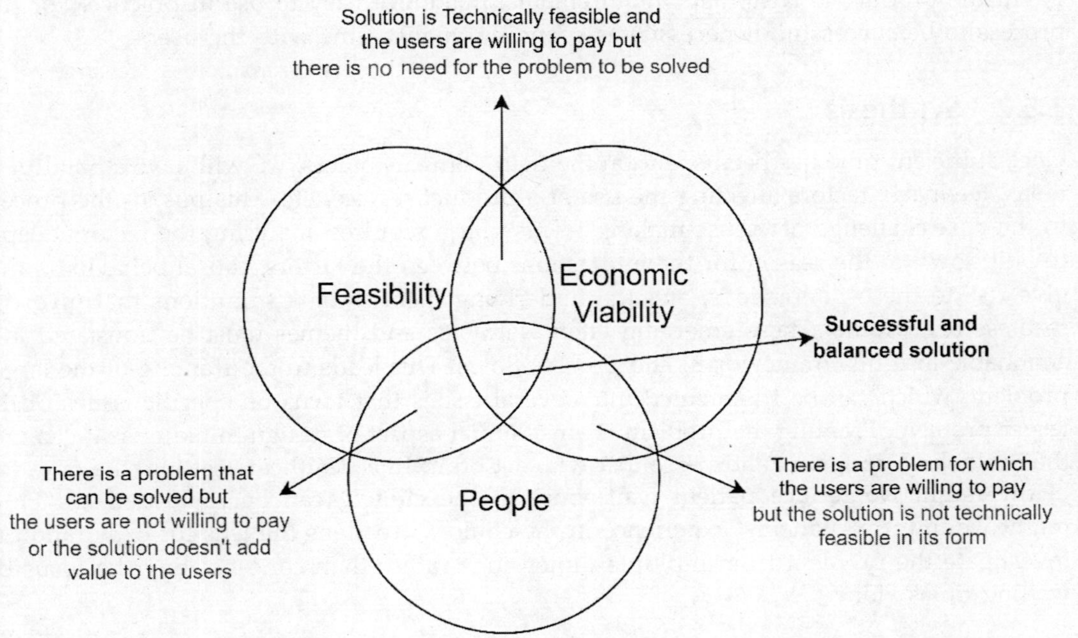

FIGURE 1.2 The Sweet Spot.

along with the people/users for whom we intend to build or innovate. Hence, we claim that the innovations are worthwhile when they consider the actual needs and situations of the users (Kelley and Kelley, 2013).

1.5 BECOMING A DESIGN THINKER

The Hasso Plattner Institute of Design at Stanford University, commonly known as the d.school, (in association with IDEO) names creation and innovation as "design thinking." New ideas emerge as one-size-fits-all methodology does not apply to almost all real-life problems. Many of the trainings have the four necessary steps as discussed subsequently. In addition, they state that these steps might require modifications and need to be tailored according to the scenario being handled (Kelley and Kelley, 2013):

1.5.1 Innovation

Innovation starts from observing the things that happen around us. The natural phenomena that occur, like when an apple fell on Newton's head, stones attracted in Magnesia, lightning created wildfires, etc., evolved the intuition of humans to use these phenomena in favour of various processes. Connecting deeply with the needs of people who face the problem helps to empathetically solve the problem by identifying factors that create the problem. We must interact with the early and extreme users to understand the challenges, difficulties, and scope for improving any product or service. Feedback helps iteratively orient the product to customers' requirements, making it easy to use in practice. For this process to be successful, it necessitates spending quality time with the users.

1.5.2 Synthesis

Once sufficient time has been spent on the field with customers, we will have a handful of ideas, feedback, factors affecting the use of a product/service, etc. This pushes the process to the next challenge of "sense-making". This phase requires analysing the factors deeply to boil down to the reason for the interactions between the factors, causal behaviours that give rise to these interactions, and the underlying theories or assumptions that give rise to these behaviours. These emerging latent variables and themes must be translated into actionable insights, frameworks, and process flows. This leads to the framing of the larger problem, which can be fragmented into several issues that focus on specific issues of the larger problem. Framing the problem is an essential aspect of design thinking as it changes the outlook of designers and personnel who act on it. In a healthcare setting, the question "How might we reduce patient wait times in the clinic?" can be rephrased as "How might we improve patients' experience in the clinic?" broadens the lens for exploration to investigate the problem from multiple dimensions rather than concentrating the focus on waiting times alone.

1.5.3 Ideation and Experimentation

This phase propels the exploration of novel thoughts to discover various feasible choices. Some promising ones undergo several iterations, prototyping, etc., to verify and validate the customer requirements and product functioning. These learning loops act as vicious cycles to test the responsiveness and robustness of the solutions. In addition, user feedback drives the process of refining solutions methodically. The period and use of resources depend on the nature of the innovation or solution. The experiments can include simulations, workflows, process flows, analytical modelling, prototyping, etc., depending on the industry and problem being served.

1.5.4 Implementation

Upon nearing the product entry to the market, a roadmap showcasing the plan to launch the product in the market is essential. This must be based on the competitors' offerings, customer preferences, pricing and affordability in the region, positioning of our product amidst its substitutes or competitors, etc. Every launch involves multiple phases, as there are competitors in every space who can deliver products and services on par with what we plan for launch. The ability to adapt to changes swiftly determines the market penetration at earlier stages of the Product Life Cycle. Amazon's entry into the Southeast Asian market underwent challenges as there was aversion from customers towards foreign brands because of the lack of cultural connections. Also, established competitors like Alibaba and Tencent increased the challenge. Though Amazon worked on this by collaborating with the local players and employing local people in their business, they explored multiple dimensions to penetrate the market. This enabled them to join hands with Small and

Medium Businesses (SMBs) by offering them cloud services through Amazon Web Services (AWS). Amazon anticipated long-term potential in cloud space as many businesses were interested in using the offering. This was possible probably because of the strategic framing of the larger question as "How can Amazon enter the Southeast East Asian market?" rather than confining their question to their core business and stating "How can Amazon enter the e-commerce space in the South East Asian market?".

1.6 DESIGN THINKING AND THE SUSTAINABLE ADVANTAGE FOR BUSINESS

Roger L. Martin, Dean of the Rotman School of Management at the University of Toronto and a senior advisor to CEOs of several companies mentioned his experience during his visit to the Research In Motion (RIM) headquarters near Toronto. This is the review and extended view of his documentation in his book "The Design of Business: Why Design Thinking is the Next Competitive Advantage". Upon reaching 176 Columbia Street, where the RIM headquarters was located, he saw similar buildings towering only eight stories' height. He could hardly differentiate the global headquarters of one of the world's most innovative companies. Though the inside entrance resembled traditional tech firms in terms of security, it lacked fancy interiors, sophisticated and attractive furniture, designs, entertainment zones, etc. The ordinarily maintained conference rooms were named after the renowned Canadian hockey legends Wayne Gretzky and Gordie Howe. This could probably be done to keep the morale of the workers high every time they look at accomplished local role models. All these attributes do not mean that RIM was negligent about design. It highlights the fact that design means more than appearance to them. They believed that design is about "making things work beautifully" and "moving knowledge along the funnel, starting from the mystery of how to enable and enhance communication in a mobile age".

Mike Lazaridis, RIM's founder, president, co-CEO, and design visionary, was one of the masterminds behind BlackBerry's success, who built a $84 million company through their wireless communication devices. Let us consider the example of BlackBerry to witness how Lazaridis solved the "paradox", the term he utters to describe the unknown and unsolved problems. His claim, "How do you solve a paradox? Well, you have to know what the paradox is", clearly portrays his thought process and the thirst to solve the core of the issue rather than addressing the symptoms with temporary fixes. In the early days, laptop users demanded smaller, handy, lightweight devices. However, reducing the standard QWERTY keypads beyond a threshold could be inconvenient for usage and typing. Also, the screen might be cluttered, considering the proportionate reduction in display size. Lazaridis carefully distinguished the problem into two components to address readability and ease of typing. The former was solved by displaying information on a screen more clearly and optimistically. He effectively delivered this when he explored, "When is a small display better? When it draws your attention to something important." The latter was solved when he answered the question, "When is a small keyboard better?" he asked. "When you can use your thumbs." This made RIM introduce a keyboard that was operable by thumb. The interface was made simpler with less but essential information.

The attention to detail and making things more comforting for users could be understood from how e-mail functionality was designed. They did not want the users to hear the receipt of a message and wait for several seconds till the message was displayed. Rather, he wanted the popup on the screen only when the message was ready to be read by the user. Lazaridis explains, "It's fundamental, but every developer we've ever hired to do this project or rewrite the code makes the same mistake. They signal you as soon as the e-mail arrives." Also, he knew that the core value of the device was not just transferring e-mails but understanding what the users wanted. So, the display design included prompts containing information about the mail's sender, the title or subject line, and a portion of the body of the mail. This allows the users to open the mail to continue reading or snooze it for later. The mix of these two functionalities, viz., enabling notifications as soon as the mail is ready to be read and displaying sufficient information for the user to quickly assess and act on it, were breakthroughs. Following this, more value was added, including the responsive keyboard and the shortcuts. The corporations started purchasing BlackBerry devices for their executives, which evidenced the success of the device for the years to come. Despite this, Lazaridis eyed the next mystery and anticipated the future needs of the customers when he came up with the idea of "a handheld device that merged voice and data." RIM initially priced the minutes of data usage. Sooner, Lazaridis and Balsille spotted that selling data was not the expertise of BlackBerry. Hence, they decided to partner with Vodafone and Verizon to utilise their expertise in wireless technology and reshape the distribution channel.

This thought extended as Lazaridis envisioned a time when an unknown competitor in the smartphone segment could compete with RIM in the corporate market. This idea motivated him to create a smaller device with a camera and music-handling abilities in addition to the existing characteristics, i.e., voice, e-mail, and web browsing. His statement to his employees, "Define for me what the ultimate BlackBerry is." led to the invention of RIM's top-selling products, the Pearl and the Curve. These products penetrated the US market before the iPhone. Lazaridis explains the major cause of the decline in iPhone sales and BlackBerry's success: "They were betting on their engine—their low-cost, high-volume, global supply chain juggernaut. They were missing the point. There will be no feature phones in the future. It will all be smartphones." In pursuing design thinking, Lazaridis resumed building the 3G Bold with advanced multimedia handling abilities like an iPod. He sensed the future inclination of customers towards touchscreen phones and knew that the existing technology could not provide the BlackBerry experience of distinguishing between navigation and touch. This rolled out sooner when they introduced technology through their Storm, which enabled users to discern scrolling or navigation from clicking the screen to confirm an action. The conscious efforts and mindfulness of leaders actively push the knowledge down the funnel at RIM. RIM's success teaches that reliability need not be undermined by validity. The mix of abductive and design thinking creates a competitive advantage that proves more beneficial than focusing on reliability and validity. It adds the flavour of innovation and improves efficiency.

1.7 NECESSITY IS THE MOTHER OF INVENTION

This success story of Airbnb was nucleated by its co-founder's need to pay rent in 2008. The business was almost on the verge of closure in 2009 when it earned about $200 per week, which was insufficient to thrive in the business. Joe Gebbia, the co-founder, started investigating the cause of reduced bookings and profit. That is when he observed a common pattern across all the listings in New York, all with low-quality and poor photographs of the rooms. This could be one of the major reasons, as these photographs are the ones the customers see on digital platforms when making payments. These gave their customers an unpleasant experience. Hence, Paul Graham, co-founder, visited some of their properties in New York and clicked photographs, renting a camera to replace the initially existing ones with better images. This initiative doubled their revenue to $400 per week. Joe, a graduate of Rhode School, understood design thinking well right from the early days. The co-founders put themselves in the shoes of customers to experience what they expect while selecting and booking rooms. This boils down to the "human-centric approach" that most pathbreaking innovations have adopted. This enhanced Airbnb's holistic and systems way of thinking, which has translated into the core focus of their business: *"its design and user experience"*. Through continuous application of the principles of design thinking in different dimensions, the co-founders converted the $400 per week earnings into a staggering $8.4 billion annual earnings, with the company spanning 192 countries (Strate School of Design, 2024).

1.7.1 Empathy

By replacing the old, unattractive images with better ones, founders Brian and Joe spent a significant amount of time undergoing the experience of the users. A large proportion of the users were looking for affordable, accessible, and unique stays. Based on the understanding, they were able to convert the thoughts of users to images that are the first points of contact/selling points for the business. This fetched more revenue than when they spent four weeks working on the codes. Another major reason for their success is continuous improvement based on the feedback from the hosts and guests regarding the stay and platform services. The 11-star framework that the brand came up with enabled them to think creatively to give an exceptional customer experience. The framework incorporates even granular details and service components offered to the customers. This helps tailor and target strategies implementation and enhances focus on the exact goal(s).

1.7.2 Design and User Experience

The interface of Airbnb is one the best in the travel industry. The user experience is enjoyable because of the ease of use and navigation across options. These are possible because the company understands the customer's capabilities, mood, and time value. The experience of staying at a stranger's place has been given an optimistic outlook by adding essential information like the stay place, host, location, proximity to transportation, and nearby sights, along with sufficient images of the entire geography. The brand ensured that enough information was fed to the customers to wipe out their sense of fear and boost their trust. The host list was also managed intuitively, such that it promoted the acceptance rate of the hosts by building connections.

1.7.3 Holistic Product Design

Brian has always believed in a "human-centric approach" that has encouraged him to give a special experience to the customers with their loved ones. Complementarily, he mentioned, "Customers are not buying our website, and they're not buying our application. That's just a storefront of communication. What they're buying is a house. And frankly, what they're buying more than the house is the host, experience of hospitality & the idea of belonging." These portray the essence of values that have acted as a strong foundation for their business. The product has been designed end-to-end to give moments to cherish for a lifetime and a sense of belonging to the stay place. The product, as Brian claims, is that "Aha" moment, which extends beyond the life cycle.

1.7.4 Sustaining the Culture

As the users are travel enthusiasts, they love to enjoy the nativity of the places they visit. To retain that, the brand has worked to retain the same right from onboarding without compromising the true culture of the places and communities. The tribes and people from other communities provide great insights to the customers to be an integral part of their culture, far away from their homes. To get a feel for what Airbnb does to their employees, their office spaces and meeting rooms are built in a way that is similar to the apartments they offer to their users. Inclusivity in terms of peoples' cultures, values, and communities has made them people together. The rating process also has propelled the connections between hosts and guests through continuous feedback and improvement. Thus, the brand has successfully transformed travel from a process to an exciting experience (Strate School of Design, 2024).

KEY POINTS TO REMEMBER

1. *Problem-solving as a human instinct:* Human beings have been solving problems and innovating since prehistoric times—from crafting stone tools to modern technological inventions. This historical perspective reminds us that design and innovation are iterative by nature: early solutions were refined over generations. Design thinking builds on this instinct, formalising a process (empathise, define, ideate, prototype, test) that mirrors how humans naturally experiment, learn, and improve solutions to meet their needs.
2. *Need for design thinking in modern business:* In today's business environment, problems are often complex, ambiguous, or not well-defined. Traditional linear problem-solving may fall short in such cases. Design thinking provides a structured

yet creative approach to tackle these challenges—it emphasises understanding the problem deeply (especially from the customer's perspective) before jumping to solutions. This approach leads to more innovative and user-appropriate outcomes, fostering trust and credibility with customers by showing that solutions are rooted in actual user needs.

3. *Human-centric and empathy-driven approach:* At the heart of design thinking is empathy—putting the user's needs, emotions, and experiences first. A human-centric approach means designers actively step into users' shoes through techniques like observation, interviews, and immersion. By genuinely understanding users' pain points and aspirations, companies can design products or services that truly resonate. This user-first mindset often uncovers latent needs and insights that would be overlooked if one focused only on technical or business aspects.
4. *Iterative learning and refinement:* Design thinking embraces an iterative process of prototyping and testing. Instead of seeking a perfect solution on the first try, teams build rough prototypes or sketches and then refine them based on feedback. This "fail fast, learn fast" mentality is crucial – early ideas are treated as experiments rather than final answers. Iteration allows teams to incorporate real-world feedback continuously, leading to solutions that are more effective and fine-tuned to user feedback by the end.
5. *Interdisciplinary collaboration fuels innovation:* Design thinking thrives on collaboration across diverse disciplines. Bringing together people with different expertise (engineering, design, marketing, etc.) leads to richer ideas and more holistic solutions. Cross-functional teams can examine a problem from multiple angles at once—a concept or prototype is vetted for technical feasibility, user desirability, and business viability in parallel. This collaborative ethos, along with an openness to wild ideas, fosters a creative environment where innovation flourishes and conventional assumptions are challenged.
6. *Empathy in action—the MRI case:* A key example from this chapter is Doug Dietz's MRI "Adventure Series" story, which demonstrates the power of empathy-driven design. By observing the fear his young patients experienced, a designer reframed the problem from "how to build a better MRI machine" to "how to create a better experience for children undergoing an MRI". The resulting solution—themed scanner environments with storytelling—dramatically improved patient satisfaction. The lesson: Deep empathy can reveal core issues (in this case, the emotional experience) that, when addressed, lead to innovative solutions without even altering the core technology.
7. *The design thinker's mindset:* Ultimately, design thinking is more than a process—it is a mindset of curiosity and openness. Key takeaways for aspiring design thinkers include embracing ambiguity (seeing ill-defined problems as opportunities), being willing to experiment and fail in order to learn, and maintaining a strong focus on the end-user throughout. By adopting this mindset, individuals and organisations can better navigate complex problems, continually learn and adapt, and drive innovation with a purpose—keeping solutions aligned with what people truly need and value.

KEY LEARNINGS

- *Historic Influence:* Design thinking has been an integral part of innovation from ancient times to date.
- *Core Elements:* Design Thinking needs to be Human-centric, iterative, and interdisciplinary.
- *Empathy:* Impactful solutions result from understanding the problem requirements from users' perspectives i.e., user experience.
- *Practical innovations:* How the real-world problems were solved in differentiated ways by viewing the problem from the users' shoes.
- *Universality:* Visualise how Design Thinking concepts could be applied across various industries and applications.

EXERCISES

1. **Conceptual Question—Defining Design Thinking:** In your own words, define "design thinking" and explain how it differs from a traditional analytical problem-solving approach. (Think about what makes design thinking unique, such as its focus on empathy, creativity, and iteration. A good answer should mention at least two distinguishing features and why they matter in solving complex problems.)
2. **Case Reflection—Lessons from the MRI Story:** Recall the Doug Dietz MRI "Adventure Series" case described in the chapter. Identify two design thinking principles illustrated by this story and explain how they led to a better outcome. For example, one principle is empathy—Doug observed children's fears and re-framed the problem around the patient experience. Another is prototyping/iteration—he experimented with transforming the MRI room into a themed adventure. Describe how each principle was applied and how it contributed to making the MRI experience less frightening for patients.
3. **Observation Exercise—Spot a Design Opportunity:** Choose a product or service you use frequently that you find could be improved (it could be anything from a mobile app to a coffee shop's ordering system). Briefly describe the current user experience and a pain point or inconvenience you notice. Now outline how you might approach improving it using design thinking:
   (a) How would you *empathise* with the users (what techniques might you use to understand their experience better)?
   (b) How might you *redefine the problem* based on user insights (present the core issue from the user's perspective)?
   (c) Suggest one innovative idea (*ideation*) that could address the problem, and describe a simple prototype you could create to test this idea (for instance, a sketch of a redesigned interface or a mock-up of a new service process). This exercise will help you practice the mindset of focusing on user needs and iterating on solutions.

4. **Discussion Prompt—Why Empathy Matters:** Write a short reflection or discuss with a peer: Why is empathy considered crucial in design thinking? Provide an example either from the chapter or your own experience where a lack of empathy led to a poor product or solution. How could applying empathy (truly understanding the user) have changed the outcome? (This prompt is to reinforce the idea that understanding the human context is not just a "nice-to-have" but often the factor that makes the difference between a product's success or failure.)

THOUGHT-PROVOKING QUESTIONS

1. Describe how empathy drives design thinking. Extend a practical problem discussed in the chapter by anticipating future challenges and probable solutions.
2. Explain the importance of evaluation and feedback in design thinking and discuss why iteration is crucial for successful innovation.
3. Analyse the case of Airbnb and explain how exceeding user expectations can drive innovation.
4. What could be potential barriers to implementing design thinking in large organisations, and how can these barriers be overcome?
5. Discuss how Roger L. Martin's insights on balancing reliability and creativity apply to a business.
6. Identify ways in which design thinking can contribute to long-term success in a business.
7. How do the examples in the chapter illustrate the importance of interdisciplinary collaboration?
8. Evaluate how integrating design thinking into traditional problem-solving methods could change the approach to strategic management.

REFERENCES

IDEO. (2024), "The Journey From Design Thinking to Creative Confidence", IDEO U, available at: https://www.ideou.com/blogs/inspiration/from-design-thinking-to-creative-confidence (accessed 7 November 2024).

Kelley, T. and Kelley, D. (2013), Creative Confidence_Unleashing the Creative Potential Within Us All, Crown Business.

Sanyal, S. and Rajendran, S. (2017), The Incredible History of India's Geography, Penguin, United Kingdom.

Strate School of Design, (2024), "Airbnb's successful design thinking story", Strate School of Design, Bengaluru, available at: https://strate.in/airbnbs-successful-design-thinking-story/.

CHAPTER 2

The Design Thinking Process

LEARNING OBJECTIVES

After reading this Chapter, the readers will be able to:

- Explain the Design Thinking framework and its key stages—Understand the five-stage model (Empathise, Define, Ideate, Prototype, Test) and its human-centred, iterative approach to problem-solving in business.
- Appreciate the role of empathy in innovation—Recognise the importance of understanding users' needs from their perspective and using techniques like interviews, surveys, and observation to help unearth valuable insights.
- Define problems effectively—Learn to synthesis research into clear problem statements or Points of View (POV) that drive focused innovation.
- Generate and manage creative ideas—Explore ideation techniques such as brainstorming and mind mapping to spur innovation and understand how businesses apply these techniques across industries.
- Prototype and test solutions iteratively—Grasp the importance of "building to think" by creating sketches, wireframes, or mockups and continuously refining solutions through user testing and feedback loops.
- Apply design thinking to real-world scenarios—Apply design thinking via case studies (e.g., in healthcare and city traffic) and practice using frameworks through exercises and reflective questions.

2.1 OVERVIEW OF THE DESIGN THINKING FRAMEWORK

Design Thinking is a user-centric, solutions-based approach to tackling complex problems. It blends desirable human perspectives with technological feasibility and business viability. In practice, design thinking encourages teams to empathise with users, define clear problems, ideate creatively, prototype early, and test iteratively. Unlike linear problem-solving methods, design thinking is often non-linear and iterative, i.e., teams may loop back to earlier stages as new insights or feedback emerge. This flexible framework has been popularised by institutions like Stanford's d.school and IDEO, and it has been successfully applied in domains ranging from product design and UX to healthcare and social innovation.

Several design thinking frameworks exist, but one of the most widely referenced is the five-stage model by the Hasso-Plattner Institute of Design at Stanford (the d.school) (Dam & Siang, 2017). Table 2.1 below summarises these key stages of the design thinking process and their objectives:

TABLE 2.1 Key Stages of the Design Thinking Process

Stage	*Objective (What happens in this stage?)*
Empathise	Understand the users' needs and context through research. Build deep empathy by observing and engaging with people to uncover their motivations and pain points.
Define	Clearly articulate the core problem based on insights from empathy. Synthesise findings into a focused problem statement (POV) that will guide ideation.
Ideate	Generate a broad range of creative and potential solutions. Brainstorm and use tools like mind mapping to explore many possibilities without judgment. Aim for quantity and novelty of ideas.
Prototype	"Build to think"—create low-fidelity representations of ideas (sketches, models, wireframes) to explore the workability of solutions. Prototypes are experimental and meant to be tested and refined.
Test	Try out prototypes with target users and gather feedback. Evaluate how well solutions match user needs; use insights to refine the prototypes or redefine the problem as needed.

This framework is human-centred at its core—it starts with empathy for the end-user and ends with solutions tested by users. Notably, design thinking is iterative: teams often cycle through the stages multiple times rather than following them in a strict sequence. For example, testing a prototype may reveal new user insights, enabling the team to redefine the problem or ideate new solutions based on feedback. By embracing this iterative loop, organisations can continuously refine ideas until a truly user-centred, innovative solution emerges.

2.2 EMPATHISE: UNDERSTANDING USER NEEDS

The first stage, Empathize, is about stepping into the user's shoes to understand their experiences and emotions. Empathy is considered the cornerstone of human-centred design.

As the Stanford d.school famously advises, *empathy is the centrepiece of a human-centred design process. The Empathize mode is your work to understand people—how they do things and why, their physical and emotional needs, how they think about the world, and what is meaningful to them."* (Trackmind, 2023). In business contexts, this means engaging with customers or end-users to uncover latent or unaddressed needs and pain points that might not be immediately obvious.

During the Empathize stage, design thinkers immerse themselves in the user's environment—observing behaviours, conducting interviews, and even experiencing the situation first-hand if possible. The goal is to gather deep insights into user motivations, frustrations, preferences, and the context in which they interact with a product or service. By doing so, teams move beyond assumptions or superficial data and discover the *"why"* behind user behaviours.

Empathising is critical because it confirms that subsequent design efforts are grounded in reality. For example, a financial services team might spend days with small business owners to learn how they manage finances, revealing pain points that a new fintech product could solve. A healthcare innovator might shadow nurses during hospital shifts to understand workflow challenges. Such insights gained through empathy fuel the creativity and relevance of solutions later in the process. Empathy connects innovation to actual human needs, setting the foundation for genuinely user-centered design.

2.2.1 Techniques: Interviews, Surveys, Observation

Design thinkers employ various research techniques to empathise with users. Key methods include:

- *Interviews:* One-on-one or group interviews allow designers to hear users describe their experiences in their own words. Open-ended, non-leading questions are used to encourage storytelling and dig into "why" users do things. For example, instead of asking, "Do you usually find online shopping easy?" a designer might ask, "Tell me about the last time you purchased a gift online." It invites the user to share a story, revealing needs or frustrations. Interviews are widely used across industries—a UX team might interview app users about their navigation patterns, while a consumer goods company might interview households about cleaning routines. Real-world example: Airbnb's founders personally interviewed hosts and guests in the early days. They discovered that poor-quality listing photos deter bookings, an insight that led them to offer professional photography—a change that significantly increased rentals (Rosenzweig, 2025). It shows how interviews can uncover a root problem and directly inform a solution.
- *Surveys:* Surveys gather feedback or facts from a larger sample of users via questionnaires. They help validate insights or spot patterns across many people. In an empathise phase, surveys might be used after initial qualitative research to quantify how specific needs or opinions are. For instance, a retail brand could survey hundreds of customers to rank the importance of different shopping features (price, convenience, experience, etc.). In industry, surveys are familiar in market research—e.g., an automaker surveying drivers about pain points in daily

commuting or a SaaS company emailing a survey about users' feature preferences. Surveys provide a breadth of data, though they should be carefully designed to avoid bias. While they lack the depth of interviews, surveys complement qualitative methods by ensuring the team's understanding isn't based on just a few voices. There are various types of sampling techniques in surveying based on various parameters, as in Figure 2.1.

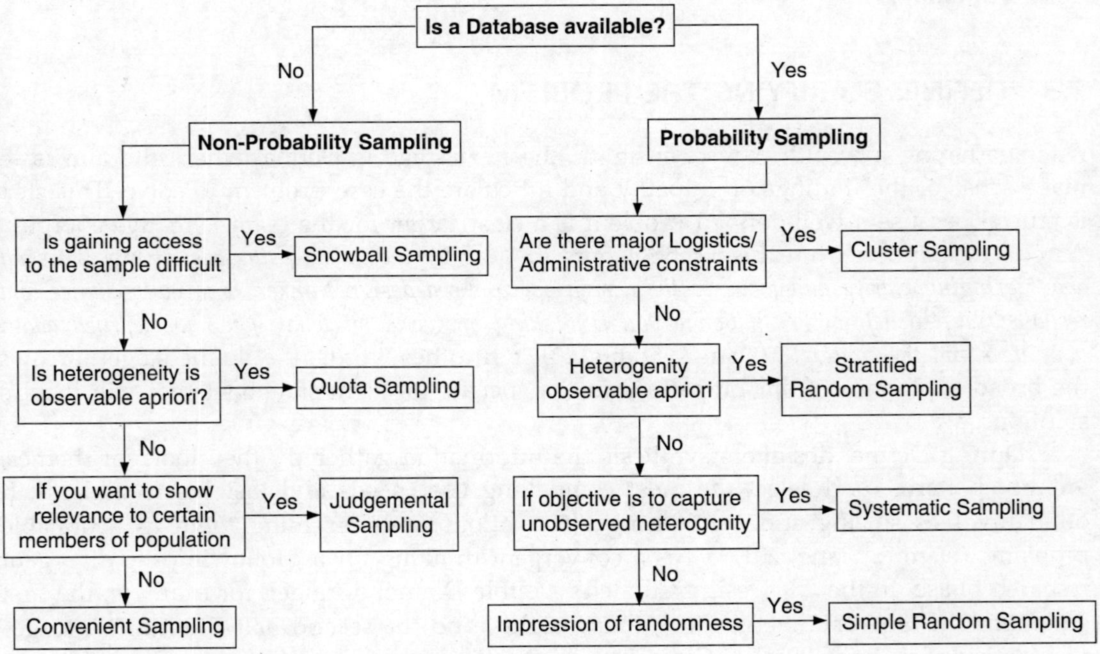

FIGURE 2.1 Sampling Techniques.

- ***Observation:*** Direct observation (contextual inquiry or field research) involves watching users engage with a product or perform relevant activities in their natural environment. This technique is powerful because people's actions don't always match what they *say*. By observing, designers can notice unarticulated needs or workaround behaviours. For example, Procter & Gamble famously sent teams into homes to watch how people cleaned floors. They observed that many consumers swept *and* mopped, a tedious two-step process. This insight led to the invention of the Swiffer, a single tool to trap dust and mop, which became one of P&G's most successful products (Rosenzweig, 2025). Observation is also used in software (through usability studies or analysing user session recordings) and in services (e.g., a bank might observe how customers navigate a branch). The key is that observation captures actual user behaviour and context. Designers look for "pain points" (signs of frustration, workarounds) and "bright spots" (where things work seamlessly) to inform opportunities. Oftentimes, inconsistencies between what users say and do reveal the most interesting insights (Perficient, 2019)– for instance, a customer might *tell* a product is fine but struggle while using it, indicating unmet needs that wouldn't surface in an interview alone.

By combining these techniques, teams gather a rich, empathetic understanding from multiple angles. In practice, an empathise phase might start with broad observations, targeted interviews, and then a survey to validate findings. The outcome is a set of user needs, insights, and personas that the team can confidently use to drive the next stage of design thinking.

2.3 DEFINE: CLARIFYING THE PROBLEM

After gathering a wealth of user insights, the next stage is Define, where the aim is to make sense of the findings of empathy and articulate the core problem to solve. This step is crucial because a well-defined problem is a clear target for the team's creative energies. As one description from the d.school puts it, *"The Define mode of the design process is all about bringing clarity and focus to the design space. As a design thinker, it is your chance and responsibility to define the challenge you are taking on based on what you have learned about your user and the context."* (Dam & Siang, 2017). In other words, the define stage narrows the broad exploration from Empathize into a specific problem statement that will inspire solutions.

During Define, designers synthesis the information gathered—they look for themes, identify patterns, and select the most compelling user needs and insights to address. It often involves sorting and condensing observations and reframing them as actionable problems (Dam & Siang, 2017). It is a convergent thinking phase, following the divergent research phase. In the UK Design Council's Double Diamond model, for example, the first "diamond" (Discover) diverges to gather insights, and the second half (Define) converges to a clear design brief (Design Council, n.d.). By the end of Define, the team should have a *point of view* on the problem: a concise summary of *who* has *what* problem and *why* it's essential.

A substantial problem definition does a few things: it focuses on a specific user or segment, expresses their core need or challenge, and is informed by deep insight—something surprising or non-obvious that the team uncovered. Crucially, the problem statement is framed without implying a particular solution so as not to bias the upcoming ideation. For example, instead of defining a problem as "we need to build a faster bicycle", a human-centred definition would be "urban commuters (who) need a quicker way to get to work (what) because crowded public transit makes their daily journey long and uncomfortable (why)." This reframing focuses on the user's underlying need (quick, comfortable commute) rather than a predetermined solution (a faster bike might be one answer, but there could be many others). Theoretical models underpinning the Define stage often stress the balance of analysis and synthesis. Tim Brown of IDEO noted that in innovation processes, *analysis* (breaking down data) and *synthesis* (combining data into patterns) are equally important. In practice, teams might use tools like affinity mapping (clustering notes from user research into themes), empathy maps, or user journey maps to analyse findings and then create frameworks like problem statements or Point of View (POV) statements to synthesise and capture the definition of the challenge.

Defining the right problem is half the battle in design thinking. A famous saying is, "A well-framed problem is half-solved." Organisations ensure they are solving the right problem by investing time in the Define stage. For instance, a company might initially frame their issue as "sales are low, we need a new marketing campaign," but user research might reveal the real issue is that customers don't understand how to use the product—pointing instead to a design or onboarding problem. Reframing the problem in human-centric terms (e.g., "new users need an easier way to get started with our product because currently many feel lost after signup") leads the team toward very different and likely more effective solutions than the original business-centric framing.

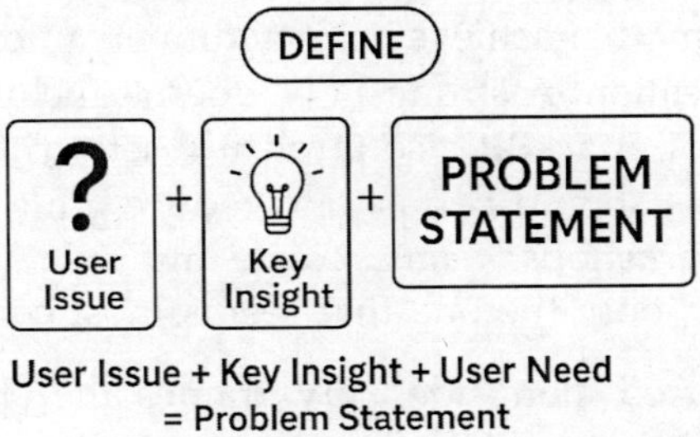

FIGURE 2.2 Problem Statement.

2.3.1 Techniques: Problem Statements, Point of View (POV)

Two key outputs of the Define stage are problem statements and POV statements, which essentially serve as anchors for the ideation phase.

1. **Problem Statement:** This is a clear, concise description of the user's need or problem that the team will address. A good problem statement is user-centered, not company-centered, and it's specific enough to be manageable but broad enough to allow creative freedom. Often, teams phrase problem statements in terms of a specific user persona. For example, instead of saying "increase app engagement," a human-centred problem statement might be: *"Young working professionals need a convenient way to organise and remember daily tasks because they feel overwhelmed by information and often miss important to-dos."* This statement identifies *who* (young professionals) and *why* (being overwhelmed leads to missed tasks) without jumping to "the solution is a task app feature." Problem statements may result from a workshop where the team distils research findings into key user needs. Why this matters: A sharply defined problem statement guides the team's brainstorming—it acts like a beacon, ensuring everyone ideates around the same challenge and criteria for success (Dam & Siang, 2017). In business case studies, teams that took time to craft a precise problem statement often found it much easier to generate relevant ideas. For instance, a bank's innovation team might define their problem as "first-time customers need to feel trust and clarity when opening an account because currently many abandon the process out of confusion." Such a statement would direct the subsequent ideation toward solutions for building trust and clarity (like simpler forms, friendly guidance, etc.).

2. **Point of View (POV):** A POV is essentially a refined problem statement that includes three elements: a specific user (who?), their need (what do they need to do?), and an insight (why?—a surprising or deeper reason uncovered in research). The d.school suggests a POV formula: "[User] needs [Need] because [Insight]." (Dam & Siang, 2017). For example: *"A busy mother of two needs a quicker way to prepare healthy dinners because our insight is that her evenings are chaotic and she feels guilty when opting for fast food."* This POV highlights the user (busy mom), need (quick healthy dinner prep), and insight (time chaos and guilt) which came from empathy work. Crafting a POV helps the team focus on a *meaningful* challenge and provides a "design vision" to rally around. It's actionable and sparks questions like "How might we help this mother achieve healthy dinners under her constraints?"—which leads directly to ideation. A strong POV doesn't include or hint at a solution but points to an angle of attack. It also implicitly sets criteria for evaluating ideas (in the above case, ideas should be fast and reduce guilt by being healthy). In many design thinking workshops, teams create multiple POV statements from their research and then choose the one that seems most compelling to proceed with.

One technique often used alongside POV frames the challenge as a "How Might We" (HMW) question. Based on the POV, the team turns the problem into an open-ended question: *"How might we [enable the user's need]?"* For example, from the POV above, one could ask: "How might we help busy parents prepare healthy dinners in less time?" The HMW phrasing purposefully suggests that a solution is possible and invites many answers . It also doesn't impose one solution path. Our example leaves room for solutions ranging from meal-planning apps to grocery delivery or cooking appliances. HMW questions are a classic bridge from Define to Ideate, ensuring the problem is framed optimally and generatively. A famous real-world example of an HMW leading to innovation is: *"How might we create a baby warming device that helps parents in remote villages give their dying infants a chance to survive?"* (Dam & Siang, 2017). This question inspired the design of the Embrace infant warmer—a low-cost, sleeping bag-like device that has saved thousands of premature babies in developing countries. It shows how a well-framed POV and HMW (focusing on *parents* and *remote villages* with *dying infants* rather than "building a cheaper incubator") opened the door to an innovative solution.

In summary, the Define stage translates empathy into focus. Techniques like crafting problem statements, POVs, and HMW questions help teams crystallise *what* user problem they are solving and *why* it matters. This stage often involves intense team discussion and synthesis, but it creates a powerful springboard for ideation when done well. It ensures that the subsequent brainstorming isn't aimless creativity but that creativity is directed at a problem that genuinely needs solving.

2.4 IDEATE: GENERATING INNOVATIVE SOLUTIONS

With a clear problem or POV, the design thinking process enters the ideation stage. Here, the objective is to generate a wide range of possible solutions—to think broadly and creatively about addressing the defined challenge. Ideation is about unleashing imagination and exploring new ideas without immediate constraints. In practice, this stage often feels energetic and free-flowing as teams look to build on each other's ideas and push beyond obvious answers.

The Ideate stage is guided by the principle that quantity breeds quality. The team increases the chances of arriving at an innovative, breakthrough solution by coming up with many ideas, including wild or unconventional ones. As Alex Osborn (the advertising executive who coined "brainstorming") famously said, *"It is easier to tone down a wild idea than to think up a new one."* (Dam & Siang, 2017). Thus, during ideation, defer judgment —no idea is immediately dismissed as too impractical. Instead, teams are encouraged to seek the unexpected, combine ideas, and stretch their thinking. This stage leverages divergent thinking; it's about expanding the solution space as much as possible before later narrowing it down.

Common approaches in ideation include structured brainstorming sessions, sketching ideas, role-playing scenarios, and other creativity techniques. Often, a facilitator will pose the "How Might We" questions defined earlier and use them as prompts for idea generation. Team members might tacitly write ideas on sticky notes first (to ensure every voice is heard), then share them for group discussion and elaboration. The environment is informal and playful—sometimes, teams use games or creativity exercises to spark fresh thinking. For example, they might do a round of "worst possible idea" (intentionally suggesting terrible solutions, which can lower inhibitions and ironically trigger good ideas) or impose fun constraints like "what if we had to solve this with 1980s technology?" to inspire novel concepts.

It's also important that ideation be inclusive and multidisciplinary. It might mean bringing people from different departments (marketing, engineering, customer service, etc.) into the brainstorming in a business setting. Each will have unique perspectives that can lead to unique solutions. A diverse team can bounce ideas off each other and build on each other's thoughts—sometimes called "Yes, and..." in brainstorming, where one idea triggers another in a positive feedback loop. The team may have dozens or even hundreds of idea notes by the end of the ideation phase. These can then be grouped and discussed to identify the most promising concepts. It's normal to then do a bit of converging—perhaps voting or ranking ideas against criteria (like which best meets the user's need or which is most feasible and innovative)—to select a few top ideas to move forward into prototyping. The key outcome of ideation is not a perfect solution but a portfolio of potential solutions and the creative confidence that the team has explored the solution space broadly.

In summary, Ideate is the stage where the team says, *"Now that we know what problem to solve, let's figure out how we might solve it—and let's consider every possibility."* It's a fun yet critical phase that harnesses creativity and sets the stage for tangible innovation in the following steps.

2.4.1 Techniques: Brainstorming, Mind Mapping

Two of the most commonly used techniques during Ideate are brainstorming and mind mapping. Both serve to generate and organise ideas, though in slightly different ways. Let's look at each and see how businesses apply them:

- **Brainstorming:** Brainstorming is a group ideation method where participants rapidly suggest ideas to solve the defined problem in a free-thinking environment. Classic brainstorming has a few simple rules: *defer judgment* (no criticism or debate on ideas during the brainstorming), *encourage wild ideas, go for quantity, build on others' ideas,* and *stay focused on the topic.* In practice, a team might have a brainstorming session for 30 minutes, using a "How Might We" question as a prompt and writing down every idea that comes to mind. Participants are encouraged to piggyback—e.g., "Alice's idea makes me think of another approach…"—hence leveraging the collective creativity of the group. Brainstorming can be unstructured or use specific techniques (round-robin sharing, brainwriting, etc.).
- **Business application:** Brainstorming is ubiquitous in creative and innovation processes across industries. Designers might brainstorm concepts for a new dashboard interface at an automotive company. In a bank, employees from different levels might brainstorm ways to improve the branch experience. Importantly, brainstorming often benefits from cross-functional input. For instance, a tech company like Google might put engineers, designers, and product managers in a room to brainstorm a new feature—the engineers contribute knowledge of what's technically possible, designers bring user perspective, and PMs add business context. This mix can yield ideas that are both novel and viable. Brainstorming sessions at IDEO are famously collaborative and visual—team members sketch ideas on the fly, post them on walls, and discuss them. The goal is to generate a large pool of ideas. After the free-form brainstorming, the team will typically discuss and converge on a subset to prototype. Brainstorming's strength lies in unlocking out-of-the-box thinking; by suspending judgment, teams often surface unexpectedly creative solutions that a more analytical discussion might never produce.
- **Mind mapping:** Mind mapping is a technique for organising thoughts in a visual diagram. Starting with a central idea or problem written in the centre, participants draw branches outward for each related idea or theme, then sub-branches for secondary ideas, and so on. This results in a "map" of ideas where

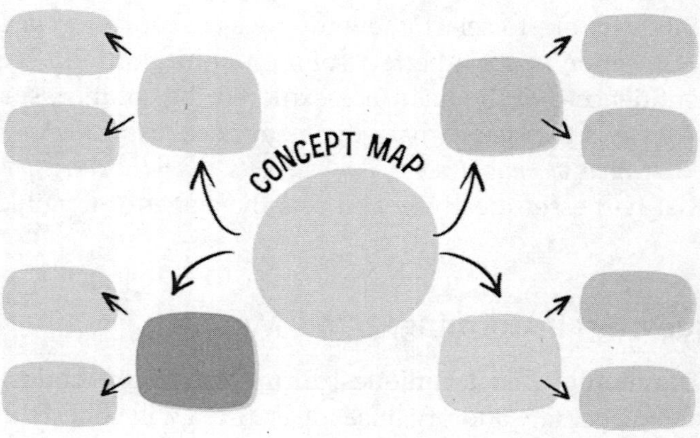

FIGURE 2.3 Mind Map.

relationships and hierarchy are visible. In design thinking, mind maps are often used to expand ideas (ideation) or organise ideas after brainstorming. For example, after brainstorming dozens of ideas, the team might create a mind map to cluster related concepts together. Alternatively, one might start with a user need in the centre and branch out all the possible ways to meet that need, exploring different categories of solutions.

✦ **Business application:** Mind mapping is common in strategy and planning sessions, not just design. For instance, an MBA team might use a mind map to brainstorm elements of a new business model—with branches for value proposition, target markets, channels, etc., then further branching into specific ideas in each category. In product development, mind maps help ensure no aspect of a problem is overlooked. Say a team is ideating on improving employee onboarding at a company; they might start with "New Employee Onboarding Experience" in the centre, then branch into "Before First Day", "First Week", and "First Month" as major phases, and ideate solutions in each (like sub-branches under "First Week" could be "mentorship", "training modules", "social integration events", each with further ideas). This structured yet flexible format helps break a big challenge into components and explore ideas within each element. Mind maps can also highlight connections between ideas—perhaps two branches reveal an opportunity to combine concepts into one solution. Many industries use mind mapping to foster creativity: advertising agencies map out campaign concepts, software teams map user needs to features and consultants map stakeholder insights when solving client problems. It's a versatile tool that primarily caters to visual thinkers. By laying out ideas spatially, it becomes easier to *see the forest and the trees*—the overall shape of the idea space and its specific ideas. Mind mapping software (or just whiteboards and sticky notes) commonly captures these diagrams during workshops.

In practice, teams often use both techniques in tandem. They might start with free-form brainstorming to get many ideas out, then use a mind map to arrange them and identify promising areas or combinations to pursue. Both brainstorming and mind mapping benefit from an environment of openness and curiosity. Additionally, both can be enhanced with external inspiration—teams might bring analogies or examples from other industries to spur ideas (a process IDEO calls "analogous inspiration") and then map those ideas out.

Ultimately, the ideation techniques help a team transition from *problem* to *solution space*. They ensure that the team has a healthy funnel of innovative concepts by the end of the ideation stage. Whether through a lively brainstorming session that yields dozens of sticky notes on the wall or a mind map that illuminates different solution pathways, these techniques drive the creative momentum of design thinking. The next challenge is turning some of these imaginative ideas into reality via prototyping.

2.5 PROTOTYPE: BUILDING TO THINK

In the Prototype stage, abstract ideas begin to take tangible form. Prototyping means creating a simplified version or model of the proposed solution. The mantra here is often *"build to think"*—by making something concrete, even if rough, you enable deeper exploration of the idea and invite feedback that wouldn't be possible with just a concept in your head. Prototypes are not final products; they are experimental artefacts intended to test design aspects and provoke learning. The significance of prototyping in design thinking cannot be overstated. It serves multiple purposes:

- **Learning:** A prototype makes the idea testable. The team and users can interact with it, which reveals what works and what doesn't. Often, building a prototype uncovers practical considerations or hidden assumptions. For example, a team designing a new mobile application may sketch out screen layouts and realise during this prototyping that an extra step is needed in the flow—insight they might not have had just by discussion.
- **Communication:** Prototypes are a communication tool. They turn vague ideas into something specific for stakeholders and team members to understand and give input. A physical model or a mock interface can align everyone's understanding of what an idea entails.
- **Iteration:** Importantly, prototypes encourage iteration because they are deliberately low investment and low fidelity at first. Since the goal is to learn, teams keep prototypes quick and cheap—think paper sketches, cardboard models, or basic digital wireframes—so they feel free to discard or change them without significant loss. It supports the fail-fast, fail-forward philosophy: it's better to identify flaws or new directions early with simple prototypes than after entirely building a product.

In design thinking, a prototype can take many forms depending on the context:

- A sketch or series of sketches can prototype a storyboard of a service (for instance, drawing the steps a customer goes through at a coffee shop to envision improvements).
- A paper interface can simulate a software app—using paper screens that a tester can "navigate" by switching them, allowing the team to test interface concepts quickly.
- A physical model made of foam, Legos, or 3D-printed parts can approximate a new physical product's shape and how one might handle it.
- A role-play or enactment in service design can prototype an experience (e.g., staff acting out a new hotel check-in process).
- Even a slide deck or video demo can serve as a prototype of an offering to gauge customer interest.

The philosophy is summed up by the saying: *"Prototype early and often."* Rather than debating which idea is best, design thinking encourages teams to prototype multiple ideas in parallel, if possible, and test them to see what resonates. Prototypes should be detailed enough to elicit useful responses, but not more. For example, if testing the information layout is the goal, a black-and-white wireframe might suffice—there is no need to polish the visual design at this stage.

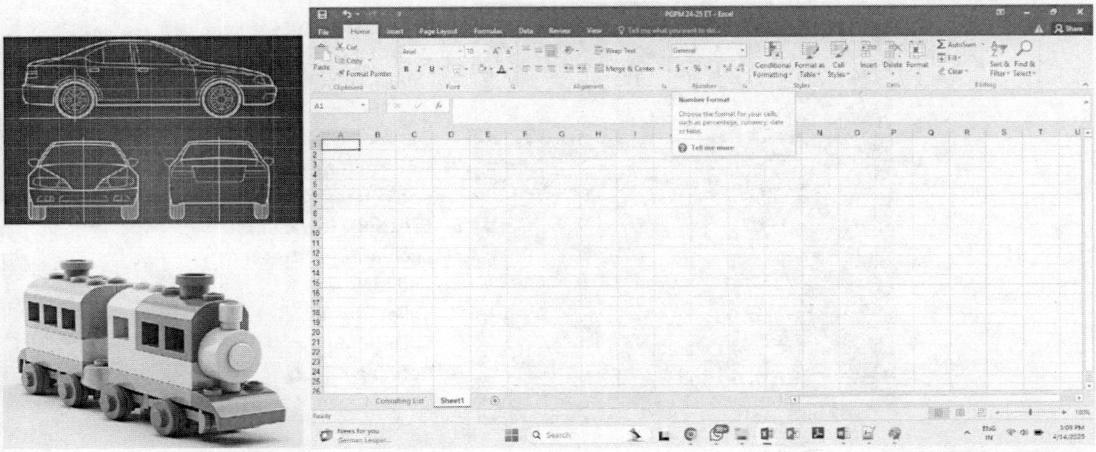

FIGURE 2.4 Design Thinking Prototype.

Prototyping also helps in refining ideas. Initial prototypes might be very rudimentary ("low-fidelity"); based on feedback, subsequent prototypes can increase in fidelity. Each time learnings are incorporated, a project might go from a sketch to a cardboard mockup, a functional but rough beta, and so on. This stepwise refinement ensures that resources are invested gradually and informed by evidence at each step.

2.5.1 Techniques: Sketches, Wireframes, Mockups

Different industries and project types will approach prototyping differently, but here are a few standard techniques and how they are applied:

- **Sketches:** Sketching is the fastest way to visualise an idea. A sketch can be anything from a quick doodle of a product shape to a detailed storyboard of a user scenario. Hand-sketching concepts in product and graphic design allows designers to explore form and function without committing to details. In the context of an app UI, sketching multiple layouts for a screen helps the team consider various arrangements before refining them on the computer.

  Sketching is universal—architects sketch floor plan concepts, advertisers sketch storyboards for commercials, and service designers sketch customer journey maps. A particular technique within sketching is "Crazy 8s," used in Google Ventures' design sprints. Each person folds the paper to get eight panels and has 8 minutes to sketch eight distinct ideas (one per panel) addressing the problem. It pushes people to think beyond their first idea. Sketches are inherently disposable, so teams feel free to ideate broadly. Even at Apple, famous for its polished products, early idea sketches and foam models were integral in nailing down the iPhone's form factor. The low cost of sketching makes it a favourite for early prototyping.

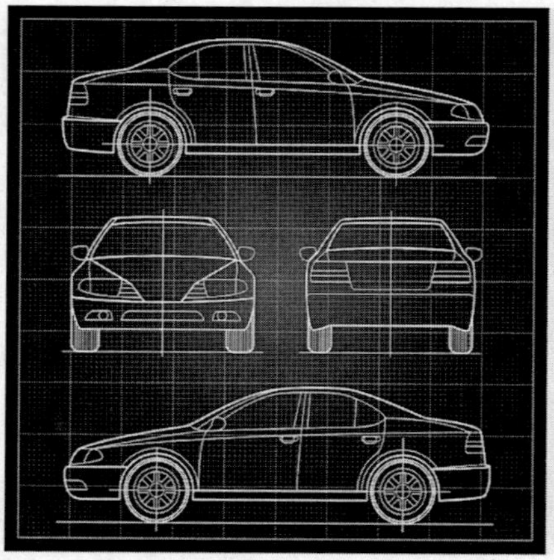

Sketching the Process Flow for New Product Development

1. Defining Problem
2. Determining entities and relationships
3. Creating Flow charts
4. Evaluating consistency and logic
5. Validating with Stakeholders
6. Refining results

FIGURE 2.5 Sketches of a New Physical Product (Car) and a New Process (Product Development flow steps).

- **Wireframes:** A wireframe is a schematic or blueprint of a digital interface, showing the layout of content and controls on each screen/page without detailed visuals. It's essentially a prototype of information architecture and interaction flow. Wireframes can be drawn on paper or created with simple digital tools. They use boxes and placeholders to represent images, text, and buttons. In software and web

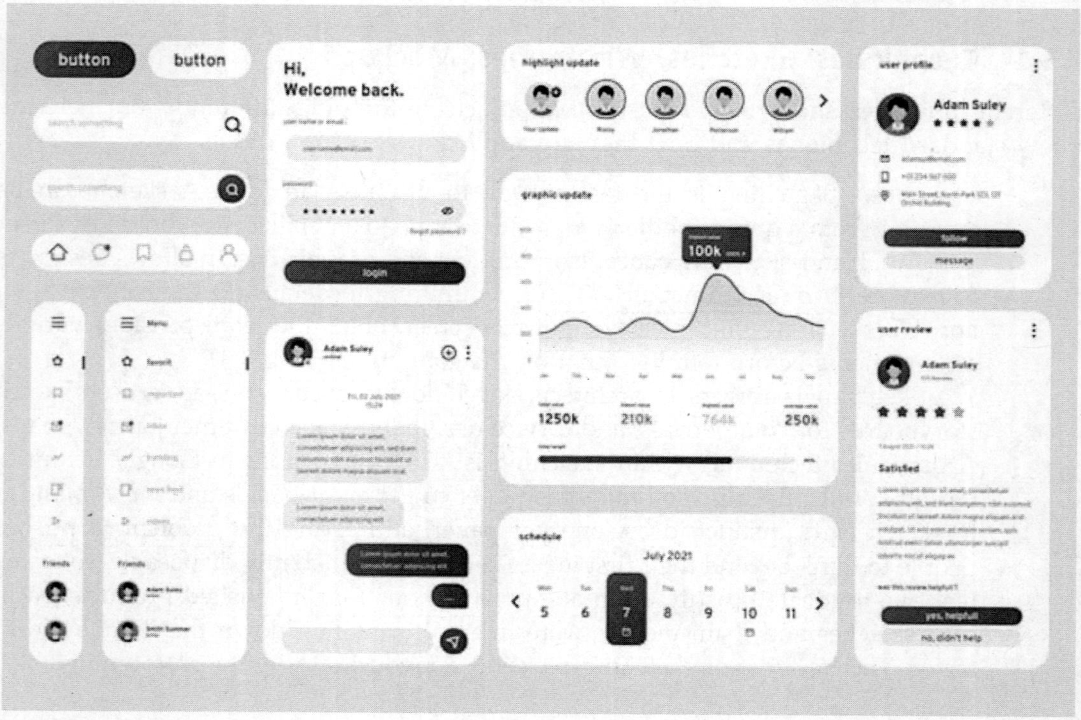

FIGURE 2.6 Wireframe.

design, wireframing is a foundational prototyping technique. For example, when a team designs a new e-commerce website, they will wireframe the homepage, product listing, checkout flow, etc., to decide what components go where and how the user navigates. This can be done quickly and reviewed with users or stakeholders to ensure the structure meets needs. Feedback like "I can't find the cart" or "This page feels too cluttered" can be gathered from a wireframe just as well as a finished UI—thereby saving the effort of pushing pixels prematurely. In industries like SaaS and mobile apps, iterative wireframing is standard; multiple versions may be tried. Often, clickable wireframes (using tools like InVision or Figma) are made, allowing a user test participant to click through a series of wireframe screens as if using the product. It tests the flow and concept without any coding.

- **Mockups:** "Mockup" can sometimes mean a mid-to high-fidelity prototype. In digital design, a mockup often refers to a more refined visualisation of an interface—showing style, colour, and content but not yet a fully working product. In product design, a mockup might be a non-functional physical model that looks close to the envisioned product. For example, a hardware startup designing a new smartwatch might create a 3D-printed mockup with the right size and shape and maybe even a screen sticker to simulate the display—it doesn't work electronically. Still, it can be worn to test comfort and aesthetics.

  In consumer electronics, companies fabricate appearance models to evaluate look and feel and to display them in focus groups for feedback. In automotive, full-scale clay models of cars are a traditional form of mockup to judge proportions before committing to manufacturing. In software, a pixel-perfect UI mockup (possibly with some interactive hotspots) can be used in user testing to get feedback on visual appeal and clarity before developers write the code.

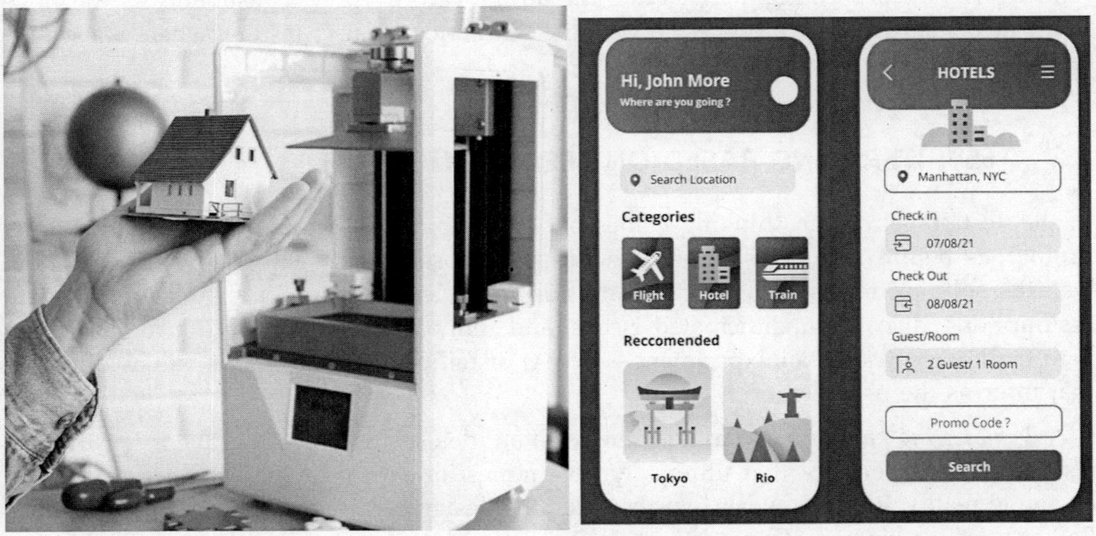

FIGURE 2.7 Prototype of a 3D printed house (scaled-down version) and a software UI.

- **Role-play and Service Prototypes:** While not mentioned explicitly in the heading, a technique for service design is worth noting—acting out or simulating the service. For instance, if designing a new airport check-in process, the team can prototype it by role-playing: one acts as the traveller, another as the agent, using props to simulate kiosks or counters. It helps identify hurdles in the experience and is effectively a "live" service prototype. Different industries adopt this: healthcare teams simulate patient intake processes, hospitality teams mockup parts of a guest experience in a conference room setting, etc., to test the human interaction elements.

Comparing how industries prototype: software/tech leans heavily on wireframes, interactive digital prototypes, and beta releases; product manufacturing often uses physical mockups and 3D prints, then functional prototypes in controlled environments; services use role-plays, pilot programs, or pop-up experiments in a small scope (e.g., a bank might prototype a new queue system in just one branch as a test). Despite differences in medium, the spirit is the same: create a representation of the idea that people can experience and do it quickly and cheaply enough that you can iterate.

One company that exemplifies prototyping is IBM, with its Enterprise Design Thinking practice. It encourages "radical prototyping," where teams even prototype business strategies (through scenarios and financial models) before a large-scale rollout. Another example: in the automobile industry, before building an expensive engine prototype, engineers might simulate it via software or build a simplified model, effectively prototyping component by component to learn incrementally.

In summary, prototyping translates ideas into reality, albeit imperfectly and incompletely. It's a process of thinking through making. By sketching, wireframing, building mockups, or enacting scenarios, design thinkers advance their solutions from concept to something testable. Prototyping reduces innovation risk by ensuring concepts are tried and refined early, incorporating insights into the design before heavy investment. As we move to the next stage, these prototypes become the centrepiece of user testing, where real-world feedback will guide further iteration.

2.6 TEST: ITERATING BASED ON FEEDBACK

In the Test stage, design thinking comes back to the users. In this phase, the team puts prototypes before real users (or stakeholders) to observe and gather feedback on how well the solution meets their needs. Testing is about learning: an opportunity to validate assumptions, discover unanticipated issues, and refine the solution. A core mindset here is to treat every test as an experiment—success or failure; the outcome is valuable insight that informs the next iteration.

Why testing matters: No matter how well an idea seems to work in theory or the lab, it's the users' experience that ultimately determines its effectiveness. Testing grounds the design in reality. It often reveals gaps between the design team's intent and user experience. For example, a fintech startup might internally prototype a new budgeting application feature and think it's intuitive. However, testing with users might show confusion about how to find or use the feature. Such insights are vital because they allow the team to fix usability issues or rethink features before a full launch. Additionally, testing can surface new user needs or context information that went unnoticed earlier, potentially sending the team back to redefine or ideate further—and that's a positive outcome in design thinking's iterative philosophy.

During tests, design thinkers observe and listen to feedback. Techniques used include:

- **Usability Testing:** Common in digital product design, a facilitator asks users to perform tasks using a prototype (e.g., "Can you sign up and create a budget in this app?") and observes where they succeed or struggle. The user might "think aloud," expressing what they find confusing or nice. Any errors, hesitations, or verbal comments are noted as areas to improve. Usability testing can be done one-on-one or remotely, and even a handful of users is usually enough to identify the major usability issues in an interface.
- **User Feedback Surveys/Interviews:** After trying a prototype, users might be interviewed or given a short survey to capture their impressions. For instance, a physical product prototype could be given to users for a week; then, the team interviews them about their experience living with it. A pilot program might be run for services, and participants will be surveyed on their satisfaction and outcomes.
- **Analytics and Feedback Loops:** Teams sometimes set up metrics to track user behaviour, especially with digital prototypes or pilot launches. For example, a beta version of a software tool might log usage data to see which features are used or where drop-offs occur. This quantitative feedback forms a loop—the design is updated, new data is gathered, and so on.

The Test phase in design thinking is inherently iterative. A prototype is rarely perfect; more often, testing illuminates needed changes. The team then cycles back—possibly to the Prototype stage to modify the design or even back to Ideate if the feedback suggests the solution approach isn't hitting the mark. In some cases, surprisingly, test feedback might even send the team back to the Empathize or Define stage if they learn that the understanding of the problem needs adjustment. It is not failure; it's progress since catching these issues early prevents costly mistakes later. The Interaction Design Foundation notes that the testing stage can reveal insights that lead the team to refine the prototype or "even go back to the Define stage to revisit the problem" (Dam & Siang, 2017).

2.6.1 Techniques: Usability Testing, Feedback Loops

Let's dive a bit deeper into the techniques mentioned and illustrate with examples:

- **Usability Testing:** This technique is most associated with software and websites, but the concept applies broadly: give users a task and watch how they interact with your prototype to accomplish it. The aim is to uncover *usability issues* (where people get confused, errors occur, etc.) and *likability issues* (whether the solution is pleasant and satisfying). In a classic usability test, the facilitator will remind the user that *"We're testing the prototype, not you,"* to make them comfortable and encourage them to speak their thoughts aloud. For example, if testing a new self-checkout kiosk prototype for a retail store, a user might be asked to scan and pay for an item. Observers might notice the user struggles to find the "Pay Now" button, indicating the UI needs redesign. Or the user might express, "I expected a confirmation screen here," telling designers that a step feels missing.

Companies like Amazon constantly run usability tests for their website changes—even small tweaks like moving a button are tested to ensure they improve and do not hurt the user experience. Car manufacturers do usability tests for in-car navigation or infotainment prototypes by letting drivers use them in a simulator and observing where attention lapses or confusion happens. Usability testing yields direct, actionable feedback for designers and is often done in multiple rounds (test, refine, test again).

- **Feedback Loops:** A feedback loop is a continuous feedback and iteration system. In product development, especially agile software development, there's an emphasis on releasing early versions (MVPs or betas) to a subset of users and then using their feedback to inform the next version. It essentially embeds testing into the development cycle. For example, many mobile applications have beta programs where enthusiastic users try new features before the official release and send feedback (either via built-in feedback forms or analytics). The team might learn that a new feature is rarely used (via analytics, a quantitative loop) and also gather qualitative feedback with reasons (via a forum or survey, e.g., users might say it's hard to find or not helpful). With that information, the team iterates—perhaps repositioning the feature in the application's navigation or tweaking its functionality—and then updates the beta for another round of feedback. This iterative loop continues until data shows the feature meets its goals (increased usage, positive feedback). In hardware or services: Feedback loops can be longer but are still used. A consumer electronics firm may do a series of user testing sessions at different prototype stages (alpha, beta units), creating a loop of test-feedback-fix over months. A restaurant chain trying a new service model (like mobile ordering) might pilot it in a few locations (gather metrics like order time, customer satisfaction surveys, etc.), refine the process, pilot again, and gradually scale up—a feedback loop on a larger scale.
- **"Fail Fast" Iteration in Startups:** Many startup cultures embrace launching something basic quickly, then iterating based on market feedback—essentially, design thinking tests and iterating ethics in a business context. For example, a startup might launch a minimal product version to see how users respond, then pivot if necessary. Case in point: Starbucks, in its early days, had a concept for its coffee shops modelled on Italian espresso bars (no seating, opera music, traditional decor). When they launched in the U.S., customer feedback and behaviour indicated this wasn't working—Americans wanted a comfortable cafe experience. Noticing this (i.e., effectively "testing" the concept in the real market), Starbucks iterated their store design—they added seating, adjusted the ambience, and introduced sizes like "Grande" and non-fat milk options. This feedback-driven pivot was crucial to Starbucks' success (Krishan, 2020). It highlights how listening to users and adapting based on feedback is vital, even beyond product design into business model and experience design.

Another technique aligned with feedback loops is A/B testing (standard in digital products). It is where two versions (A and B) are released to see which performs better. It's a real-time test of specific design decisions (like button colour or wording) on a subset of users. While more of a quantitative experiment than a holistic design thinking test, it underscores the idea of continuously using feedback to improve the design.

In any testing approach, the key is to remain open-minded and agile. The design team must resist the urge to defend their prototype if users struggle; instead, they say, "Thank you, this is valuable to know", and take notes. After testing, the team reviews the feedback and decides what changes to make. It might involve quick fixes or might prompt rethinking a feature entirely. It is common to cycle through multiple prototype-test iterations. Each iteration ideally gets the solution closer to meeting user needs and providing a delightful experience.

Testing also helps in *measuring success relative to the defined problem*. Remember the POV and success criteria established in Define? During tests, the team can check if those are being met. For instance, if the POV was about helping a busy mom cook dinner faster, the test might measure if the prototype saves time or reduces stress for her when tried. If not, go back to the drawing board. If yes, that's validation to proceed.

By the end of the Test stage (or multiple test iterations), the team should have high confidence in their solution's desirability, usability, and effectiveness. The insights gained ensure that when the solution is fully implemented, it's far more likely to succeed because it has been shaped by real user input at every step.

2.7 ITERATIVE NATURE OF DESIGN THINKING

One of the defining characteristics of design thinking is its iterative, non-linear nature. Rather than a strict sequence of steps that you execute only once, the process is more like a continuous cycle or loop of learning and improving. Teams frequently loop back to previous stages based on findings in later stages. This flexibility is a significant strength, as it allows the solution to evolve in step with a more profound understanding.

The design thinking process is often depicted as an iterative loop. After testing, teams may circle back to Empathise or Define, refining their understanding of the users' needs and problems. Each iteration of the Empathize–Define–Ideate–Prototype–Test yields new insights, gradually converging on an optimal solution.

In practice, iteration might look like this: After testing a prototype (Stage 5), the team realises that the problem wasn't framed quite right—users are indicating a different underlying need. The team then goes back to the Define stage (Stage 2) to reframe the problem or to Empathise (Stage 1) to gather more insights on that newly uncovered need. Then they ideate (Stage 3) again for that reframed problem, prototype (Stage 4) a refined concept, and test (Stage 5) again. This cycle can repeat several times, gradually honing in on a truly effective solution.

Iteration is not a failure; it's intentional. Design thinking embraces a "learn as you go" philosophy. Early iterations are expected to be rough, so rapid prototyping and frequent testing exist to improve through feedback. Each loop through the stages reduces

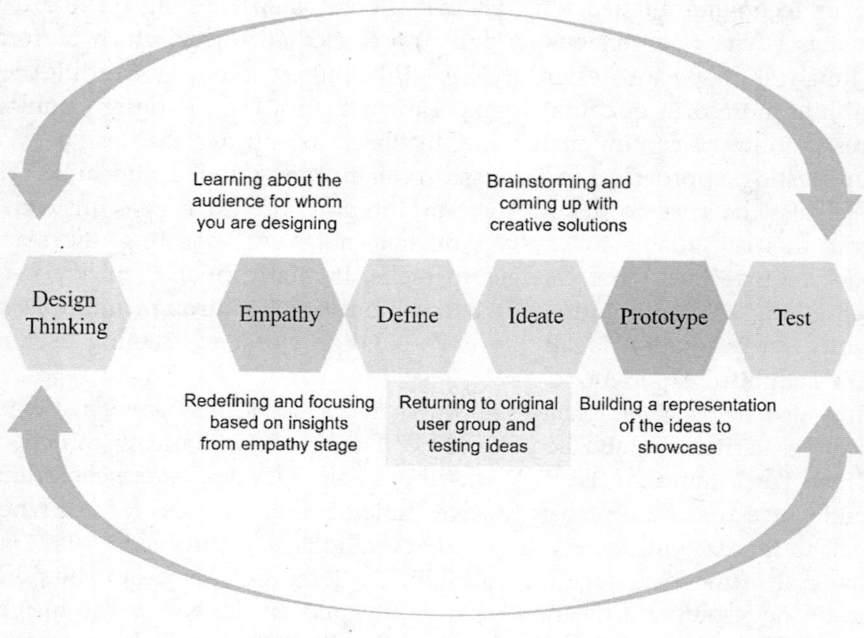

FIGURE 2.8 The Design Thinking Process.

uncertainty. It's far better to iterate on paper and in prototypes than to launch a fully built product and then discover fundamental issues. By iterating, teams save time and resources in the long run and end up with a solution that has been validated and refined.

Moreover, the process itself is fluid. Sometimes, teams might do a mini-iteration within a single stage. For instance, they might prototype and test multiple versions in quick succession (micro-iterations) during the Prototype stage. Or they might iterate between Empathize and Define a few times at the project's start as they refine their understanding of the user's world.

Another aspect of iteration is that design thinking isn't just executed once for a project and then done. Even after launching a product or solution, the design thinking mindset encourages continuous observation (empathising with users as they use the solution in real contexts) and iteration to improve further or adapt to changing needs. In other words, the end of one cycle can feed into the beginning of the next cycle in an ongoing innovation process. Many modern companies adopt this continuous design and improvement cycle as a part of agile methodologies or continuous improvement programs.

Consider a case where iteration was key: Netflix, in its early days, started as a DVD-by-mail service. As the environment changed (streaming became viable, user behaviours shifted), Netflix's team essentially re-entered the Empathize stage—understanding emerging user desires for instant access—and redefined their problem ("How might we deliver entertainment instantly?"). They ideated and eventually pivoted to streaming. They have continued to iterate the service, using A/B tests and user feedback loops on features like personalised recommendations (a feature that went through many design iterations using user data). This iterative evolution is why Netflix remains successful—they treat design as ongoing, not one-and-done.

To summarise, iteration is integral to design thinking's DNA. The process is depicted not as a straight line but often as a loop or a series of loops (as shown in Figure 2.8), reinforcing that each phase can lead back to an earlier phase. Embracing iteration means embracing continuous learning and flexibility. It requires a culture where team members are comfortable with ambiguity and change and see each product version not as a final verdict on success or failure but as a stepping stone toward a better solution. This iterative approach helps teams navigate complexity and uncertainty, which is why design thinking is suited to tackling wicked problems where the best answer is not obvious.

SCAN ME

Scan to watch the lecture—The design thinking process.

Readers are encouraged to watch the lecture on the design thinking process by following this link: https://youtu.be/7ZIgRE7oNvo. Alternatively, they can use the QR code below to access the lecture.

CASE STUDIES: Healthcare and City Traffic Scenario

To see how the design thinking process comes together in real life, let's examine two case studies from different domains: one in healthcare and another in urban traffic. Each illustrates how the stages of design thinking were applied and the outcomes achieved. Notably, one is a global example, and the other is an Indian scenario, highlighting that design thinking is universally applicable yet locally adaptable.

Healthcare Case Study:

Improving Hospital Shift Handoffs (Global Example—Kaiser Permanente, USA)

One famous example of design thinking in healthcare comes from Kaiser Permanente, a large American healthcare provider, which collaborated with IDEO to improve the way nurses exchanged information during shift changes. Initially, Kaiser's challenge was that nurse shift handoffs were inefficient and inconsistent. Nurses often spent up to 45 minutes per shift in a backroom handing over patient information, which delayed incoming nurses from seeing patients and led to communication gaps (Seoane, 2018). The problem affected patient care—patients felt unattended and sometimes lost vital information.

- **Empathise:** A project team, including Kaiser's nursing staff and IDEO designers, started by observing and interviewing nurses and patients. They shadowed nurses through shift changes to witness the process and its pain points. They empathised with nurses juggling many tasks, patient waiting, and uncertainty during these changeovers. Nurses expressed frustration that they spent so much time away from patients while doing handoff, and each nurse had their own way of note-taking, which sometimes confused colleagues.

- **Define:** Synthesising these observations, the an apparent problem was *"Nurses need a more efficient, standardised way to hand over patient information at shift change because the current process is too long and varies widely, causing delays and potential miscommunication."* A POV statement might have been in design thinking terms: "Busy hospital nurses need a way to quickly and reliably transfer critical patient information to the next shift because currently patients wait unattended and information isn't consistently shared." The insight was that moving the handoff closer to patients and standardising it could improve efficiency and care quality.
- **Ideate:** The team brainstormed numerous ideas. These ranged from creating a digital tool for handoff to redesigning the workflow entirely. Many ideas centred on engaging patients in the process or using checklists to ensure consistency. They considered having nurses do shift change at the patient's bedside instead of a conference room so that the incoming nurse could meet the patient immediately and the patient could overhear or even contribute to the discussion (increasing transparency and trust).
- **Prototype:** One of the promising ideas was a "bedside handoff" combined with a standard template for information. The team prototyped this by creating a simple checklist for nurse handovers and role-playing a bedside shift change in a hospital ward. To ensure consistency, they also prototyped a documentation tool that both nurses would fill in together during the bedside handoff. It might have been done initially on paper forms or a whiteboard as a low-fidelity prototype of the process and tools.
- **Test:** They then tried the new handoff process in a real hospital unit (on a small scale)—effectively a pilot test. Nurses performed shift changes at patients' bedsides, using the checklist and engaging patients by inviting questions or comments. Observers noted what happened: for example, nurses initially felt awkward involving patients, and some patients were passive. The feedback from nurses was that the process took about the same time or slightly less than before (since both nurses were present and did not repeat work), and patient feedback was very positive—they felt more informed and cared for. However, some tweaks were needed in the checklist to cover all necessary info, and nurses suggested adding a quick update to patients at the end. The team iterated on these details and tested again.

These design thinking efforts resulted from the Nurse Knowledge Exchange (NKE) protocol that Kaiser rolled out across many of its hospitals. The new solution involved nurses conducting shift-change briefings at the patient's bedside, encouraging patient participation, and using a standardised electronic worksheet to record information. It dramatically reduced nurses' time searching for information and reduced shift-change duration. More importantly, it improved patient care: nurses began their shift already familiar with their patients, and patients felt safer and more engaged (since they literally "met" the incoming nurse as the shift started). After implementing this design, Kaiser reported increased patient satisfaction and reduced communication-related errors. The solution was so successful it was rolled out to over 8,000 hospitals and became a model of best practice in healthcare (Lockwood & Papke, 2017).

This case highlights design thinking in action: deep empathy (shadowing nurses), reframing the problem (from "nurses take too long to hand off" to "how might we involve patients and streamline communication?"), ideating with input from frontline staff, quickly prototyping a new workflow (not just a product), and testing in a real environment with iteration. It shows that even processes and experiences can be prototyped and refined just like physical products. Kaiser's case is now cited widely as an example of how human-centred design can transform healthcare delivery.

City Traffic Scenario Case Study: Redesigning a Dangerous Road Junction (Indian Example—Sunguvarchatram Junction, Chennai)

In India, a compelling case emerged from an educational initiative where a design thinking club of engineering students tackled a pressing local problem: a notoriously dangerous road junction on the outskirts of Chennai. The Sunguvarchatram junction on a busy highway connecting Chennai and Bengaluru had a high incidence of accidents—dozens of fatalities and injuries each year (School of Design Thinking, n.d.). The challenge was how to make this junction safer for all commuters.

A batch of 17 students, guided by faculty from a School of Design Thinking in Chennai, applied the design thinking process to this real-world traffic problem:

- **Empathise:** The students began by collecting data and observing the junction in person. They spent time at the site at different hours, noting traffic flow, driver behaviour, signage, and road conditions. They also consulted accident records and spoke informally with commuters (drivers, pedestrians) and traffic officials to understand the circumstances of accidents. Importantly, they performed a "journey mapping" exercise for drivers: mapping out a driver's experience approaching and crossing the junction. It helped them capture the emotional highs and lows. For instance, they observed that drivers often felt anxious and confused when approaching the intersection due to poor signage and lighting, especially at night. They empathised with truck drivers who complained about sudden cross-traffic and local villagers who needed to cross the highway on foot or two-wheelers. Through immersive observation and some interviews, the students gained a human perspective on why accidents were happening (beyond what statistics alone would tell).
- **Define:** After analysis, the students identified core problems. One major insight was that the root cause of many accidents was driver distraction and reduced concentration at the junction, exacerbated at night by poor visibility and lack of

clear signals. The junction had a "star" road pattern rather than a grid, meaning multiple roads converged asymmetrically, giving drivers limited options to avoid conflicts (Kunal, 2018). Additionally, some of the basic safety infrastructure was lacking or not maintained. For example, warning signs and reflectors were either absent or not functioning, and there were no speed-calming measures. They framed the problem: *"Commuters (especially at night) need a safer way to pass through the Sunguvarchatram junction because the current road layout and lack of safety measures lead to high distraction and collision risk."* In technical terms, the problem encompassed human factors (driver behaviour, decision-making under stress) and design factors (road design and signals). The students' Point of View might have been: "Drivers travelling at night need clear guidance and a forgiving road design at the junction because they currently face sudden hazards and have difficulty anticipating cross-traffic." The group also recognised multiple stakeholders: drivers, local pedestrians, and industries in the area that contributed to unusual traffic patterns (like slow trucks turning).

- **Ideate:** The interdisciplinary student team brainstormed a host of possible solutions. They didn't limit themselves to one category—ideas spanned infrastructure changes, technology interventions, and policy/ enforcement. Some brainstormed ideas included installing rumble strips and better street lighting to grab drivers' attention, redesigning the intersection into a roundabout (traffic circle) to slow down vehicles naturally, adding large reflective signboards far ahead of the junction to warn drivers, creating a pedestrian overpass or underpass, deploying blinking warning lights or speed cameras, and even community measures like reflective stickers on local tractors or trucks. They used tools like brainstorming divergence and then convergence; for instance, they prioritised ideas using Stephen Covey's urgency vs. importance matrix to focus on ideas that could have high impact quickly (like immediate sign and lighting fixes) and also considered bold ideas that might require more time (like re-routing traffic flow or redesigning the junction physically).
- **Prototype:** Some solutions could be prototyped on paper or in a simulation. The students created a simple scaled model of the junction to simulate how a roundabout might work, moving toy cars through it to identify potential issues. They prototyped sign designs and placement for awareness solutions—essentially making printouts of large warning signs ("Accident-prone zone ahead—slow down") and even temporarily placing them to gauge visibility. For technology ideas, they conceptualised how a "blinking light system" could work by using flashlights to mimic the effect at night and standing at various distances to see if it caught attention. They also prototyped the user experience of the journey: one team member drove through the junction following a proposed new signage placement to see if it felt safer or prompted earlier slowing. These quick-and-dirty prototypes (some were just exercises or visual mocks) helped them refine the feasibility of ideas. For example, they realised that a full roundabout might not be feasible due to space constraints with nearby buildings, but a partial median redesign could channel traffic better.

- **Test:** With cooperation from the local Road Transport Office (RTO), the students could implement low-cost trial measures and observe outcomes. They placed temporary reflective drums and markers at critical spots to guide lanes and tested these over a few days, observing whether drivers adjusted their paths at night. After these changes, they also conducted a small survey of regular commuters (like local auto-rickshaw drivers or truckers who frequented the route), asking if they noticed a difference or had suggestions. The feedback was encouraging—drivers reported better awareness of the junction when reflective markers and signage were in place, though they still suggested that enforcing speed reduction was necessary. The temporary measures also revealed some tweaks needed (one sign that was placed too near the turn needed to be placed further back).

After several weeks of research and testing, the student team compiled their recommendations and findings into a report for the RTO. Their solution set was multi-faceted: immediate actions like installing rumble strips, repainting faded lane markers, adding solar-powered blinking warning lights and convex mirrors for blind turns; medium-term actions like improving junction lighting, placing informative signboards well in advance of the junction, and trimming obstructions blocking drivers' view; and long-term suggestions like redesigning the junction geometry to a safer layout (if possible an island or signalised intersection), and community education for local drivers about the risks. They even suggested timing changes like restricting heavy truck movement during peak local traffic hours to reduce conflict.

The impact of this case was twofold. First, it demonstrated the power of human-centred, systematic thinking on an infrastructure problem—something often left to engineers alone, but here approached with empathy and user perspective. Secondly, some of the students' recommendations were taken up by authorities: reportedly, reflective signage and better lighting were put into practice, and discussions on structural improvements were initiated. Even modest changes showed results: in the following year, accident rates at that junction reduced (according to anecdotal reports in the case study follow-up, though comprehensive data would be needed to quantify). Equally important, this case became an educational example in India of applying design thinking to civic issues, inspiring similar approaches for other community problems.

Comparing it globally, this local project parallels how design thinking was used in places like New York City to redesign street intersections for pedestrian safety via the "Vision Zero" initiative—empathising with pedestrians and drivers, prototyping changes with paint and plastic bollards, testing outcomes (accident data), then making permanent design changes. The Sunguvarchatram project shows that the same principles of iterative, user-focused design can improve something as concrete as road safety in an Indian context with limited resources.

We see that design thinking is not linear in the healthcare and traffic case studies. There were loops of going back and forth—Kaiser's team likely revisited their ideas and prototypes multiple times with nurses; the student team iterated between observation and trying solutions at the junction. Both cases also illustrate cross-disciplinary collaboration (nurses and designers, engineering students and transport officials), which enriched the outcome. Most importantly, the teams arrived at practical, innovative solutions that addressed the true needs by focusing on the humans at the centre of the problem—patients and nurses in one, drivers and commuters in the other.

Readers are encouraged to watch below two lectures presented by authors on two different scenarios where design thinking plays a crucial role.

- Design thinking for enhancing hospital efficiency—https://youtu.be/5VPzHw6ZcFs. Viewers can scan the QR code below to watch it.

Scan to Watch the Lecture—Design Thinking for Enhancing Hospital Efficiency.

- Explore traffic congestion and design thinking by watching this video: https://youtu.be/L6W-JBPPuh0. Viewers can use the QR code below to access it.

Scan to watch the lecture—Design Thinking for traffic congestion.

KEY POINTS TO REMEMBER

1. *Design thinking Framework (Empathise–Define–Ideate–Prototype–Test):* This is a flexible guide, not a rigid recipe. Always understand the human context (empathise) before jumping to solutions. *Empathise with users, clearly define the problem, ideate broadly, build prototypes, and test with users* while remaining willing to loop back as needed.
2. *Human-Centered & Empathy-Driven:* The heart of design thinking focuses on people—their needs, behaviours, and emotions. Use techniques like user interviews,

observations, and immersion to uncover insights. A solution is only as good as understanding the user behind it.

3. *Define Stage—The Power of Framing:* Spend effort to synthesise research into a sharp problem definition. A well-framed problem (often captured in a POV statement) guides the team and fuels creativity. Ensure the problem statement is user-centric (e.g., "Users need a way to X because Y"), not solution-centric.
4. *Ideation—Quantity and Openness:* Aim for volume and diversity when generating ideas. Encourage wild ideas and defer judgment. Techniques like brainstorming and mind mapping help teams think out of the box and explore all possible solutions. Collaboration across disciplines leads to richer ideas.
5. *Prototype Early, Prototype Often:* Embrace a mindset of "build to learn." Create quick, low-cost prototypes—whether sketches, role-plays, or models—to make ideas tangible. Prototyping is a means to explore options and provoke feedback, not to polish the final product. It's fine to prototype multiple concepts in parallel.
6. *Test and Iterate:* Always put prototypes in front of real users. Observe and listen to their feedback. Use usability testing or pilot programs to see how well the solution fits. Crucially, be ready to iterate—use what you learn to refine the solution. Iteration might mean minor tweaks or a significant pivot; that adaptability is key to getting it right.
7. *Non-Linearity and Flexibility:* The process stages are not one-way checkpoints but modes you can revisit. If new insights emerge during testing, loop back to redefine the problem or ideate anew. This iterative approach ensures the final solution is well-tuned to user needs and context.
8. *Broad Applicability:* Design thinking isn't just for product designers—it applies to services, processes, business models, and social issues. The case studies showed its use in a hospital setting and traffic safety. Design thinking provides a structured but creative approach in any scenario where human experience can be improved.
9. *Collaboration and Mindset:* Successful design thinking requires a collaborative team culture and a mindset open to experimentation and failure. It blends analytical thinking (making sense of research) and creative thinking (generating and exploring ideas). It also values storytelling—capturing user stories and envisioning solution scenarios—to humanise organisational problems and solutions.

Keep these key points in mind as a checklist or guiding principles when approaching a design thinking problem. They ensure that you maintain the integrity of the process and maximise its effectiveness in arriving at innovative, user-centred solutions.

KEY LEARNINGS

- *Design thinking is an iterative, user-centered process:* It taught us that by continually looping through understanding users, defining problems, ideating, prototyping, and testing, we can handle complex problems and refine solutions that truly fit users' needs. Unlike linear problem-solving, design thinking's iterative nature means improvement is continuous and informed by real-world feedback.

- *Empathy is essential for innovation:* One of the strongest takeaways is the importance of stepping into the user's shoes. By using empathy techniques (interviews, observations, etc.), we uncover latent needs and insights that drive meaningful innovation. A deep understanding of the user anchors the entire design process.
- *Problem framing drives solution quality:* We learned that how you define the problem largely determines the creativity and relevance of solutions. Investing time to synthesise research into a sharp POV or problem statement ensures the team's efforts are focused on solving the right challenge. A well-defined problem is a springboard for great ideas ("A problem well stated is a problem half solved").
- *Brainstorming and mind mapping enhance creative output:* We saw the value of divergent thinking tools in generating many ideas and broadly exploring solution spaces. Brainstorming breaks conventional thinking patterns by encouraging wild ideas without judgment, and mind mapping helps organise and extend thinking around a problem. These techniques, especially in diverse teams, can yield innovative concepts that one person might not conceive.
- *Rapid prototyping and testing reduce risk:* A key learning is the mantra "fail fast to succeed sooner." Creating prototypes—whether a sketch, a mock interface, or a role-play—and testing them early with users allows us to identify flaws and opportunities before significant resources are spent. Each test provides actionable feedback, turning "failures" into learning. This approach de-risks innovation because we make course corrections early and often.
- *Iteration leads to better outcomes:* Both theory and case examples reinforced that iteration is not a wasted effort but rather the path to excellence. The healthcare and traffic case studies demonstrated that initial solutions can be improved dramatically through user feedback and redesign cycles. The willingness to return to the drawing board upon new insights is a hallmark of success in design thinking. Over time, iterative refinement leads to solutions that are user-approved and effective in context.
- *Design thinking is applicable beyond product design—it's a problem-solving mindset:* We learned that the principles can be applied to services, business processes, policy challenges, and more. It's a versatile toolkit. Managers can use design thinking to tackle business model innovation, customer experience design, organisational change, or any scenario requiring creative problem-solving with a human touch.
- *Collaboration and stakeholder involvement are crucial:* Design thinking isn't a solo activity; it thrives on multidisciplinary teamwork and involving stakeholders (like end-users or clients). This collaborative approach yields more ideas and builds buy-in for solutions, as stakeholders feel heard and see their feedback incorporated.
- *Mindset shift:* Perhaps the most important learning is a mindset one—to remain *curious, empathetic, and unafraid of ambiguity or failure.* Design thinking encourages us to view problems through the lens of possibility ("How might we...?") and to treat every prototype or test as an experiment—success is learning, regardless of the outcome. Adopting this mindset can make us more resilient and creative managers.

These key learnings equip us with a framework and confidence to systematically yet creatively approach messy, open-ended problems. In a business environment, mastering design thinking means we can lead teams to innovate, stay aligned with customer needs, and iterate solutions until they truly resonate and deliver value.

EXERCISES

1. **Design Thinking in Everyday Life:** Identify a small everyday problem you face (e.g., your morning routine is hectic, or managing email is overwhelming). Apply the design thinking stages on your own:
   (a) *Empathise:* Reflect on your needs or interview a family member with the same issue.
   (b) *Define:* Write a clear problem statement (what's the core issue and why?).
   (c) *Ideate:* List at least 10 ideas (no matter how wild) to solve it.
   (d) *Prototype:* Pick one idea and create a quick prototype. For example, if it's a routine problem, sketch a new schedule or set up a mock "morning dashboard" on paper.
   (e) *Test:* Follow your prototype for a day or two and note what works or doesn't. Iterate once and see if it improves.
   (f) Write a short reflection on what you learned from the process, especially any surprising insights from empathising or testing.
2. *Interview and Empathy Exercise:* Pair up with a classmate. Each one of you think of a product or service you find frustrating. Conduct a 15-minute empathy interview with each other about that experience. Ask open-ended questions like "Can you describe the last time that happened?" and dig for feelings/ motivations. After interviewing, each of you should summarise:
   (a) What are your partner's key needs/pain points (what matters most to them?)?
   (b) One insight you uncovered (something not evident at first). Then, together, brainstorm at least 5 "How Might We" questions based on your findings (e.g., "How might we make online grocery shopping less confusing for new users?"). This exercise builds empathy and problem-framing skills.
3. *Brainstorming Session (Group exercise):* Form teams of 4–5. Choose one of these challenges:
   (a) Improving the experience of attending online classes.
   (b) Reducing food waste in the campus cafeteria.
   (c) Enhancing the hotel check-in process for business travellers. Warm up with a quick ice-breaker (e.g., each person shares the wackiest product they've seen). Then, spend 10 minutes in pure brainstorming mode for the chosen challenge. Follow brainstorming rules (defer judgment, go for quantity, encourage wild ideas). Aim to generate at least 30 ideas as a team. After brainstorming, cluster similar ideas (maybe using a mind map or affinity diagram). As a team, pick one or two favourite idea clusters and flesh them out—what would that idea

entail? Present your top ideas to the class. Focus on how the brainstorming rules and teamwork led to ideas you might not have thought of alone.

4. *Rapid Prototyping Challenge:* In this exercise, speed is key. Individually or in pairs, take one of the ideas from the brainstorming session (yours or another team's) and create a prototype in 15 minutes or less. Use your materials: paper, post-its, cardboard, role-play with a script, a slide mockup, etc. For example, sketch the screens if the idea was a new mobile app; if it's a new cafeteria process, role-play it with your partner and record it on video. After 15 minutes, have each person/ pair share their prototype with another pair as "testers." The testers interact with the prototype (ask questions, act as users) and give one positive feedback and one suggestion for improvement. Then, switch roles.

   Discussion: What did you learn about the idea by prototyping it? Did it change your perception of the solution?

   This exercise underscores the value of prototyping and feedback under time constraints.

5. *Case Study Reflection:* Revisit the case studies in Section 2.8 (Healthcare and City Traffic). Break into small groups and pick one of them.

   Discuss and answer:

   (a) How did empathy play a role in the success of this case? Identify specific empathy findings that guided the solution.
   (b) What could have been a likely "How Might We" question they used to ideate solutions?
   (c) Name one prototype they tried and what feedback or result it yielded.
   (d) If you were on that design team, what is one additional idea you might have suggested? (Be creative!) Each group shares a quick summary of their discussion. The aim is to deepen understanding by actively dissecting real examples.

By engaging in these exercises, you will practice empathy, problem framing, ideation, prototyping, and testing tangibly. They are designed to simulate the flow of design thinking on small personal scales and slightly bigger real-world contexts. Through these, you should gain confidence in applying the methodology and experience first-hand the kinds of insights and improvements it can generate.

THOUGHT-PROVOKING QUESTIONS

Reflect on the chapter content and consider the following questions to assess your understanding and provoke further thought:

1. **Empathy and Business Value:** Why is empathy such a crucial component of design thinking, and how can truly understanding user needs lead to competitive advantage for a company? Can you give an example of a situation where a lack of empathy might result in a failed product or service?

2. **Problem Definition:** Explain what a POV statement is in your own words. Given a scenario—for example, "college students often skip breakfast"—formulate a possible POV statement and a corresponding "How Might We" question to illustrate the Define stage.
3. **Brainstorming Dynamics:** What are the key rules of brainstorming, and what is their purpose? Describe a time (in a class project, workplace, or other group) when group discussion was dominated by critique or hierarchy. How might applying brainstorming principles change the outcome in such a scenario?
4. **Prototyping Fidelity:** There is a saying, "Prototype low-res to test big ideas, prototype high-res to test small details." What does this mean? At what stage in the design thinking process would you use a very low-fidelity prototype versus a more refined prototype? Provide an example of each and what you'd be trying to learn.
5. **Iteration in Action:** Design thinking is iterative. How would you convince a sceptical manager used to linearly executing projects that iterative testing and refinement will save time or money in the long run? Support your argument with insights from the case studies (e.g., what might have happened if Kaiser had implemented a solution without testing it with nurses first?).
6. **Application beyond Design:** Pick a business domain (such as operations, strategy, or marketing) and discuss how design thinking could be applied there. For instance, how could an operations manager use design thinking to improve a process on a factory floor? What stages would they go through, and who might they be involved with?
7. **Global vs. Local Context:** Compare the healthcare and traffic case studies. What does each illustrate about adapting the design thinking approach to the context (one in a corporate healthcare environment, one in a public sector/ local community setting)? What challenges unique to each context did the design thinking process help navigate?
8. **Measurement of Success:** If you were implementing design thinking in a company project, what metrics or indicators might you use at the end to determine if the process was successful? (Consider both the outcome—the effectiveness of the solution—and the process—team engagement, number of iterations, etc.)

These questions are meant to stimulate critical thinking about the design thinking process. Some have straightforward answers from the chapter, while others ask you to apply concepts or take a stance. Discussing these in class or pondering them in writing will help solidify your grasp of design thinking and how to leverage it in real-world scenarios.

REFERENCES

Dam, R. F., & Siang, T. Y. (2017). Define and Frame Your Design Challenge by Creating Your Point of View and Ask "How Might We". Interaction Design Foundation. Retrieved May 15, 2024, from https://www.interaction-design.org/literature/article/define-and-frame-your-design-challenge-by-creating-your-point-of-view-and-ask-how-might-we

Dam, R.F., & Siang, T.Y. (2017). The 5 Stages in the Design Thinking Process. Interaction Design Foundation. Retrieved May 15, 2024, from https://www.interaction-design.org/literature/article/5-stages-in-the-design-thinking-process

Dam, R.F., & Siang, T.Y. (2021). Stage 2 in the Design Thinking Process—Define the Problem by Synthesising Information. Interaction Design Foundation. Retrieved May 15, 2024, from https://www.interaction-design.org/literature/article/stage-2-in-the-design-thinking-process-define-the-problem-by-synthesising-information

Design Council. (n.d.). Framework for Innovation (Double Diamond). Design Council (UK). Retrieved May 15, 2024, from https://www.designcouncil.org.uk/our-resources/framework-for-innovation/

Interaction Design Foundation. (2025). Design Thinking (DT). Interaction Design Foundation—Topics. Retrieved May 15, 2024, from https://www.interaction-design.org/literature/topics/design-thinking

Krishan, K. (2020, April 3). Do It Again: The Iterative Design Thinking Process. ZEUX Innovation Blog. Retrieved May 15, 2024, from https://www.zeuxinnovation.com/articles/iteration-design-thinking/

Kunal. (2018, August 13). How can design help solve Bangalore's traffic problem? UX Collective (Medium). Retrieved May 15, 2024, from https://uxdesign.cc/bangalore-traffic-short-case-study-7206b53ccc40

Lockwood, T., & Papke, E. (2017, November 13). How Kaiser Solved the Problem of Hospital "Ghost Towns". Fast Company. Retrieved May 15, 2024, from https://www.fastcompany.com/90150616/how-kaiser-solved-the-problem-of-hospital-ghost-towns

Perficient. (2019, January 16). Design Thinking: Empathy & Observation (Pt 3). Perficient Blogs. Retrieved May 15, 2024, from https://blogs.perficient.com/2019/01/16/design-thinking-empathy-observation-pt-3/

Rosenzweig, M. (2025, January 17). Design Thinking examples: 5 case studies. Triangility Magazine. Retrieved May 15, 2024, from https://triangility.com/design-thinking-examples-3-case-studies/

Saavedra Seoane, M. (2018, July 26). Success stories about the application of Design Thinking in the health field. DesignThinking.gal Blog. Retrieved May 15, 2024, from https://designthinking.gal/en/success-stories-about-the-application-of-design-thinking-in-the-health-field/

School of Design Thinking. (n.d.). Application of Design Thinking to Make Commuting Safer. SoDT Case Study. Retrieved May 15, 2024, from https://www.d-thinking.com/case-studies/application-of-design-thinking-to-make-commuting-safer

Trackmind. (2023, February 14). 5 Steps of Design Thinking—Part 1: A Crash Course in Empathy. Trackmind Solutions Blog. Retrieved May 15, 2024, from https://www.trackmind.com/design-thinking-empathy/

CHAPTER 3

Problem-Solving in Business

LEARNING OBJECTIVES

In this Chapter, we explore the significance of problem-solving in business and various approaches to tackling business challenges. After reading this Chapter, the readers will be able to:

- Understand the importance of problem-solving in business and recognise how effective problem-solving can drive success (and how poor problem-solving can lead to failure).
- Differentiate between structured and unstructured problem-solving approaches and identify the most appropriate situations.
- Gain familiarity with common problem-solving frameworks and methodologies used in business and understand their broad applications.
- Explain the hypothesis-driven approach to problem-solving, as used in consulting and data-driven decision-making, and apply it to real business scenarios.
- Apply structured problem-solving techniques, including forming issue trees and using the Mutually Exclusive, Collectively Exhaustive (MECE) principle, to break down complex problems logically.
- Perform root cause analysis using tools like the 5 Whys and Fishbone diagrams to identify underlying causes of business problems and propose effective solutions.

3.1 IMPORTANCE OF PROBLEM-SOLVING IN BUSINESS

Problem-solving is a critical skill in business because every organisation inevitably encounters challenges. The way a company addresses its problems often determines its success or failure. Effective problem solvers can analyse complex situations, think critically, and generate creative solutions to overcome obstacles. Strong problem-solving promotes efficiency, innovation, and resilience in a dynamic marketplace, enabling businesses to navigate uncertainties and maintain a competitive edge. For example, companies use problem-solving to improve processes, address customer needs, resolve conflicts, and adapt to market changes, which drive organisational success.

The impact of problem-solving (or lack thereof) is evident in real-world business outcomes. One famous success story is Netflix's decision to reinvent its business model. In 2007, faced with shifting consumer preferences away from DVDs, Netflix boldly pivoted to online streaming. This well-considered problem-solving move, recognising the trend and investing in streaming Technology, propelled Netflix to dominate the entertainment industry. Similarly, Apple's introduction of the iPod in 2001 addressed a problem in portable music consumption. Despite scepticism, Apple's innovative solution (combining a user-friendly device with an online music store) transformed the music industry and set the stage for Apple's future growth. These examples highlight how proactive problem-solving can identify opportunities and drive major business innovations (Nelson, 2023).

Conversely, ineffective problem-solving can spell disaster. Kodak's failure to adapt to the digital photography revolution is a classic example. Kodak invented one of the first digital cameras, but management viewed it as a threat to their film business and failed to embrace digital Technology fully. This inability to solve the strategic problem of digital disruption, essentially a refusal to change the business model, led to Kodak's rapid decline and bankruptcy. The Kodak story underscores that inaction or wrong decisions in the face of problems (in this case, technological change) can leave even a market leader obsolete. In summary, problem-solving is not just a routine workplace skill; it is fundamental to making sound business decisions, avoiding pitfalls, and capitalising on opportunities for long-term success (Nelson, 2023).

3.2 STRUCTURED AND UNSTRUCTURED PROBLEM-SOLVING

Approaches to business problem-solving can be broadly categorised as structured or unstructured. A *structured problem-solving* approach is systematic and methodical: the problem solver follows a defined process or framework to analyse the issue step by step. By contrast, an *unstructured problem-solving* approach is more ad-hoc and relies on intuition, experience, or improvisation without a formal plan. In practice, many managers blend both styles, but understanding the distinction is essential for choosing the right approach in a given situation.

Structured problem-solving typically involves clearly defining the problem, gathering and analysing data, generating options, and implementing solutions in a logical sequence. It often employs analytical tools or frameworks (which we introduce in this chapter) to ensure nothing is overlooked. This approach is ideal for complex or high-stakes problems because it imposes rigour and completeness. For example, if a manufacturer faces a recurring quality defect, a structured method would be to investigate potential causes systematically (using data and root cause analysis) and then implement a fix. Such a method reduces the chance of jumping to conclusions or missing key factors.

Unstructured problem-solving, on the other hand, relies on informal techniques and judgment. It might involve brainstorming freely, trial-and-error, or drawing on one's prior experience to make a quick decision. This approach can be practical for simple problems or when time is limited. For instance, a startup founder dealing with a minor website glitch might simply apply her experience or intuition to fix it on the fly rather than conduct a complete analysis. Unstructured methods can also spark creativity. In the early ideation phases, teams often brainstorm in an open-ended way to generate novel ideas without the constraints of a formal process.

It's essential to match the approach to the problem. Experts note that problem-solving should not default to unstructured thinking for significant issues. A structured approach is recommended to ensure thorough analysis if a challenge is complex, has serious consequences, or occurs frequently. However, for minor or one-off problems, an elaborate structure may not be worth the effort—an unstructured quick fix based on intuition might be "good enough." For example, research suggests unstructured techniques (like relying on personal experience or a quick discussion) may be acceptable when a problem is low in severity and unlikely to recur. In summary, structured approaches bring rigour and are best for complex, critical problems, whereas unstructured approaches offer speed and flexibility for simpler ones. Skilled business leaders know when to apply each style: they might brainstorm creatively to explore a new product idea (unstructured) but use a structured process to diagnose why sales dropped last quarter.

3.3 INTRODUCTION TO FRAMEWORKS AND METHODOLOGIES

Given the importance of solving business problems systematically, many frameworks and methodologies have been developed to guide the problem-solving process. A problem-solving framework is essentially a structured blueprint—it provides a step-by-step approach or a set of principles that can be followed to analyse an issue and formulate a solution. In business, using formal frameworks ensures that teams approach problems consistently and comprehensively rather than relying on ad-hoc thinking. These frameworks are taught in business schools and employed in industry because they encapsulate best practices and can be applied to various scenarios.

There are numerous frameworks and methodologies, each suited to different problems. For example, companies often use the Plan-Do-Check-Act (PDCA) cycle or Six Sigma's Define, Measure, Analyse, Improve, Control (DMAIC) methodology in process improvement and quality management. The PDCA cycle is an iterative framework that guides teams to plan a change or solution, implement it, check the results, and act on what is learned—repeating the cycle for continuous improvement (Wevalgo, n.d.). DMAIC, on the other hand, is a data-driven framework used to improve existing processes by following five phases (defining the problem, measuring current performance, analysing root causes, improving by implementing solutions and controlling to sustain the gains). These structured methodologies benefit operational problems where improving efficiency, quality, or cost is the goal.

For strategic and complex business problems, management consultants often employ their own set of frameworks. These include market analysis frameworks (like the 3C's—

Company, Customers, Competitors), decision matrices, and the use of logic trees (introduced later in this chapter). We will see that consultants emphasise breaking problems into components and ensuring analyses are *MECE* to cover all aspects logically. Another widely used framework is design thinking, an iterative methodology for solving problems creatively and human-centred. It encourages understanding user needs, brainstorming ideas, prototyping, and testing solutions. While design thinking is more exploratory and user-focused, it is still structured with defined stages (empathise, define, ideate, prototype, test).

It's worth noting that no one framework fits all problems. Each methodology has its strengths and ideal applications. For instance, a Lean Six Sigma approach might excel at reducing manufacturing defects, while design thinking might be better for developing an innovative new service. Businesses often choose a framework that aligns with the nature of their problem—or they combine elements from multiple frameworks. The common thread is that using a framework brings discipline to problem-solving. It helps teams identify the real problem, explore causes and alternatives, and implement solutions in a way that results can be evaluated and learned from. In later chapters, we will delve into specific methodologies in detail; for now, it's essential to recognise that frameworks provide a roadmap for solving problems and are invaluable in academic and real-world business settings (Chapman, 2025).

3.4 HYPOTHESIS-DRIVEN APPROACH

One powerful strategy, especially popular in consulting and analytics-driven projects, is the hypothesis-driven approach to problem-solving. In a hypothesis-driven approach, you begin by formulating a hypothesis, an educated guess, about the root cause of the problem or the likely solution. Instead of starting with exhaustive data gathering, you start with a plausible theory and then seek to test it. Top consulting firms like McKinsey, Bain, and BCG widely adopt this approach to tackle complex challenges efficiently (Rescon Partners, 2024). It helps focus the analysis on what matters most, avoiding the trap of boiling the ocean (analysing everything under the sun without direction).

Here's how it works: Suppose a business's profits are declining. Rather than randomly analysing all aspects of the company, the team might hypothesise, for example, that "profits are down because customer churn has increased due to poor customer service." That hypothesis becomes the starting point. The team will then gather data specifically to confirm or refute this hypothesis. It might include checking customer satisfaction ratings, service response times, and churn metrics. If the hypothesis is validated (data shows customer defections correlate with service complaints), the analysis can concentrate on fixing customer service. If the hypothesis is rejected, the team formulates and tests a new hypothesis (maybe pricing issues or a new competitor is the cause). This iterative loop continues until the actual cause is identified (MConsultingPrep, 2024).

The hypothesis-driven Method has several advantages. First, it streamlines analysis by focusing only on the most likely causes, saving time and resources. Teams don't waste effort collecting irrelevant data; they stay targeted at verifying the hypothesis. It helps prevent analysis paralysis, where one gets bogged down in data without making decisions.

Second, it encourages iteration and refinement. Each test of a hypothesis yields new information, which might lead to adjusting the hypothesis or forming new ones. By the end of the process, the conclusions are well-supported by evidence. Third, starting with a hypothesis can drive meaningful team conversations and alignment. It gives everyone a clear initial direction ("We think the problem is X, let us investigate that first"), which keeps the problem-solving focused on the critical issues rather than meandering through unrelated analyses.

Real-world business applications of the hypothesis-driven approach abound. The scientific Method used in R&D and the lean startup method of rapid experimentation are both hypothesis-driven at their core—form and test a hypothesis quickly. In management consulting, a classic example might be entering a new market: consultants will hypothesise which customer segment or product will be most profitable and then research that in depth. In data analytics, an analyst might hypothesise that "a decrease in website traffic is due to a recent change in Google's search algorithm" and then check the timing and sources of traffic data to confirm it. Another example comes from marketing: at Rescon Partners, consultants use hypothesis-driven problem-solving to improve Account-Based Marketing strategies. They start by hypothesising about a target account's needs or pain points and focus research on those assumptions rather than collecting all possible data about the account. This way, they quickly zero in on actionable insights that can inform personalised marketing campaigns.

The key to using the hypothesis-driven approach is to base your initial hypothesis on informed judgment (prior knowledge, preliminary data, experience); it should be an "educated guess," not a wild guess. From there, staying objective is crucial. If the data does not support the hypothesis, one must be willing to pivot to a new hypothesis rather than clinging to the original theory. When done correctly, hypothesis-driven problem-solving leads to faster and more effective decision-making, making it a favourite approach in high-paced business environments where time and information are limited.

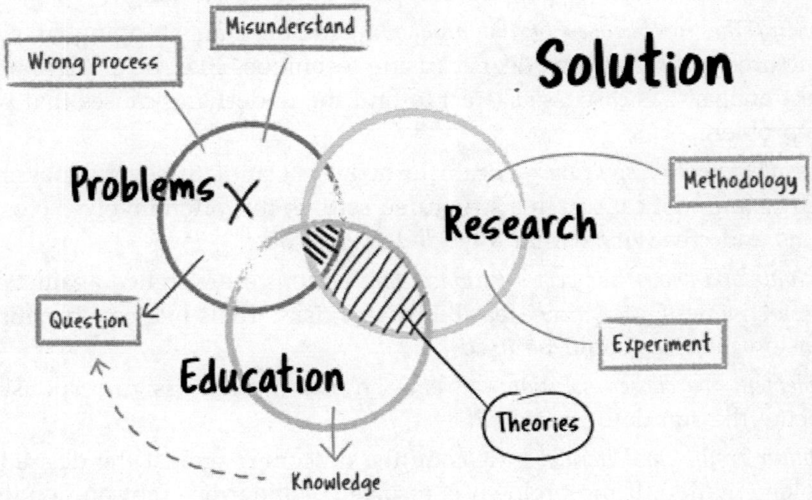

FIGURE 3.1 Hypothesis.

The diagram highlights how problems in business arise from misunderstandings, wrong processes, or lack of clarity. To tackle these issues, the hypothesis-driven approach brings together three essential elements, problems, education, and research. Problems create questions, education builds foundational knowledge, and research applies that knowledge through methodology and experimentation. The overlap of these three areas helps form meaningful theories and guide toward effective solutions. This approach believes that real insight and direction often come from where informed learning, questioning, and testing meet. That's where a working hypothesis is formed and refined, leading teams closer to the actual solution.

3.5 STRUCTURED FRAMEWORKS

Structured frameworks provide a step-by-step methodology for solving problems and making decisions. Unlike a single hypothesis or idea, a framework offers an end-to-end process that guides the team from problem definition to solution implementation and evaluation. Many businesses formalise their problem-solving to ensure consistency and thoroughness in decision-making (McKinsey & Company, 2019). By following a structured framework, managers can approach issues methodically, which helps clarify the problem, avoid missed factors, and document the rationale behind decisions.

Most structured problem-solving frameworks share common phases. A typical step-by-step methodology might include:

1. *Identify or define the problem clearly:* It means articulating what is wrong or what decision needs to be made in specific terms (e.g., "customer satisfaction scores have fallen 10% in the last quarter" rather than a vague "customers are unhappy").
2. *Analyse the current situation and gather data:* Understand the context: when and where the problem is occurring, how big the gap is, and who is affected. It could involve data collection, process mapping, or benchmarking.
3. *Identify the root causes of the problem:* Rather than stopping at symptoms, a structured approach digs deeper (using techniques like the 5 Whys or cause-and-effect analysis, as discussed later) to find the underlying causes that truly explain the problem.
4. *Develop potential solutions:* Brainstorm and formulate several possible ways to address the root causes. In a structured setting, this often involves cross-functional teams and creativity within a guided framework.
5. *Evaluate and choose the best solution:* The options are weighed against criteria such as effectiveness, cost, time, feasibility, and risks. Tools like cost-benefit analysis or decision matrices could be used.
6. *Implement the chosen solution:* Create an action plan, assign responsibilities, and execute the solution controlled.
7. *Monitor results and iterate:* Measure the outcomes against the desired goals after implementation. If the problem is resolved, standardise the solution; if not, refine the approach or try an alternative solution.

For example, the Business Development Bank of Canada (BDC) recommends a 7-step structured problem-solving process similar to the above sequence. The steps are: (1) identify the problem, (2) describe the situation, (3) take temporary countermeasures (to contain immediate damage), (4) find the root cause, (5) propose solutions, (6) implement an action plan, and (7) check the results. By following such a process, companies ensure they are not just "putting out fires" temporarily but fixing issues permanently. One of BDC's advisors notes that many firms waste effort on constant firefighting because they never address root causes in a structured way, resulting in the recurrence of the same problems. The structured framework forces the team to pull out the problem "by the roots" rather than repeatedly trimming the leaves (Business Development Bank of Canada, n.d.).

Structured frameworks often incorporate continuous improvement loops. For instance, after Step 7 (check results), a team might loop back if the results are unsatisfactory. It is where frameworks like PDCA come into play, as mentioned earlier. PDCA is a classically structured framework: during the "Plan" phase, you define and analyse the problem. In "Do", you implement a solution on a small scale. In "Check", you evaluate the outcome, and in "Act", you standardise the solution or adjust and repeat the cycle. From manufacturing to healthcare, many organisations embed such cycles in their culture for continuous problem-solving and improvement.

The benefit of using structured frameworks is evident in decision quality. When teams diligently follow steps to identify root causes and evaluate options, they are far less likely to overlook critical factors. Consider a company facing high employee turnover (people quitting). An unstructured approach might lead a manager to assume, "Oh, it's just about salaries," and raise pay, only to find that turnover remains high because the real issue is poor leadership and work culture. A structured framework would have systematically gathered data (exit interviews, industry benchmarks), identified multiple root causes (perhaps compensation, manager behaviour, lack of career growth, etc.), and then addressed each in a targeted way. The final decision, which might include manager training programs, more apparent career paths, and compensation adjustments, would be more likely to solve the actual problem. Structured frameworks help businesses make well-informed, transparent, and accountable decisions (McKinsey & Company, 2019). They turn problem-solving into a repeatable process that can be taught, refined, and scaled across the organisation.

3.6 ISSUE TREE ANALYSIS

One of the most valuable tools for tackling complex problems is the issue tree (also known as a logic tree). An issue tree is a diagram that breaks down a broad problem into progressively smaller, more manageable sub-problems (issues) in a tree structure. The purpose of an issue tree is to map out all possible drivers or causes of a problem in a structured way, which ensures a comprehensive analysis. This technique is especially favoured in consulting because it provides a visual and logical layout of the problem space (MConsultingPrep, n.d.).

An issue tree typically starts with the core problem statement at the top (the trunk) and then splits into major categories or components (the first level of branches). Each branch can further be divided into sub-branches as we delve deeper using smaller questions or identify contributing factors. The process continues until you reach a level where the issues are specific enough to be directly analysed or tested. A well-constructed issue tree is *mutually exclusive and collectively exhaustive,* meaning each branch is a distinct aspect of the problem (no overlaps), and together, the branches cover all possible aspects of the problem (no significant gap is left out). We will discuss the MECE principle more in the next section, as it is crucial for issue trees.

To illustrate, consider a classic business problem: "Profits are down." It is a broad problem that many things can lead to. An issue tree for this problem would start by breaking "Profit" into two fundamental components: Revenue and Cost (since Profit = Revenue—Cost). It gives two first-level branches: one for revenue and one for costs. Next, each of those branches can be broken down further. One typical breakdown for revenue is Price and Quantity (because revenue = price × quantity sold). Another way to break down revenue is by customer segments or product lines if those are more relevant. One could break it down for cost into Fixed Costs and Variable Costs or categories like Cost of Goods Sold, Marketing, Overhead, etc., depending on the business. At each subdivision, you continue to ask, "What could cause this element to be off?" and make those causes into sub-branches.

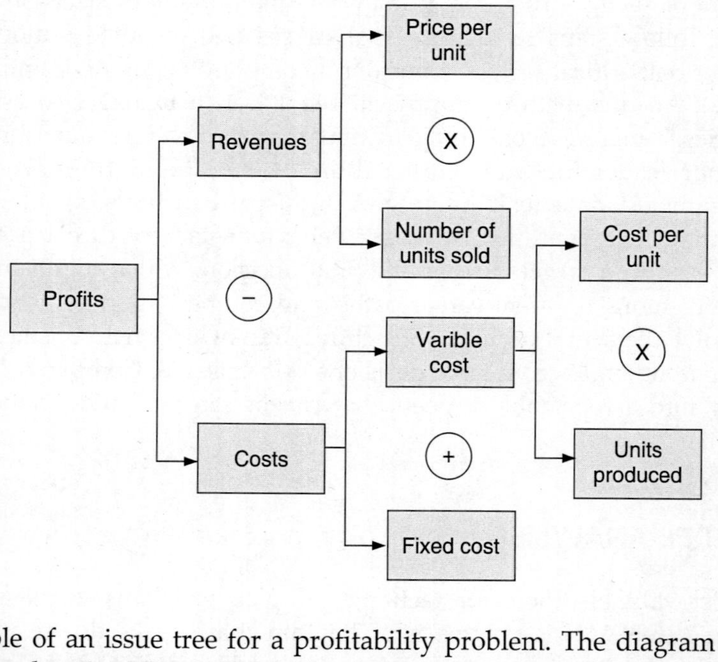

An example of an issue tree for a profitability problem. The diagram illustrates how Profits can be broken into Revenues (split into price per unit and number of units sold) and Costs (split into Variable Cost and Fixed Cost, with variable cost further dependent on cost per unit and Units produced). By mapping out the problem, a business can isolate which branch, i.e., revenue or cost, and which sub-component drives the profit decline. In a real analysis, each final node (price, volume, cost per unit, etc.) will be investigated using data to determine where the issue lies.

In the context of issue tree analysis, business examples abound. Let us take the case of Harley-Davidson, the motorcycle company we introduced earlier. Suppose Harley-Davidson is experiencing "negative profit" (losses) in a particular year. A consulting team might create an issue tree to diagnose why profits are negative. The top node is "Profit decline at Harley-Davidson," which splits into "Revenue decline" and "Cost increase." Further, the Revenue branch could split into issues like "Loss of existing customers" and "Failure to acquire new customers". The Cost branch might be divided into "Higher production costs" and "Higher marketing costs," etc. Now, each can be examined: why are existing customers leaving? Why aren't new customers coming? Is it due to competition, changes in consumer preferences, or something about Harley's product? In Harley's real case during the pandemic, the analysis (through this kind of breakdown and data testing) revealed that a key issue was losing its core older customers (many of whom stopped buying bikes or even passed away due to the pandemic) and not attracting younger riders. The issue tree helped pinpoint that the revenue decline was not due to competition (since competitors were also struggling, indicating the market as a whole was down). Instead, it was a demographic and product appeal problem. This insight led to solutions focused on pricing adjustments to boost short-term sales and a longer-term strategy to refresh the brand for younger customers (MConsultingPrep, n.d.).

The power of an issue tree lies in its clarity and thoroughness. By laying out the problem in a tree diagram, it becomes easier to discuss and assign analysis tasks. Each branch can be investigated (often, different team members take different branches). The tree also serves as a checklist to ensure no significant possibility is overlooked—if the tree is MECE, then analysing each branch means you've covered the whole problem. For instance, in the Harley example, once the team had branches for "fewer existing customers" and "fewer new customers," they could hypothesise reasons under each and test them (e.g., check sales data by age group, check if competitors gained Harley's customers, etc.). This systematic approach is far more effective than a vague discussion like "Maybe our bikes aren't selling because of the economy? Or maybe our marketing is bad?" The issue tree forces specificity: is it an external issue (economy, competitors) or an internal issue (product, marketing, cost structure)? Each becomes a branch to explore.

Consultants use issue trees to diagnose problems (the "why" trees) and to answer other questions. There are "how" trees for mapping out how to achieve a goal and "which" trees for making choices among options. For example, a "how" tree might break down the question "How can we increase market share?" into branches like "Increase share in existing markets" and "Enter new markets" and further sub-branches under each strategy. A "which" tree might structure a decision like "Which new product should we launch?" into criteria and sub-criteria. In all cases, the visual tree format helps tackle the question in a structured manner.

In summary, Issue Tree Analysis is a cornerstone of structured problem-solving. Breaking a complex problem into a hierarchy of issues helps business teams be methodical and MECE in their analysis. The result is often a deeper understanding of the problem and a clear roadmap for analysis. Each branch of the tree becomes a smaller problem to solve or a hypothesis to test. When combined with a hypothesis-driven approach, teams will often draw an issue tree and then put a "priority dot" on the branch they hypothesise is the problem, focusing their efforts first. If that hypothesis is wrong, they move to the next branch. This way, the issue tree and hypothesis work in tandem to solve even the toughest business problems in a logical, evidence-based way.

3.7 MECE PRINCIPLE

When building issue trees or any structured breakdown of a problem, one guiding rule that consultants and analysts swear by is the MECE principle. Let us break down what that means and why it's valuable.

- **Mutually Exclusive (ME):** Each category or item in a grouping should be distinct with no overlap. In other words, no element should fall into two categories simultaneously.
- **Collectively Exhaustive (CE):** Cumulatively, the categories or items should cover all possible options or components, leaving no gaps. Everything relevant must be captured in one of the categories.

Applying MECE to problem-solving ensures that you organise information without redundancy and omission when you break a problem into parts (as in issue trees or frameworks). It makes the analysis more precise and more reliable.

Consider an example: Imagine you are investigating the causes of declining sales for a company. You might initially list some possible causes, such as marketing issues, sales team performance, customer satisfaction, pricing, and online strategy. At first glance, this may seem like a decent list, but is it MECE? Likely not. There's overlap and gaps. "Marketing issues" and "Online strategy" could overlap (online strategy is part of marketing). "Sales team performance" and "Customer satisfaction" differ, but customer satisfaction could be affected by marketing, sales or product issues—it's not a separate category but rather an outcome. Also, this list might miss other big buckets like product quality or external market factors. A non-MECE breakdown can lead to confusion, double-counting, or overlooking key drivers.

A MECE way to categorise the causes of declining sales could be:

- External Market Changes (e.g., economic downturn, new competitors, changing customer preferences in the market)
- Customer Behavior (e.g., changes in customer needs, customer usage patterns, customer demographics)
- Internal Operational Efficiency (e.g., issues in sales force effectiveness, marketing execution, distribution problems)
- Product Offering (e.g., product not meeting customer needs, quality issues, outdated features)
- Finance/Pricing (e.g., product is priced too high, discounts removed, customers find better value elsewhere)

This set of categories is more likely to be MECE. Each category addresses a different aspect of the business (external, Customer, internal Process, product, financial), so they have minimal overlap. Together, they cover virtually all areas that could lead to sales decline. Any specific cause you think of should fit neatly into one of these buckets. For instance, "Our prices are too high" falls under Finance/Pricing; "A competitor released a more innovative product" falls under External Market Changes; "Our website's user experience is poor" might be considered an Internal Operational issue or perhaps part of Product Offering if the website is part of the product experience.

Why is MECE so important? When analyses are MECE, logic is easier to follow, and communications are clearer. Each branch can be explored in a MECE issue tree without worrying that "maybe this cause is partially considered elsewhere." It also ensures logical completeness, i.e., you've considered all possible angles. For businesses, this thoroughness is key: if you miss a cause of a problem because your breakdown wasn't exhaustive, you might end up proposing a solution that doesn't solve the issue.

Let us connect MECE back to the issue tree analysis. When we broke down profit into Revenue and Cost earlier, that's a MECE breakdown (revenue and cost factors are distinct, and together, they cover all of the profit). If we break down "Revenue" into "Volume and Price," those are MECE revenue components. If we further break down "Volume" into, say, "Volume from existing customers" and "Volume from new customers," again, we aim for MECE. We wouldn't want overlaps like "Volume from retail channel" and "Volume from new customers" on the same level because new customers could come from the retail channel, which would be double counting or overlapping categorisation. Instead, we'd choose one basis of breakdown and stick to it (either by customer type or by channel, but not both at the same level).

Another scenario: Suppose a company is brainstorming ways to increase profit. A non-MECE list of ideas might mix categories: "increase sales, reduce costs, improve marketing, launch new products." A MECE list at the top level would likely separate into "Grow Revenue" and "Cut Costs" (which are MECE). Under "Grow Revenue," you could further list "Sell more to existing customers," "Gain new customers," and "Increase prices," which are mutually exclusive ways to grow revenue. Under "Cut Costs," you might list "Improve operational efficiency" and "Negotiate cheaper supplier contracts," etc. By structuring ideas this way, you avoid confusion and can evaluate options systematically.

The MECE principle is heavily emphasised in management consulting training because it improves problem structuring and communication. Presentations to executives are clearer when issues and recommendations are MECE—it avoids ambiguity. In a business context, using MECE categories can also help divvy up work among team members without overlap. For instance, if a task is to analyse market entry options, one analyst can examine "Organic entry" vs. "Partnership" vs. "Acquisition" (which are MECE entry modes) without stepping on each other's toes.

Let us consider a case of Amazon trying to penetrate the South East Asian market. They need to have a structured approach to cover the potential customers as much, without any overlap. There are multiple possible ways in which they can segment their market and service offerings based on the type of product/ service considered. Figure 3.2 explains various ways of segmenting the market without overlaps, ensuring complete coverage of potential customers.

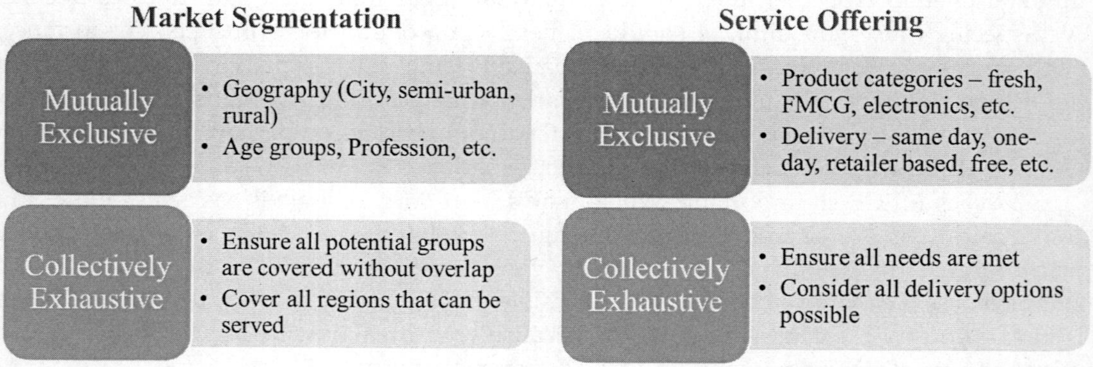

FIGURE 3.2 MECE segmentation.

Presented below are some of the problem instances along with possible market segmentation and service offerings. These could provide directions for the readers to think in line and understand different ways of segmenting their market and offerings.

PROBLEM STATEMENT 1: Amazon needs to effectively tailor its marketing and product offerings to address the diverse customer base in Southeast Asia.

Market segmentation: Segmentation by Customer Demographics

- *Urban Professionals:* Prefer fast, premium services and are likely to prioritise convenience over cost.
- *Suburban Families:* Focus on value, large-basket grocery shopping, and prefer economical delivery options.
- *Rural Consumers:* Face logistical challenges, so affordability and accessibility of delivery services are critical.

Service offering:

- Offer tailored services like same-day delivery for urban professionals.
- Family-sized grocery bundles for suburban customers.
- Cost-effective logistics options for rural areas.

PROBLEM STATEMENT 2: Amazon needs to differentiate itself in a crowded market with local and global competitors.

Instance 2: Segmentation by Competitor Positioning

- *Local Competitors:* Strong brand loyalty and regional knowledge.
- *International Competitors:* Strong supply chains and familiarity with global best practices.
- *Other E-commerce Players:* Likely agile and localized.

Service:

- ✦ Identify where to focus resources (mapping)
- ✦ Competitive pricing and superior international products to compete with Local competitors
- ✦ Superior logistics, technology, etc., to outperform International Competitors
- ✦ Logistics expertise and innovation for E-commerce rivals

To summarise, MECE is a guideline for logical thinking. When breaking down problems, segments, or data, strive to make your categories mutually exclusive (each thing falls into one bucket only) and collectively exhaustive (all relevant things are accounted for in one of the buckets). It leads to cleaner analysis and ensures you don't miss critical pieces. It is the secret sauce behind many consulting frameworks and equally applies to everyday business analysis. By keeping your problem-solving MECE, you enforce rigour and clarity, ultimately leading to better solutions.

3.8 ROOT CAUSE ANALYSIS

Solving a business problem often requires looking beyond the immediate symptoms and identifying the root cause. Root cause analysis is digging deep into a problem to find the foundational cause (or causes) leading to the observed issue. Addressing root causes is crucial because it allows you to fix the problem permanently rather than just patching symptoms temporarily. Several structured tools are commonly used for root cause analysis in business, and two of the most popular are the 5 Whys technique and the Fishbone Diagram (Ishikawa Cause-and-Effect Diagram).

The 5 Whys Technique: This simple yet powerful Method was famously developed at Toyota as part of its quality improvement process. As the name suggests, the technique involves asking "Why?" repeatedly around five times, though the exact number is not fixed, to move past symptoms and uncover the underlying cause of a problem. Each answer forms the basis of the subsequent "why" question. The idea is that by the time you've asked *why* five times (digging into why the initial cause happened, why that happened, and so on), you will have arrived at an actionable root cause.

A classic real-world example of the 5 Whys comes from Amazon and its founder, Jeff Bezos. During a visit to an Amazon fulfilment centre, Bezos learned of an incident where an employee's thumb was injured by getting caught in a conveyor belt. He led the team through a 5 Whys analysis on the spot (Management Study Guide, n.d.):

1. Why was the employee's thumb caught in the conveyor? Because he was chasing his bag that went down the conveyor.
2. Why was his bag on the conveyor? Because he placed it there, and the conveyor unexpectedly started.
3. Why did he put his bag on the conveyor? He was using the conveyor as a table to hold his belongings.
4. Why did he need to use the conveyor as a table? Because there was no regular table or surface at his workstation where he could put his bag.

At this point, by the fourth "why," it became clear that the root cause of the injury was the lack of a simple table or shelf for personal items. If an appropriate surface was provided, the employee wouldn't have used the conveyor as a makeshift table. Bezos' team determined that the solution was to give tables at the appropriate stations (and possibly reinforce safety training) to prevent such incidents. In other words, a seemingly complex issue (worker injury in a high-tech warehouse) had a rather humble root cause (no table for the worker's bag), and the fix was straightforward and low-cost—something they might have missed without the 5 Whys process.

This example shows how 5 Whys can peel away layers of symptoms (injured thumb, bag on conveyor, conveyor turned on) to reveal a fundamental cause (no table). In a business setting, you might use 5 Whys for problems like "Why are deliveries always late to the customer?" or "Why did we miss our revenue target this month?" By iteratively asking why, we could discover the root causes, such as a broken internal process or a miscommunication, that needs to be addressed directly. The 5 Whys technique is valued for its simplicity and ability to quickly direct attention to what needs fixing. However, it's worth noting that 5 Whys is most effective for relatively straightforward problems; complex problems might have multiple root causes and may require more elaborate analysis (or repeating 5 Whys for different symptom chains).

A condensed description of Amazon's problem instance is presented using 5 Whys. Amazon is facing persistent delivery delays, but the root cause of the problem isn't immediately clear. The goal is to drill down to the root cause by repeatedly asking "why.".

Assumptions:

- Surface-level issues (e.g., late deliveries) are symptoms of deeper operational problems.
- Addressing the root cause will have a ripple effect, improving overall performance.
- Each "why" leads to a deeper understanding of the problem.

Challenges:

- Ensuring that the process doesn't stop prematurely, leaving the real root cause unaddressed.
- Involving all relevant stakeholders to get to the bottom of the issue.
- Implementing corrective actions once the root cause is identified.

Analysis:

1. Why 1: Why are deliveries late?
   Warehouses are not stocked in time.
2. Why 2: Why aren't warehouses stocked in time?
   Suppliers are delayed in sending goods.
3. Why 3: Why are suppliers delayed?
   Long lead times due to inefficient transport routes.

4. Why 4: Why are transport routes inefficient?
   Warehouses are located far from supply hubs.
5. Why 5: Why are warehouses located far from supply hubs?
   Poor planning during site selection/Less cost at far away sites/cheap labor, etc.

Solution Steps: Relocate or open additional warehouses closer to key suppliers, improving stocking times and reducing delivery delays.

Pointers for Discussion

- Start understanding the problem from multiple business perspectives of implementation and break it down into multiple problem statements (issues).
- Each problem statement that we see is a sub-component of our larger case. We use appropriate frameworks to solve each of them.

Fishbone Diagram (Ishikawa Diagram): The fishbone diagram is another popular tool for root cause analysis, especially when a problem likely has multiple contributing causes. It's called a fishbone diagram because it resembles a fish's skeleton: the head of the fish is the problem (effect) you're looking at, and the bones branching off are categories of potential causes with sub-branches for specific causes. Kaoru Ishikawa, a Japanese quality control expert, pioneered this diagram to brainstorm and organise potential causes of quality problems systematically. In business, fishbone diagrams are used in various contexts, from manufacturing defects to service delays to customer complaints.

To create a fishbone diagram, write the problem statement on the right (the "head" of the fish). Then, you draw a horizontal line to the left, which is the spine, and branch off major cause categories. Ishikawa originally suggested the "6 M's" for manufacturing as common categories: Manpower (People), Methods, Machines, Materials, Measurements, and Milieu (Environment). These categories can be adjusted depending on the context (for example, some use 4 M's or replace specific categories for service industries). Under each category, you then brainstorm possible causes related to that category and draw them as smaller lines (like ribs) off the branch. You can further ask "why" for each cause and add sub-causes as smaller branches of those lines, creating a tree of causes for each category.

For example, imagine a manufacturing team investigating why a particular product has a high defect rate. The team might set up a fishbone diagram with categories: Machine, Method, Material, Manpower, Measurement, and Environment. Under Machine, they list potential causes like machine calibration issues, equipment wear and tear, etc. Under Method, they list incorrect assembly procedures or lack of a standard process. Under Material, perhaps there is variability in raw material quality. Manpower could include insufficient training or operator error. Measurement might cover inadequate testing or false readings. Environment could consist of temperature or humidity affecting production. By laying all this out, the team can visually see all plausible causes of defects organised by type. They can then investigate each branch (perhaps they find that under "Machine," a piece of particular equipment is frequently miscalibrated, causing errors).

A business case using a fishbone diagram could be one in which a call centre is experiencing poor customer satisfaction. The problem ("low customer satisfaction scores") is at the head of the fish. The team might choose categories like People, Process, Technology, and Customer (or Policy, if relevant). Under People, possible causes are new hires' lack of training and high staff turnover. Under process, causes include the lengthy call handling procedure and lack of a callback system for missed calls. Under Technology, causes include frequent phone system dropouts and slow computer systems causing delays. Under Customer, causes may be changing customer expectations or inconvenient operating hours. By mapping these out, the company can systematically address each angle; perhaps they discover through this analysis that the most significant issues are process-related (calls take too long because agents have to navigate 10 different screens—a process fix) and technology-related (the phone system drops calls). Those become the root causes to fix (simplify the agent workflow and upgrade the phone system).

In both the 5 Whys and fishbone diagram, we see an emphasis on structured inquiry. Instead of just tackling what's immediately apparent, these techniques force a team to explore deeper or broader. Often, businesses combine approaches where they might brainstorm causes with a fishbone diagram and then apply the 5 Whys to drill down on a particularly likely cause chain. Additionally, data often supports root cause analysis (for example, Pareto charts might be used to identify the most frequent cause among those identified).

Let us consider an example where Amazon addressed their delivery delays using the Fishbone technique. Amazon is experiencing logistical delays in delivering perishable groceries, which is impacting customer satisfaction and competitive positioning in the new market.

In this case, the delivery delays was the outcome and the contributing causes were grouped based on multiple dimensions, the various functional areas in the facility.

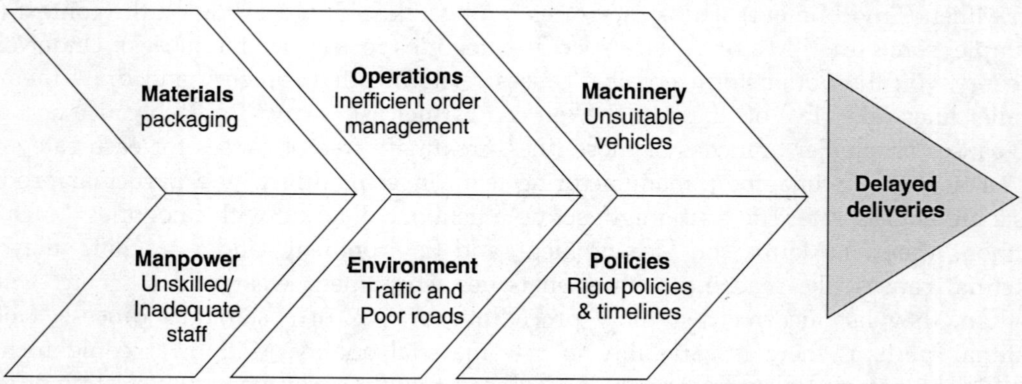

FIGURE 3.3 Fishbone Diagram.

TABLE 3.1 Root Cause Analysis using Fishbone diagram

	Problem	*Analysis*	*Solution*	*Considerations*
Materials	Packaging issues for perishable goods are causing spoilage during transit.	Inspect packaging	Change the design, use advanced insulation to prevent damage and temperature control.	Trade-off between warehouse storage equipment vs. transportation cost (for sophisticated transport) vs. insulation and packaging costs.
Operations	Inefficient order management processes lead to picking delays in warehouses.	Investigate the workflow from order placement to fulfillment to find bottlenecks.	Automate order management systems to streamline picking, reduce errors, and improve fulfillment speed.	Consider employing workers for picking orders, tracking errors, etc. Analyze the level of automation required in these processes.
Machinery	Delivery vehicles are outdated or unsuitable for transporting perishable goods.	Evaluate fleet for temperature control and other sensors.	Invest in cold storage in vehicles to maintain freshness.	Investing in cold storage transport vs. outsourcing to 3PL providers vs. placing regional warehouses closer to customers to reduce lead time.
Manpower	Lack of adequate staff or poorly trained staff.	Assess staffing levels and employee training programs.	Hire additional staff during peak periods and conduct training on handling perishables and expediting delivery.	Offering training programs to staff vs. level strategy (hiring temporary workers during peak periods).
External	Traffic congestion and poor infrastructure in urban areas cause unpredictable delivery times.	Examine the delivery routes and infrastructure	Implement route optimization and plan delivery to avoid peak congestion periods.	3PL or using maneuverable vehicles in city or planning delivery during less congested periods.
Policies	Management's rigid policies on delivery timelines do not fit to local market conditions.	Review Amazon's delivery policies and compare them to competitors' flexible models.	Allow more adaptable delivery windows based on real-time data on traffic and order volumes.	Offer flexible delivery slots vs. discounts for choosing delivery in lean traffic periods (sustainable customer).

Root cause analysis ensures that problem-solving efforts address the *real* problem, not just a symptom. Techniques like 5 Whys and fishbone diagrams are invaluable in this regard. They have been used in countless organisations to save costs and time by eliminating recurring problems. A culture that asks, "Why did this happen, and why is that, and why is that?" is a culture that learns and improves continuously rather than one that repeatedly fixes the same issue. Whether it's an operational glitch, a strategic misstep, or a customer complaint, finding root causes is the first step to developing effective, lasting solutions.

CASE STUDY: Real-Time Business Case: Walmart's Operational Challenges in 2024

Introduction

Walmart, one of the world's largest retailers, operates in a dynamic and highly competitive environment. In 2024, Walmart faces several operational challenges impacting its business performance. As a global retail giant with a vast supply chain, multiple product categories, and a firm reliance on customer satisfaction, Walmart must continuously refine its business strategies to maintain its competitive edge.

This case study will explore three key problems Walmart is facing, each analysed using a structured problem-solving approach:

1. Declining In-Store Sales—Hypothesis-Driven Approach
2. Rising Supply Chain Costs—Issue Tree Analysis
3. Increase in Online Order Returns—Root Cause Analysis

By applying these methodologies, Walmart can address its business challenges systematically, leading to effective solutions and long-term growth.

PROBLEM 1: Declining In-Store Sales (Hypothesis-Driven Approach)

Context and Business Impact

Over the past two years, Walmart has observed a gradual but significant decline in in-store sales, even as its e-commerce platform continues to grow. This shift has raised concerns for the management team, as Walmart has historically relied on its physical stores for most of its revenue. The decline in foot traffic and in-store spending has impacted overall profitability and store performance, particularly in urban locations where customers seem to be shifting toward alternative shopping experiences.

Recognising the urgency of this issue, Walmart's executive team decides to apply a hypothesis-driven approach to identify the primary reason behind declining in-store sales. Instead of investigating all possible causes extensively, the company formulates an initial hypothesis based on industry trends and customer behaviour data.

Step 1: *Formulating the Hypothesis*—The initial hypothesis suggests:
"Walmart's in-store sales are declining because customers prefer the convenience of e-commerce and same-day delivery services, reducing the need for physical store visits."

This hypothesis is based on observed changes in consumer behaviour, where digital shopping and home delivery services have seen exponential growth across the retail industry.

Step 2: *Testing the Hypothesis*—To validate this hypothesis, Walmart gathers relevant data from multiple sources:

1. *Customer Footfall Data:* Analysing trends in in-store visits over the past three years to confirm whether foot traffic has dropped significantly.
2. *Customer Surveys & Interviews:* Administering direct interactions with customers to understand their shopping preferences.
3. *Sales Trends Across Channels:* Comparing in-store sales to e-commerce performance to see if customers simply shift from one channel to another.
4. *Competitor Analysis:* Examining whether similar retailers, such as Target and Costco, are also experiencing declining in-store sales or if Walmart is being uniquely affected.

Step 3: *Results and Hypothesis Refinement*—The analysis provides key insights:

1. Footfall data confirms that in-store traffic has dropped by 18% over the last two years, correlating with increased online transactions.
2. Customer surveys reveal that 40% of respondents prefer shopping online for non-grocery items, citing convenience and price comparison as primary reasons.
3. Sales data indicates that while in-store purchases have declined, Walmart's online sales have grown by 27%, suggesting a channel shift rather than an outright loss of customers.
4. Competitor analysis shows that while Target has experienced a similar trend, Costco has maintained its in-store sales by offering exclusive deals and premium membership perks.

Given this information, Walmart refines its hypothesis:

"In-store sales are declining primarily because customers prefer online shopping for convenience, but a lack of exclusive in-store incentives and promotions at Walmart has accelerated the shift."

Step 4: *Implementing Solutions*—To address this challenge, Walmart implements strategic measures:

1. *Enhancing In-Store Experience:* Introducing limited-time, in-store-only promotions and interactive shopping experiences to make physical visits more valuable.
2. *Integrating Online and Offline Shopping:* Expanding the "Buy Online, Pick Up in Store" (BOPIS) program to encourage hybrid shopping.
3. *Optimising Product Placement:* Prioritising high-demand products in in-store layouts to improve the customer journey.

Outcome

Within six months, foot traffic stabilised, and in-store sales saw a 5% increase, particularly in categories where in-store discounts and promotions were introduced. The hypothesis-driven approach allowed Walmart to focus first on the most likely cause, ensuring a rapid and targeted solution.

PROBLEM 2: Rising Supply Chain Costs (Issue Tree Analysis)

Context and Business Impact

As a retail giant with an extensive global supply chain, Walmart faces mounting pressures due to rising supply chain costs, impacting profit margins. Increasing freight charges, higher wages for logistics workers, and supplier price hikes have contributed to a 10% increase in operational costs over the past year. To maintain its Everyday Low Price (EDLP) strategy, Walmart must identify the core areas driving cost escalation and implement cost-saving measures.

To systematically analyse the issue, Walmart's logistics and finance teams employ Issue Tree Analysis to break down the problem into its key components.

Step 1: *Constructing the Issue Tree*
The problem is: "Why are Walmart's supply chain costs rising?"

Since, Total Supply Chain Cost = Freight Costs + Labor Costs + Supplier Costs + Inventory Costs,

The issue tree branches into the following:

1. Freight Costs
    - Rising fuel prices
    - Port congestion and delays
    - Higher shipping rates from carriers
2. Labor Costs
    - Increased wages for warehouse and delivery workers
    - Higher turnover leads to training expenses
    - Increased overtime due to labor shortages
3. Supplier Costs
    - Global raw material shortages
    - Currency fluctuations impacting imports
    - Supplier price increases
4. Inventory Costs
    - Overstocking leads to excess storage costs
    - Inefficiencies in demand forecasting
    - Higher warehousing costs

Step 2: *Prioritising the Investigation*
Upon analysing Walmart's financial reports and supplier contracts, the company determines:

1. Freight costs have risen by 15% due to shipping disruptions and higher fuel prices.

2. Labour costs have increased by 12% due to wage hikes and high attrition in warehouse jobs.
3. Supplier price hikes are the single most significant contributor to cost increases, with an average increase of 18% across categories.

Since supplier price hikes have the highest cost impact, Walmart prioritises negotiating new supplier contracts and increasing sourcing efficiency.

Step 3: *Solution Implementation*

1. *Negotiating Bulk Purchase Discounts:* Through volume-based pricing, Walmart strengthens partnerships with major suppliers to secure better rates.
2. *Optimising Freight Logistics:* Investing in regional warehouses and alternate shipping routes to reduce reliance on costly freight options.
3. *Labour Productivity Enhancements:* Deploying automation in warehouses to reduce dependency on manual Labor.

Outcome

Within a year, supply chain costs decrease by 7%, helping Walmart preserve its low-price advantage. The issue tree analysis provided a precise breakdown, allowing the company to focus on the most impactful cost drivers.

PROBLEM 3: Increase in Online Order Returns (Root Cause Analysis)

Context and Business Impact

With the growth of e-commerce, Walmart has seen a 22% increase in online order returns, leading to higher reverse logistics costs and customer dissatisfaction. Unchecked return rates not only impact profitability but also affect inventory management and warehouse efficiency.

To determine the fundamental cause of high return rates, Walmart's customer service and operations teams apply Root Cause Analysis (5 Whys technique).

Step 1: *Applying 5 Whys*

1. Why are online order returns increasing?
   - Because customers frequently return items they claim "did not match expectations."
2. Why did the products not match expectations?
   - Because customers often report misleading product images or descriptions on the website.
3. Why are product descriptions inaccurate?
   - Because some third-party sellers upload their descriptions without Walmart's verification.
4. Why aren't descriptions verified before listing?
   - Because Walmart's marketplace system currently allows automatic product uploads for certain vendors.

5. Why does Walmart allow this system?
   - Because the process was designed for speed, vendor onboarding was prioritised over product accuracy.

Root Cause Identified:

The lack of stringent product listing verification for third-party sellers is the key driver behind increased returns.

Solution Implementation

1. Introducing stricter quality checks for third-party sellers.
2. Enhancing AI-powered image verification to ensure accuracy.
3. Launching Customer review-based flagging for misleading listings.

Outcome

Return rates decrease by 10% within six months, improving operational efficiency and customer trust.

KEY POINTS TO REMEMBER

1. *Effective problem-solving drives business success:* How a business addresses its challenges often determines its fate. Companies that excel at problem-solving can innovate and adapt, leading to success (e.g., Netflix's strategic pivot to streaming when faced with a DVD decline), whereas poor problem-solving can lead to failure (e.g., Kodak's inability to adapt to digital photography). The key point is that solving the right problem at the right time—and doing so methodically—is fundamental to sustaining a competitive advantage in any industry.
2. *Structured vs. unstructured approaches:* Not all business problems are alike. Some are well-defined and benefit from a structured problem-solving approach—following a clear process or framework to reach a solution. Other problems are novel or ill-defined, requiring a more unstructured or creative approach, where flexibility and intuition play a bigger role. Effective managers recognise when to apply structured methods (for thoroughness and clarity) and when to allow a more open-ended exploration. Often, a blend of both—structured analysis plus creative thinking—yields the best results for complex business challenges.
3. *Leveraging frameworks and methodologies:* Over time, businesses and consultants have developed proven problem-solving frameworks to guide analysis (such as PDCA, DMAIC, or the 3C's model). Using a framework brings discipline and ensures a comprehensive look at the issue, rather than an ad-hoc or haphazard approach. Key point: *Frameworks serve as roadmaps*—they break down the problem-solving journey into manageable stages (defining the problem, analyzing causes,

exploring solutions, etc.), helping teams cover all bases. However, it's also understood that no single framework fits every problem; skilled problem solvers may combine elements of multiple frameworks as needed.

4. *Hypothesis-driven analysis:* A critical approach highlighted in this chapter is the hypothesis-driven method, commonly used in consulting. Instead of starting with exhaustive data gathering, you begin with a hypothesis—an educated guess about the root cause or best solution—and then test it. This approach directs focus to the most relevant facts quickly and prevents analysis paralysis. The takeaway: formulating and iteratively testing hypotheses can make problem-solving more efficient and pointed, as teams validate what's true or false and converge on an effective solution faster than by exploring everything at once.
5. *Issue trees and MECE thinking:* Breaking complex problems into smaller parts is essential. An issue tree (logic tree) is a tool that maps out a problem into branches and sub-branches (sub-problems), ensuring a logical structure. A well-constructed issue tree follows the MECE principle—Mutually Exclusive, Collectively Exhaustive—meaning each sub-problem is distinct (no overlap) and together they cover all possible causes of the problem (no gaps). This key point stresses that using issue trees helps teams systematically identify where to analyze further, and it provides clarity by showing how different facets of a problem relate. It's a visual checklist that nothing important has been overlooked.
6. *Root cause analysis—digging deeper:* Solving a problem thoroughly requires identifying its root cause, not just addressing symptoms. Techniques like the 5 Whys (asking "Why?" repeatedly to peel back layers of cause-and-effect) or Fishbone diagrams (visualizing multiple potential causes under categories like people, process, technology, etc.) are invaluable. They prompt teams to investigate underlying reasons for an issue (for example, discovering that a decline in sales is due not just to a poor marketing campaign, but to a deeper issue like changing customer needs or a product quality problem). The key reminder is that treating root causes leads to lasting solutions, whereas treating symptoms may only provide temporary relief.
7. *Adaptability and continuous improvement:* A final takeaway is the importance of flexibility in problem-solving. Business environments change and sometimes an approach needs to be adjusted. Skilled problem-solvers stay adaptable—they can pivot from one framework to another or iterate on their analysis as new information comes to light. Additionally, problem-solving in business is an ongoing, continuous improvement effort; even after implementing a solution, it's important to monitor results and be ready to tackle follow-up problems. This dynamic, proactive attitude, combined with the structured techniques learned (like hypothesis testing and MECE thinking), equips readers to handle business challenges methodically and creatively.

KEY LEARNINGS

- *Critical Skill:* Problem-solving is an essential capability for business success. Effective problem-solving enables companies to overcome challenges, innovate, and adapt, whereas poor problem-solving (or failing to solve the right problem) can lead to business failures. Real-world examples like Netflix's successful pivot and Kodak's downfall illustrate the high stakes of good vs. bad problem-solving.
- *Structured vs. Unstructured:* Problem-solving approaches can be structured (systematic and data-driven) or unstructured (relying on intuition and spontaneity). Structured approaches follow clear steps and are best for complex, recurring, or high-impact problems because they ensure thorough analysis. Unstructured approaches, while faster and more flexible, are suited for simple or urgent issues where a quick, experience-based fix may suffice.
- *Frameworks and Methodologies:* Businesses leverage numerous problem-solving frameworks (like PDCA, DMAIC, design thinking, etc.) to tackle issues consistently. Frameworks provide a roadmap, from defining the problem to implementing solutions, which helps teams not miss critical steps. Selecting the appropriate methodology (or combination) depends on the problem context, but all frameworks aim to improve decision-making through structure.
- *Hypothesis-Driven Thinking:* A hypothesis-driven approach focuses on problem-solving by starting with a possible explanation and then seeking evidence to confirm or refute it. This approach, used heavily in consulting, avoids wasted effort on unanalysed data and enables faster insights. It is iterative and dynamic as the team efficiently zeroes in on root causes or viable solutions while hypotheses are tested.
- *Issue Trees and MECE:* Breaking down problems using issue trees helps deal with complexity by splitting problems into parts in a visual, logical structure. A well-constructed issue tree follows the MECE principle, where the branches are Mutually Exclusive and Collectively Exhaustive, ensuring clarity (no overlaps) and completeness (no gaps) in analysis. This structured breakdown is invaluable for identifying where to focus analysis and ensuring all possible causes or options are evaluated.
- *Root Cause Analysis:* Techniques like the 5 Whys and Fishbone Diagram are key to drilling down to the underlying causes of a problem rather than just addressing symptoms. 5 Whys involves repeatedly asking "why" to peel back layers of causes, often revealing a simple root cause behind a complex issue (as demonstrated by the Amazon warehouse example with the missing table). Fishbone diagrams facilitate brainstorming multiple potential causes organised by category, providing a comprehensive view of factors contributing to a problem. By identifying root causes, businesses can implement solutions that prevent issues from recurring, leading to long-term improvements.

EXERCISES

1. *Issue Tree Brainstorm—Declining Profits:* You are an external consultant hired by a mid-size retail company whose profits have declined for two years. Construct an issue tree to break down the problem of declining profits. Consider the top-level branches (at least revenue-related and cost-related factors) and sub-branches (specific causes under each). Identify one branch you hypothesise is the main cause, and describe the data or analysis you would perform to test that hypothesis.
2. *Structured vs. Unstructured Scenario:* Imagine you are a manager at a software firm facing two different problems. Problem A: A major client's project is delayed due to unforeseen technical hurdles. Problem B: Team morale has dropped slightly this month. For each problem, decide whether a structured or unstructured problem-solving approach is more appropriate. Justify your choice and outline your approach. (For example, for the chosen structured problem, list the steps you would take in order; for the unstructured one, explain how you might address it quickly via experience or brainstorming.)
3. *Hypothesis-Driven Analysis—New Product Launch:* Your company's new product is underperforming (lower sales than expected). Apply a hypothesis-driven approach by stating an initial hypothesis for the underperformance (e.g., "Our product is priced too high for this market segment") and then outline a plan to test this hypothesis. What data would you gather, and how would you evaluate the results? What would your next hypothesis be if the data disproves your initial hypothesis?
4. *Using MECE in Practice:* You reduce customer wait times at a bank's branches. To ensure a MECE approach, list all potential areas where delays could occur in the customer service process (e.g., queueing, transaction processing, staffing, etc.) in an MECE manner. Once you have the categories, pick one category and suggest specific improvements or analyses for that area. Explain why making the list MECE helps in tackling the problem systematically.
5. *Whys Application—Manufacturing Case:* A factory has a problem: a machine keeps breaking down, causing production stoppages. The obvious symptom is "Machine X broke down three times this week." Perform a 5 Whys analysis (as an exercise, write out a chain of at least five whys) to explore what could be the root cause of the Machine's frequent breakdowns. Based on your final "why" answer, propose a solution that addresses the root cause. How would this solution prevent the breakdowns from recurring?
6. *Fishbone Diagram—Service Quality:* A hotel has been receiving poor reviews, specifically regarding slow room service delivery. Develop a mini fishbone diagram (you can describe it in words or bullet points for each category) to identify possible causes of slow room service. Use categories such as Manpower, Methods, Machines (equipment), and Environment. Under each category, list at least two possible causes (for example, under Manpower: "insufficient staffing during peak hours" and "lack of training in service efficiency"). After listing causes, pick the cause you believe is most critical and describe a plan to verify and address it.

7. *Framework Selection Challenge:* For each of the following business challenges, name a structured problem-solving framework or tool that would be appropriate to use and explain why:
   (a) A startup is trying to decide which of three international markets to enter first.
   (b) A manufacturing firm wants to systematically reduce defect rates in its production line.
   (c) A non-profit organisation is brainstorming ways to increase its fundraising revenue.
   (d) A tech company must diagnose why their mobile app's user engagement has dropped in the last month.
   (e) These exercises are designed to let you apply the chapter's concepts to realistic scenarios. They range from creating problem structures and hypotheses to choosing the right tools. In tackling them, practice being clear, logical, and MECE in your thinking, and remember to focus on root causes and data-driven validation of your ideas.

THOUGHT-PROVOKING QUESTIONS

Why is effective problem-solving so critical in business? Provide an example of a business decision that led to success because of good problem-solving and an example of a failure that resulted from poor problem-solving. What lessons can be drawn from those examples?

1. **Structured vs. Unstructured Approaches:** In your own words, describe the difference between a structured problem-solving approach and an unstructured approach. If a company faces a novel problem it has never seen before, how might it balance structured analysis with unstructured creativity? Can these approaches complement each other?
2. **Framework Familiarity:** Identify two problem-solving frameworks mentioned in this chapter (for example, DMAIC, design thinking, PDCA, etc.). For each, briefly outline its steps and give a scenario in which each would be the preferred Method. Why do you think that framework is well-suited to that scenario?
3. **Hypothesis-Driven Approach in Action:** Explain the hypothesis-driven problem-solving approach. How does starting with a hypothesis change the way one gathers and analyses data? Consider a scenario such as declining online sales on an e-commerce website. Propose a hypothesis for the decline and outline how you would investigate it using the hypothesis-driven Method.
4. **Issue Trees and MECE Check:** What does an issue tree (or any list of factors) mean to be "MECE"? Create a simple issue tree for the problem "Employee turnover is high at Company X." Ensure your first-level branches are MECE, and give one example of a non-MECE breakdown versus a MECE breakdown for this problem.
5. **Root vs. Symptom:** Define a "root cause" and explain why addressing root causes is more effective than addressing symptoms. Consider a customer service example: customers are unhappy because of long call centre wait times. What

might be a symptom-focused solution versus a root-cause-focused solution? Which is likely to yield better long-term results and why?

6. **Applying 5 Whys:** Pick a common business problem (such as "project deadline was missed" or "monthly sales target was not met") and demonstrate how you would apply the 5 Whys technique to find a potential root cause. What challenges might you encounter when using 5 Whys, and how can you ensure the team reaches a meaningful root cause, not just a superficial answer?
7. **Interpreting a Fishbone Diagram:** If a fishbone diagram for a factory's low productivity pointed to "Machine downtime", "Worker training", "Material quality", and "Scheduling method" as major categories of causes, what kind of specific causes might fall under each of these categories? How would you prioritise the causes to be addressed first? Describe how you would verify if a suspected cause from the fishbone diagram is indeed a root cause.

REFERENCES

Business Development Bank of Canada. (n.d.). A 7-step structured problem-solving process to deal with your business challenges. BDC Operational Efficiency. Retrieved July 10, 2024, from https://www.bdc.ca/en/articles-tools/operations/operational-efficiency/7-steps-solve-operational-problems.

Chapman, R. (2025, April 7). A Comprehensive Guide to Process Improvement Methodologies: Enhancing Business Efficiency. Leading Business Improvement. Retrieved July 10, 2024, from https://leadingbusinessimprovement.com/a-comprehensive-guide-to-process-improvement-methodologies/

Management Study Guide. (n.d.). Five Whys Analysis. ManagementStudyGuide.com. Retrieved July 10, 2024, from https://www.managementstudyguide.com/five-whys-analysis.htm

McKinsey & Company. (2019, September 13). How to master the seven-step problem-solving process. McKinsey Insights (Podcast Transcript). Retrieved July 10, 2024, from https://www.mckinsey.com/capabilities/strategy-and-corporate-finance/our-insights/how-to-master-the-seven-step-problem-solving-process.

MConsultingPrep. (n.d.). Issue Tree in Consulting: A Complete Guide (With Examples). MConsultingPrep. Retrieved July 10, 2024, from https://mconsultingprep.com/issue-tree.

Nelson, L. (2023, August 7). The Importance of Decision-Making Process in Business. AFA Education Blog. Retrieved July 10, 2024, from https://afaeducation.org/blog/the-importance-of-decisionmaking-process-in-business/

Rescon Partners. (2024, November 6). Hypothesis-Driven Problem Solving: A Key Approach at Rescon Partners. Rescon Partners Insights. Retrieved July 10, 2024, from https://www.resconpartners.com/hypothesis-driven-problem-solving-a-key-approach-at-rescon-partners/

Wevalgo. (n.d.). Comparison of Problem-Solving Methods and Techniques. Wevalgo Know-How. Retrieved July 10, 2024, from https://www.wevalgo.com/know-how/opex-assessment-tools/problem-solving.

CHAPTER

4 Advanced Problem-Solving Techniques

LEARNING OBJECTIVES

After reading this Chapter, the readers will be able to:

- Understand and apply key strategic problem-solving frameworks—Grasp the concepts of Value Chain Analysis, First-Principles Thinking, Systems Thinking, Scenario Analysis, and the Balanced Scorecard, and know when to apply each in business contexts.
- Align theory with practice—Learn how these techniques are used in real-world companies (from startups to multinationals) to drive efficiency, innovation, and strategic decision-making.
- Holistic decision-making—Develop the ability to analyse business problems from multiple perspectives—operational, financial, customer, and long-term—ensuring solutions do not create new issues but build sustainable competitive advantage.
- Strategic planning under uncertainty—Gain skills in preparing for future scenarios and uncertainties (e.g. market shifts, crises) using systematic methods, improving resilience and adaptability.
- Performance alignment—Learn to align an organisation's strategic objectives with day-to-day operations and metrics, ensuring that all levels of the business work toward common goals.

4.1 VALUE CHAIN ANALYSIS

Value Chain Analysis is a framework introduced by Michael Porter in 1985 to analyse the sequence of activities by which a firm creates value for its customers. The value chain encompasses *primary activities* (inbound logistics, operations, outbound logistics, marketing

& sales, and service) and *support activities* (procurement, technology development, human resource management, and firm infrastructure) that produce a product or service together. Porter noted that each activity in the value chain is a "basic unit of competitive advantage". In other words, how each activity is performed determines costs and contributes to differentiation. By examining each step, companies can identify where they add value or incur costs and optimise accordingly.

Businesses use Value Chain Analysis to gain competitive advantage by *optimising operations and reducing inefficiencies*. As Porter described, the goal is to *deliver the most value to customers at the lowest cost*, thereby increasing the firm's margin. It involves scrutinising each activity to find opportunities for cost reduction (e.g. streamlining production or logistics) and value enhancement (e.g. improving product quality or customer service). For instance, a firm might discover through value chain analysis that its warehousing process is incurring unnecessary costs; improving inventory management (an inbound logistics activity) can reduce waste and expense, leading to a cost advantage. According to an IBM summary of Porter's work, maximising the value in each activity is *key to market success*. Companies that effectively refine their value chain can either become cost leaders or differentiators in their industry (or both).

Real-world example—Amazon: Amazon's business illustrates how value chain improvements drive competitive advantage. Amazon has built a *robust, technology-driven value chain* that integrates advanced IT systems, efficient operations, and customer-centric processes. The result is that Amazon's value chain "not only enhances profitability but also ensures that the company remains adaptable to changing market demands". For example, Amazon's heavy investment in automated warehouses (operations) and its proprietary delivery network (outbound logistics) has driven down fulfilment times and costs. Simultaneously, its customer service excellence (service activity) and use of customer data in marketing have enhanced customer satisfaction and loyalty. By continually refining each link in its value chain, Amazon achieves cost efficiencies (which it can pass on as low prices) and superior customer experience. This combination underpins its competitive advantage and strong financial performance (Ferreira, 2023). In short, Amazon's case demonstrates that *value chain analysis* is not a theoretical exercise but a practical tool to pinpoint and strengthen the activities that contribute most to a company's value creation and profit.

Cross-industry application: The principles of value chain analysis apply across industries, but different industries focus on different activities to gain an advantage. For example, in a *manufacturing* business, operations (production efficiency) may be the critical value-adding activity, as seen in companies like Toyota, which excel at lean manufacturing. Outbound logistics and inventory management (getting products to stores or customers quickly and cost-effectively) are often paramount; Walmart and Amazon have gained advantages through world-class logistics systems. In contrast, a *technology* or software company may benefit from product development and marketing activities focusing on innovation and customer acquisition. As one analysis notes, *the importance of each part of the value chain varies by business type*: for a distributor, inbound and outbound logistics are vital, whereas for a pure retailer, outbound logistics might be less critical (since stores are the point of sale). The "operations" may be service delivery in service industries. For a hotel chain, the operations activity includes guest check-in, housekeeping, etc., which must be managed efficiently for cost control and quality. Despite these differences, the core idea remains: by breaking the business into its component activities and examining each, managers in any industry can discover where inefficiencies exist or where improvements can yield a competitive edge. Companies, from manufacturers to tech giants, routinely analyse value chains to find these opportunities. In sum, Value Chain Analysis is a versatile framework that, when applied thoughtfully, helps organisations in any sector pinpoint where to cut costs, invest resources, or re-engineer processes for maximum value creation.

Readers are encouraged to watch the lecture **https://youtu.be/uMV_gyAd9Ro** to understand value chain analysis, quickly. Alternatively, below the QR code can be scanned:

SCAN ME

Scan to watch the lecture—Value chain analysis.

4.2 FIRST-PRINCIPLES THINKING: DECONSTRUCTING PRINCIPLES

First-principles thinking is rooted in the ancient Greek philosophical tradition, most notably discussed by Aristotle, who referred to "first causes from which a thing is known." First-principles thinking is a problem-solving approach that involves breaking a problem down to its most fundamental truths and building solutions from those basics rather than making decisions by analogy or precedent. In modern problem-solving, this mindset translates into breaking down a complex issue into its most basic elements by stripping away inherited assumptions, conventional wisdom, or analogies based on the past, and then building solutions from the ground up. As Elon Musk famously explained, *"I think it's important to reason from first principles rather than by analogy… [With first principles] you boil things down to the most fundamental truths … and then reason up from there."*. It means questioning every assumption and "rule of thumb" about a problem until you reach the true core elements. By starting from these first principles (facts or laws of nature) and reasoning upward, one can devise radically new solutions not bound by legacy thinking. This method is powerful in business and innovation because it forces a rethink of conventional solutions and can reveal possibilities (and cost savings) that a more incremental, analogy-based approach would miss.

This method begins with identifying and distinguishing the parts of a problem, much like disassembling a machine to understand how each part contributes to its function. It then moves to challenging assumptions and eliminating biases. Once the noise is cleared, establishing the root causes becomes possible, leading to deeper understanding rather than surface-level fixes. These root causes, or "first truths," act as a foundation on which to build. Next comes the task of organising and prioritising these problem components within the broader context or the "big picture," ensuring that the problem is not viewed in isolation. Once the pieces are clear and placed in context, the thinker proceeds to identify relationships between parts. This reveals how actions taken on one element may affect another. Finally, with clarity on all fronts, the problem-solver is in a position to assemble a suitable solution, not based on replication, but on sound logic and fresh construction from first principles.

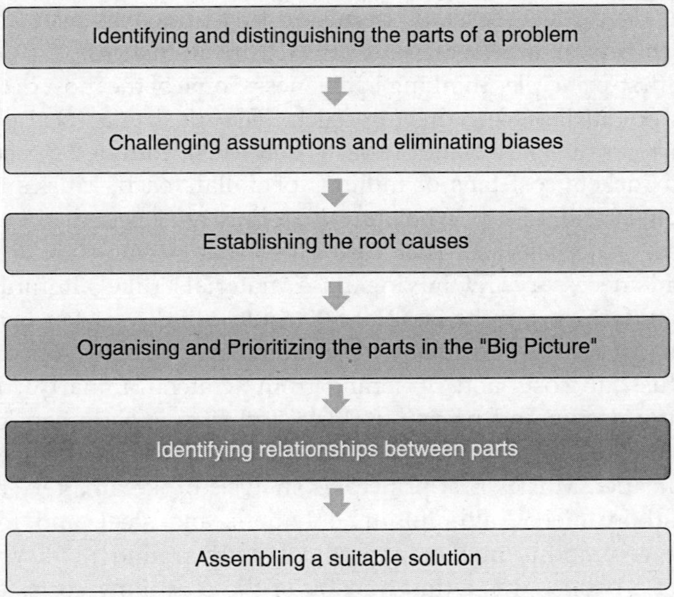

FIGURE 4.1 Systematic thought Process.

This structured sequence of analysis, clearly depicted in Figure 4.1, provides a rational, often transformative, pathway to solutions. It demands granularity (zooming into fine details to see nuances others might miss), depth (tracing the true origins of a problem rather than its symptoms), and diversity (considering wide-ranging perspectives to anticipate risk and opportunity). For instance, understanding why product adoption varies across Southeast Asia involves breaking the issue into cultural preferences, infrastructure readiness, regulatory environments, and purchasing power, each a part to be analysed, rather than relying on analogies from Western markets. Similarly, a company like Amazon may observe low global sales of certain SKUs not due to price or marketing flaws, but because the products lack "nativity", a deep cultural resonance with local buyers. These insights are rarely visible without peeling back the layers to examine what truly drives outcomes.

In today's volatile business environment, first-principles thinking equips managers and entrepreneurs with the cognitive flexibility to reimagine what's possible. Whether it is reinventing supply chains, designing new pricing models, or entering new markets, this approach builds reasoning "upward" from evidence and logic rather than "sideways" from precedent. It is not just an intellectual exercise, but a competitive strategy for navigating uncertainty, complexity, and disruption with clarity and originality.

The importance of first-principles thinking in problem-solving lies in its ability to spur innovation and breakthrough solutions. Discarding assumptions allows entrepreneurs and managers to see problems in a new light and solve challenges that are thought to be unsolvable. First-principles thinking "takes much more mental energy" but can lead to *novel or even groundbreaking results*. It is fundamentally a creative process: instead of accepting "best practices" as given, first-principles thinkers rebuild the solution from the ground up. This approach has deep roots (Aristotle discussed first principles over 2300 years ago) but has gained modern prominence because it can disrupt industries.

Examples of first-principles thinking in business: Some of the most dramatic innovations in recent decades are attributed to this approach. *Elon Musk* is a vocal proponent and has applied first principles at SpaceX and Tesla. When Musk founded SpaceX, the aerospace industry assumed rockets cost tens of millions of dollars each. Musk's team started with physics fundamentals and asked: What raw materials are needed to build a rocket, and how much do those materials cost? They discovered that buying standard aerospace-grade components wasn't necessary. By buying base materials (like aluminium, copper, and titanium) and manufacturing in-house, SpaceX could build a rocket for about 2% of the typical price. This shocking result (a 98% cost reduction) was only uncovered by refusing to accept the status quo costs and reasoning from scratch. Similarly, Musk applied first principles to battery design and pricing at Tesla. Industry experts had long assumed that battery packs would always be expensive (around $600 per kilowatt-hour) and could not be dramatically cheaper. Musk's first-principles analysis broke a battery down into its raw materials, viz., carbon, nickel, aluminium, polymers, and steel, and found that buying those materials on commodity markets would cost only around $80/kWh. In other words, the *intrinsic* cost of a battery was a tiny fraction of the prevailing costs. This insight drove Tesla's strategy to vertically integrate battery production and invest in new manufacturing techniques to approach that theoretical cost floor. Indeed, by redesigning battery cells and building the Gigafactory, Tesla has driven battery costs closer to those fundamental limits, giving it a considerable cost advantage in electric vehicles. As noted in one article, the takeaway is that by attacking problems from a fundamentally different angle, first-principles thinking lets companies make far *better decisions* free from the compromises of conventional wisdom (Baer, 2015).

First-principles thinking is not only for famous billionaires; startups and forward-thinking companies of all sizes increasingly embrace it. In startup cultures (such as Silicon Valley), first-principles thinking is often ingrained: entrepreneurs tackling new markets often *cannot* rely on prior industry playbooks (because they may be inventing something entirely new). Instead, they question everything. This mindset has enabled startups to disrupt established industries by doing things in fundamentally different ways. For example, the founders of DoorDash applied first principles to on-demand delivery logistics, and the company devised a hyper-efficient model that incumbents hadn't envisioned (Buildd.co, n.d.). Startups in emerging tech sectors (AI, blockchain, etc.) regularly use first principles to navigate uncharted territory.

In contrast, established corporations can find first-principles thinking challenging because of ingrained routines and "we've always done it this way" mindsets. However, large companies that encourage first-principles reasoning in R&D or strategy teams can also achieve transformative innovation. For instance, Google's secret research lab "X" is known for first-principles experimentation (like Project Loon's internet balloons). First-principles thinking can also be used within big companies to drastically cut costs or re-imagine supply chains, much like a startup would. Still, it requires strong leadership support to challenge internal orthodoxies.

Startups vs. established firms: Startups often have an advantage in using first principles because they start with a clean slate. As one startup founder put it, *First-Principles Thinking is "all about break[ing] down the [problem], reframe it and logically build the solution from scratch"—actively questioning every assumption and stripping down to the fundamentals before building up*. This approach is a survival skill in the "wild" startup world where playbooks don't exist, and copying others can lead to stagnation (CoreVoice, n.d.). In contrast, established corporations might default to reasoning by analogy ("This new product is like product X we launched last year, so use the same process"). The risk is that they miss novel solutions or cost savings. That said, many big companies are trying to cultivate first-principles thinking. For example, when Ford was near bankruptcy in 2006, CEO Alan Mulally asked leaders to justify every part of the business from scratch, essentially a first-principles reevaluation, which helped turn the company around. Some corporations run internal incubators or hackathons to get employees to think outside the box and challenge assumptions like a startup.

Cultural context—Silicon Valley vs. India: First-principles thinking is often associated with Silicon Valley's innovation culture, where questioning the status quo is encouraged. Entrepreneurs like Musk, Peter Thiel, and others explicitly preach first-principles reasoning as the key to disruptive innovation. In India's startup ecosystem, there has traditionally been a strong culture of "Jugaad"—a Hindi term meaning an improvised, frugal solution born from ingenuity. Jugaad is about being resourceful: *"Seek opportunity in adversity, do more with less, think and act flexibly, keep it simple..."*. In many ways, jugaad philosophy complements first principles thinking as both approaches challenge the notion that big budgets or existing methods are needed to solve a problem. Indian startups often combine first-principles engineering with jugaad's frugality to create innovative, cost-effective products suited to local needs. A classic example is the $2,000 Tata Nano car development, where engineers questioned the necessity of every feature found in standard cars (from the number of cylinders to having a glovebox) to strip the design down to its affordable essentials. The result was an ultra-low-cost vehicle for the Indian mass market (though its commercial outcome was mixed, the engineering approach was groundbreaking). Similarly, India's space agency ISRO, operating under severe budget constraints, used first principles to build and launch the Mars Orbiter Mission in 2014 at just $74 million (far cheaper than similar missions). They reconsidered everything from propulsion to materials, exemplifying frugal first-principles innovation. Culturally, while Silicon Valley startups might use first principles to push technological frontiers, Indian innovators often use them to radically reduce cost and complexity, aligning with "do more with less." Both settings demonstrate that first-principles thinking is a universally applicable tool, whether you're aiming to make batteries cheaper (Tesla) or water purifiers ultra-affordable for villages (Indian social enterprises), breaking a problem down to first principles can reveal a path that conventional thinking would never illuminate.

Here is a nutshell illustration of the First Principles Thinking process:

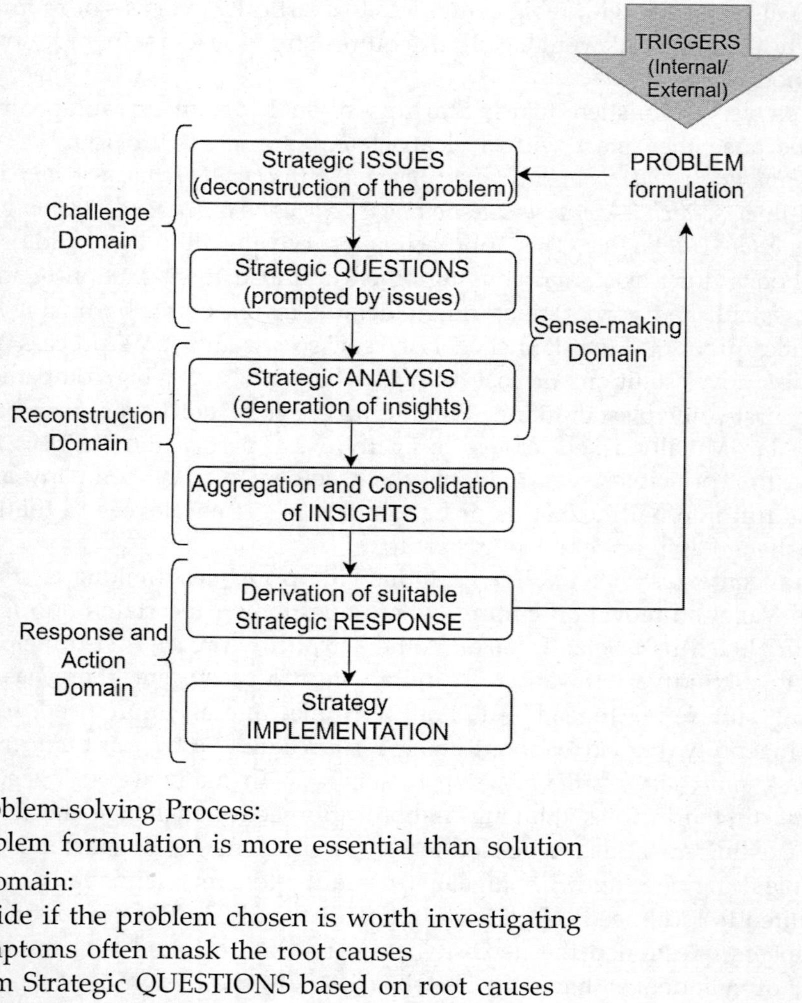

Strategic Problem-solving Process:

- ✦ Problem formulation is more essential than solution

Challenge domain:

- ✦ Decide if the problem chosen is worth investigating
- ✦ Symptoms often mask the root causes
- ✦ Form Strategic QUESTIONS based on root causes

All the Strategic Issues framed are:

- ✦ Not equally important
- ✦ Evolve over time
- ✦ Interconnected
- ✦ QUESTIONS are reshaped as the problem requirements change

Sense-making domain:

- ✦ Meaning is established through the responses to questions
    - Formal analyses based on data collected
    - Informal—Intuition or heuristics

- ✦ These three dovetail to the derivation of plausible outcomes
- ✦ Interpretation and Filtering of the outputs
- ✦ Ascription to acquire meaning in the greater context

Reconstruction domain:

- ✦ Assimilation and integration of insights
- ✦ Consider missing pieces in the puzzle and the capability of the firm reconstruct

Response domain:

- ✦ Formulation and evaluation of RESPONSES
- ✦ Preceding analyses need to be narrowed into viable strategic options

4.3 SYSTEMS THINKING

Systems Thinking is a holistic approach to problem-solving that views an organisation (or any problem domain) as a *system* of interrelated components. Instead of isolating small parts of a process, systems thinking considers the *whole* and the *interconnections*, recognising that changes in one area can affect others (sometimes unintended). In business, this means understanding that departments, processes, people, and external factors are all part of a broader system and must be understood in relation to one another. A concise definition is: *"Systems thinking is an approach to problem-solving that looks at problems as part of a system. When working with an organisational structure, like a supply chain, the system combines the people, structures, processes, and environment that work together (or don't) to create a desired outcome."* . In other words, systems thinking encourages managers to see the forest rather than just the trees. Rather than optimising one team or one step in isolation, one examines how the *entire* process flows and how action in marketing might impact operations, customer satisfaction, etc. The goal is a *healthy system* that delivers the desired outcome instead of an unhealthy system that delivers unintended consequences.

Systems thinking in business problem-solving is crucial when dealing with complex or long-term challenges, where a change in one business element can ripple through many others. It helps leaders recognise interdependencies and anticipate the *long-term implications* of decisions. Without a systems perspective, well-intentioned solutions can backfire. For example, a company might institute a new performance KPI to improve one metric, only to find it causes dysfunctional behaviour elsewhere, a classic unintended consequence of not thinking systemically. It is noted that "solutions…may often lead to more complex problems" if the broader system dynamics are not understood. Systems thinking forces consideration of feedback loops (how does the output of one part of the system affect the input of another) and delays (an action today might have effects next quarter or next year).

Definition: "Collection of interacting components/ actors where the total outcome is more than that of the individuals separately".

Greek Philosophy states that *"the whole is more than the sum of the parts"*

System: Car, Human beings, School, etc., are all systems; they have a purpose

Not a system: Sand spilt on the floor is not a system (No interaction/collective purpose)

Businesses use systems thinking to understand any intervention's short-term and long-term impacts. A key aspect is distinguishing symptoms from root causes. Systems thinkers dig into *why* problems occur by examining the structure producing the behaviour. They are wary of quick fixes that only address symptoms. For example, if customer churn rates rise, a non-systems approach might immediately blame the sales or support teams. A systems approach would map out the entire customer experience system, including marketing promises, product quality, after-sales support, competitor actions, etc., to see *which interactions in the system* are causing dissatisfaction. Perhaps an issue with product usability (an R&D/design problem) leads to customer frustration, which shows up in support calls and cancellations. Solving churn might require a product change rather than just retraining support reps. By viewing problems in context, a company avoids the trap of siloed fixes that can create *"catastrophic consequences"* down the line. As one practitioner put it bluntly, many managers have a *"conceit"* that their linear, local fixes will solve problems. Still, often, they address symptoms rather than the underlying system, so issues recur or pop up elsewhere.

The 2008 Global Financial Crisis stands as a cautionary tale of what happens when systems are misunderstood or viewed in isolation. What began as a downturn in the U.S. housing market, triggered by an increase in borrowers defaulting on home loans, rapidly cascaded into a worldwide economic collapse. The root of the issue lay not just in faulty financial products or housing speculation, but in a widespread failure to understand how interconnected the components of the financial system truly were. Key actors operated on incorrect assumptions, such as the belief that economic growth would continue indefinitely, while engaging in actions that intensified risk: lenders relaxing their standards to win business, regulatory institutions falling short of enforcing safeguards, and financial institutions borrowing heavily to expand their loan books. When the tide turned and borrowers defaulted en masse, the entire system teetered under the weight of its own complexity. House prices fell due to oversupply, financial institutions began to fail, and the world economy was thrust into recession.

This episode starkly illustrates the essence of systems thinking, a framework for viewing problems not as isolated events, but as parts of dynamic systems where elements interact, influence one another, and generate emergent outcomes. In contrast to reductionist approaches that break problems into independent fragments, systems thinking insists on seeing the whole picture: understanding how feedback loops, interdependencies, and delays shape behaviour over time. It is this broader, relational perspective that helps managers avoid the trap of addressing symptoms while ignoring causes or generating solutions that inadvertently create new problems elsewhere.

At the heart of systems thinking is the recognition that everything is connected to something else; nothing exists in isolation. Every action taken in one part of a system affects other parts, sometimes in surprising or delayed ways. This is why the failure of subprime mortgage borrowers in the U.S. housing market could ripple through to affect banks in Europe, trigger job losses in Asia, and unsettle government policies worldwide. Such ripple effects are predictable only when we understand the nature of the system.

Systems can be open or closed, depending on their interaction with the environment. Open systems, such as economies, organizations, and communities, interact continuously with their surroundings, adapting and evolving. Closed systems, by contrast, are self-contained and do not exchange matter or energy with their environment, though in business contexts, true closed systems are rare. Moreover, systems are often classified as hard or soft. Hard systems are technical and mechanical, think of a car engine, where each part has a defined role and predictable interaction. In contrast, soft systems involve human factors, perceptions, and behaviours. For example, the act of driving a car involves the driver, traffic conditions, pedestrian behaviour, and road signals, all of which form a complex web of soft system interactions.

In a business context, a school is not merely a building (hard system), but a soft system where the values, expectations, and motivations of students, teachers, and administrators interact to create outcomes. Similarly, a company's supply chain is not just a logistical process; it includes suppliers' capacities, customer preferences, geopolitical risks, and climate factors. Each component may behave differently depending on the context, making prediction difficult unless the system is understood holistically.

The core value of systems thinking lies in its ability to help managers see patterns, not just events. It encourages the search for underlying structures and root causes, rather than reacting to surface-level symptoms. In doing so, it prevents short-term fixes that create long-term harm and enables solutions that strengthen the entire system. Whether applied to crisis management, supply chain optimisation, sustainability, or strategic planning, systems thinking equips leaders with the lens to navigate complexity with clarity, anticipate consequences, and build resilient organisations.

Unilever's sustainable supply chain: A striking example of systems thinking in action is Unilever's approach to sustainability through its *Unilever Sustainable Living Plan (USLP).* Launched in 2010, the USLP aimed to decouple Unilever's growth from its environmental footprint and increase its positive social impact. Achieving such ambitious goals requires a systems-thinking mindset. Unilever had to examine its entire value chain and extended ecosystem, not just make incremental changes in one area. The company used systems thinking to *"analyse the environmental and social impacts of its operations, products, and value chain"* end-to-end. For example, Unilever tackled greenhouse gas emissions by conducting life-cycle analyses of products from raw material sourcing to manufacturing to consumer use and disposal. This analysis revealed that a significant portion of emissions for products like soap or shampoo occurred not in Unilever's factories but when consumers used the product (heating water for a shower, etc.). Such insight, which lies outside the traditional organisational boundaries, is a direct product of systems-level thinking. Unilever responded by campaigning for consumer behaviour change and innovating products (like shampoos that rinse out with less water), addressing the overall water use system. They also worked closely with suppliers (upstream in the value chain) to reduce deforestation related to palm oil and with distributors and customers (downstream) to reduce waste.

Another example is Unilever's initiative to improve the livelihoods of smallholder farmers in its supply chain. Rather than demanding suppliers cut costs or risks, Unilever took a systems view of rural farming communities. They identified challenges farmers faced (access to finance, training in sustainable practices, market access) and collaborated on solutions to create a more resilient agricultural system. By investing in training and resources for farmers, Unilever ensured a long-term sustainable supply of quality raw materials (like tea, vegetables, etc.), benefiting both the farmers and Unilever. This win-win outcome was visible only when looking at the entire system, not just a transaction. The results of Unilever's systems approach have been impressive as the company reports that the Sustainable Living Plan has *reduced environmental impact (e.g. GHG emissions, water use) and improved social conditions* (for communities and workers involved) *while also driving business growth and innovation* (ESG&, 2023). Many of Unilever's "sustainable living" brands (managed with these systemic goals) outpaced the growth of other brands, proving that doing good and doing well can coincide when managed as part of a whole system. Unilever's experience underscores that tackling complex problems like sustainability or large-scale supply chain resilience requires viewing the company as part of a larger system, including communities and the environment, rather than an isolated entity.

Adoption across industries and geographies: Systems thinking initially gained popularity in fields like environmental management and engineering (through system dynamics models and thinkers like Jay Forrester and Peter Senge). Today, it is increasingly adopted in business strategy and operations across industries. *Manufacturing and supply chain management* have naturally gravitated to systems thinking because of the tightly coupled processes involved; a change in a factory can affect suppliers, distributors, and customers in unforeseen ways. The best supply chain companies explicitly use systems thinking. For example, an industry review noted that *many of the top 25 supply chains in the world (companies like Dell, Ford, Procter & Gamble, Apple, McDonald's, Amazon, Unilever, Intel, etc.) are well-known examples of systems thinking in practice.* These companies see their supply chain as an integrated system and optimise it end-to-end (often sharing data with suppliers, coordinating production with demand forecasts, etc.). In *technology and software,* systems thinking is evident when companies consider user feedback loops and platform effects; for instance, a social media company must think about system dynamics (how user engagement, content, and ad revenue feed back into each other). *Healthcare organisations* use systems thinking to improve patient outcomes by looking at the entire patient journey through the health system (this has given rise to the field of "systems medicine" and more holistically designed care processes). Geographically, systems thinking has been embraced by many European companies, partly influenced by sustainability focus and regulations. For example, Dutch and Scandinavian firms often integrate systems thinking in their emphasis on circular economy (designing products for reuse and recycling requires seeing the full system of production and disposal). Japanese management practices, too, have long implicitly used systems thinking. The concept of "Lean" in the Toyota Production System is about seeing the production process as an interrelated system and eliminating waste holistically. In developing economies, systems thinking is increasingly recognised as essential for tackling infrastructure development and urban planning where business, government, and society intersect.

In summary, systems thinking is becoming a global best practice for managing complexity. Whether it is a German automotive manufacturer mapping out an entire product life-cycle to meet EU recycling laws or a Singaporean city planner coordinating transportation, housing, and business districts, the principle is understanding the interdependency system before acting. Organisations that adopt systems thinking tend to be better at *long-term strategic planning* because they can anticipate second- and third-order effects of decisions (e.g., how a new product cannibalises another or how increasing warehouse throughput might bottleneck shipping if not concurrently addressed)—those who do not take a systems perspective risk solving one problem only to create another unintentionally. As business environments become more complex and fast-changing, seeing the big picture is an increasingly vital leadership skill.

Let us have a glimpse at another example of a Chemical Manufacturing company.

This case study focuses on the supply system between an international chemical manufacturing company producing dynamite, and quarries who buy sticks of dynamite to blast rock faces to make gravel. The manufacturing company produces dynamite from two inert liquids by mixing them together to create an explosive. The explosive liquid has to be stored somewhere safely before it is plasticized by adding plasticizers. The plasticizing process resembles that of making a dough. The plasticized explosive liquid becomes dynamite. The dynamite needs to be stored somewhere safely until it is transported and delivered to the customers, i.e. the quarries.

Defining Objectives:

1. Reimagine the Supply Chain and delivery to serve better
2. Enhance safety
3. Reduce Non-Value Addition activities

Tasks as Consultants:

1. Identify the Non-Value Addition activities in the current Supply Chain of the customer.
2. Apply Systems Thinking to provide innovative solutions.
3. Apply any other frameworks to strengthen the analyses.

Solution offered:

1. Development of the Mobile Manufacturing Unit (MMU)
    - A specialized truck equipped with separate tanks for two inert liquids, enabling safe transport of raw materials.
    - On-site mixing of the inert liquids to create the explosive directly at the quarry location, eliminating the need for pre-made dynamite.

Solution offered:

1. On-Demand Blasting Service
    - Quarries simply request the amount of rock they need fragmented, and the MMU team handles the blasting process on-site.
    - The MMU applies the explosive directly into drilled holes in the rock face, bypassing the need for quarries to store or handle dynamite.

Outcomes/What it means to the Customer?

Enhanced Safety and Reduced Security Costs

1. Eliminating the transport of ready-to-use explosives reduces the need for stringent security measures.
2. Quarries are freed from storing hazardous materials on-site, minimizing risk and compliance requirements.

Increased Efficiency and Cost Reduction:

1. Simplification of the supply chain by removing the plasticizing, storage, and transport stages for dynamite.
2. Reduces logistical costs, streamlines the blasting process, and lowering operational expenses for both players.

Outcomes/What does it mean to the Customer?
Shift to a Service-based Business Model

1. The Chemical manufacturer transitioned from a product-based to a service-based model, providing a "rock-on-the-ground" outcome rather than just selling dynamite.
2. Builds stronger customer relationships by aligning more closely with their core objectives and operational needs.

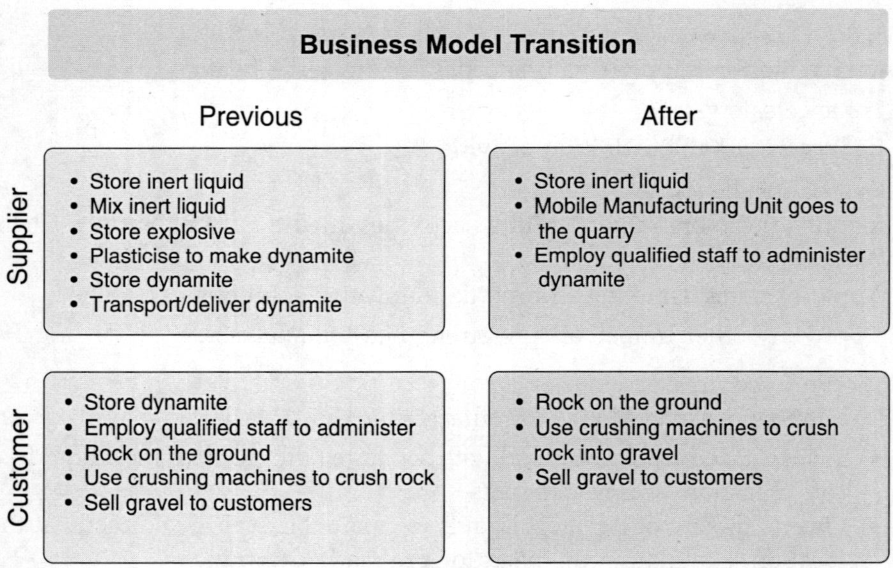

FIGURE 4.2 Business Model Transition.

4.4 SCENARIO ANALYSIS

Scenario Analysis (or Scenario Planning) is a strategic planning technique for dealing with uncertainty by developing a set of plausible future scenarios and exploring how the organisation would fare under each. Unlike forecasting (which tries to predict the most likely future), scenario planning embraces the uncertain future and considers multiple "what if" narratives. Typically, a small number of distinct scenarios bracket a range of outcomes (e.g., best case, worst case, and moderate case, or scenarios driven by different key variables like regulatory environment, market growth, etc.). Each scenario is essentially a story about how the future might unfold based on different assumptions about critical uncertainties. The role of scenario analysis in strategic planning is to *broaden managers' thinking* about the future, improve preparedness, and test how strategies would perform under very different world conditions. A key point is that scenario analysis is not about predicting exactly what will happen but about making robust decisions across a range of possible futures. Scenario planning's origins in military and corporate strategy (pioneered by Herman Kahn at RAND and later popularised by Royal Dutch/Shell) stress shaping the mental models of decision-makers. One case study of Shell's approach noted, *"At Shell, the aim of scenario planning was not to predict the future but to modify the mental model of decision-makers faced with an uncertain future."*. By envisioning even unlikely but possible developments, leaders can challenge their assumptions ("Would our current strategy survive if X happened?") and devise contingency plans.

In today's fast-moving economy, businesses operate in an environment marked by constant change, technological disruption, and evolving customer expectations. The pace of industrial transformation is accelerating, driven by digital innovation, globalisation, and emerging societal demands. To survive and thrive in such a complex and dynamic setting, organisations must go beyond rigid planning and embrace strategic flexibility, the capacity to adapt, respond, and pivot in real time. This requires more than just quick decision-making; it demands a continuous loop of learning, adaptation, and reinvention.

A powerful conceptual model that encapsulates this need for agility is the OODA Loop, developed by U.S. Air Force Colonel John Boyd. Originally designed to evaluate fighter pilots' decision-making capabilities under combat pressure, the OODA Loop has since become a foundational framework in business strategy and competitive thinking. OODA stands for Observe, Orient, Decide, and Act, representing a recurring cycle that leaders and organisations must navigate to remain responsive and competitive in uncertain environments.

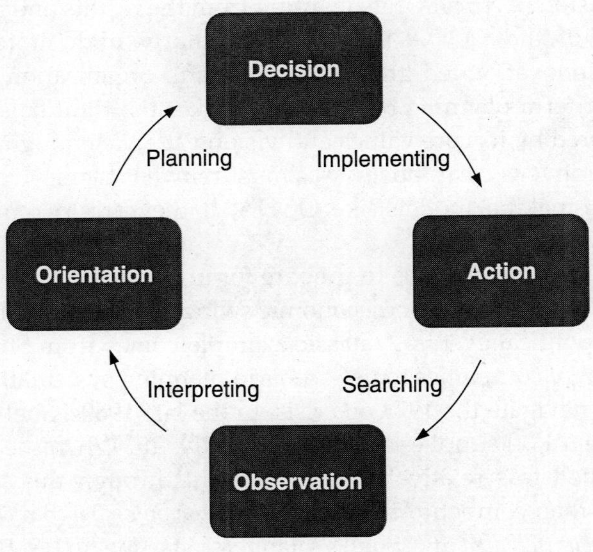

FIGURE 4.3 OODA framework.

The Observe phase involves collecting data from the external environment, market trends, customer behaviour, competitor actions, regulatory changes, as well as from within the organisation itself. This step is crucial in turbulent contexts where patterns shift rapidly and old assumptions can become obsolete overnight.

Next is Orient, arguably the most critical and complex stage. It involves interpreting the observations in light of the organisation's culture, values, capabilities, and mental models. This is where strategic sensemaking occurs, analysing what the observed signals mean and framing the problem through the lens of both historical experience and real-time insights. Orientation shapes the quality of the decisions that follow.

Decision follows as the organisation selects a course of action based on the available data and strategic framing. This choice is never made in a vacuum; it is informed by the orientation process and weighed against possible risks and opportunities.

Finally, in the Act phase, the decision is implemented. But the cycle doesn't end here. The results of the action feed back into the system, generating new observations and triggering another loop of analysis and adaptation.

This cyclical structure creates a feedback loop that is particularly suited for volatile environments. Businesses that can cycle through OODA faster than their competitors gain a decisive advantage. They are able to act while others are still deliberating. This notion, known as getting inside the opponent's decision loop, was vital in aerial combat and is equally relevant in modern industries disrupted by startups, consumer shifts, or regulatory surprises.

For companies, the metaphor of the fighter pilot is apt: navigating high-stakes, fast-changing situations where milliseconds can mean the difference between winning and losing. Firms must build internal systems that sense the environment (Observe), analyse and interpret signals accurately (Orient), make clear strategic choices (Decide), and execute with speed and precision (Act), all while learning from the results and adjusting accordingly.

The relevance of the OODA Loop is particularly high in today's era of digital transformation and innovation-led growth. A successful organisation is no longer one that merely excels at long-term planning but one that strikes the right balance between stability and flexibility, anchored by its core values and vision yet agile enough to evolve in response to change. The imperative is clear: businesses must reinvent themselves continually, guided by adaptive decision-making models like OODA, if they are to remain competitive in a turbulent, fast-growing world.

Businesses use scenario analysis to prepare for uncertainties and market shifts beyond their direct control. For example, macroeconomic swings, technological disruptions, changes in regulation, or geopolitical events. A classic example comes from Shell in the 1970s. Shell was one of the first large companies to use scenario planning systematically, and it famously helped the company navigate the 1973 oil crisis. In the late 1960s, Shell developed scenarios in which Middle Eastern oil supplies were significantly cut. When the 1973 OPEC embargo and oil shock hit, Shell was relatively ready, thought through this "crisis scenario", and could respond faster than competitors. Indeed, *while the oil embargo rocked the world economy, Shell "seemed to have anticipated it."* Shell's planners, starting in 1965, had created a new long-term planning activity using Herman Kahn's scenario methods. The power of their scenario work was not in predicting the exact timing of the crisis but in *recognising the possibility* and mentally rehearsing responses. It gave Shell a strategic advantage (it shifted investment and supply sourcing according to its scenarios). Since then, Shell's scenario planning team has continued to produce long-term energy scenarios (famously looking 20–30 years ahead) to inform its strategy on issues like oil demand, renewable energy, and climate change. For instance, in the mid-2000s, Shell published scenarios like "Scramble" vs. "Blueprints": *In the "Scramble" scenario, policymakers worldwide pay little attention to energy efficiency or climate until supply crises force reactive change (leading to energy price spikes and chaotic adaptation). In the "Blueprints" scenario, early coordinated actions on energy policy and carbon pricing drive clean technology development and a smoother transition to lower emissions.* Considering both, Shell could plan a flexible strategy of investing in renewables and gas (beneficial in a Blueprints world) and maintaining oil capabilities for a Scramble-type world. This example shows how scenario analysis helps in long-term growth strategy (positioning the company for success under different future market conditions, such as high-carbon vs. low-carbon future). Notably, scenario planning has enabled Shell to survive multiple upheavals in the energy sector over decades, partly by avoiding strategic rigidity. They don't bet on a single forecast but rather prepare for several eventualities.

Another well-known use case is how scenario analysis is employed in the tech industry and telecoms. For example, a smartphone manufacturer in 2010 might have created scenarios around different rates of mobile internet adoption, different competitor moves (if, say, a tech giant from another sector entered phones), or various consumer preference shifts. By planning for a scenario where consumers prioritise price vs. one where they prioritise innovative features, the company can develop product strategies and supply chain plans for each and then watch real trends to see which scenario (or which combination of scenarios) is emerging.

Scenario analysis is also extremely valuable in crisis management and risk planning. Companies and governments use it to rehearse responses to low-probability but high-impact events, called *"war gaming"* or *stress testing*. For instance, banks must do scenario-based stress tests (what if unemployment rises X%, what if a liquidity crunch occurs. Will the bank remain solvent?). As a timely example, consider the COVID-19 pandemic: Very few businesses *predicted* a global pandemic would strike in 2020. However, those that had previously run *"pandemic" or "global disruption" scenarios* in their planning were far better positioned to respond. Experts have noted that COVID-19 was largely unexpected but not completely unimaginable. *It could be visualised and prepared for through scenario planning.* Some companies (and government agencies) did have "global pandemic" as one of their scenarios on the shelf, informed perhaps by SARS in 2003 or flu pandemic models. Those who did could activate contingency plans (for example, moving operations remotely, shoring up supply redundancies, etc.) faster than those who had never considered such a scenario. A commentary from Oxford Saïd Business School observed that firms using scenario planning were *"much better prepared to seize opportunities"* during the COVID economic contraction. For example, some manufacturing firms quickly pivoted to producing medical supplies, and certain retailers swiftly implemented e-commerce and delivery models effectively because they had anticipated something like a sudden collapse of in-person business. It highlights scenario analysis as a long-term strategy and crisis resilience tool.

Case study—*Multinational vs. regional use:* Large multinational corporations tend to institutionalise scenario planning as part of their strategy cycles, whereas smaller regional companies might use it more informally (or sometimes overlook it). Multinationals operate in complex, volatile environments across different countries with different risks. So, they often have dedicated teams to develop scenarios for global economics, geopolitical shifts, technological disruptions, etc. For example, HP and IBM in the 2000s created scenarios about the future of computing (cloud vs. local, open-source prevalence, etc.) to guide their investments. Airbus and Boeing routinely use scenario analysis for air travel demand under various oil price and GDP growth situations, as decisions on launching new aircraft programs involve 10-20-year outlooks. We have already discussed Shell, an archetype of an MNC that continuously uses scenario planning (Shell's scenario team has produced over 30 rounds of global scenarios since the 1970s). An online case study notes, *"Major corporations and research firms often develop and share future scenarios specific to an industry's future or to address major global problems. Shell…continues to be the leader in scenario planning."*. Conversely, a regional or mid-sized company might focus on more immediate, local uncertainties. For example, a regional dairy processing company might do scenarios for local milk supply (good harvest vs. drought affecting feed) or local market demand changes, but perhaps not broader global scenarios. There is sometimes a misconception among smaller firms that formal scenario planning is a luxury only big companies can afford. It is a *dangerous misconception as even startups and SMEs benefit from scenario thinking* and need not be resource-intensive. For instance, a regional retail chain could scenario-plan the entry of a global competitor into their market or an economic downturn in their city and then develop strategies (like strengthening customer loyalty programs or diversifying product lines) that would help in those scenarios. Many regional companies learned this the hard way during events like COVID-19 or sudden regulatory changes. Those who had thought through "What if we have to shut our stores?" could move sales online or via delivery quickly, whereas others were caught unprepared.

To illustrate, consider two companies in the same industry, one global and one regional: Ford Motor Company (global) versus a hypothetical regional car dealership network. As a multinational company, Ford uses scenario analysis to prepare for things like electrification trends, global recession scenarios, or new tariffs in different markets. The regional dealership might use scenario analysis for more localised questions. For example, a scenario where a new highway diverts traffic away from their location or a scenario where a new competitor dealership opens in town. The *scope* and *scale* of scenarios differ, but the method is similar. Both can anticipate changes and plan responses.

Scenario planning for growth vs. crisis: It is useful to distinguish between scenario analysis for *opportunity/ growth* and crisis/ risk management, though they overlap in practice. For long-term growth strategy, companies use scenario analysis to test the robustness of their strategic plans against different futures. For example, a company considering a large investment (like building a new factory) will analyse scenarios such as "high market growth" vs. "stagnant market" vs. "decline" and see under which scenarios the investment pays off. It informs a go/ no-go decision or adjustments (maybe building a smaller scalable facility to hedge against a low-growth scenario). They might also explore best-case scenarios to ensure they can scale up if things go better than expected. This kind of scenario work ensures the strategy is flexible and can be adjusted as the future unfolds.

On the other hand, crisis scenario planning is about being ready for specific adverse events. It is common in enterprise risk management, e.g., in cyberattack scenarios and natural disaster scenarios. Companies often create playbooks for scenarios like "our data centre is breached" or "a key supplier fails" so they can respond swiftly if it ever occurs. An example is how many multinational firms had "Brexit scenarios" prepared years before the UK left the EU. They ran scenarios on supply chain delays at borders, regulatory divergence, etc., allowing them to relocate certain operations or secure alternate logistics before any worst-case disruptions hit. In sum, scenario analysis supports crisis management by forcing organisations to imagine and prepare for challenging situations (so they aren't scrambling with no plan if it happens). It supports strategic planning by illuminating which strategies will succeed across various futures (so the company is not overcommitted to one future that may not happen).

In practice, good scenario planning often yields a set of 3-4 detailed scenarios, with names like "Boom," "Bust," and "Steady," or thematic titles like Shell's "Scramble" and "Blueprints." Managers then discuss: *If scenario X unfolds, what would we wish we had done? What strategy would we pursue?* Those insights lead to strategic moves that make sense in multiple scenarios, sometimes called *robust strategies*. Additionally, scenario analysis can highlight trigger points or early indicators (for example, if interest rates start rising rapidly, we might be heading toward our "inflation shock" scenario, time to enact the corresponding contingency plan). Ultimately, scenario analysis is valuable in improving the quality of strategic conversations and decisions despite uncertainty. As one Harvard Business Review article title aptly put it, it helps managers start "Living in the Futures", making them more agile and less surprised no matter what tomorrow brings.

Let us now see a case of Amazon entering the Southeast Asian market from a OODA framework perspective.

SCENARIO 1: *High Competition with Localized Preferences and Payment Barriers*

Inception: Amazon entered Southeast Asia via Singapore with fast delivery options but faced stiff competition from established players like Lazada and Shopee, which had deep local market knowledge and adaptable payment solutions.

Observations:

- High market share held by local e-commerce platforms with strong customer loyalty.
- Varied digital adoption and limited credit card penetration across regions.

Orientations to Business:

- Adapt offerings to better suit local preferences.
- Consider more flexible payment solutions, recognizing the regional disparity in digital financial adoption.

Future Scenario Planning:

- *Rapid adoption:* Rapid and limited digital adoption scenarios.
- *Intensified Competition:* Local competitors grow their market share with aggressive tactics.

Probable Decisions:

- Launch a localized Amazon Prime with region-specific benefits and pricing.
- Expand payment options—COD and mobile wallet.

Implementation Methods:

- Partner with local fin-tech companies for payment solutions.
- Tailor the Prime subscription model to include exclusive benefits for popular local categories.

Action in Real System:

- Monitor adoption rates of new payment options and adjust strategies based on customer feedback.
- Invest in customer education campaigns to promote digital payment methods and Amazon Prime benefits.

Scenario planning can also be viewed as a response to the stimulus encountered by the system(s). it determines the capability to respond to these changes, that define the fitness for survival. Higher the responsiveness, better chances of survival. There are two key aspects namely responsiveness and robustness that need to be balanced through the stimulus cycles. While responsiveness believes in effecting the changes faster, robustness, on the other hand is the likelihood that an organization need not change to meet an uncertain event/environment. It governs the potential for success under varying conditions. The systems become more robust and responsive when subject to multiple vicious cycles.

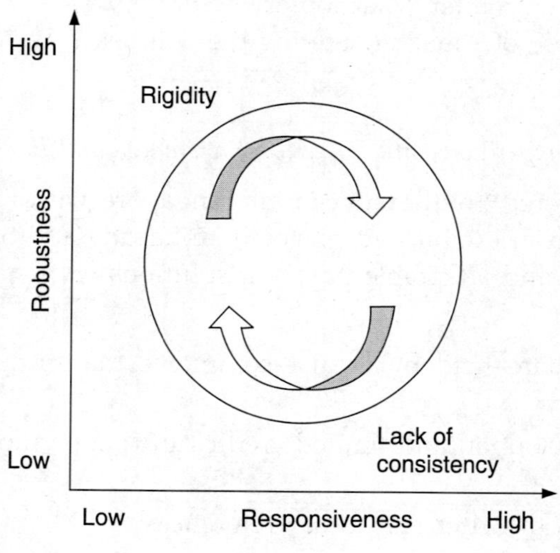

4.5 BALANCED SCORECARD

The Balanced Scorecard (BSC) is a strategic performance management framework developed by Robert Kaplan and David Norton in the early 1990s, designed to give managers a more "balanced" view of organisational performance beyond just financial measures. Kaplan and

Norton observed that traditional metrics (like quarterly financials) were lagging indicators and often encouraged short-termism. So, they introduced the BSC to include additional perspectives critical to long-term success. The classic Balanced Scorecard encompasses four performance perspectives: Financial, Customer, Internal Business Processes, and Learning & Growth (sometimes called Organizational Capacity or People). The organisation sets objectives, measures (KPIs), targets, and initiatives for each perspective. By looking at all four areas, companies ensure they are balancing short-term and long-term priorities. For example, in addition to financial metrics (profit, revenue growth), a BSC will track things like customer satisfaction and retention (Customer perspective), process efficiency and quality (Internal perspective), and employee skills or innovation (Learning & Growth perspective). These non-financial metrics are often drivers of future financial performance. As an Investopedia summary puts it, the BSC *"takes into account four perspectives essential to value creation...: the financial perspective as well as a focus on customers, internal business processes, and learning and growth."*. By including all four, the scorecard links the company's overarching strategy (e.g., becoming number one in customer service in our industry) to concrete metrics and actions across these domains.

One can think of the Balanced Scorecard as a framework to translate strategy into operational terms. Managers start with the high-level *strategic vision* and then determine what that means in each perspective. For instance, if the strategy is innovation leadership, the Learning & Growth perspective might include targets for R&D spending or employee training in new technologies; the Internal Process perspective might track product development cycle time; the Customer perspective might measure percentage of revenue from products launched in the last 3 years; and the Financial perspective would, of course, track the revenue growth or ROI from innovation. The BSC forces this kind of holistic thinking. Kaplan and Norton described it as a way to *"clarify and translate vision and strategy into action"*. Providing a comprehensive set of metrics aligns business activities with the strategic goals and facilitates better performance monitoring.

Using the BSC to align strategic objectives with operational goals: One of the Balanced Scorecard's core strengths is exactly that alignment. It ensures that what people do day-to-day (operational activities) connects to what the organisation tries to achieve (strategic objectives). For example, a strategic objective might be "Improve Customer Loyalty." On a balanced scorecard, this could appear under the Customer perspective with a specific KPI like *Net Promoter Score* or *repeat purchase rate*. Then, the internal process perspective might aim to "enhance service quality" with KPIs like service response time or defect rate, which drive customer loyalty. Learning & growth might include "Employee training in customer service" with a measure of training hours completed. Financial might include "increase customer lifetime value" as an outcome measure. By doing this, *the BSC ties the high-level goal ("better customer loyalty") to concrete actions at the process and employee level,* creating a *line of sight* for employees. They can see how doing their job well contributes to strategic success. The BSC is a communication tool as much as a measurement tool: it *"provides a comprehensive framework, helping organisations translate vision into actionable goals, ensuring all facets of the business work towards common objectives."*. Many companies find that implementing a BSC breaks down silos because it creates shared goals across departments (e.g., the IT department has objectives on the scorecard that relate to customer and financial outcomes, not just internal IT metrics). It also introduces accountability beyond financial results. A call centre manager, for instance, knows that improving customer satisfaction scores is as important as keeping costs within budget since both are on the scorecard.

Perspectives in practice: To illustrate, consider the four perspectives in a *BSC for a retail chain*:

- *Financial:* Increase same-store sales growth, Improve profit margin, etc. (lagging indicators of success).
- *Customer:* Achieve a top-tier customer satisfaction index, increase customer retention, and improve online review scores. (These reflect how the company is perceived by customers, which drives financial results.)
- *Internal Processes:* Reduce inventory stockouts, Shorten checkout time, Improve supply chain delivery accuracy, etc. (Operational metrics that drive customer satisfaction and efficiency.)
- *Learning and Growth:* Increase employee training hours in product knowledge, Improve staff engagement survey scores, Upgrade IT systems uptime, etc. (Capabilities that enable better processes and customer service in the long run.)

By measuring these, leadership can tell a "story" of performance. A well-designed BSC will have *cause-and-effect links*: e.g., "Increasing employee training (Learning) will improve service quality (Internal), which will raise customer satisfaction (Customer), which in turn will boost sales (Financial)." Such linkages validate that the strategy is working across all levels. If one part of the chain is weak (say, customer satisfaction isn't improving despite better process metrics), management can investigate and adjust strategy or execution accordingly.

CASE STUDY: BSC Implementation in a Fortune 500 Company

One famous early adopter of the BSC was Mobil's North America Marketing & Refining division, which used it in the 1990s to execute a new strategy and saw significant performance gains (Kaplan & Norton wrote a Harvard case on it). To provide a contemporary example, consider Ford Motor Company (a Fortune 500 manufacturer), which adopted the BSC to rejuvenate its operations. Ford's leadership recognised that they needed to go beyond financial turnaround and improve product quality and internal efficiency to achieve sustainable success. Using the BSC, Ford set objectives and measures in all four areas. For instance, under Internal Processes, they focused on streamlining operations (measuring things like manufacturing cycle time and defect rates); under Learning & Growth, they invested in employee development and engagement (measured by training programs and employee satisfaction indices); under customer, they tracked vehicle quality ratings and customer loyalty; and under Financial, they of course watched profitability and cash flow. This balanced emphasis yielded tangible improvements. Over a few years, Ford dramatically *enhanced product quality and reduced costs*. Their warranty repair rates fell (indicating better quality), and manufacturing efficiency rose, contributing to a return to profitability. According to case analysis, *Ford's use of the Balanced Scorecard helped it "enhance product quality and reduce costs," this holistic approach enabled Ford to overcome significant challenges and become more competitive.* In other words, Ford achieved a true turnaround by not just chasing short-term financial fixes but also focusing on the underlying drivers (process and people). The BSC provided the framework to monitor and drive this multi-faceted effort, aligning the entire organisation (from factory floor to corporate offices) around the strategy of operational excellence and quality improvement. Many other large corporations report similar benefits. For example, Apple Inc. in the late 1990s (after Steve Jobs' return) implicitly used a balanced scorecard approach, focusing not only on financials but also on the *innovation pipeline (Learning & Growth), internal design and supply chain efficiencies (Internal Process), and user experience (Customer)*, which led to improved product outcomes and, eventually, spectacular financial results. Apple is often cited as a success story where aligning the organisation around a broad set of strategic performance objectives (not just profit) led to sustained competitive advantage.

Adaptation for different organisation sizes: Small and large corporations can benefit from the BSC, though their implementations will scale differently. A small or mid-sized business (say, a local restaurant chain or a niche software firm) might use a *simplified* scorecard, perhaps with fewer metrics, but balanced objectives are still valuable. Surveys show that organisations of all sizes widely use the BSC: *about 61% have fewer than 500 employees, and only 9% have over 10,000 employees*. It indicates that small companies find it useful because it gives structure to their strategy execution. For a small business, the BSC can prevent the common pitfall of focusing only on immediate financial survival; it reminds them to also track things like customer satisfaction or employee skills that will drive long-term success. For example, a small tech startup might set a customer satisfaction goal as part of its early scorecard. Even if revenue is small, they are building the foundation for growth.

On the other hand, large corporations benefit from the BSC in managing complexity. A big company might have dozens of departments and matrixed teams; the BSC provides an overarching framework so that, for instance, the IT department's goals support the business unit goals, which support the corporate strategy. It also helps communication as large companies often use a "cascading" approach, where high-level scorecard objectives cascade down to departmental and individual scorecards, creating top-to-bottom alignment. For instance, the strategy may set a goal to improve customer experience; the retail division has a scorecard objective to enhance in-store experience; a store manager's scorecard might include a target for customer wait time or store cleanliness audit scores. This cascade ensures everyone knows their part in achieving the strategy. The benefit for a large corporation is coherence; everyone isn't pulling in different directions or optimising only their silo. Studies (like 2GC's annual surveys) have found that a majority of organisations believe the Balanced Scorecard helps influence business actions and is "extremely or very useful" in practice.

Furthermore, the BSC encourages a long-term view even in a quarterly-driven corporate world. By incorporating Learning & Growth metrics, including innovation, training, and culture, executives are reminded to invest in the future. A small company might be tempted to cut training during tough times, but a BSC would flag that as undermining a key perspective. Likewise, a big company might be tempted to squeeze processes to hit a quarterly number. Still, the BSC might reveal that customer satisfaction is dropping, indicating an early warning to fix issues before the brand is damaged.

In summary, the BSC has proven to be a *game changer* in how organisations plan and measure success. It shifts the conversation from "Did we hit our financial target?" to "*Are we doing the right things in all areas to build a thriving organisation?*" Linking strategic goals with day-to-day metrics creates a bridge between the boardroom and the frontline. Whether in a small business (where it can bring discipline and strategic focus) or a large enterprise (where it drives alignment and strategic communication), the BSC helps ensure that strategy isn't just a lofty statement but a living guide for operational decisions. Companies that successfully implement it often report clearer focus, better teamwork across functions, and improved performance monitoring. However, it is important to note that the BSC is not a one-time project requiring continual updates and adaptation. One case study noted that organisations must *customise the scorecard to their context and update it as the business evolves* to keep it effective. When used dynamically, the BSC becomes an integral part of the management system, aligning the entire organisation from strategy formulation to execution and feedback.

KEY POINTS TO REMEMBER

1. *Value Chain Analysis for competitive advantage:* Value Chain Analysis breaks down a company's activities (from inbound logistics and operations to marketing, sales, and service) to see where value is added and costs are incurred. The key point is that by examining each link in the chain, managers can identify opportunities to reduce costs or enhance value. For instance, improving an inefficient manufacturing process or strengthening customer service can lower expenses or increase customer satisfaction. *Bottom line:* Optimising individual activities in the value chain leads to a stronger overall competitive position, whether through cost leadership or differentiation.
2. *First-Principles Thinking—Back to basics:* First-principles thinking is about distilling a problem to its fundamental truths and building up solutions from scratch, as if no preconceived assumptions existed. This technique encourages questioning every assumption ("Why must this be done this way?") and is a driver of innovative solutions because it frees thinkers from the limits of existing practices. *In essence:* By understanding the basic elements of a problem, one can generate breakthrough ideas that reimagine products or processes (a mindset famously used in fields like engineering and entrepreneurship to achieve big leaps rather than incremental improvements).
3. *Systems Thinking for holistic solutions:* Systems Thinking entails viewing problems in a business as parts of an interconnected whole. Rather than fixing an issue in isolation, a systems thinker examines how different parts of the organisation (or external factors) interact and influence each other. This key point reminds us that

changes have ripple effects: a decision in one department could unintentionally cause issues in another if the system relationships aren't considered. By using systems thinking, managers strive for solutions that optimize the entire system (not just a part), avoid unintended consequences, and create long-term, sustainable improvements that align with the organisation's broader objectives.

4. *Scenario Analysis (planning for uncertainty):* Scenario Analysis (or scenario planning) is a strategic tool to prepare for an uncertain future. Instead of relying on a single forecast, teams develop multiple realistic scenarios (e.g. best case, worst case, and several in-between) based on key variables that could change (such as market conditions, regulatory shifts, or technological advances). The important takeaway is that thinking through these scenarios in advance helps organisations stay agile and ready—if one of the imagined futures begins to materialize, the company has a playbook of strategies it can quickly implement. This approach reduces surprise and panic in volatile environments and leads to more robust strategic plans that have considered risks and opportunities ahead of time.
5. *Balanced Scorecard—Aligning strategy with action:* The Balanced Scorecard is a framework for translating a company's vision and strategy into a coherent set of performance measures across four perspectives: Financial, Customer, Internal Processes, and Learning & Growth. The key point is that success shouldn't be measured by financial metrics alone. By setting objectives and KPIs in all four areas, managers ensure that, for example, customer satisfaction, internal efficiency, and employee development are all progressing in support of long-term strategy. In essence, the Balanced Scorecard helps align day-to-day operations with strategic goals—every level of the organisation knows what success looks like beyond just profit, fostering better strategic execution and balance in performance outcomes.
6. *Using the right tool for the right problem:* This chapter presented multiple advanced techniques, and a central takeaway is that each has its specific use-case and strengths. Effective problem-solvers mix and match these tools as needed. For instance, one might use first-principles thinking to conceptualize a radical new solution, then apply value chain analysis to assess where it adds value, and finally use a Balanced Scorecard to monitor implementation. The overarching point is that mastering these diverse techniques enables a manager to approach complex problems from multiple angles—strategic, operational, financial, human—and to ensure that solutions are well-rounded, thoroughly analysed, and successfully implemented.

KEY LEARNINGS

- Value Chain Analysis is a framework that breaks down a company's activities and finds competitive advantages. Firms can identify inefficiencies or strong points by examining each step, from inputs to outputs. The real-world application shows that optimising the value chain drives profitability. For example, Amazon achieved cost savings and speed by refining logistics and leveraging technology in every part of its value chain. Different industries focus on various value chain segments (e.g., a manufacturer on production efficiency, a retailer on supply chain and merchandising)—still, all benefit from a holistic view of value creation and where it can be improved.

- First-principles thinking is about questioning assumptions and reconstructing problems from fundamental truths. It encourages creativity and radical innovation, as seen in SpaceX reducing rocket costs to a fraction of industry norms and Tesla re-imagining battery economics. The key learning is that by not accepting "industry standard" constraints, businesses can sometimes achieve ultra-low-cost products or completely new business models that were thought impossible. This approach is especially useful in dynamic or emerging fields, and it is a reminder that continuous improvement sometimes requires stepping back and redesigning from scratch. In practice, first-principles thinking can be applied by continually asking "why" and "what if we start over?" for any challenging problem.
- Systems Thinking teaches that in business, everything is interconnected. Optimising one department or metric in isolation can lead to sub-optimal outcomes or unintended side effects elsewhere. Adopting a systems perspective means looking at the big picture and understanding how processes, people, and external factors interact. The success of efforts like Unilever's sustainability initiative underscores that tackling complex problems (sustainability, efficiency, etc.) requires addressing the entire system (supply chain, consumer behaviour, stakeholder incentives) rather than a single facet. By understanding cause and effect across the whole business, managers can implement changes that produce lasting benefits and avoid "fixes that fail" (where a short-term fix creates a long-term issue). Tools like causal loop diagrams, feedback analysis, and cross-functional teams help in practising systems thinking.
- Scenario Analysis prepares organisations for an uncertain future by asking "What would we do if...?" for multiple plausible scenarios. The lesson is that planning for various outcomes makes a company more agile and resilient, even if the future doesn't unfold exactly as one scenario. Shell's ability to handle the oil shocks and its continued use of scenarios for future energy markets demonstrate that scenario planning can yield a competitive advantage in the face of volatility. Another learning is the importance of recognising early indicators—scenario planning often identifies what signs to watch (e.g., a shift in customer preference or a regulatory change) that signal which scenario might be emerging so the company can pivot accordingly. For MBA students and managers, scenario analysis underscores the value of flexibility: rather than betting the farm on one forecast, develop strategies that perform well across various possible worlds (or have contingencies ready for each).
- Balanced Scorecard provides a structured way to translate strategy into action by balancing financial and non-financial goals. A major insight is that "what gets measured gets managed". By setting targets in Customer, Internal Process, and Learning & Growth areas, companies ensure short-term financial concerns do not overshadow those drivers of success. The BSC teaches that long-term financial

success comes from excelling in customer satisfaction, efficient and quality processes, and continuous improvement/learning. Cases like Hilton Hotels and Ford showed that implementing a BSC led to improvements in service quality and operational efficiency, which drove profitability. Another takeaway is the importance of alignment: the BSC cascades strategic objectives down through the organisation, creating line-of-sight for employees. This alignment means everyone understands how their role impacts larger goals, which improves execution. Thus, the BSC is as much about communication and cultural change as it is about measurement. It fosters a performance culture where multiple facets of excellence are valued. Small and large organisations can adapt the BSC to instil discipline in following through on strategy.

- Overall, these advanced problem-solving techniques are complementary. A modern, high-performing company might use all of them in concert. For instance, a firm could use *first-principles thinking* to design a new product, apply *systems thinking* to ensure the product's launch is supported by the entire organisation (and supply chain) without hiccups, use *scenario analysis* to anticipate market reception under different conditions and track the ongoing execution with a *BSC* to ensure the strategy stays on course. The common thread is structured, thoughtful analysis for moving beyond gut feeling or single-metric management to robust frameworks proven in theory and practice. By mastering these techniques, MBA graduates and business leaders can tackle problems systematically yet creatively, leading to more innovative solutions and sustainable competitive advantages in their careers and companies.

EXERCISES

1. *Value Chain Analysis Exercise—Retail Coffee Business: Case Scenario:* You are a consultant for a growing coffeehouse chain facing eroding profit margins. The company's COO provides you with information on their sourcing costs (coffee beans, dairy), operations (barista labour, drink preparation processes, equipment maintenance), outbound logistics (distribution of beans and supplies to stores), marketing expenditures, and customer service feedback.

   Task: Perform a *value chain analysis* for this coffeehouse. Identify at least three activities in the value chain where the company can reduce costs or add value. For each activity, propose an initiative, for example, negotiating better prices for beans (Procurement), streamlining the drink-making process to serve customers faster (Operations), or improving the app ordering system (Marketing/Sales). Explain how it would improve the company's competitive position. Be prepared to explain how changes in one part of the value chain might impact other parts (for instance, will faster service require different training in HR? Will cheaper suppliers affect quality?). This exercise will test your ability to break down a business and find improvement opportunities using Value Chain Analysis.

2. *First-Principles Thinking Challenge—Electric Scooter Startup: Scenario:* You co-founded a startup making electric scooters for urban transportation. Each scooter's battery is currently the most expensive component, and industry norms suggest a fixed minimum cost per battery. However, a rival has suddenly released a model with a much longer battery life at a similar price, threatening your market share.

   Task: Use *first-principles thinking* to brainstorm how you might radically improve your scooters' battery performance or cost. Start by listing assumptions your team has held (e.g., "We must use lithium-ion chemistry," "Battery must be one unit," "Charging must be done by plugging into an outlet"). Challenge each assumption—could you use a different battery chemistry or form factor? Could you enable battery swapping stations to use smaller batteries? Could regenerative braking significantly extend the range? For each idea, break down the problem: identify the fundamental goals (e.g., provide energy for X miles) and explore alternatives from the ground up. Develop one proposal that would dramatically lower costs or improve the range (for example, a new design using modular batteries or sourcing raw materials differently than Tesla did by analysing commodity prices). Present your proposal, explaining how you arrived at it from first principles and why it is not just copying what competitors do. This exercise encourages you to question industry conventions and find innovative solutions.

3. *Systems Thinking Simulation—E-commerce Supply Chain: Context:* An e-commerce company experienced a successful sales promotion that unfortunately led to delivery delays and many customer complaints. In the debrief, different managers blamed their issues: the warehouse said *couriers* were the problem, the delivery team said *inventory forecasting* was wrong, customer service said they weren't informed of delays, etc.

   Task: Conduct a *systems thinking analysis* of the company's operations to understand how this promotion's execution failed. Map out the key components of the order fulfilment system: marketing (which ran the promotion), the online ordering system, inventory management, warehouse packing, courier shipping, and customer communications. Draw a causal loop diagram (or simply outline relationships) showing how these components interact. For instance, the promotion (Marketing) led to a surge in orders beyond forecast (Inventory issue), which led to stockouts (Warehouse delay), which caused late shipments (Courier backlog) and, ultimately, customer complaints (Customer Service overload). Identify at least two *feedback loops* or interdependencies (e.g., a delay in warehouse processing might cause an overload in customer support calls, which distracts warehouse managers with escalation emails—a reinforcing feedback loop of chaos). Now propose two systemic solutions: one could be better cross-department coordination before promotions (so inventory and warehouse prep are aligned with Marketing), and another might be building slack capacity that can absorb order surges. Explain how your solutions address the problem at the systems level rather than just treating one symptom. This exercise tests your ability to see the big picture and recommend changes that improve the entire system's robustness, not just one silo.

4. *Scenario Planning Exercise—Global Expansion Decision: Scenario:* A mid-sized clothing retailer based in India is considering expanding into two new markets: Latin America and Southeast Asia. The CEO is unsure which region to focus on and is concerned about each uncertainty.

   Task: Perform a *scenario analysis* to help guide this decision. First, identify 2–3 key uncertainties that would significantly impact success in these markets. For example, economic growth rates, competitive landscape (entry of global fast-fashion giants), and trade policies/tariffs in each region. Develop two contrasting scenarios for the future of each target region (you can do a total of four scenarios, two per region). For Latin America, perhaps create a "Booming Middle Class" scenario (high growth, stable politics, great consumer spending) and an "Economic Turbulence" scenario (recession, currency volatility). For Southeast Asia, it may be a "Regional Free Trade & Digital Adoption" scenario vs. a "Protectionism and Offline Retail persist" scenario. In groups, describe each scenario's conditions in narrative form. Then, analyse how the company's strategy should differ in each scenario: e.g., in the booming scenario, the company should invest in many physical stores, whereas in a recession scenario, it should use a low-cost online-only entry. After considering the scenarios, discuss which market (Latin America vs. SE Asia) offers more robust opportunities across scenarios. Does one region have more favourable outcomes in most scenarios? Finally, make a recommendation (with the recognition that it is based on scenario analysis, not certain predictions). This exercise will require you to think about macro factors and make strategic suggestions resilient to different futures.

5. *Balanced Scorecard Exercise—Aligning Operations with Strategy: Context:* You are the new strategy manager of a healthcare clinic network. The clinic's strategy is "Exceptional Patient Experience with Efficient Operations for Affordable Care." However, the current organisational focus seems skewed. The finance department pushes revenue generation (more tests, more patients) even if waiting times increase, and there is little tracking of patient satisfaction.

   Task: Design a *Balanced Scorecard* for the clinic network that balances these priorities. Break into teams, each team developing objectives and one or two sample metrics for each of the four perspectives: Financial, Customer, Internal Process, Learning, & Growth. Ensure the objectives align with the overall strategy given. For example, under *customer,* you might set an objective to "Achieve top-quartile patient satisfaction" with metrics like patient survey scores or repeat visit rates. Under *internal Processes, an objective could be to "Improve service efficiency" by measuring the* average waiting time or throughput of patients per day (without quality loss). *Financial* might include "Maintain profitability" or "Grow revenue per doctor" but balanced with cost of care metrics. *Learning & growth* could emphasise "Continuous training in patient care" (measure: hours of staff training, or employee engagement scores, since happy staff often yield happy patients). Once each team drafts its scorecard, compare them: Do they all reflect the strategy of exceptional experience + efficiency? Discuss how hitting targets in one perspective affects the others (for instance, does investing in Learning & Growth by training staff improve Customer satisfaction? Yes, likely, that's a cause-effect link to note). Each team should also suggest one initiative for improvement based on the scorecard. For example, if wait times are too high (Internal Process issue), propose adding an online check-in system or hiring a triage nurse; if staff engagement is low (Learning & Growth issue), propose a new incentive program. This exercise teaches translating a broad strategy into specific, balanced performance measures and actions. It will illustrate the importance of not defaulting only to financial metrics, especially in a mission-driven field like healthcare, and how aligning all areas via a scorecard can drive strategic success.

THOUGHT-PROVOKING QUESTIONS

1. **Integrative Thinking:** Consider a situation where a company simultaneously faces declining customer satisfaction and rising costs. Which techniques (Value Chain Analysis, First-Principles Thinking, Systems Thinking, Scenario Analysis, Balanced Scorecard) would you apply first to diagnose and address the issue, and why? How might these approaches complement each other in holistically solving the company's problem?
2. **Challenging Assumptions:** Identify a product or service in today's market that you believe is constrained by *industry assumptions*. What are those assumptions, and how could first-principles thinking be used to upend them? For instance, choose something like "air travel," "university education," or "food delivery". What do most players take for granted that a fresh startup might question? Outline a brief first-principles strategy for an innovator in that space.
3. **Avoiding Unintended Consequences:** Provide an example (real or hypothetical) of a well-intentioned business change that produced unintended negative consequences because of a lack of systems thinking. (For example, a bank that introduced an incentive for tellers to open new accounts might lead to tellers being overly aggressive, upsetting customers and hurting satisfaction.) How could systems thinking have prevented the issue? What steps should the company take now to fix the systemic problem?
4. **Scenario Planning and Bias for Action:** Critics of scenario planning sometimes argue that it can lead to "paralysis by analysis," where managers waffle between scenarios and delay decisions. Do you agree? How can companies ensure scenario analysis leads to *actionable strategies* rather than indecision? In your answer, describe how a firm might use scenario outcomes to formulate a core strategy with contingency plans (as opposed to waiting to see which scenario occurs). Consider the balance between preparedness and the need for commitment.
5. **Balanced Scorecard Trade-offs:** The Balanced Scorecard requires balancing objectives across different perspectives. Sometimes, improving one metric can hurt another (for example, increasing production output might risk quality drops,

affecting customer satisfaction). As a manager, how would you handle a situation where two scorecard metrics appear to conflict? Provide a specific example (say, Internal Process vs. Customer perspective conflict) and discuss a decision-making approach to resolve the trade-off. How might the scorecard be adjusted to mitigate such conflicts in the future (perhaps by adding a metric that captures both aspects, like "defect rate" to ensure output increases don't sacrifice quality)?

REFERENCES

Baer, D. (2015, January 5). Elon Musk Uses This Ancient Critical-Thinking Strategy To Outsmart Everybody Else. Business Insider. Retrieved September 20, 2024, from https://www.businessinsider.com/elon-musk-first-principles-2015-1.

Buildd.co. (n.d.). How SpaceX, Amazon, Zerodha and DoorDash use First Principles Thinking to problem solve. Buildd Product Insights. Retrieved September 20, 2024, from https://buildd.co/product/examples-of-first-principles-thinking.

CoreVoice. (n.d.). First Principles Thinking: Problem Solving for Startups. CoreVoice Blog. Retrieved September 20, 2024, from https://www.core77.com/posts/25743/

ESG&. (2023, April 30). How Systems Thinking Can Help Us Build a More Resilient Future. ESG & Eco. Retrieved September 20, 2024, from https://esgand.eco/understanding-sustainability-how-systems-thinking-can-help-us-build-a-more-resilient-future/

Ferreira, J. (2023, July 10). Amazon Value Chain Analysis. Business Model Analyst. Retrieved September 20, 2024, from https://businessmodelanalyst.com/amazon-value-chain-analysis/

Gebbia, J. (n.d.). How Design Thinking Transformed Airbnb from a Failing Startup to a Billion-Dollar Business. First Round Review. Retrieved September 20, 2024, from https://review.firstround.com/how-design-thinking-transformed-airbnb-from-failing-startup-to-billion-dollar-business.

Handa, A., & Vashisht, K. (2017, February 6). How IBM Is Embracing the Future Through Design. UXmatters. Retrieved September 20, 2024, from https://www.uxmatters.com/mt/archives/2017/02/how-ibm-is-embracing-the-future-through-design.php

Harvard Business School Online. (n.d.). 5 Examples of Design Thinking in Business. HBS Online Blog. Retrieved September 20, 2024, from https://online.hbs.edu/blog/post/design-thinking-examples.

IBM. (2020, January). Value Chain Analysis: Core Concepts and Key Activities. IBM Think Blog. Retrieved September 20, 2024, from https://www.ibm.com/think/topics/value-chain-analysis.

Ignatius, A. (2015, September). How Indra Nooyi Turned Design Thinking Into Strategy: An Interview with PepsiCo's CEO. Harvard Business Review. Retrieved September 20, 2024, from https://hbr.org/2015/09/how-indra-nooyi-turned-design-thinking-into-strategy.

Network for Business Sustainability. (n.d.). The Challenge of Change: 3M, Six Sigma and Corporate Culture. NBS Knowledge. Retrieved September 20, 2024, from https://nbs.net/the-challenge-of-change-3m-six-sigma-and-corporate-culture/

Nichols, D. (2018). Going to Extremes—how Nike found their latest innovation. The Brandgym. Retrieved September 20, 2024, from https://thebrandgym.com/going-to-extremes-how-nike-found-their-latest-innovation/

Randall, K. (2020, June 8). PepsiCo's Design Thinking Approach to Organizational Innovation. R&D Today. Retrieved September 20, 2024, from https://www.rndtoday.co.uk/design-thinking/pepsicos-design-thinking-approach-to-organizational-innovation/

Sayyadi, M., & Provitera, M. (2024). Inside Tesla: A Rare Glimpse of Tesla's Mysterious Innovation Culture. The European Business Review. Retrieved September 20, 2024, from https://www.europeanbusinessreview.com/inside-tesla-a-rare-glimpse-of-teslas-mysterious-innovation-culture/

CHAPTER 5

Design Thinking Process Implementation

LEARNING OBJECTIVES

Design Thinking has become a cornerstone methodology in business education and industry practice for driving innovation. After reading this Chapter, the readers will be able to:

- Understand the value of extreme customers—Identify who "extreme users" are and why they provide crucial insights beyond the average customer.
- Learn how to foster an innovation culture—Discover leadership strategies and cultural elements that encourage creative problem-solving and calculated risk-taking in organisations.
- Gain a step-by-step integration plan—Grasp a clear process for implementing design thinking in teams, including collaboration techniques, cross-functional teamwork, and iterative experimentation.
- Explore diverse applications—Examine how design thinking can be applied to product development, service design, and high-level business strategy, with examples from multiple industries (technology, healthcare, fintech, etc.).
- Manage change and overcome resistance—Recognise common barriers to adopting design thinking and learn tactics to overcome organisational and psychological resistance to change.
- Study a real-world transformation—Analyse a detailed case study of SAP, illustrating how a global enterprise scaled design thinking across the company and compare it with other large firms' experiences.
- By the end of this chapter, you should be able to apply design thinking principles in various business contexts practically, lead teams through the design thinking process, and embed this mindset into an organisation's DNA.

5.1 LEARNING FROM EXTREME CUSTOMERS

Defining Extreme Customers: In design thinking, *extreme customers* are those users at the far ends of the usage spectrum. They are the outliers whose needs or behaviours differ significantly from the mainstream. These include *lead users* (who face needs before others do), power users who push a product's limits, or users with special needs due to disabilities or unique environments. For example, a power user might use a software tool 10 hours a day and discover performance issues that no casual user would. In contrast, a user with a disability might require alternative interactions that reveal general usability improvements. Studying such extremes forces teams to challenge assumptions and can uncover latent needs, as research shows this approach can drive innovation beyond conventional constraints. By designing for the needs of extreme users, companies often create solutions that benefit the broader user base, referred to as the *edge-effect* of innovation.

Why They Are Crucial: Extreme customers magnify problems and opportunities. They often experience pain points more intensely or use products in unconventional ways, making underlying issues more visible. Observing how they adapt or "hack" products can inspire new features or offerings. For instance, many assistive technologies (voice recognition, text-to-speech, etc.) were initially developed for users with disabilities but ended up adopted by the mainstream (think of how voice assistants like Siri or Alexa owe their lineage to such innovations). Designing with extreme cases in mind encourages *inclusive design*. Solutions that work for extremes tend to be flexible and robust enough to improve the experience for *all* users. Extreme users also help test robustness. For example, if a product holds up under extreme conditions or usage, it will perform reliably for average users. In short, these fringe perspectives stretch creativity and prevent complacency by forcing designers to consider a wider range of scenarios than the "average" user would generate.

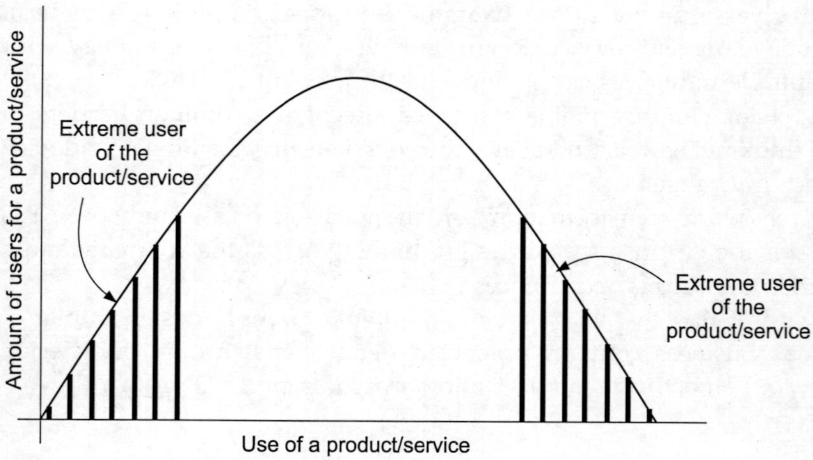

FIGURE 5.1 Illustration of extreme users at the edges of a typical user distribution. Designing for the needs at the fringes (striped areas) can spur ideas that also improve the product for the mainstream middle (Wikipedia, n.d.).

Gaining Insights from Extremes: Organisations can systematically leverage extreme customers through targeted research. One approach is ethnographic research, which involves observing extreme users in context to see how they interact with a product in real life. For example, a medical device company might shadow a triathlete with a prosthetic leg (an extreme user of running shoes) to observe workarounds and unmet needs. Another method is participatory design workshops involving extreme users in brainstorming solutions. Companies also analyse user modifications: when passionate users rig or modify products, those adaptations signal opportunities (e.g. video gamers building custom controllers to play despite disabilities). Engaging early adopters or lead users in beta testing is equally valuable. Their feedback often foresees what the mass market will desire months or years later. The key is to actively seek out those on the spectrum's edges (the tech geek pushing every feature, the customer using a product in a harsh environment, the person excluded by current designs) and learn from their extreme use cases.

Real-World Business Cases: Leading Companies have Tapped Extreme users to Spark Innovation

Nike's FlyEase line is a prime example. For its hands-free GO FlyEase sneaker, Nike drew inspiration from disabled athletes who couldn't use traditional laces. By collaborating with an extreme user who lacked hand dexterity, Nike's team invented a shoe to put on and off without hands. Originally, it solved a problem for those with disabilities but also created convenience for everyday customers (Taylor, 2019). This "extreme" innovation embodied Nike's inclusive ethos and opened a new market segment, showing how designing for extremes can yield breakthrough products with broad appeal.

Airbnb provides another case: In its early days, struggling to gain traction, Airbnb's founders zeroed in on a small group of *early users* in New York City. They noticed an extreme pain point wherein the hosts had poorly lit, amateur photos that turned off potential renters. In a now-famous design thinking move, the founders flew to New York, met these hosts, and personally took high-quality photos of their spaces. This hands-on empathy with their "extreme" early adopters solved the immediate problem (better images doubled their weekly revenue) and proved the value of deep user insight, ultimately saving the company (First Round Review, 2015).

Likewise, Apple has long leveraged extreme user insights, particularly around accessibility. The company's Voice Over screen reader and other assistive features were designed for visually or motor-impaired users. Though these were some extreme cases of smartphone interaction, these features have improved the overall product, benefitting all users with features like voice dictation and Siri. By addressing the needs of initially excluded users (e.g., the blind or those who cannot use touch screens), Apple fulfilled a social imperative and gained unique innovations that set its products apart. These cases illustrate that extreme users, whether *power users, early adopters, or users with disabilities,* often point the way to the next big innovation.

Industry Comparisons: Different industries target different "extremes" to innovate. In healthcare, extreme users might be patients with rare conditions or chronic illnesses, and providers study them to design solutions that eventually improve care for all patients. For example, a hospital might redesign its pediatric MRI service after observing that claustrophobic or autistic children (extreme patient needs) are uncomfortable during scans. It is a famous instance that led to the redesigning of the GE Healthcare Adventure Series, which made MRI rooms child-friendly and reduced the need for sedation (Harvard Business School Online, 2022). In technology and software, extreme users are often early adopters or tech enthusiasts who push a platform to its limits. Tech firms like Google often release beta products to these users, whose heavy use and feedback drive refinements before mass rollout. Companies might look at extreme trendsetters or extremely loyal customers in retail and consumer goods to spark ideas. For instance, high-end fashion brands observe avant-garde street wear communities to inspire designs that trickle into mainstream fashion. Conversely, they also study extreme *non-users* (people who refuse a product) to understand barriers. Industries like automotive have even looked at extreme environments: engineers design off-road vehicles by studying drivers in the harshest terrains (desert racers, Arctic explorers) to ensure durability and performance enhancements that ultimately benefit the average driver (e.g., better traction systems). While the specifics vary, a bank might examine super-users of a finance app versus a non-profit studying community with no access to its services. The principle holds across sectors: reaching out to the fringes of your user base yields fresh insights that core markets won't reveal. By comparing approaches, we see that *healthcare organisations* often emphasise empathy and inclusive design (to ensure no patient is left behind), *tech companies* harness lead users for feature innovation, and *consumer product firms* watch extreme enthusiasts and sceptics to drive product and experience innovation. In all cases, extreme customers act as a litmus test for innovation opportunities, helping businesses break out of the assumptions of the average user.

5.2 BUILDING A CULTURE OF INNOVATION

Innovation is not just a process; it's a cultural phenomenon. An organisation's culture can significantly accelerate or impede the adoption of design thinking. To successfully implement design thinking, companies must foster an innovation culture: a work environment that encourages creativity, experimentation, and empathy at all levels. Key elements of such a culture include a shared belief in the *value of new ideas*, openness to failure as a learning opportunity, collaborative teamwork across silos, and an inherent customer-centric mindset. Research with global executives finds common cultural traits associated with innovation success: high tolerance for risk, intellectual curiosity, a non-hierarchical structure, and empowerment of employees. In one study, 91% of surveyed senior executives listed characteristics like "intellectual courage, risk-taking, and a flexible, non-hierarchical structure" as vital for an innovative culture (Sayyadi & Provitera, 2024). These traits mirror design thinking principles–which thrive in environments where people feel safe to propose wild ideas, challenge the status quo, and empathise deeply with users.

Leadership Strategies for Fostering Innovation: Leadership plays a pivotal role in shaping culture. Innovative companies often have leaders who *model* the creative behaviours they want to see. For instance, top management at Google gave employees "20% time", which is permission to spend 20% of their work hours on passion projects outside their routine jobs. It communicated trust and encouraged bottom-up innovation, resulting in products like Gmail and AdSense that originated from employees' side projects. Leaders can promote a culture of innovation by explicitly rewarding experimentation (even if a particular experiment fails) and reframing failures as learning. At 3M, a long-established innovator, leadership historically allowed scientists to tinker (15% free time for research) and celebrated "happy accidents". The Post-it Note is a classic outcome of a "failed" experiment that leadership recognised as a potential product.

On the other hand, leaders must be careful with initiatives like Six Sigma or other efficiency drives that, if over-emphasised, can stifle the free-thinking needed for innovation. 3M's experience in the early 2000s is instructive: a new CEO imposed strict Six Sigma metrics on all processes, which clashed with 3M's innovation culture. Employees complained that an overemphasis on efficiency and precision was "getting in the way of real invention," with new product revenue stagnating. Subsequent leadership relaxed those controls to restore a balance between creative exploration and disciplined execution (Network for Business Sustainability, 2018). The lesson is that leaders must actively balance structure and freedom by implementing just enough processes to harness innovation without smothering it. Effective strategies include setting *big, inspiring goals* (e.g., Elon Musk's directive at Tesla to "think in notches of 10x improvement" encourages radical ideas over incremental ones), flattening hierarchies so that junior voices with bold ideas are heard, and creating formal channels for idea-sharing (hackathons, innovation labs, etc.). Leaders at Tesla are noted for pushing intellectual risk-taking and empowering employees at all levels to contribute ideas while maintaining a high bar for execution. They exemplify *intellectual courage* that permits challenging their teams to attempt what others deem impossible (like landing rockets or building electric cars at scale), and crucially, they back those bets with resources and vocal support. In summary, leadership that champions design thinking will consistently emphasise *customer focus* ("the user comes first" as a mantra), allocate time and resources for innovation (Google's 20% time or Hack Weeks), and publicly recognise creative efforts, thereby signalling to the entire organisation that innovation is genuinely valued.

Examples from Innovative Companies: Several companies are repeatedly cited as models of an innovative culture: Google, 3M, and Tesla among them. Google cultivates innovation through open information sharing (e.g. weekly all-hands "TGIF" meetings where any employee can ask founders questions), an idea that transparency breeds trust and stimulates ideas. Google's campus environments are famous for playful spaces and amenities. Far from trivial perks, these send the message that creativity and well-being are essential to performance. More substantively, Google's internal incubator programs and the acceptance of moonshot projects (Google X's self-driving cars, Loon balloons, etc.) demonstrate a top-down endorsement of big thinking. The result is a workforce that feels permission to pursue unconventional ideas, aligning with design thinking's ethos of exploring alternatives without fear. 3M, by contrast, offers a longer historical perspective: as early as the 1940s, 3M established a norm that up to 15% of an engineer's time could be used for exploratory projects (the origin of products like Scotch Tape and the adhesive behind Post-its). 3M also formed informal "innovation committees" and internal venture capital funds to seed employee ideas. Their culture motto was "FedEx Days," which means to deliver something overnight and encourage quick prototyping. Notably, 3M leadership tolerated *mistakes as part of discovery*, a hallmark of design-thinking-friendly cultures. When that balance tipped (during the Six Sigma era), 3M saw a dip in radical innovation, reinforcing how delicate and vital the culture is to innovation outcomes (Network for Business Sustainability, 2018). Tesla exemplifies a more top-driven but still innovative culture. Elon Musk's leadership is known for setting audacious visions (e.g. accelerating the transition to sustainable transport), insisting on first-principles thinking, and expecting employees to solve problems in ways never done before. Employees at Tesla often work under intense pressure. Still, many are motivated by the bold mission and the fact that unconventional thinking is put into practice quickly (e.g. designing new manufacturing processes or reimagining car sales without dealers). A key cultural aspect of Tesla's flat communication is that Musk has encouraged engineers to email or talk to anyone else to solve a problem, regardless of hierarchy, and to remove barriers to innovation. It is quite different from traditional automakers' siloed cultures. Additionally, Tesla operates with a "bias for action" by rolling out prototypes and iterative improvements via over-the-air updates to cars at a pace legacy companies struggle to match. Despite industry differences, all these companies share common threads: leadership that visibly supports innovation, employees who feel empowered to experiment, and a shared purpose or vision that fuels passion for innovation.

Regional Cultural Differences: Corporate culture is also influenced by national and regional culture, which affects how design thinking is adopted across North America, Europe, and Asia. In North America (especially the U.S.), there is often a cultural glorification of risk-taking and entrepreneurship. American business culture tends to tolerate failure (to a point) as a learning step. Silicon Valley's "fail fast, fail forward" mantra epitomises this. This attitude aligns well with design thinking, which requires iterating through failures to reach reasonable solutions. An American startup, for instance, might celebrate a "post-mortem" of a project that flopped, extracting lessons for the next venture. As one observer quipped, Americans *"glorify risk-taking and always have…we roll the dice to beat the odds"*, indicating that trying bold ideas is ingrained in the culture.

In contrast, many European business cultures have traditionally been more cautious and methodical. Failure in some European contexts carries more stigma, and there can be a preference for thorough planning over rapid experimentation. For example, a German manufacturing firm might emphasise precision and reliability so strongly that proposing a half-baked prototype (common in design thinking's early phases) feels uncomfortable. Hierarchies in Europe also tend to be more formal. However, Europe is diverse: Nordic countries often promote egalitarianism and consensus (which can favour collaborative design thinking), while some Southern European or older industrial cultures might be more top-down. Recent trends show that Europe is catching up in encouraging entrepreneurial thinking, but companies in certain regions may need to consciously counteract employees' fear of making mistakes.

Asia Presents another Dimension: East Asian cultures (in countries like Japan, China, and South Korea) historically have higher *power distance*, i.e., respect for hierarchy is strong and often a more collective mindset. Employees may be less inclined to voice unconventional ideas in front of seniors, which can inhibit the free-flowing brainstorming that design thinking encourages. Moreover, a fear of "losing face" can make people less willing to prototype something imperfect or admit an approach failed. For instance, Japanese corporate culture has excelled at continuous improvement (kaizen), focusing on refining existing processes, but has sometimes struggled with the more radical, ambiguity-embracing design thinking style (Bennett, 2019). That said, many Asian companies are adapting: some Chinese tech firms and Indian startups are adopting Silicon Valley-like cultures of agility. There's also evidence of blending approaches—for example, a Korean corporation might run design thinking workshops but adapt facilitation techniques to fit local norms, ensuring junior team members feel safe contributing despite hierarchy.

Comparative Impact: North American teams might dive into design thinking with enthusiasm for their creative freedom, needing perhaps more guidance on focusing efforts (to avoid chaos), whereas a European team might need more encouragement to break out of analysis paralysis and take leaps of faith. An Asian team could benefit from modified workshop formats that assure no one is singled out for blame if an idea fails, creating a "safe space" within a traditionally formal culture. Ultimately, while *design thinking principles are universal, empathy, creativity, and iteration, how an organisation fosters these can vary by region.* Companies must be mindful of these cultural starting points. For example, when IDEO works with clients globally, they often adjust their training: in the U.S., they might emphasise channelling abundant ideas into execution. In Europe, they might work on loosening strict adherence to initial plans, and in Asia, they often start by securing strong executive endorsement to permit participants to experiment. Despite regional differences, success stories abound: Scandinavian firms have wholeheartedly embraced design thinking in service design; American companies lead in disruptive product design; and some Asian enterprises (like Singapore's government agencies or Alibaba in China) have built hybrid cultures that leverage both traditional discipline and new design-driven innovation techniques.

In summary, building a culture of innovation requires *intentional effort*: leadership must set the tone, the structure must bend to allow creativity and local cultural norms should be acknowledged and, when necessary, nudged toward the open, user-focused, and experimental mindset that design thinking thrives on.

5.3 STEPS FOR INTEGRATING DESIGN THINKING INTO YOUR TEAM

Adopting design thinking in an organisation is not a one-off event but a journey. It involves introducing new practices and mindsets into team workflows. Here is a structured step-by-step approach to implementing design thinking in teams, along with best practices for collaboration and iteration:

1. ***Educate and Evangelise:*** Begin by building awareness and understanding. Provide training workshops to introduce the design thinking process. Typically, the Empathize, Define, Ideate, Prototype, and Test stages so that team members can grasp the methodology (Dam & Siang, 2017). Use hands-on exercises during training so that people experience what it's like to empathise with users, brainstorm,

and build quick prototypes. It's often effective to start with a small pilot group of enthusiastic participants (perhaps a cross-functional innovation task force) who can later become in-house evangelists. Many companies create *internal design thinking champions* or hire experienced design thinking coaches (like how IBM hired design experts to jump-start its program). This stage aims to demystify design thinking and generate buy-in by highlighting success stories and quick wins. Leadership should explicitly endorse the effort. For example, a manager might kick off the training by saying, "We're investing in this because we believe deeply in user-centred innovation." This top-down support encourages team members to take the training seriously and embrace the upcoming changes.

2. ***Start with a Real Project (Pilot):*** After initial training, moving from theory to practice is crucial. Identify a project suitable as a *design thinking pilot*. Good candidates are problems that are user-centric, somewhat open-ended, and important but not mission-critical (so there is space to experiment without excessive risk). For instance, a software team might pick to improve the onboarding experience for new users; a bank's team might choose to redesign the account opening process. Form a cross-functional team for this project including members from different departments (e.g., a designer or UX specialist, a product manager, an engineer, a marketing or operations person, etc.). Cross-functional collaboration is key because it brings diverse perspectives to the problem and breaks down silos. As the team kicks off the project, have them apply the design thinking steps rigorously, conduct user interviews or observations (Empathise) to gather insights, synthesise findings into user personas or point-of-view statements (Define), run creative brainstorming sessions possibly with sketching (Ideate), build a simple prototype or storyboard

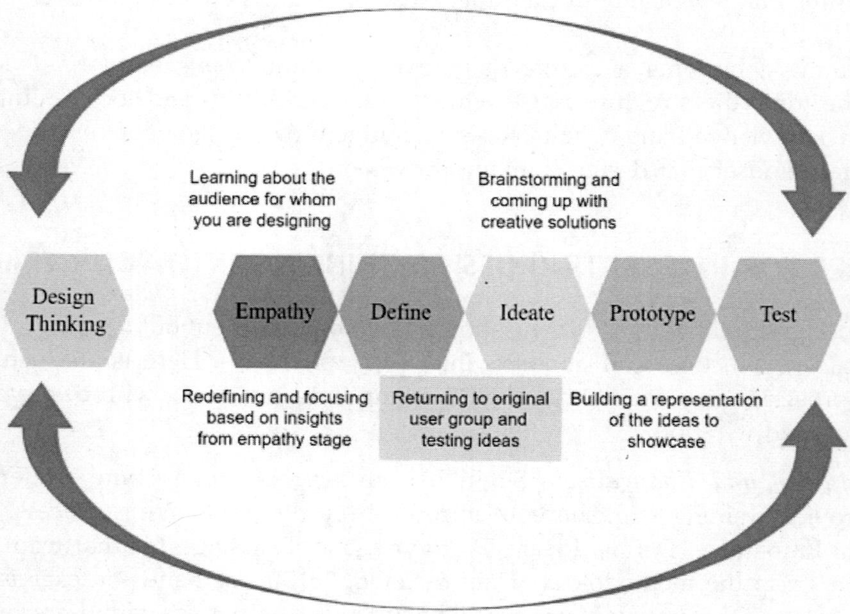

FIGURE 5.2 The iterative design thinking process.

(Prototype), and then get it in front of users for feedback (Test). This cycle might repeat several times, refining the solution. Throughout the pilot, encourage the team to document their process and learnings. This will be valuable for demonstrating the approach to others later.

3. ***Iterate and Refine (Practice of Experimentation):*** Emphasise an *iterative mindset* during the project. In traditional project management, teams might be inclined to plan extensively and execute once. In design thinking, teams should plan for multiple small experiments. For example, if the prototype in the pilot doesn't resonate with users, that's expected, go back a step, ideate new solutions, or redefine the problem with new insights. Encourage rapid cycles to build *minimum viable prototypes* (as simple as a paper sketch interface or a role-playing script for a service interaction) and test them internally or with a few friendly customers. Each iteration is a chance to learn. Cultivate a team norm that critique is about the idea, not the person, to maintain psychological safety. Best practices include holding regular debriefs after user testing sessions to discuss what worked and what didn't and then deciding what changes to make as a group. This collaborative, looped approach should become the team's new habit. A practical tip is to time-box iterations: give the team two days to prototype and one day to test, then repeat. It prevents analysis paralysis and keeps momentum (design thinking favours action, as captured by the motto "prototype as if you know you're right, test as if you know you're wrong"). Over time, as the team sees improvements in the solution with each iteration, it reinforces the value of an iterative, user-focused approach.
4. ***Embed Collaboration and Cross-Functional Work:*** Design thinking thrives on diverse inputs, so make cross-functional teamwork the norm. In the pilot, note how having varied expertise in the room leads to richer ideas. Maybe the customer service rep offers an insight that sparks a tech solution from the engineer that the designer then refines visually. To institutionalise this, adjust team structures and meeting cadences. For example, multidisciplinary project squads for future initiatives should be created rather than homogeneous departmental teams. Encourage open brainstorming sessions where marketing, ops, finance, and R&D folks jointly ideate on a customer problem to break down the "silo mentality" that can stifle innovation. Best practices for collaboration include using *visual collaboration tools* (like Miro or whiteboard walls covered in sticky notes) so everyone can contribute and see connections, as well as rotating team leads or facilitators from different backgrounds to ensure balanced participation. Additionally, adopt the practice of user journey mapping or service blueprinting in workshops, which naturally requires input from multiple departments (since a customer's journey cuts across touchpoints owned by different teams). By routinely involving multiple functions in design discussions, you create a culture where collaboration isn't a forced exercise but the default way work gets done. It shall result in a hallmark of organisations successfully practising design thinking.
5. ***Scale and Integrate:*** Once the pilot project yields a result (e.g., a new prototype service or a redesigned process) and ideally a positive outcome (say, improved user satisfaction in tests or a successful small-scale launch), use that success to

build momentum. Share the success story across the organisation through a demo day, an internal case study, or presentations to other groups. It showcases what design thinking looks like in action and the value it can bring. Next, identify additional projects and form new teams to tackle them using design thinking. At this stage, some companies formalise the effort by creating an *Innovation Lab* or *Center of Excellence* to support teams or adopting toolkits (like IBM did with an internal "Design Thinking Toolkit" for all employees). It's also essential to integrate design thinking into existing processes. For instance, if your company follows a product development stage gate process, consider adding an early 'empathise/user research' stage or making prototypes and user-testing feedback a prerequisite for concept approval. If strategy offsites usually involve just PowerPoints and data, integrate design thinking exercises like persona creation or rapid prototyping of strategy ideas. This integration ensures design thinking isn't seen as a separate silo or one-time workshop but as *part of how the company solves problems*. A key best practice here is to continue executive support. Leaders should allocate resources (budget, time) for ongoing design thinking initiatives and perhaps even tie some performance evaluations or OKRs to innovation/user-centric metrics to signal their importance.

Best Practices Summary: Throughout integration, certain best practices improve the odds of success:

(a) Maintain customer focus—keep real users involved at every stage, through interviews or test groups, so teams stay grounded in empathy.
(b) Promote an experimental mindset—celebrate teams that try bold ideas (have an "Innovation Award" or simply highlight lessons learned from a failed experiment in company newsletters to normalise risk-taking).
(c) Use frameworks and templates—teams new to design thinking benefit from structures like empathy maps, "how might we" question templates, and ideation rules (defer judgment, go for volume, etc.) to guide their sessions.
(d) Ensure diversity in teams—diversity of background, gender, expertise, etc., leads to more creative outcomes; design thinking teams should be assembled with this in mind.
(e) Provide spaces and tools—if possible, create physical (or virtual) collaboration spaces stocked with whiteboards, sticky notes, and prototyping materials (or their digital equivalents) to signal that it's a creative zone. For instance, companies like SAP and IBM set up dedicated studios or *"Design Garages"* to give teams an inspiring environment separate from day-to-day cubicles (Tangram Interiors, 2017).
(f) Iterate on the integration itself—gather feedback from teams about the design thinking adoption process and refine training, tools, or support accordingly. In essence, treat the rollout of design thinking *as a design challenge* too: empathise with employees, identify pain points in working this new way, and ideate and test improvements to the program.

CASE STUDIES: IDEO and IBM

Renowned design consultancy IDEO is often held up as a gold standard for how cross-functional teamwork and iterative prototyping can become second nature. On an IDEO project (say, redesigning a shopping cart, as in a famous Nightline documentary), the team is deliberately composed of engineers, a psychologist, a retail expert, etc. They follow a structured brainstorm (with rules like "one conversation at a time" and "encourage wild ideas"), then split into sub-teams to prototype different concepts in a matter of days. They might create multiple rough prototypes (a cart focused on child safety, another on easy scanning of items) and then combine the best elements after testing them in a mock supermarket. This fluid teamwork, lack of ego (ideas stick or twist based on merit and user feedback), and quick cycles are vivid examples of design thinking integration. While not every company is IDEO, many emulate its practices to boost their innovation capacity. IBM provides an example of scaling design thinking in-house. Around 2013, IBM began a company-wide program to infuse design thinking into its product teams. They hired hundreds of designers and embedded them into development squads, shifting the ratio from 1 designer per 72 software programmers to about 1:8. IBM also trained over 100,000 employees in its customised design thinking methodology, hosting intensive "boot camps" for new hires and even seasoned executives (Handa & Vashisht, 2017). Multi-disciplinary teams at IBM started adopting rituals like *"hills"* (IBM's term for stating user-centric goals), *"playbacks"* (regular sessions where teams present their work in progress to get feedback from peers and stakeholders), and using dedicated studios for workshops. A case study of IBM's Cloud products noted that after integrating design thinking, the teams accelerated their development cycles and improved the usability ratings of their software. The collaborative ethos even extended to involving clients in the design process (similar to IBM's "co-create with clients" approach). IBM's success shows that even a very large, historically formal organisation can pivot to embrace design thinking by systematically training people, restructuring teams (each product team has at least one designer and often a user researcher), and altering processes to include iterative user testing. The outcome was not just sleeker software but a cultural shift in how teams approached problem-solving, i.e., more open, user-focused, and iterative. For instance, IBM reported that applying design thinking reduced the time to align with project requirements and significantly reduced development rework. These examples reinforce the importance of collaboration, iteration, and leadership support in making design thinking an everyday practice in teams.

By following these steps and practices, any team, whether in a startup or a large corporation, can start to integrate design thinking into its DNA. The journey often starts small, with one team and one project. Still, as the mindset and successes spread, it can transform how the entire organisation innovates and delivers value to customers.

5.4 DESIGN THINKING FOR PRODUCT DEVELOPMENT, SERVICE DESIGN, AND BUSINESS STRATEGY

Design thinking is a versatile approach that can be applied to various domains, from designing tangible products to crafting intangible services to rethinking business models and strategy. While the core principles remain the same (human-centricity, creativity, prototyping, etc.), the application can look different across product, service, and strategy contexts. Let's explore each:

Product Development: Design thinking places the end-user at the center of the process when developing physical or digital products. The team seeks to deeply understand user needs, pain points, and desires in order to inform product features and design choices. For example, in consumer electronics, design thinking might involve observing how users interact with a gadget daily, identifying frustrations, and then iterating on prototypes to refine ergonomics or functionality. A classic case is GE Healthcare's MRI machine redesign for pediatric patients. The MRI scanner is a complex, expensive product that was traditionally engineered for performance, but using design thinking, GE's team (led by designer Doug Dietz) spent time empathising with the children who had to undergo MRIs. They discovered these young patients were terrified by the clinical, noisy machine and the dark room. Through user-centric research (including talking to children and child-life specialists), they reimagined the MRI experience as the "Adventure Series." They painted MRI machines and rooms in themes like pirates or outer space, added playful elements, and guided children through a story. The result was a dramatic increase in patient satisfaction. The *product* itself wasn't technically altered, but the holistic *user experience* of the product was redesigned.

Sedation rates for kids plummeted, and hospitals saw better outcomes. It demonstrates that product development with design thinking goes beyond features, encompassing the context of use and emotional experience. Another product example is Oral-B's toothbrush, in which Oral-B's designers used design thinking to question user behaviour rather than just adding high-tech features for their next electric toothbrush. They found that many users felt anxious about brushing (wondering if they did it well) and didn't necessarily want a music-playing, data-tracking toothbrush. Instead, through user research, the design team recommended simpler innovations like making the charger more travel-friendly and adding connectivity to remind users to replace brush heads (Harvard Business School Online, 2022). These insights, uncovered by focusing on real user needs, led to a more successful product than a gadget with unnecessary bells and whistles. In software product development, design thinking might manifest through extensive User Experience (UX) research and iterative interface design. Teams develop personas, map user journeys, and prototype interfaces (wireframes to interactive mocks) that are continually validated with target users. Companies like Apple are known for obsessive user-focused product design. For example, the development of the first iPhone involved observing how people used their phones and iPods, leading to the revolutionary touch interface and visual voicemail, addressing user frustrations they didn't even articulate.

In summary, for product development, design thinking ensures the product is desirable to users (solves the right problem elegantly) and is technically feasible and economically viable. It often leads to breakthrough features or designs that differentiate the product. As evidence, many modern product teams follow a design thinking-like process, starting with empathy research, then defining the product vision through the lens of user needs, brainstorming creative solutions (possibly with industrial designers, engineers, and users co-creating), prototyping (from 3D prints for physical products to beta apps for digital), and testing with users to iterate. This approach is now common at companies such as Dyson (which famously prototypes vacuum components hundreds of times, observing how people clean their homes) and Microsoft (which uses design sprints to prototype new software features based on user feedback rapidly).

Service Design: Service industries (like hospitality, travel, healthcare, finance, retail, etc.) use design thinking to innovate not a physical product but the *end-to-end customer experience* and processes that deliver a service. Service design often involves mapping the customer journey, identifying each touchpoint a customer has with the service, and then improving or reinventing those interactions to be more user-friendly and delightful. Design thinking helps organisations step into their customers' shoes. A well-known example is Airbnb. Airbnb's service is an online platform connecting hosts and guests, but the company applied design thinking to refine every aspect of this service experience. In its early years, Airbnb's designers created storyboards (like comic strips) of the entire guest experience, from booking to check-in to leaving a review, to identify emotional highs and lows. It led to numerous service tweaks like developing a robust review system (to build trust in the community), offering professional photography for hosts (to set guest expectations and improve listings, as mentioned earlier), and customer service improvements. Airbnb's continual focus on the user's journey considers *extreme users,* such as hosts with unique spaces or guests on long-term stays. It allows them to transform hospitality without owning a single hotel.

Another case is in Financial Services: Banks have used design thinking to improve the mortgage application process (a complex, anxiety-inducing service interaction for customers). By mapping that journey, banks discovered pain points like confusing forms and long waiting times for approval. Empathising with customers (some banks have executives go through the application as if they were customers themselves) has led to simplifications such as more intuitive online applications, proactive communication updates ("your loan is in stage 3 of 5"), or even entirely new services like on-demand chat support to answer applicants' questions.

Uber Eats provides a modern example of service design innovation. The food delivery app's team conducted research through a program called "Walkabout," where designers would embed themselves in cities and observe the food delivery ecosystem, from restaurants' kitchen operations to couriers' navigation and customers' meal unpacking. Insights from this immersive empathy work led to features like the *delivery partner app* enhancements (they noticed drivers struggling with parking in busy areas, so the app was modified to provide specific delivery instructions and optimal parking spots for pickups/drop-offs) (Harvard Business School Online, 2022). By understanding the service from all user perspectives, viz., restaurant, courier, and customer, UberEats introduced innovations that smoothed out the process. Service design often must consider multiple stakeholders (unlike a product used by one end-user, a service might involve a customer, a frontline employee, back-office systems, etc.). Design thinking facilitates co-creation among these stakeholders. Hospitals, for instance, have applied design thinking to improve patient discharge processes, involving nurses, doctors, patients, and family caregivers in brainstorming and prototyping a better workflow (resulting in clearer instruction booklets for patients, follow-up call services, etc., which reduce readmission rates). The outcome of design thinking in service design is usually a combination of new touchpoint designs (e.g., a mobile app or a kiosk), process changes (like a sequence of steps or roles of service staff), and sometimes entirely new offerings (for example, when banks noted that under-served customers were intimidated by branches, they prototyped "micro-branches" in community centres to meet them where they are).

Business Strategy and Decision-making: Applying design thinking at the *strategy level* is an emerging and exciting area. Traditionally, business strategy has been the domain of analytical frameworks, spreadsheets, and top-down planning. However, design thinking introduces a more iterative, human-centred approach to strategy formulation. It means treating strategy not as a static plan but as a creative design challenge: understanding the needs of stakeholders (customers, employees, partners), generating possible strategic initiatives, prototyping those initiatives (perhaps as pilot programs or simulations), and testing to gather feedback before scaling. One application is in corporate strategy for growth or transformation. IBM, for instance, used design thinking principles when shifting its strategy toward cloud and AI in the 2010s. Rather than just deciding on the boardroom, IBM involved clients and employees through workshops to envision the future of enterprise AI products by effectively *prototyping the strategy*, developing early versions of AI-driven solutions with key clients, and learning from those experiments.

Another example comes from Intuit, the financial software company known for TurboTax and QuickBooks. Intuit's CEO, Scott Cook, introduced "Design for Delight," a design thinking-inspired approach in product teams and business model innovation. One outcome was the creation of QuickBooks Online (a cloud version), which was informed by a deep understanding of small business owners' needs for mobility and collaboration. Intuit also incubated completely new strategic ventures, like the SnapTax mobile app, by empowering small teams to use empathy and experiments to tap into new markets (SnapTax arose when an Intuit team observed young adults wanting to do taxes entirely on their phones. It seemed a strategic departure from their main desktop software but an important move to capture a new segment). Fintech startups likewise often use design thinking to define their strategy: they start by identifying an unmet customer need (e.g., "millennials need a simpler way to save money"), brainstorm various service concepts, test a minimum viable product, and then iterate their business model. It is essentially strategy by design. Even at the highest level, setting vision and corporate direction, design thinking encourages more adaptive and user-driven strategies. A specific technique is scenario prototyping: instead of just analysing market data, strategists might craft narratives or even mock-ups of what a future customer experience could look like if certain strategies are pursued, then use feedback on those narratives to choose a direction. Another technique is empathy for the ecosystem: for example, if a company is shaping a platform strategy, it might interview not just end-users but also partners/ developers to design a strategy that aligns incentives for all participants (akin to how Apple designed its App Store strategy by considering developer experience deeply, not only the end-user).

The design thinking approach to strategy can be seen in how Netflix evolved its business model. Initially, as a DVD rental-by-mail service, Netflix's leadership (Reed Hastings and team) continually focused on user behaviour and technology trends, empathising with emerging customer needs. They realised people disliked the inconvenience of physical returns (pain point) and that internet streaming could solve it. By *prototyping* a streaming service (even when infrastructure was nascent) and observing uptake, Netflix pivoted its strategy to streaming, well ahead of competitors. Later, noticing that existing studios didn't fully meet customers' appetite for diverse content, Netflix pursued original content creation, which was a risky strategic leap at the time. Instead of doing this purely from boardroom analysis, Netflix heavily uses data (what people watch or want) and even tests the waters with smaller content investments before going big on the original series. Each move shows elements of design thinking: user insight driving strategic vision, willingness to experiment (e.g., piloting an original show like *House of Cards* after seeing data on binge-watching), and iterating the strategic plan (today Netflix continuously refines its content strategy based on subscriber feedback and viewing behaviour) (Harvard Business School Online, 2022). In essence, design thinking brings a *hypothesis-driven, user-tested* mentality to strategy: rather than assuming we know what will work in the market, craft a hypothesis (a new service, a new business model), test it in a controlled way (a pilot market or prototype), learn from that, and then invest further or pivot. It is analogous to the Lean Startup methodology, which aligns with design thinking that aims to treat strategy and business models as something you validate through design prototypes (like MVPs) and feedback.

Comparative Utilisation: Product-focused versus service-focused companies can utilise design thinking somewhat differently. A product-focused company (say, a smartphone manufacturer or an automobile company) often emphasises design thinking in *R&D and product design teams*. The tangible nature of products means there's heavy use of physical prototyping, industrial design thinking, and user testing in labs or usability sessions. Timelines might be longer (because building physical prototypes can take time), but each iteration is crucial to avoid costly mistakes in production. These companies also use design thinking to integrate hardware, software, and aesthetic design. For instance, a car manufacturer might involve engineers and ethnographers to observe how drivers interact with infotainment systems and then iterate the interface. A service-focused company (like a retail bank, an airline, or a hospital) might deploy design thinking more in *operations, customer experience, and strategy teams*. They prototype changes to service touchpoints (like a new check-in process at an airport tested at one terminal before global rollout or a new telemedicine service piloted in one region for a hospital system). Because services involve humans delivering service, there is also an element of employee experience design that involves simultaneous staff training with new scripts or tools. The iterations can be faster in some ways (a bank can pilot a new account opening workflow in a few branches for a month and get data, which is quicker than, say, fabricating a new hardware prototype). However, service design must ensure internal buy-in and training, another complexity layer. Design thinking helps by including frontline employees early in the service design (co-creating solutions so they are practical). Another difference is that product companies might measure the success of design thinking by metrics like product adoption rates, usability scores, or a decrease in support calls. In contrast, service companies may look at customer satisfaction (NPS scores), churn rates, or process efficiency improvements as evidence that a design thinking-inspired change works. Yet, these lines blur as most companies are a mix of products and services. For example, Apple is product-centric but has services (Apple Store customer service, Apple Music, etc.) and applies design thinking across both dimensions, resulting in the meticulous design of devices and the integrated service ecosystem. Starbucks, a service business (coffee retail), treats its store layout, application, and ordering process as products to be designed via user research, helping it effectively productise the service.

In all cases, design thinking ensures that whether we're developing a gadget, a service process, or a business strategy, we start with humans and end with innovative solutions tailored to their needs. The approach increases the likelihood that products truly *delight* users, services *wow* customers in consistency and ease, and strategies *connect* with real market desires and adapt to change. The many case studies across industries, from healthcare devices to fintech apps to entertainment media, illustrate that design thinking is not confined to any one field but is a universal language of innovation.

5.5 OVERCOMING RESISTANCE TO CHANGE

Implementing design thinking often requires a shift in mindset and ways of working. Resistance can emerge with any change. Organisations might face scepticism from employees ("Is this just the latest fad?"), reluctance from management who are used to traditional processes or inertia in the company culture that favours the status quo. Leaders must anticipate and proactively address these barriers to successfully embed design thinking.

Common Barriers and Resistance: One major barrier is cultural resistance. If an organisation has a traditional hierarchical, risk-averse culture, employees might be uncomfortable with the ambiguity and experimentation of design thinking. For example, in a firm where employees are used to strictly defined roles and following management directives, suddenly asking teams to self-direct a brainstorming session or talk to customers can cause anxiety or pushback. People may think, "This is not how we do things here," or fear that deviating from established procedures could be career-limiting. Another form of resistance is the "*not invented here*" syndrome. If an outside consultant or new executive introduces design thinking, long-time staff might resist it simply because it's new and came from outside their ranks. There can also be misunderstandings about design thinking wherein engineers might think, "This is just about post-its and not rigorous," or analysts may feel that qualitative user research is inferior to hard data. Additionally, some may perceive design thinking as extra work on top of their regular duties. This leads to pushback due to resource and time constraints ("We're already busy; we don't have time for workshops"). Practical issues like budget for prototyping or travelling to meet users can also be barriers if not addressed. Psychological resistance emerges as design thinking asks people to expose unpolished ideas (which can be ego-threatening) and to have their prototypes potentially fail in testing (which can be uncomfortable in a culture that penalises mistakes). There's also organisational resistance in the form of processes or KPIs that conflict with experimentation (e.g., if employees are only rewarded for billable client hours, they won't spend time on exploratory empathy research).

Strategies to Overcome Resistance: Overcoming these challenges requires top-down and bottom-up efforts. A critical strategy is to secure a leadership championship. When executives and managers actively participate in design thinking training and projects, it signals to everyone that this is not just a buzzword of the month. Leaders should *communicate a clear vision* of why the organisation is adopting design thinking. For instance, "We need to become more customer-centric to stay competitive; design thinking will help us do that by unlocking creativity at all levels." They should also model the desired behaviour where a senior leader openly brainstorms wild ideas or admits, "I don't know the answer. Let's prototype and find out," which grants permission for others to do the same. Tying design thinking to the company's purpose can motivate employees (e.g., a healthcare CEO might frame it as, "This will help us care for patients better"). Another strategy is to start small to demonstrate quick wins. Pick a project with a manageable scope and apply design thinking, then showcase the result. Early tangible successes are the best antidote to scepticism. When colleagues see, for example, that a design thinking-led pilot improved customer satisfaction by 20% or cut internal process time in half, it creates buy-in. It's important to measure and communicate these wins. Also, consider addressing the sceptics by involving them: sometimes, the biggest naysayers can become the biggest advocates if invited to participate and see the value first-hand. If an engineer thinks it's fluff, invite them to a user interview session; the insights they hear may flip their perspective. Educating everyone on *what design thinking is and isn't* helps dispel myths, for instance, clarifying that it's not at odds with data-driven decision-making but complements it with qualitative insight.

Organisations should build a safe environment for experimentation to combat the fear of failure. This can be done by explicitly reframing failure as learning. Some companies adopt practices like "fail fairs" or regular debriefs where teams discuss what they learned from experiments that didn't pan out. This approach normalises that not every idea will succeed, and that's okay. Creating a *sandbox,* a space or limited context to try ideas without jeopardising core operations to help people experiment without fear. For example, a bank might use one branch as an innovation test bed; staff there know they can try new service approaches that would later be rolled out. Recognising and rewarding effort and creativity, not just successful outcomes is key. Suppose an employee tries a new approach to solve a problem (like prototyping a new form), which doesn't work. In that case, managers should praise the initiative and encourage refining the idea rather than punishing the attempt.

Organizationally, aligning processes and metrics with design thinking is important. If current KPIs discourage taking time for innovation, adjust them. Some companies add an objective for managers to complete a certain number of customer empathy activities or innovation experiments per quarter, signalling that time spent on design thinking is valued. Training programs can equip employees with new skills (interviewing users facilitating ideation) so they feel more confident and less resistant when asked to do these activities. It's also helpful to integrate design thinking with existing frameworks rather than portraying it as a wholesale replacement. For instance, showing how design thinking can work within an Agile software development process (they are quite complementary) or how insights from design thinking can feed into quarterly business planning. It reduces the sense that "we're throwing away everything we know." Many companies create hybrid processes (like "Lean UX" or "Agile + Design Thinking" playbooks) to ease the transition.

Importantly, leadership needs patience and persistence as cultural shifts take time. Employees might not all jump on board after the first workshop. Hence, continuous encouragement, coaching, and highlighting of positive examples is needed. Change agents or a core design thinking team can mentor others, gradually building a critical mass of practitioners. There will be pockets of faster and slower adoption, focusing on enabling the willing and converting the middle rather than forcing everyone simultaneously. Over time, as more success stories emerge and as customers respond positively, the initial resistance tends to wane.

Case Examples of Overcoming Resistance: Let us consider a couple of scenarios. When design thinking was first introduced at IBM, it *clashed with the existing engineer-centric culture,* and many veteran engineers and project managers were resistant. They thought it was distracting from writing code or "for designers, not for me." IBM overcame this with a strong executive mandate (the CEO made it a strategic priority) and by hiring new design talent to work alongside the old guard, essentially seeding the culture with fresh perspectives. Early on, there was cynicism. Employees learned the methods in workshops but returned to their desks where traditional metrics hadn't changed, leading to frustration. IBM managed to turn the tide by tightly integrating design thinking into real projects with customer involvement. Sam Yen, IBM's design leader, realised that to convince internal teams, he had to get customers directly involved and excited. IBM invited their enterprise clients to participate in design thinking sessions to co-create solutions. When IBM's sales and engineering staff saw how much clients loved this collaborative approach ("the customers made us scale it," Yen noted), it reframed design thinking from an internal mandate to an external demand. In other words, field teams could no longer resist as their most important customers were asking for workshops and user-centric deliverables. This smart tactic turned resistance into receptiveness by leveraging customer pull. Over a few years, IBM went from resistance to over 100,000 employees trained and tangible business outcomes. They measured that design thinking projects cut time to market by three fourths and yielded a 301% ROI, which quieted critics because the data spoke loud and clear.

Another example: SAP, in its early design thinking rollout, found that many employees were enthusiastic during training but didn't apply it afterwards because their bosses didn't ask for it, and they fell back into routine. There was a "valley of death" after the hype. SAP addressed this by aligning design thinking with strategic projects and creating physical spaces (d.school-inspired "AppHaus") where cross-functional teams could physically get together and work in new ways to make the change tangible. They also formed an internal network of coaches to support teams. They publicised these internally when initial small successes (like a better UX for an SAP software module) emerged. Slowly, pockets of adoption grew into a company-wide movement backed by the co-founder Hasso Plattner's constant advocacy. The comparison of IBM and SAP to other firms shows that having top-level sponsorship, training plus practice, and evidence of value are universal levers to overcome inertia.

On an individual level, sometimes the turning point is when a resistant person participates in a design thinking activity with a real user and experiences the "aha!" moment. For example, a finance executive reluctant to embrace design thinking might sit in on a user empathy interview for the first time and hear a customer express a pain that translates directly to a new business opportunity, depicting that direct contact can convert sceptics into believers. Organisations can facilitate these encounters, ensuring that even senior, traditionally-minded executives regularly engage with customers or end-users in the design process.

In sum, overcoming resistance to design thinking is about managing human factors of change. Communicating the why, enabling people with how, starting small, proving value, and integrating into the work fabric. With persistence, the early resistance often gives way as people see that design thinking isn't a threat to their jobs or a waste of time but rather a powerful way to make their work more impactful and their customers happier. Many companies that initially struggled have later reported that design thinking became a unifying language across departments and a source of pride. However, reaching that point requires navigating the initial headwinds carefully and empathetically (ironically, applying empathy to your employees and colleagues as much as to customers).

CASE STUDY: SAP—Scaling Design Thinking Across a Global Enterprise

To illustrate how design thinking can be implemented at scale, consider the case of SAP, one of the world's largest enterprise software companies. In the mid-2000s, SAP faced a challenge common to many mature tech firms: its products were powerful but often criticised for being complex and not user-friendly. The company's leadership, notably co-founder Hasso Plattner, believed that a greater focus on end-users and innovation was needed to maintain a competitive edge. Thus, SAP embarked on a journey to infuse design thinking throughout its global organisation, a massive enterprise with tens of thousands of employees across continents.

Background: SAP's interest in design thinking was partly sparked by Plattner's involvement with Stanford University's d.school (which he helped fund) and the Hasso Plattner Institute in Germany (Vetterli, C., & Plattner, 2015). He saw the approach's potential and became a key sponsor for bringing it into SAP. Around 2004–2005, SAP began experimenting with design thinking in small pockets. By 2010, SAP formally launched initiatives to train employees in design thinking and apply it to software development projects. Sam Yen, a Stanford design program PhD, joined SAP and eventually became Chief Design Officer, leading the internal adoption effort (Stanford Graduate School of Business, 2016).

Initial Challenges: Early on, SAP encountered internal friction. The company had a strong engineering culture focused on reliability and rich feature sets, unlike IBM's culture clash. Many developers and product managers were not used to directly engaging with end-users or iterating prototypes; the norm was to gather requirements from business analysts and proceed with building according to spec. So when design thinking workshops were introduced, some employees were enthusiastic, but many did the training and then didn't apply it, falling back into old habits. Sam Yen noted that employees would express interest in leveraging design thinking "but never seemed to follow through with it" in day-to-day work (Stanford Graduate School of Business, 2016). SAP's teams were saying the right things, but cultural inertia was holding them back. There was also some executive scepticism outside of Plattner's circle as middle managers questioned if spending time on "post-it note sessions" would delay development or if customers wanted to participate in co-design.

Strategies and Tactics for Scaling: SAP approached scaling design thinking with a multi-pronged strategy: grassroots engagement + executive support + structural changes. On the grassroots side, they ran a series of programs and events to engage the broader employee base. For instance, SAP organised innovation jams and design thinking weeks where employees could form teams to tackle any idea using design thinking, like internal hackathons. It gave people a low-risk chance to practice the methods on something they cared about. They also set up an internal community of practice to encourage employees passionate about design thinking (including many who went through d.school training) to act as ambassadors and coaches for their colleagues. On the executive side, SAP's board fully backed the effort: design thinking progress became a topic in strategy meetings, and success stories were highlighted from the top. Leaders conveyed that design thinking was integral to SAP's innovation strategy, not just a side experiment.

One key realisation Sam Yen had was making design thinking relevant to everyone's day job. Initially, they tried bottom-up and top-down approaches to generate enthusiasm. They discovered that *just* engaging employees wasn't enough if their bosses weren't on board, and *just* getting executive buy-in wasn't enough if employees didn't know how to execute. So, they adjusted their tactics. A breakthrough move was when SAP decided to involve customers directly in their design thinking initiative. They launched the SAP Co-Innovation Program, where strategic customers were invited to SAP to work together on real business challenges using design thinking. For example, SAP might bring in a few executives and end-users from a client company, pair them with an SAP development team, and run a multi-day design thinking workshop to prototype solutions for a new analytics dashboard tailored to that client's needs. These sessions created immediate value for important customers (strengthening relationships and showing SAP's commitment to user-centricity) and offered hands-on training and mindset change for SAP's employees. When an SAP product manager saw how excited a customer was to be *asked* about their needs and to collaborate on a prototype, it underscored the power of the approach. Sam Yen recalled that they thought, *"Why don't we introduce our most strategic customers to design thinking, so we can co-define our futures together?"*. It turned design thinking from a theoretical exercise into a practical necessity for keeping customers happy. As a result, scepticism within SAP eased: engineers and managers started seeing design thinking as a tool to achieve better client results, not just an internal mandate. It moved it from what some called an "ivory tower" initiative to something very grounded in business outcomes.

Structurally, SAP has also established dedicated design thinking teams and spaces. They opened physical, creative spaces like the SAP AppHaus in Heidelberg and other locations—funky, open environments deliberately unlike typical corporate offices. These spaces served as innovation hubs where project teams (often including customers) could immerse in design thinking workshops free from daily distractions. The AppHaus model was significant: it demonstrated SAP's willingness to invest in the infrastructure for innovation and signalled to employees that this was a new way of working. SAP also integrated designers into product units (much as IBM did) by hiring many new UI/UX designers and giving them equal footing with engineers in product decision-making. Early on, SAP's development teams might have one designer for dozens of engineers; over time, those ratios improved, and designers took on leadership roles in projects, ensuring that design thinking practices (like user research and prototyping) were not optional but part of the development cycle.

Challenges Faced: Scaling across a global enterprise wasn't without hiccups. SAP had teams from Palo Alto to Bangalore to Walldorf, as different regions have different work cultures (linking back to our point on regional differences). The German headquarters team, for instance, had to balance the traditional meticulous engineering culture with the more free-form design thinking approach. Some teams initially treated design thinking as a "phase" (do a workshop at the start, then revert to normal) rather than a continuous mindset. It took education to change this. Maintaining momentum was also an issue, as initial enthusiasm can fade if not continually fed. SAP tackled this by embedding design thinking into various corporate processes. They made it part of employee onboarding, ensuring that every new hire, whether in sales or development, got a taste of design thinking in their orientation, so they knew this was how SAP works. They also incorporated it into their project management methodology (e.g., before writing a single line of code, teams were expected to conduct empathy interviews, define user personas, etc., as a formal checkpoint).

Another challenge was measuring impact. Executives wanted to see results from this investment. SAP gathered success stories. For example, one team used design thinking to simplify a CRM software interface, which led to higher adoption by end-users at client companies; another team co-designed a new mobile app with a customer, which became a product used by many others. They also measured internal metrics like employee engagement. They discovered that anecdotal feedback indicated that employees found work more meaningful when they connected with end-users and saw the direct impact of their solutions. Over time, SAP's product UX improved significantly, garnering better customer feedback. The development cycles in some areas were shortened, and co-innovation created customer-specific solutions faster. All this data and storytelling was fed back to reinforce the program's value.

Results: Today, SAP is often cited as a successful example of a large-scale design thinking adoption. It transformed from a company known for clunky enterprise UIs to one that won awards for design (SAP's Fiori design system, which offers a clear, consistent user experience across their applications, is a fruit of this effort leading to a unified UX paradigm created with extensive user input). More importantly, design thinking helped SAP change its culture to be more customer-centric and innovative. The company reports that cross-functional collaboration is stronger; engineers now regularly visit customers and understand their context, something uncommon before. SAP's Design Thinking initiative also had an external ripple effect: many of SAP's clients learned the approach through collaboration, spreading design thinking into other industries (e.g., a manufacturing company that worked with SAP might have been inspired to use design thinking internally for their processes). The case underscores several key takeaways:

- *Leadership Sponsorship and Vision:* Hasso Plattner's role was crucial. Without a top champion, the effort might have fizzled. His vision made design thinking part of SAP's identity.

- *Training and Tools:* SAP invested in educating its workforce and giving them the means (like AppHaus spaces and toolkits) to practice design thinking, not just talk about it.
- *Integrating into Real Work:* Using strategic customer projects as the vehicle, SAP tied design thinking to tangible outcomes (product improvements, innovations) that mattered to the business, which helped convince the sceptics.
- *Cultural Patience:* The transformation wasn't overnight. It took years of persistence, experiments, and adjustments. SAP had to learn from failures along the way. For example, when one tactic to engage teams didn't work, they tried another.

Comparing SAP's approach with other large enterprises: IBM's approach, as discussed, was similarly large-scale, but IBM invested extremely heavily in hiring designers to embed within teams and developed its own branded framework ("IBM Design Thinking" with distinctive practices like "hills, playbacks, sponsor users"). IBM's change was somewhat more top-down initially, and they quantified business impact rigorously (Forrester study citing 300% ROI) to justify the program. In the consumer goods arena, PepsiCo took another route by creating a Chief Design Officer role (Mauro Porcini), who built a design and innovation culture in a traditionally marketing-driven company by setting up design hubs. He had top leadership backing to infuse design thinking in product packaging, advertisements, and brand strategy. PepsiCo's scale was smaller (in terms of design team size) but very influential in shifting mindset from being product-centric (just colas and chips) to human-centric (thinking about the experience of snacking, health trends, etc.). Procter & Gamble (P&G) earlier had attempted something similar under A.G. Lafley by embracing design thinking for product innovation around the mid-2000s but faced challenges sustaining it when leadership changed. That shows how continuity of vision (which SAP had with Plattner's continued involvement) is important; at P&G, when Lafley left, some of the momentum was lost as new leaders had different priorities. Having institutionalised the approach, SAP was less dependent on one person over time.

In contrast to some companies that treat design thinking as a silo (like an innovation lab separate from core operations), SAP tried to avoid that by eventually saying, *"Design thinking is how we all work,"* not just the innovation team. Not every enterprise achieves broad integration. Some end up with great innovation labs that don't influence the main business. SAP and IBM are examples where design thinking scaled beyond labs into the mainstream of product development and customer engagement.

KEY POINTS TO REMEMBER

Key Takeaways from SAP's Transformation:

1. Scaling design thinking requires aligning it with corporate strategy—SAP did this by making it part of its mission to improve user experience and co-innovate with customers.

2. Top-down and bottom-up must meet in the middle—leadership set the mandate and provided resources, while employees on project teams embraced the methods to create wins; one without the other would have failed.
3. Overcoming inertia needs proof and persistence—early frustration (the "valley of death" where people had training but no implementation path) was overcome by changing tactics (involving customers and adjusting processes).
4. Cultural change is the hardest part—but once the mindset shifted (e.g., SAP engineers routinely think about end-users, not just features), the organisation unlocked a new level of innovation. In SAP's case, this cultural change is evidenced by a quote from an SAP participant at d.confestival: *"It can't be an additional layer to what people do. It has to be what they do"* (Tangram Interiors, 2017). It indicates that design thinking became embedded in daily routine, which is the ultimate mark of success.
5. Comparison with others: SAP's journey echoes elements of IBM's and others, reinforcing that while tools and terminology may differ, the core success factors, viz., leadership, training, integration, customer focus, and patience, are similar.

In conclusion, the SAP case demonstrates that even a large, globally distributed enterprise with a traditionally technical focus can reinvent its culture and processes around design thinking. The company improved its products' usability and client satisfaction and invigorated its workforce with a more creative, purpose-driven way of working. This case provides a blueprint for other organisations looking to scale design thinking: start with a strong vision, empower people through training and real projects, involve customers for credibility, and relentlessly drive the change into the company's everyday habits.

KEY LEARNINGS

- **Extreme Users Drive Innovation:** Designing for the *extreme ends* of your user spectrum can unlock breakthrough ideas. By paying attention to early adopters, power users, or users with special needs, companies can discover unmet needs that mainstream users don't articulate. For example, Nike, which designed a hands-free shoe for disabled athletes, created a product popular with a broad audience, illustrating that solutions for extreme cases often benefit everyone. The key insight is to *embrace outliers* instead of ignoring them, as they can reveal opportunities for product and service innovation that give your business a competitive edge.
- **Culture is King for Innovation:** Implementing design thinking is as much about cultural change as process change. Innovative outcomes require an environment where people feel safe to take risks, hierarchy does not stifle ideas, and customer-centric thinking is ingrained. Companies like Google and 3M show that giving employees freedom (20% time, tolerance for failure) and support (resources, cross-team collaboration) yields tangible innovations. Conversely, overly rigid or metric-driven cultures can smother creativity, as seen when 3M's overemphasis on Six Sigma initially hurt innovation until a balance was restored. The lesson is that

leadership must actively cultivate a culture of curiosity, openness, and empowerment to realise the benefits of design thinking.

- **Practical Integration is Essential:** Design thinking should be woven into the fabric of team workflows, not done as a one-off workshop. A structured approach helps start with empathy research, clearly define the problem, ideate broadly, prototype quickly, and test with users in an iterative loop. Collaboration across functions (mixing perspectives from marketing, engineering, operations, etc.) is crucial to avoid silos and ensure feasibility and viability are considered alongside desirability. Organisations should enable this with supportive measures, from providing creative workspaces to adjusting project management methods. It aids the teams to practice design thinking routinely. When IBM embedded a designer in each team and mandated user-testing "playbacks," it operationalised the approach at scale. The overarching takeaway is that *process and teamwork adjustments make design thinking sustainable*, turning initial enthusiasm into consistent practice.
- **Broad Applicability—Products, Services, Strategy:** Design thinking isn't just for product design. Its principles extend to service innovation and crafting business strategy. Focusing on user journeys can dramatically improve services (e.g., GE Healthcare's kid-friendly MRI or UberEats optimising delivery for local conditions). At the strategy level, maintaining a human-centred outlook helps companies pivot correctly (Netflix continually evolved by empathising with customer pain points around renting, viewing, and content choices). The key learning is to *apply design thinking when facing a complex, human-centric problem, whether* choosing a new business model or improving a customer support process. It pushes organisations to test assumptions and iterate solutions in any domain, reducing risk and increasing alignment with stakeholder needs.
- **Managing Change and Overcoming Resistance:** Introducing design thinking can cause resistance, as people may be set in their ways or wary of a new approach. Successful adoption requires change management with strong communication of *why* the change is needed, training and coaching on *how* to do it, and gradual demonstration of *results*. Leadership must champion the effort, and employees must feel safe when trying new behaviours. Creating quick wins through pilot projects is an effective tactic to convert sceptics, involving customers or end-users to validate the approach (when clients rave about a co-creation workshop, it's hard for internal staff to dismiss its value). It's important to anticipate common barriers like fear of failure or siloed thinking and address them, for instance, by altering incentive structures or publicly celebrating learned-from failures. The overarching insight is that *empathetic leadership must understand employees' and stakeholders' viewpoints during the change to embed design thinking successfully*. Companies like SAP and IBM learned to tweak their rollouts (involving strategic customers, adjusting training, etc.) when initial efforts hit a wall, reminding us that implementing innovation methodologies is an iterative process.
- **Enterprise Scaling Lessons:** The SAP case showed that scaling design thinking enterprise-wide is possible if done holistically. Key factors included top-level sponsorship, widespread skill-building, alignment to tangible projects, and

persistence over time. A notable insight is the power of involving customers in the innovation process to create internal buy-in. SAP turned design thinking from an internal initiative into a collaborative approach demanded by their customers. Creating infrastructure (like SAP's AppHaus spaces or IBM's design studios) and integrating design thinking into corporate DNA (onboarding, performance metrics, etc.) cemented the change. The takeaway for large organisations is to treat the adoption of design thinking like a multi-year transformation program by resourcing, evangelising, integrating, and measuring it. The payoff is substantial when done well, as IBM's 300% ROI on design thinking projects is evidence of that. It resulted in faster development, better products, improved customer satisfaction, and a more innovative workforce.

This chapter highlighted that design thinking is a powerful approach but requires *the right mindset and environment*. Organisations can successfully implement design thinking and drive significant innovation by learning from extreme users, fostering an innovation-friendly culture, following a collaborative and iterative process, applying it across products/ services/ strategy, and skillfully managing change. These learnings are universally applicable; whether you're an MBA student tackling a case or a manager leading a team, the human-centred, experimental, and collaborative design thinking principles can be your playbook for solving complex problems and creating value.

EXERCISES

1. **Extreme User Interviews**—*Hands-on empathy research:* Pick a common product or service in teams of 3–5 (e.g., a coffee maker, a banking app, a grocery store layout). Identify one "mainstream" user and at least one "extreme" user for that context. For example, a mainstream user of a coffee maker is a typical office worker coffee drinker. At the same time, extremes could be a coffee aficionado who uses it 10 times a day or an individual with a disability affecting their hands. Each team member should conduct a short interview (10–15 minutes) or observation with one user (extreme or mainstream), focusing on their needs, pain points, and hacks/ workarounds. Regroup and create an empathy map or list of insights, comparing the extreme vs. mainstream findings. As a team, discuss: *What did the extreme user reveal that the regular user did not? How might those insights inspire design ideas?* Finally, each team should present two innovation opportunities for the product/ service derived from the extreme user's perspective (citing user insight). This exercise builds skill in user research and shows the value of extremes in sparking innovation.
2. **Culture of Innovation Assessment**—*Analyse and recommend.* Assume you are a consultant brought in to assess the innovation culture of Company X (you can use a well-known company or a fictional composite). First, individually list observable indicators of Company X's culture (e.g., office layout, decision-making processes, risk tolerance, stories of past projects). Then, as a team, use a framework (like a

checklist of innovation culture attributes, e.g., "Are failures tolerated? Do cross-functional teams meet regularly? Do employees have time for side projects? Is user feedback integrated into work?") to evaluate Company X. Identify barriers to innovation in the current culture (maybe strict hierarchy, or fear of leadership criticism, etc.) and enablers (perhaps a strong sense of mission or diverse talent). Now, together, formulate three concrete recommendations to foster a stronger innovation culture at Company X. These could range from leadership actions (e.g., institute quarterly "no bad idea" town halls where any employee can pitch) to process changes (e.g., reward teams for attempting bold projects) to environment tweaks (e.g., create an open innovation lab space).

Each recommendation should be justified: *Explain how it addresses a specific cultural barrier or leverages an enabler.* For instance, if Company X is risk-averse, a recommendation might be "Implement a Failure Wall—a place where teams post lessons from failures—to destigmatise taking risks," explaining how this symbol and practice encourages psychological safety. This exercise will make you think critically about the link between culture and innovation outcomes and practice prescribing realistic interventions.

3. **Team Design Challenge (Product to Service)**—*Cross-functional collaboration and iteration:* Break into cross-disciplinary teams (ensure each team has a mix of backgrounds, if possible: marketing, finance, engineering, etc., and mimic cross-functional). Each team is given a design challenge prompt: "Redesign the campus cafeteria experience to be more enjoyable and efficient" or "Design a solution to improve personal financial saving habits for young professionals." Over a 2-hour workshop (which can be broken into segments), teams will go through a mini design thinking cycle:

   Empathise: Each team member shares a quick personal perspective or story related to the topic (or uses a provided persona/ user story). Alternatively, conduct a 5-minute interview with another student outside the team representing the target user.

   Define: As a team, synthesise one clear problem statement (Point-of-View). For example, "Busy students need a quicker way to get healthy food between classes because current wait times are long, causing them to skip meals or choose unhealthy snacks."

   Ideate: Conduct a rapid brainstorming session (10 minutes timed) to generate as many ideas as possible and encourage wild ideas. Use techniques like "Yes, and…" to build on ideas and defer judgment (no criticism during brainstorming). Aim for at least 20 ideas on sticky notes.

   Prototype: Choose one promising idea (or combine elements) and create a simple prototype. If it's a service, role-play the scenario or sketch a storyboard; if it's a product or app, draw the interface or build a paper mock-up. Keep it low-fidelity.

   Test: Each team then swaps prototypes with another team or presents to a couple of volunteers acting as users. Gather feedback: What did they like? What questions or confusions arose? Did it solve their need? Teams then get 5 minutes to discuss how they would iterate the design based on feedback (write down one improvement).

Afterwards, have each team briefly present their journey: the problem they focused on, the prototype they came up with, and one key thing they learned from user feedback that they would change. This exercise simulates a compressed design sprint, reinforces each step's importance, and highlights teamwork and iterative learning. In the debrief, reflect on how having different functional perspectives in the team influenced the ideas (did a finance-minded person bring a practicality check, did a designer-minded person push for user emotion, etc.). It mirrors real-world cross-functional collaboration in innovation projects.

4. **Service Blueprint Creation**—*Applying design thinking to service design:* Using a known service (for example, "A day using a city bike-share service" or "Checking into a hotel and staying for a night"), teams will create a service blueprint. Map out the customer's journey step by step (from service discovery, initial sign-up or arrival, use of the service, to post-service follow-up). For each step, identify the customer's actions, the front-stage interactions (what the customer directly sees/ does, e.g., an app screen or a receptionist), the back-stage processes (what the company does behind the scenes, e.g., database verification, housekeeping preparing a room), and pain points or delight points at each step. Use a large paper or whiteboard to draw this blueprint collaboratively. Once the current state service is mapped, apply design thinking to ideate improvements. As a team, mark two moments where the customer pain is significant or the experience falls short. Generate ideas to improve those moments (perhaps using "How Might We" questions, e.g., "How might we reduce wait time at hotel check-in?"). Choose one idea and sketch or describe a *modified blueprint* for that part of the service (e.g., implementing a mobile check-in with a digital key for the hotel). Then, discuss implementation: what would need to change in the back-stage processes or employee roles to make that happen? Finally, each team shares one improvement idea and why it enhances the user experience. This exercise ties together understanding an existing service (empathy and definition), creative thinking for improvement (ideation), and considering operational feasibility (practical strategy). It shows the interplay of design thinking with process design and strategy.
5. **Overcoming Resistance Role-Play**—*Develop change leadership skills.* Students pair up (or in triads) to role-play scenarios where they must convince a stakeholder about design thinking or handle a resistant team member.

   Example scenarios:

   (a) You are a team lead introducing design thinking to your team. Role-play a conversation where one team member, Alex, is sceptical ("We've done fine without this; why do we need sticky notes to solve problems?"). Practice responding with empathy and persuasive reasoning. Try techniques like acknowledging Alex's concerns ("I understand it seems new and different…") and then explaining benefits with evidence ("...but in our pilot, we solved a problem in 2 days that previously took weeks, because we got direct user input.").

(b) You are a product manager pitching to your VP why the next project timeline should include a 1-week design sprint. The VP is concerned about meeting the deadline. Role-play making the business case. Perhaps cite how upfront user research and prototyping can save time by catching issues before development (maybe use an analogy or case as proof). The VP (the other student) will raise typical concerns ("This sounds expensive," "What if it delays us?"), and the one pitching must address them. After 5–10 minutes, swap roles or discuss. Then, as a whole class, debrief the following: What arguments or approaches seemed practical? How can you handle resistance not with confrontation but with constructive dialogue? This exercise builds skills in *change management communication*. It forces students to articulate the value of design thinking pragmatically and practice active listening and empathy even with colleagues, essentially using design thinking (empathy, understanding needs/fears) to sell design thinking!

6. **Case Analysis—Learning from SAP and IBM**—*Comparative case study:* Students are divided into small groups, each assigned either the SAP or the IBM case. Each group will identify the following from their case:

   (a) *Initial Situation*—what challenges or environment existed that made the company adopt design thinking;
   (b) *Key Actions*—what did leadership and teams do to implement it (training, structural changes, etc.);
   (c) *Challenges*—what resistance or difficulties arose;
   (d) *Outcomes*—what were the results (cultural, product outcomes, financial, if any)?

After about 20 minutes, form new groups that contain someone from an SAP group and someone from an IBM group (i.e., the Jigsaw method). They share summaries and then together *compare and contrast* SAP vs. IBM. The group discusses questions: *What common success factors do you see? What differences in approach (perhaps due to industry or company history) do you note? If a third large enterprise adopts design thinking, what lessons from these cases are most important?* Finally, each mixed group shares one key recommendation they'd give to a hypothetical large company CEO about to embark on a design thinking initiative, backed by evidence from SAP/ IBM (e.g., "Make sure to measure and publicise early wins—IBM did a study showing 301% ROI which helped keep support high"). This exercise reinforces learning from real cases and encourages critical thinking on how context influences implementation.

Through these exercises, MBA students will actively practice the concepts from empathy and ideation techniques to change management and strategic thinking, solidifying their understanding in a practical, team-based way.

THOUGHT-PROVOKING QUESTIONS

1. **Extreme Users and Innovation:** *Consider a product or service you use frequently.* Who might be an "extreme user" of it, and what unusual needs or behaviours might they have? How could you engage that extreme user to improve the product for all users?

   Discussion Points: Identify extreme users, extrapolate insights, and understand how designing for extremes relates to inclusive design.

2. **Innovation Culture Critique:** Why might a highly hierarchical organisation struggle to implement design thinking, and what steps could leaders take to change that gradually?

   Angle: Connect cultural traits (power distance, fear of failure) with barriers to design thinking; challenge students to propose realistic leadership actions (like Google's 20% rule or rewarding experimentation).

3. **Integrating into Process:** *Design thinking emphasises iteration.* How does this iterative approach conflict with traditional planning methods in business, and how can teams reconcile the two?

   Follow-up: Have you seen or experienced a situation where sticking rigidly to a plan caused a problem that an iterative approach might have avoided? What does that teach about flexibility in implementation?

4. **Design Thinking in Services vs. Products:** How does applying design thinking to a service (e.g., improving airline boarding) differ from using it to a physical product (e.g., a new suitcase design)? In what ways is it the same?

   Hint: Consider tangibility, stakeholder involvement (employees in service), prototyping methods (role-play vs. 3D models), etc. Students should articulate both unique challenges and universal principles.

5. **Measuring Success:** Companies like IBM and SAP invested heavily in design thinking. What metrics or indicators would you use as an executive to decide if this investment is paying off?

   Prompt critical thinking: Is it speed to market, user satisfaction scores, employee engagement, innovation revenue, or something else? How do qualitative outcomes (better team collaboration) translate into quantitative value? Students can reference the cases (IBM's ROI study), SAP's improved UX feedback, etc.) when formulating answers.

6. **Overcoming Individual Resistance:** Imagine you are a team leader, and one of your senior team members openly dismisses design thinking activities as "fluff". What would you say or do to handle this?

   This question gauges the ability to apply influence techniques and empathy: Students might answer with approaches like showing evidence, inviting them to participate and lead part of a session, or linking design thinking to that person's own goals (e.g., "I know you care about quality, this method can reduce rework…").

7. **Global Implementation Challenges:** SAP had to implement design thinking across different countries and cultures. What cultural factors should a multinational consider when rolling out an innovation program, and how might they adapt their approach in North America vs. Asia?

   Probe understanding: Use knowledge from section 5.2 about regional differences. Students should mention communication style, hierarchy, and attitudes toward risk and give examples of adaptations (maybe more leadership directive in high power-distance cultures vs. more grassroots in individualistic cultures).

8. **Design Thinking and Strategy:** "Design thinking is only for product design, not for setting business strategy." Do you agree or disagree? Provide reasoning or examples to support your view.

   Encourage critical thought: Students might disagree, citing how empathy with customers can reveal strategic opportunities (like Netflix's pivot or Intuit's SnapTax innovation). Some may agree partially, noting that hard strategic decisions also need market analysis and financial modelling (they can discuss integrating the two).

9. **Exercises Reflection:** Having engaged in the hands-on exercises (extreme user interview, team design challenge, etc.), what was one aspect of design thinking that you found challenging to apply, and how did your team address it?

   Personalise the learning: Students reflect on their experience—maybe brainstorming is more challenging than expected due to judgment, or interviewing felt awkward (e.g., the need for psychological safety in brainstorming or that good questions matter in interviewing).

10. **Case Connection:** From the SAP case study, identify one decision or tactic crucial to SAP's success in scaling design thinking. How might that apply to a different company or context (for example, a startup or a non-profit)?

    It ensures comprehension of the case: Students might pick "involving customers in co-design", "creating AppHaus innovation spaces", or "strong executive evangelism," etc., and then generalise it. For instance, a startup could involve its early adopters in a design sprint for the roadmap, or a non-profit could create a cross-departmental innovation task force with leadership backing.

    These questions encourage students to critically analyse and apply the chapter's concepts, relating them to real situations and reflecting on their exercise experiences. The answers will demonstrate their understanding of design thinking implementation and readiness to use these ideas in their careers.

REFERENCES

Bennett, R. (2019, October 10). Design Thinking vs. Engineering: Complementary Disciplines, Different Cultures. Sutherland Labs Blog. Retrieved November 5, 2024, from https://www.sutherlandlabs.com/blog/design-thinking-engineering-complementary-disciplines-different-cultures/

Dam, R.F., & Siang, T.Y. (2017). Design Thinking. Interaction Design Foundation Topics. Retrieved November 5, 2024, from https://www.interaction-design.org/literature/topics/design-thinking

First Round Review. (2015). How Design Thinking Transformed Airbnb from Failing Startup to Billion-Dollar Business. First Round Review. Retrieved November 5, 2024, from https://review.firstround.com/how-design-thinking-transformed-airbnb-from-failing-startup-to-billion-dollar-business

Handa, A., & Vashisht, K. (2017, February 6). How IBM Is Embracing the Future Through Design. UXmatters. Retrieved November 5, 2024, from https://www.uxmatters.com/mt/archives/2017/02/how-ibm-is-embracing-the-future-through-design.php

Harvard Business School Online. (2022). 5 Examples of Design Thinking in Healthcare and Business. HBS Online Blog. Retrieved November 5, 2024, from https://online.hbs.edu/blog/post/design-thinking-examples

Kelley, T. (2001). The art of innovation: Lessons in creativity from IDEO, America's leading design firm (Vol. 10). Crown Currency.

Network for Business Sustainability. (2018). The Challenge of Change: 3M, Six Sigma and Corporate Culture. NBS.net. Retrieved November 5, 2024, from https://nbs.net/the-challenge-of-change-3m-six-sigma-and-corporate-culture/

Sayyadi, M., & Provitera, M. (2024). Inside Tesla: A Rare Glimpse of Tesla's Mysterious Innovation Culture. The European Business Review. Retrieved November 5, 2024, from https://www.europeanbusinessreview.com/inside-tesla-a-rare-glimpse-of-teslas-mysterious-innovation-culture/

Stanford Graduate School of Business. (2016). SAP Design Thinking (Case Study Part I). Stanford GSB Case Studies. Retrieved November 5, 2024, from https://www.gsb.stanford.edu/faculty-research/case-studies/sap-design-thinking-part

Tangram Interiors. (2017, September 25). D.confestival: The Future of Design Thinking. Tangram Interiors Blog. Retrieved November 5, 2024, from https://www.tangraminteriors.com/blog/d-confestival-the-future-of-design-thinking

Taylor, D. (2019, March 4). Going to Extremes—How Nike Found Their Latest Innovation. The Brandgym Blog. Retrieved November 5, 2024, from https://thebrandgym.com/going-to-extremes-how-nike-found-their-latest-innovation/

Vetterli, C., & Plattner, H. (2015, August 20). Ten Years of Support for Design Thinking: An Interview with Hasso Plattner. ThisIsDesignThinking.net. Retrieved November 5, 2024, from https://thisisdesignthinking.net/2015/08/ten-years-of-support-for-design-thinking-an-interview-with-hasso-plattner/

Wikipedia. (n.d.). Extreme users. Wikipedia. Retrieved November 5, 2024, from https://en.wikipedia.org/wiki/Extreme_users

CHAPTER 6

Visualisation, Ethnography and Journey Mapping in Design Thinking

LEARNING OBJECTIVES

After reading this Chapter, the readers will be able to:

- Visualisation as a communication tool—Explain the importance of visualisation in design thinking and how translating ideas into sketches, diagrams, or prototypes helps teams communicate concepts clearly. Understand how visual thinking enables a shared vision (by reducing misinterpretation) and invites feedback, aligning stakeholders around tangible ideas.
- Ethnography for deep user insight—Describe what ethnography means in a design thinking context and how to conduct basic ethnographic research. Learn to immerse in the user's environment through observation and interviews to uncover users' behaviors, motivations, and pain points–especially needs that users may not explicitly articulate—and see how these insights inform better design decisions.
- Journey mapping the user experience—Understand how to create a user journey map (or experience map) that charts the end-to-end interactions a person has with a product or service. Be able to identify each touchpoint, along with the user's goals, feelings, and frustrations at every step. Learn how journey mapping reveals pain points and opportunities for improvement in the overall user experience that might be missed when looking at individual parts in isolation.
- Integrating tools for empathy-driven design—Appreciate how visualisation, ethnography, and journey mapping work together to strengthen empathy and user-centric innovation. By the end of the chapter, readers will be able to apply these tools in combination, for example, using ethnographic findings to inform a journey map, or visualising solutions for issues uncovered in a journey—thereby ensuring that design solutions remain firmly grounded in real user experiences.
- Real-world application and best practices—Recognise real-world examples of these methods in action (such as IDEO's rapid visual prototyping, Ford's use of ethnographic research for car design, or Airbnb's storyboarding of the guest experience). Learn best practices for using each tool effectively (e.g., staying objective when observing users, iterating a journey map with actual user feedback) and be aware of common pitfalls to avoid when employing these techniques.

6.1 INTRODUCTION

Understanding users means knowing their needs, behaviours, and pain points, which is the cornerstone of the design thinking process. Design thinking is a human-centred approach to innovation that begins with empathy for the end-user and iteratively develops solutions through ideation, prototyping, and testing. Successful innovation hinges on deeply understanding the people you're designing for. By prioritising user insights, teams can ensure that products and services resonate with real-world use cases rather than abstract assumptions.

Visualisation, ethnography, and journey mapping are three key tools in design thinking that facilitate a deep understanding of users. *Visualisation* uses images, sketches, and prototypes to express ideas tangibly. It is not limited to artistic drawing; it's about "visual thinking", unlocking a different part of the brain to explore concepts beyond words. *Ethnography* is a research method drawn from anthropology involving immersive observation and qualitative inquiry into users' lives and contexts. It helps designers discover how people *behave and why, often revealing latent needs that user*s may struggle to articulate. *Journey mapping* (also called experience mapping) is the creation of a visual narrative of the end-to-end user experience, highlighting each touchpoint a user has with a product or service and noting their goals, actions, and emotional highs and lows along the way. Together, these tools form a powerful toolkit for any design thinker. Visualisation brings ideas to life, ethnography grounds ideas in reality, and journey maps connect individual interactions into a coherent user experience story.

In real-world applications, these tools have had a significant impact. Global design firm IDEO, for example, uses visual prototyping to test product ideas rapidly. This practice helped reinvent the humble shopping cart by quickly building and iterating physical mock-ups in response to user feedback. Automaker Ford has employed ethnographic research to understand how drivers in different markets use their vehicles, leading to design decisions (from dashboard features to horn durability) aligning with local user behaviour. Platforms like Airbnb have relied on journey mapping and storyboarding to overhaul their service experience, mapping out every step of the host and guest interaction to identify gaps and opportunities for improvement. These examples highlight how visualisation, ethnography, and journey mapping drive innovation by keeping the design process rooted in a rich understanding of user perspectives. In the following sections, we delve deeper into each tool, examining their roles in design thinking, techniques and best practices, case studies of industry applications, and how they can be integrated to create user-centred designs in any sector.

6.2 VISUALISATION IN DESIGN THINKING

In design thinking, visualisation serves as a bridge between abstract ideas and tangible solutions. By visualising concepts through sketches, diagrams, or prototypes, teams can communicate and develop ideas in ways that pure text or verbal discussion cannot. Jeanne Liedtka, a leading design thinking scholar, notes that visualisation pushes us beyond using words alone, reducing misinterpretation by aligning everyone around a standard visual reference. Team members are far less likely to walk away with different mental models when a concept is drawn out or prototyped. For example, simply saying, "We need a new customer service platform" might evoke disparate images in the minds of IT, marketing, and operations teams. However, drawing a rough interface or user flow for that platform creates a shared vision and invites concrete feedback. Visualisation externalises thinking, making ideas "lookable" and thus easier to critique, refine, and build upon collaboratively.

Key visualisation techniques in design thinking include sketches, wireframes, and storyboards. Sketching is a quick and low-fidelity way to brainstorm or communicate an idea. These can be hand-drawn renderings of a physical product or interface, often done in the early ideation stage to generate many concepts. The goal is not artistry but clarity. Even simple stick-figure drawings or rough schematics can convey a user flow or product concept. Wireframes are skeletal outlines of digital interfaces (or sometimes service touchpoints) focusing on layout and functionality rather than visual design. Wireframes commonly use boxes and placeholders to denote where content, images, or buttons will go, giving a sense of structure. They help teams consider how a user might navigate a website or app, for instance, without the distraction of colour and fonts. Wireframes are a staple in UX design for mapping the information architecture and ensuring that key elements are positioned effectively. Storyboards borrow from filmmaking and narrative arts. They are sequential panels or illustrations depicting a scenario of a user interacting with a product or service. In a storyboard, characters (often representing user personas) are shown step-by-step as they encounter a problem, use a design solution, and experience the outcome. This technique puts a human story to the design, emphasising context, chronology, and emotion. It helps teams visualise a static product and experience using it over time. Storyboards are especially useful for capturing intangible elements like the user's mood or environment at each stage of an interaction. By mapping out these narratives, designers ensure they consider the user's journey (much like a journey map, but in a more narrative, visual format) even as they brainstorm solutions.

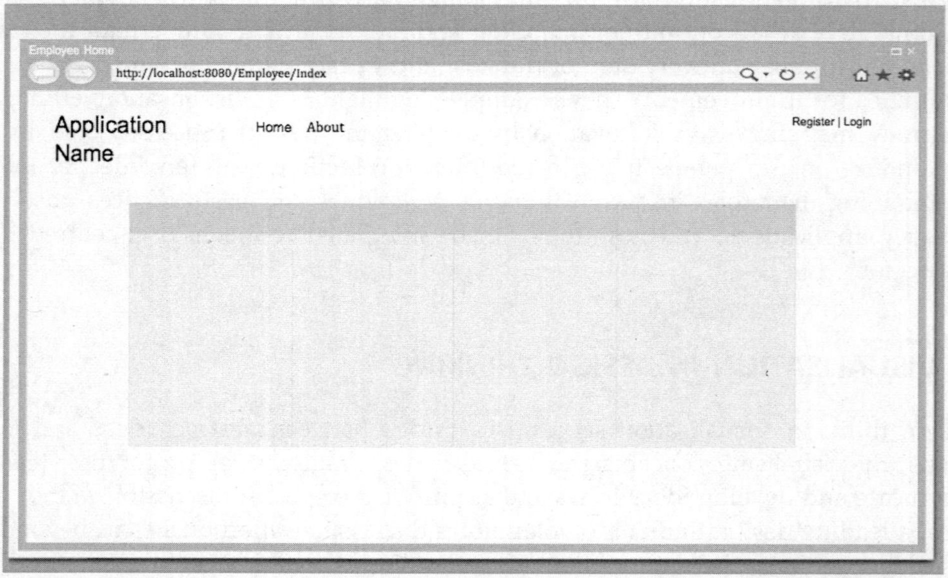

FIGURE 6.1 A basic wireframe example for a web interface.

Wireframes are a visualisation form that outlines content and functionality without graphic distractions. In this simple wireframe, one can see placeholders for the application name, navigation menus ("Home", "About"), and a grid layout for content. Such visual schematics allow designers and stakeholders to discuss layout and flow early in the design process, ensuring that key information and controls are positioned logically before investing in high-fidelity design.

Visualisation plays multiple roles in ideation and prototyping. Quick sketches or diagrams enable the team to generate many concepts rapidly during ideation. Instead of writing a paragraph to describe each idea, a sketch can often be created in seconds to convey the essence. For example, a new kitchen appliance concept might be sketched to show its form factor and how a user would operate it. These visuals fuel creative discussion and invite team members to build on each other's ideas ("What if the handle were on this side?" or "Could this screen be larger for elderly users?"). In the prototyping phase, visualisation becomes even more critical. Teams create low-fidelity prototypes like paper prototypes of an application, cardboard mock-ups of a device, or role-play scripts for a service to test how the idea works in practice. The mantra here is "fail fast to succeed sooner." By quickly making ideas tangible, design thinkers can put them in front of users and gather feedback when changes are inexpensive. A rough visual prototype may expose unanticipated user confusion or use errors, which can be fixed in the next iteration. This iterative loop of visualise → get feedback → refine is at the heart of design thinking. It leverages the fact that people respond more concretely to something they can see and interact with rather than an abstract description.

One famous case study of visualisation in action is IDEO's use of visual prototyping in product design, often illustrated by their 1999 shopping cart project. IDEO was challenged to reinvent the traditional shopping cart in this project (featured on an ABC Nightline special). This product has seen little change in decades despite issues with safety and usability. The IDEO team started by interviewing and observing shoppers (ethnography, which we will discuss later) and then rapidly moved to visualise solutions. In a fast-paced brainstorming session, team members sketched dozens of cart ideas: modular baskets, improved wheels for manoeuvrability, child-safe seats, etc. Rather than debate these on a whiteboard for too long, they almost immediately began building physical prototypes of the most promising ideas using foam, metal scraps, and everyday materials. Within days, the team had a rough prototype of a new cart design with features like detachable plastic baskets (to allow shoppers to carry a basket around and then easily dock it back on the cart) and a horizontal handlebar for better control. This tangible prototype was taken to a grocery store for testing, and the shoppers pushed it around, tried to nest it, loaded items, and so on, providing invaluable feedback. One iteration revealed that the cart was still hard to steer through tight aisles, so the team visualised a solution by attaching wheels that turned 90 degrees. Another iteration addressed child safety by adding a swing-up child seat with a seatbelt. The design evolved based on real user interaction by visually prototyping and testing in rapid cycles. Ultimately, the final design featured a nestable cart frame with removable baskets, improved ergonomics, and greater safety, addressing the identified issues. IDEO's visual approach did not just result in a novel cart; it demonstrated how quickly moving to visualisation (sketches and prototypes) can accelerate learning. The project has since been cited as a model for rapid prototyping and user feedback integration (CliffsNotes, n.d.). More broadly, it highlights how visualisation in design thinking isn't about making things look pretty; it's about making ideas testable and concrete. By seeing and touching the idea, designers and users can engage with it, leading to insights that would never surface in a purely conceptual discussion.

Beyond products, visualisation aids in service design and strategy as well. Storyboards, for example, were used by Airbnb's founders to reimagine their entire guest experience (as we'll explore later), and companies like Apple have famously sketched customer retail journeys to design their store layouts. Even abstract concepts like a new business model can be visualised using diagrams or comics to tell how value flows to the customer. The act of visualising forces clarity: any gaps or implausible elements in the idea become evident when you try to draw them. It is why visualisation is a key tool in the ideation (expanding and communicating ideas) and prototyping (testing and refining solutions) phases of design thinking. It engages team creativity, surfaces misalignment early, and creates artefacts (sketches, mock-ups) that can be shared with users and stakeholders to gather feedback. In sum, visualisation translates empathy and imagination into something actionable. It is how inklings become innovations on the drawing board and in the workshop before they ever reach production.

Readers are encouraged to watch the lecture by visiting the link - https://youtu.be/Y7QGe51j6a0. Alternatively, the presented QR code can be scanned.

SCAN ME

Scan to watch the lecture—Visualization.

6.3 ETHNOGRAPHY IN DESIGN THINKING

If visualisation brings ideas to life, ethnography brings designers into the user's life. In the context of design thinking, ethnography means going out into the field to observe and engage with people in their natural environment as they interact with products or services (or as they experience problems needing solving). The purpose is to develop a deep, nuanced understanding of user behaviour, motivations, and frustrations. Unlike a structured survey or focus group conducted in a lab, ethnographic research is typically open-ended and contextual. The researcher might be a silent observer in the back of a grocery store aisle watching how shoppers choose cereal or an active participant riding with a truck driver for a day to see how they organise their route. By doing so, the designer-as-ethnographer can capture insights that users may not articulate in interviews. It's about discovering the *unspoken* truths of user experience.

Ethnography helps answer the crucial "why" behind user behaviour. Rather than discovering what a user does or whether they like something, ethnography digs into how they do things and why those habits, preferences, or pain points exist. It is invaluable in design thinking's Empathise phase. It grounds the entire innovation process in reality. Often, users may not be fully aware of their own latent needs. As the oft-cited quote (apocryphally attributed to Henry Ford) goes, "If I had asked customers what they wanted, they would have said a faster horse." True or not, the sentiment underscores that people may describe solutions based on what they know rather than the actual need (in Ford's era, a need for faster travel). Ethnography tries to observe the need or problem in action, unfiltered by the user's self-reporting biases, thus equipping designers to define the problem more accurately.

Key ethnographic methods in design thinking include participant observation, in-depth interviews, and field studies (often collectively termed field research). In *participant observation*, the researcher immerses themselves in the users' environment and may even participate in the same activities as the user. For example, a designer interested in improving the experience of air travel might spend time in airports, not just watching passengers but going through the process of checking in, going through security, waiting at the gate, etc., as a participant. This method yields firsthand insight into interactions and routines. *Interviews* in ethnographic research are typically open-ended and may occur in the user's context (at their home, workplace, or wherever relevant), often following or interwoven with observation. Instead of a formal questionnaire, ethnographic interviews feel more like guided conversations. The researcher might ask the user to show how they perform a certain task and talk through it. These interviews can be semi-structured, combining some prepared questions with improvised probes that follow the user's train of thought. Observing actions and listening to users' explanations provides both behavioral data and the users' perspective. Additionally, ethnographers may collect artefacts or documents. For instance, a designer studying healthcare workflows might gather copies of forms nurses have to fill out or take photos of how patients organise their pillboxes at home. All these forms of data give a rich picture of the user's world. The Interaction Design Foundation summarises that ethnographic research "involves immersing oneself in the natural context of individuals to collect qualitative insights into their behaviour and culture," emphasising observation and engagement in real-world settings. This immersive quality is what sets ethnography apart from other research methods; by letting go of one's presumptions and "stepping into the user's shoes" (and environment), a designer can discover needs that would not surface in a conference room discussion.

Ethnography has proven particularly powerful in uncovering user behaviour nuances that lead to breakthrough designs. For example, ethnographic research at Intel in the early 2000s famously revealed how people in emerging markets were sharing mobile phones within families and communities, which helped inspire new phone features and business models (e.g. multiple address books on one device). In the automotive industry, Ford Motor Company leveraged ethnography to gain deeper consumer insights—a notable case involved understanding how drivers perceived the performance of the Ford Mustang. After a redesigned Mustang in the late 1990s, it received complaints that it "felt less powerful" than the previous model. Ford was puzzled because the new engine was more powerful on paper. To solve this mystery, Ford dispatched ethnographers to ride along with Mustang drivers and observe. Through interviews and ride-along observations, the research team discovered that drivers equated "power" with sensory experiences like the roar of the engine, the vibration in the steering wheel, and the visual cues of a sporty design. Though technically superior, the new model was more sound-dampened and had a subtler design, thus delivering a muted sensory experience. With this insight, Ford's designers returned to the drawing board. They made stylistic changes to the Mustang's exterior (making it look more aggressive and "fast" even when stationary) and engineered a more satisfying engine growl (Smith & Davis, 2022). The result was a car that *felt* powerful to drivers, validating that the ethnographic insight, viz., power is visceral, not just numerical, was on point. This case underscores how ethnography can uncover the real meaning behind user feedback and guide design decisions that align with user experience, not just engineering specs.

Consider ethnographic research for emerging markets, as in Ford's work in developing regions. Designing for emerging markets often requires shedding assumptions that hold in a company's home market. Ethnography is crucial: it brings designers face-to-face with different cultural contexts, usage conditions, and constraints. In practice, Ford has a human-centred design initiative known as *D-Ford* (short for Design Ford), which conducts ethnographic research worldwide to inform product development (Bell, 2021). Through these studies, Ford learned, for instance, that drivers in some countries like India use their car horns far more frequently than drivers in North America or Europe, not out of aggression but as a regular part of communicating on crowded roads. One report noted that in Mumbai, an average driver honks *in two weeks* as much as a typical German driver might in an entire year. An automaker that didn't appreciate this might release a car in India with a horn designed for infrequent use, leading to premature failure and customer frustration. Luxury carmaker Audi famously had to equip its India models with special, extra-durable horns to withstand this reality (Jaafari, 2016). Ford's ethnographers similarly observe and take note of such local behaviours. Another insight from emerging market research might be how owners repurpose car interiors. One ethnographic study found that in India, drivers often install after-market curtains and ambient lighting in cars, reflecting a desire for a living room-like comfort in chaotic traffic jams. Noticing this, designers can preemptively consider privacy screens or dimmable cabin lights in future models. Ethnography in emerging markets also uncovers constraints such as infrastructure gaps (e.g., how do you design an SUV for a region with few paved roads? What do rural drivers do if a vehicle breaks down far from service centres?). By immersing in the daily life of emerging-market consumers, Ford's design teams have developed features tailored to those needs, from more robust suspension and cooling systems (for rough roads and hot climates) to simple, intuitive dashboards that accommodate drivers who may be first-time car owners. These adaptations underscore a broader point that ethnography prevents a one-size-fits-all design mentality. It pushes companies to meet users where they are, literally and figuratively. As Usha Raghavachari of D-Ford describes, keeping the consumer at the centre through global ethnographic research "significantly de-risks the investment in future products" (Bell, 2021). It ensures that products are grounded in real user contexts and needs, no matter how far they might be from the designers' own experiences.

It's worth comparing ethnographic research in consumer-facing industries vs. B2B (business-to-business) settings, as the approach can differ. In consumer markets (like retail, automotive, or home appliances), ethnography often involves *individuals or families* and focuses on personal, day-to-day contexts. The researcher might observe a single person shopping or a family cooking dinner, and the insights tend to revolve around convenience, comfort, aesthetic preferences, emotional triggers, etc. In contrast, B2B ethnography usually occurs in workplaces or operational environments and involves *professional users* (employees) or multiple stakeholders. For example, a B2B ethnographic study might involve shadowing warehouse workers to understand a supply chain software's usability or observing doctors and nurses in a hospital to inform the design of a new medical device. Access and complexity differ in B2B as they involve gaining permission to observe employees or processes that might require navigating corporate gatekeepers, and organisational policies or workflows could influence usage behaviours. The insights in B2B contexts often relate to efficiency, safety, or integration with other systems (e.g., how a new piece of machinery fits into an assembly line). Whereas a consumer ethnographer might note a user's unspoken frustration assembling a piece of furniture (leading to a redesign of the product or instructions), a B2B ethnographer might note communication breakdowns between departments using software (leading to a redesign of the interface or data flow). Both aim to improve user experience, but *the "user" in B2B is also an employee with specific job goals.* One practical difference is that in consumer ethnography, the pain points might be confusion, discomfort, or delight. In contrast, in B2B ethnography, pain points often translate to lost time, errors, or workarounds that indicate a flawed process. Table 6.1 highlights some of these differences:

TABLE 6.1 Ethnography in Consumer vs. B2B Contexts

Aspect	*Consumer Ethnography*	*B2B Ethnography*
Setting	Natural home, retail, or public environments—e.g., observing a shopper in a mall or a user in their living room. The context is personal life.	Workplace or operational environments—e.g., factory floor, office, hospital. The context is the professional setting, often with complex workflows.
Participants	Individuals, families, or small friend groups acting as end-users/consumers. Typically, the person observed is the decision-maker and user of the product.	Employees or teams within an organisation. Multiple user roles (end-user, manager, IT support) may be observed when understanding a single service. Users might not be the ultimate decision-makers (purchasers) for the product.
Focus of Insights	Personal needs, convenience, aesthetic preferences, and emotional drivers. How does the product fit into the user's lifestyle, and what are the user's feelings (enjoyment, frustration) during use?	Efficiency, productivity, safety, and integration with work processes. How does the product/service fit into existing workflows, and how does it impact job performance or collaboration?

Aspect	*Consumer Ethnography*	*B2B Ethnography*
Challenges Observed	Usability issues, unmet latent needs in daily tasks, workarounds or "hacks" consumers devise. For example, a user repurposing a product to serve a need indicates a gap in the market.	Process bottlenecks, communication gaps, user errors or training issues. For example, staff create manual Excel logs outside a system, indicating that the official tool doesn't meet all their needs. Also, organisational constraints or compliance requirements affect use.
Example Outcome	Insight: Shoppers struggle to carry baskets when they get heavy. Design response: Create carts with detachable baskets (as in IDEO's cart project).	Insight: Factory workers ignore an alert system because it's too frequent and noisy. Design response: Redesign the alert interface to prioritise critical warnings and provide context so it aids rather than annoys.

In both cases, ethnography's strength lies in uncovering the reality of use, but the reality can look very different in a home vs. a business. A savvy design thinker will tailor the ethnographic approach to the context: for consumers, that might mean spending an afternoon as a "fly on the wall" in someone's kitchen. For B2B, it might mean attending daily team meetings in a corporate office for a month. The end goal is the same: gain empathy by seeing through the users' eyes. This empathy fuels the next stages of design thinking (Define, Ideate, etc.) by ensuring the problem definition is accurate and the ideas generated are relevant.

To summarise, ethnography in design thinking brings the voice and context of the user directly into the process. It complements other research and data by providing rich stories and observations. There are challenges as ethnographic research can be time-consuming, and it requires researchers to interpret qualitative data without letting their own biases intrude. But when done well, the payoff is profound. Ethnography can reveal small details that make a big difference. It helps teams avoid false assumptions (designing for how they *think* people use a product versus how they use it). Whether it's watching how a nurse improvises with tape to mark settings on a medical device (inspiring a more user-friendly control knob) or seeing how rural families in an emerging market share a single smartphone (inspiring multi-user profiles in Android), ethnography turns real human behaviour into design inspiration. In the following section on journey mapping, we will see how the insights gathered (often through ethnography) can be synthesised into a clear depiction of the user experience and how that depiction can guide innovative solutions.

6.4 JOURNEY MAPPING IN DESIGN THINKING

Design thinking strongly emphasises viewing experiences holistically from the user's perspective. Journey mapping is a tool that enables precisely that: it is a visual representation of the process a user goes through to accomplish a goal, charting each step or "touchpoint" and capturing the user's experience at each one. A journey map (also known as a customer journey map or user journey map) typically lays out the sequence of stages (for example, discover → purchase → usage → support) and, for each stage, details what the user is doing, what channels or interfaces they interact with, what they are thinking or feeling, and where pain points or delights occur. The goal is to create an end-to-end narrative from the user's eyes—from the very first moment they become aware of a product/service, through the process of engagement, and on to the end of the experience (which could be purchase or repeat usage, or even leaving the service). By doing so, journey maps help design teams identify opportunities for improvement and innovation at each step, especially at points where the user's experience breaks down.

A hallmark of journey mapping is its attention to emotional highs and lows throughout the user's experience. An effective journey map doesn't only note what the user does but also how they feel. Their level of satisfaction, frustration, confusion, or happiness at each stage. For instance, consider the journey of a hotel guest during booking. They might feel excited but anxious about whether the hotel photos are accurate; during check-in, they might feel impatient waiting in line; upon entering their room, they may feel delighted if it exceeds expectations or disappointed. These emotional curves are crucial because they highlight "moments of truth"., which are the points that can make or break the overall experience. A common visualisation on journey maps is a line graph tracking user sentiment over time, often dipping down at pain points and rising at moments of satisfaction. Design thinking teams pay special attention to those dips (to ideate fixes that raise them) and to the peaks (to reinforce or extend them). As one guide puts it, journey mapping focuses on tracing the customer's journey with special attention to emotional highs and lows, aiming to uncover needs that customers themselves might not voice. For example, a customer might never explicitly say, "I feel anxious when I don't get shipping updates for my online order." Still, a journey map of online shopping might reveal a low point of uncertainty in the waiting period between purchase and delivery. This insight could spur an idea to send proactive tracking updates as a solution addressing an unmet emotional need.

Steps in creating a journey map generally include:

1. *Identifying the user persona and scenario* to map
2. *Outlining the high-level stages* of the journey
3. *Listing the touchpoints, actions, and channels* the user engages in at each stage
4. *Mapping the user's thoughts and emotions* at each step (including pain points and delights)
5. *Identifying opportunities* for improvement at each stage.

Let us break this down with an example. Suppose we are mapping the journey of a rental car customer picking up a car at an airport. First, we clarify the persona (e.g., a business traveller, Alex, who frequently rents cars on trips) and the scenario (renting a car for a 3-day trip, booked online in advance). Next, we outline the stages: Booking → Arrival at the Airport → Shuttle to Rental Center → Pick Up Car → Use Car → Return Car → Post-Rental.

For each stage, we list touchpoints and actions: Alex interacts with the rental company's website during booking. His actions include searching vehicles, entering dates, and payment; during *Arrival*, Alex looks for signage to the rental shuttle; during *Pick Up*, Alex waits in line at the rental counter, shows ID, receives keys and paperwork, inspects the car, etc. We note the channels: website, physical signs, bus, rental counter, and parking lot. Now, crucially, we annotate Alex's experience: During *booking*, perhaps Alex feels confident if the website is clear, but maybe frustrated if there are hidden fees (pain point: "price changed at check-out; felt annoyed"). During *Arrival*, Alex is tired from a flight and feels anxious about finding the shuttle on time (pain point: "hard to find shuttle stop at the airport, no clear directions"). At *Pick Up*, perhaps Alex feels impatient waiting and then hurries if the agent upsells insurance (pain point: pressured decision). Once in the car and on the road (*Using the car*), Alex feels relieved and satisfied if the car is clean and has the requested GPS. At *Return*, maybe Alex feels a bit stressed locating the drop-off area, but there's relief once it's done and the final bill matches expectations. After leaving (*Post-Rental*), Alex might receive an email receipt and feel content if everything went smoothly or upset if an unexpected charge appears (like a refuelling fee). By laying this out, we can visualise Alex's emotional journey: perhaps a dip around Arrival/ Pickup due to confusion and wait, a rise during usage, and a small dip at Return if minor stress occurs.

Now we have a map. The final step is to draw insights and opportunities from it. We might highlight the shuttle sign issue as an *opportunity:* Provide clearer instructions or a mobile notification in-app guiding the customer to the rental shuttle (this addresses the low point at Arrival). We might also see an opportunity to streamline the counter process via a self-service kiosk or a "skip the counter" program for business travellers to alleviate the wait and pressure at Pick Up. Journey mapping makes these gaps evident by putting the entire experience on one page.

To illustrate a real case, let's turn to Airbnb's journey mapping for guest and host experiences. Airbnb famously undertook a comprehensive journey mapping (and storyboarding) project around 2011–2012, code-named *"Snow White."* The founders realised that to scale their service, they needed to deeply understand the end-to-end experience of their two key user groups, viz., guests and hosts. They identified about 15 key moments in the guest journey, from the time a person first hears about Airbnb, through searching for a place, booking, travelling, checking in, the stay itself, and finally leaving a review and remembering the trip. They did the same from the host's perspective: listing a space, receiving a booking request, hosting the guest, and after the guest departed. These moments were illustrated in storyboards (large drawings) to visualise what the guest or host would be doing and feeling. For example, one frame shows a *host receiving a reservation request* on the Airbnb app and feeling excited that someone wants to stay at their place (but also a bit anxious to vet the guest's profile). Another frame depicts a *guest arriving at a listing*, feeling a mix of adventure and concern ("Will the place be like the pictures? Will the host be welcoming?"). By mapping these journeys, Airbnb identified several pain points. One major insight was that the offline portions of the experience were critical and under-served. For instance, after booking but before check-in, guests often felt unsure about the neighbourhood or how to plan their trip locally, which leads to an emotional low of uncertainty that could sour the experience. In response, Airbnb created features like Neighborhood Guides (rich local information to help guests get comfortable with where they would be staying). They also noticed hosts worried about how to make guests feel welcome or struggled with managing keys. It led to improvements like template messages for hosts to communicate with guests and, eventually, the development of self-check-in guides and smart lock integration. Journey mapping showed Airbnb exactly *which frames of the experience* had gaps. As Nathan Blecharczyk (Airbnb co-founder) explained, this process was galvanising as it got everyone in the company aligned on the ideal guest and host experiences. It became a "litmus test" for prioritising projects. If an idea didn't improve one of the journey frames, maybe it was less important (Sequoia Capital, 2023). Over time, Airbnb's continuous attention to the guest/host journey led to service innovations such as 24/7 customer support, the Airbnb Experiences offering (to enrich the travel journey beyond accommodation), and improved review systems for trust, all targeted at key moments on the journey map.

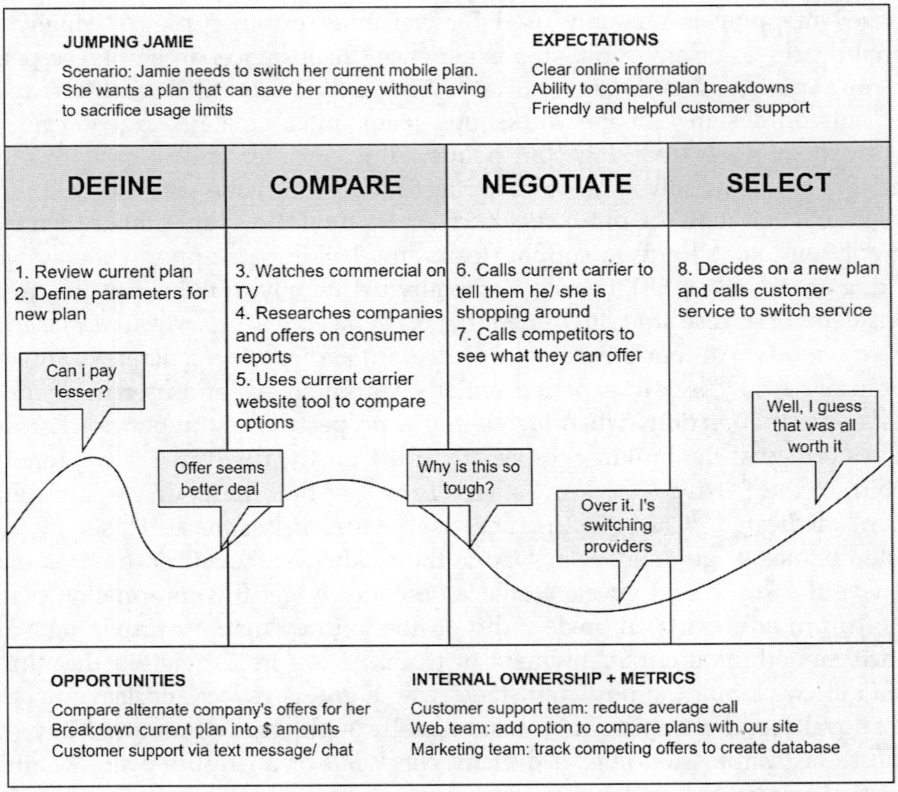

FIGURE 6.2 Excerpt from a customer journey map example ("Jumping Jamie")—illustrating stages of a mobile service sign-up and the user's emotional journey.

This simplified journey map shows the process a persona ("Jumping Jamie") goes through when switching her mobile phone plan. The top row outlines the stages (Define, Compare, Negotiate, Select) under which specific user actions are listed (e.g., reviewing the current plans, researching options, calling providers). The wavy line across the stages represents Jamie's emotional highs and lows. For instance, during the "Compare" stage, we see a dip accompanied by a quote, "Ugh, why is this so difficult?!" indicating frustration when Jamie finds it hard to compare plans. Later, at the final "Select" stage, the line peaks as Jamie decides on a new plan, with a quote, "Well, I guess that was all worth it." indicating relief and satisfaction. At the bottom, the map highlights *Opportunities* (e.g., the company could offer a tool to compare plans for her) and *Internal Ownership & Metrics* (which teams in the company own each part of the journey and how success is measured) (Sprout Social, 2020). This journey map helps the service provider identify exactly where the user is unhappy (frustration during comparison) and what features or support might alleviate that (perhaps a simplified comparison tool or clearer pricing). It also ensures different departments (marketing, customer support, etc.) understand their role in improving Jamie's experience end-to-end. Journey maps like this are instrumental in design thinking because they convert raw research (from user interviews or observations) into a strategic visual to guide design decisions.

Journey mapping is not only used for consumer experiences; it's equally valuable for internal processes or any multi-step experience (for instance, an employee onboarding journey or a patient healthcare journey). The map becomes a baseline to discuss improvements. In design thinking workshops, teams often create a large journey map on a wall with sticky notes, marking pain points with red notes and ideas with green ones along the timeline. This collaborative mapping ensures everyone sees the "big picture" of the user's interaction with the product/service across time and space, rather than each team focusing only on their slice (e.g., support team only looking at support calls, website team only looking at the online UI). It fosters empathy by literally drawing out the user's story.

Consider a brief case study to cement the concept: *Airbnb's guest journey mapping yields service improvements.* We touched on some outcomes earlier. One concrete example is how Airbnb improved the check-in experience. Early journey maps and user feedback showed that guests often felt anxious when arriving at a property. They might not know how to get the keys or access the building, especially if the host wasn't physically present. It was a pain point in the "Arrival/Check-in" stage of the guest journey. Airbnb introduced their application's dedicated "Check-in Instructions" feature in response. Hosts could upload step-by-step photos or guidance (e.g., "Go to the lockbox at the left of the gate, enter code 4231, retrieve the key"), and guests would automatically get this information before their trip. This feature addressed an anxiety dip on the journey map by providing clarity and reassurance, smoothing a critical moment of truth. Also, Airbnb realised that the journey doesn't end at check-out; the post-stay stage (where guests reflect and leave reviews) was crucial for loyalty and acquiring new customers through word-of-mouth. They identified that a guest's last impression (e.g., a difficult check-out or a dispute over cleaning) could taint the memory of the entire trip. By mapping out even post-stay feelings, Airbnb put policies to simplify check-out (standardising expectations, encouraging hosts to be reasonable with cleaning tasks, etc.). They added small touches like sending a "Thank You" email to guests after their stay, prompting them to leave a review while subtly celebrating their trip. The outcome of these interventions, informed by journey mapping, was an increase in overall ratings and repeat usage, as guests felt the platform cared about every stage of their travel experience, not just the booking.

To demonstrate how a journey map can be structured, consider Table 6.2, which breaks down a generic user journey (as an example, booking and staying at an Airbnb, from the guest's perspective) into stages with actions, emotional highs/lows, and pain points:

TABLE 6.2 Simplified Journey Map for an Airbnb Guest

Journey Stage	*Example Guest Actions*	*Guest Emotions (Highs/Lows)*	*Key Pain Points Identified*
Planning (Pre-booking)	Browse listings on the Airbnb website; filter by date, location, and price; read reviews; discuss with travel partner.	*Emotion:* Excitement at seeing nice options, but can be overwhelmed by too many choices. Curiosity about different homes.	*Overwhelm:* "Too many listings to compare, not sure which one to pick." *Trust concern:* "Will the place look like these photos?"
Booking	Send an inquiry or instant book chosen listing; enter payment info; receive a confirmation email.	*Emotion:* Relief at securing a place; happiness if the booking was easy. Some anxiety about payment or reservation being accepted.	*Unclear fees:* "Service fees and cleaning fees bumped up the price at check-out—frustrating." *Uncertainty:* "Hoping the host approves my request quickly."
Pre-Arrival (Waiting)	Communicate with the host for check-in details, arrange transportation, and pack for a trip.	*Emotion:* Building anticipation for the trip, but potential nervousness if the host responds slowly.	*Communication delays:* "Host hasn't replied to my question about parking—feeling anxious." *Info gap:* "Not sure how to get from the airport to the apartment."
Check-In	Find the property; meet the host or retrieve keys from the lockbox; enter and settle in.	*Emotion:* Momentary stress finding or accessing the place; then hopeful and curious when stepping inside. High if all goes smoothly ("This place is great!") or low if there are issues.	*Wayfinding:* "Had trouble finding the building entrance at night." *Access issues:* "Lockbox code didn't work initially, panicked for a moment."
Stay (Experience)	Use the accommodation (sleep, cook, relax); possibly contact the host or customer service if needed; explore the neighbourhood.	*Emotion:* Enjoyment during good moments (cosy home, good amenities). Any issues (e.g., Wi-Fi down) cause frustration. Overall, it is a mix of comfort and the usual travel fatigue. Peaks if something exceeds expectations (e.g., extra clean, thoughtful host gesture).	*Amenities problem:* "The Wi-Fi was hard to connect to—took an hour to resolve." *Unmet expectation:* "The water pressure was low—annoying surprise."

Journey Stage	*Example Guest Actions*	*Guest Emotions (Highs/Lows)*	*Key Pain Points Identified*
Check-Out	Follow the host's check-out instructions (e.g., tidy up, lock door), perhaps meet the host to return the keys, and travel to the next destination.	*Emotion:* Bittersweet if the trip ends—satisfaction if the stay was good, or eagerness to leave if not. It could be a bit stressful to make an early check-out time.	*Rushed feeling:* "Check-out was at 10 AM, so I felt rushed to clean up and leave." *Uncertainty:* "Was I supposed to take out the trash or not? Instructions weren't clear."
Post-Stay	Leave a review for the host; receive the host's review as a guest; tell friends/ family about the trip.	*Emotion:* Reflective—if largely positive, the guest feels happy and nostalgic, boosting the likelihood of a good review and telling others. Any lingering bad feelings (small issues) might fade or could colour their memory if significant.	If something bad happened (e.g., the deposit was charged unfairly), *anger* or disappointment afterwards. Otherwise, a potential pain point is the effort of writing a review ("Should I bother?").

This hypothetical journey map in Table 6.2 shows how mapping out stages and user feelings can point to specific improvements. For instance, the overwhelm in the Planning stage suggests an opportunity for Airbnb to improve filtering or provide personalised recommendations (to reduce choice paralysis). The uncertainty in Pre-Arrival transportation could be mitigated by Airbnb sharing local transit info or offering an airport pickup service partnership. Each pain point on the map is essentially a design prompt. It illustrates why journey maps are so valuable in design thinking: they translate raw research into a structured story, from which many "How Might We" questions naturally flow (e.g., "How might we reassure users about what to expect (trust) during the Planning stage?" or "How might we make Check-In effortless even if the host isn't present?").

Journey mapping as a tool also encourages *cross-functional discussion*. Using Airbnb again: improving a guest's journey might involve website engineers (for the booking interface), the trust and safety team (for background checks and secure payments), customer service (for 24/7 support), and the host community (since hosts also play a role in the guest's experience). Having a single map of the journey allowed Airbnb to coordinate all these functions toward a common objective: to make each guest's journey as smooth and delightful as possible. It's a living document wherein user behaviour changes as new features roll out, and/ or the journey map can be updated. Some organisations treat journey maps as strategic assets, reviewing them regularly and measuring improvements at each stage (for example, tracking Net Promoter Score at each major touchpoint to see if design changes yield better sentiment).

In summary, journey mapping in design thinking combines storytelling and analysis. It takes the empathy gained from research (often ethnographic research) and frames it in a timeline highlighting where design can make a difference. It's significant because users don't judge experiences solely on one moment. Just like a terrible check-in can sour a hotel stay, a fantastic customer support call can redeem an earlier frustration. Journey maps ensure no part of the user experience is overlooked. By methodically identifying touchpoints, pain points, and emotional peaks/ valleys, journey mapping allows design teams to prioritise efforts where they matter most. The Airbnb case demonstrates how a thorough journey mapping exercise can lead to numerous targeted solutions that elevate the entire experience. Whether applied to customers, patients, employees, or any "user" journey, this tool focuses on delivering a cohesive and positive experience throughout, which is a core aim of design thinking.

Readers can watch a quick video on the journey mapping by visiting the link—https://youtu.be/SCHqtm3avBs

Alternatively, the below presented QR code can be scanned to watch the lecture.

SCAN ME

Scan to watch the lecture—Journey Mapping.

6.5 INTEGRATING THESE TOOLS IN DESIGN THINKING

Visualisation, ethnography, and journey mapping each provide unique value, but they are highly complementary in practice and often work best in concert. In a user-centred design project, one can think of ethnography as *input*, journey mapping as *processing/synthesis*, and visualisation as *output*, with overlaps at each phase of the iterative design thinking cycle. By integrating all three, teams create a robust pipeline from user insights to solution ideation to implementation, continually looping back whenever new insights emerge.

Consider how a design thinking team might employ all three tools in a single project, say, redesigning a retail store experience for a major retailer. The project might begin with ethnographic research as design researchers go into stores and observe shoppers and staff in action. Through this, they notice, for example, that customers frequently abandon their search for certain products because they can't find them or they get frustrated waiting for help. Researchers conduct a few in-depth interviews on-site, learning that shoppers often come in with a specific goal (like "I need a birthday gift") but struggle to navigate the store's layout or signage. These raw insights, like a map scribbled in a notebook showing where people wandered and quotes like "I wish there were a directory," form the empathic foundation. Next, the team creates a journey map of the in-store shopping journey. It plots stages such as Entry (customer enters a store, grabs a cart), Navigation (looking for items, browsing aisles), Decision (making purchase decisions, perhaps trying items or reading labels), Check-out, and Post-Purchase. The team annotates this map using ethnographic data about customers' actions and feelings. They highlight that during *Navigation,* many customers hit a low point: confusion and frustration in finding products. Pain points include poorly labelled aisles and a lack of staff assistance on the floor. Conversely, there's a slight emotional uptick at Check-out if the line is short and the cashier is friendly. Armed with this synthesised view, the team moves to ideation, where *visualisation* becomes key. They brainstorm ideas to fix and visualise the navigation pain point: one group sketches an improved signage system (e.g., colour-coded sections, overhead maps, a mobile application integration to guide customers). Another group storyboard is a concept where, upon entering, customers can input what they seek into a kiosk or application and get a personalised store map. The storyboard shows a character walking directly to aisle 8 with the application in hand and smiling. Yet another idea is to change the store layout. Hence, the team draws a floor plan diagram to illustrate a new arrangement of sections that clusters popular items or aligns with how people naturally shop (maybe grouping "gift ideas" from various categories in one area for convenience). All these visuals, including the sketches of signs, wireframes of an app, and floor plan diagrams, allow the team to evaluate and combine solutions quickly. They might even build a quick prototype by printing new signs and temporarily placing them in a test store aisle to see if shoppers navigate better or use tape on the floor to mock up a new layout path. This integration of tools can happen rapidly: ethnography yields insights, journey mapping identifies where to act, visualisation prototypes the fix, and then back again. For example, test the prototype in-store (a form of observational research) to gather more ethnographic insight on how the new idea works, possibly leading to another iteration of the journey map with the improvements.

A real-world example of redesigning a retail experience using all three tools comes from a large big-box retailer (consider a company like Target or Walmart, though we will describe it generically). This retailer noticed declining customer satisfaction scores in their home goods department. They formed a design thinking task force. First, they did ethnographic observations: researchers spent weeks in various store locations, watching how shoppers behaved in the home goods aisles (bedding, kitchenware, decor). They discovered some intriguing patterns. For instance, shoppers often pick up an item (say a kitchen utensil), look around as if comparing or considering, then place it back and leave the aisle empty-handed. Interviews revealed that customers were overwhelmed by choices and lacked information (one said, "There are 50 types of spatulas... I don't know which is good, so I'll think about it or buy later online"). The research also showed people frequently couldn't locate staff to ask questions, and some eventually walked out without buying what they came for. With this rich data, the team created a journey map of the in-store shopping experience for a home goods customer. It highlighted stages like Need Recognition (customer realises they need a spatula at home), Store Entry (motivated, with a mental list), Product Search (scanning the aisle), Evaluation (comparing options), Decision, and Check-out/Exit. The map showed a drop in the *Evaluation* stage with a big pain point labelled "Analysis paralysis—too many options, not enough info." Another pain point was that at store entry, customers didn't know which aisle to go to for specific items (some wandered multiple departments). With these defined, the team ideated solutions. They visualised a few: one was a simplified signage system (e.g., larger category signs like "Cooking Essentials" visible from the entrance and subcategory signs like "Spatulas and Spoons" directly above that section). They drew mock-ups of what these signs would look like and even printed some sample signs. Another idea was an "expert tip" tag on the shelf, which had a little card with a quick recommendation ("Our chef's choice for non-stick pans") and needed to be sketched based on how it could appear next to a product. They also prototyped a store map brochure that customers could grab at the entrance, showing where major categories were. The most tech-forward idea was an in-store navigation application; they wireframed the app screens (store map with a dot and a search bar to find products).

Testing these ideas, they implemented a pilot in a few stores: new overhead signs and shelf info tags were installed (low-tech visualisation put into reality), and they stationed an associate as a "guide" at the entrance to hand out the paper maps. Ethnography came back into play as they observed shoppers in these pilot stores. The results were very positive, as researchers saw fewer "lost" faces and more direct paths to products, and customers spent less time wandering and more time engaging with products. One ethnographic insight post-change was a customer exclaiming, "Oh, that's where it is!" upon seeing the new sign, a small anecdote that confirmed the signage helped. Metrics later showed those stores had a 15% increase in customer satisfaction scores and a 7% boost in sales for that department after the redesign (Insight7, n.d.). The retailer then rolled out the changes chain-wide, integrating a digital solution (eventually a mobile application feature to locate items). This case exemplifies how ethnography (initial observations) identified the root problems, journey mapping clarified *when and where* in the experience to intervene (navigation and decision stages), and visualisation/prototyping produced concrete solutions (signage, info displays, maps) that were tested and refined. Each tool fed into the next, creating a cycle of insight and improvement.

Integration of these tools is also powerful for cross-industry innovation. A team in one industry can apply the trio to a different context by focusing on the user journey. For instance, consider applying journey mapping in a perishable food logistics context: one could map the "journey" of produce from farm to grocery shelf, identifying touchpoints (harvest, transport, warehouse, store) and pain points (delays, temperature fluctuations, handling damage). Ethnographic research might involve riding in delivery trucks or observing workers in a distribution centre, revealing that much time is lost during manual inspections. The visualisation could then prototype a solution, such as a new labelling system or a sensor dashboard to track production conditions. Similarly, a fintech startup might use these tools to design a new app: ethnography through contextual interviews with target users (e.g., small business owners managing finances) yields insights into their tasks and frustrations; journey mapping outlines the steps those business owners take to, say, send an invoice or apply for a loan (including emotions like anxiety about cash flow); visualisation comes into play as the team sketches wireframe and storyboards how their fintech application will fit into that journey (perhaps notifying the user at a critical moment or simplifying a multi-step process into one tap). By iterating among the three, viz., research, mapping, and prototyping, the fintech product is more likely to hit the mark for user needs from the outset.

A key point about integration is iteration. These tools are not one-and-done; they cycle. After implementing changes, new ethnographic observation can verify improvements or uncover new issues, prompting an updated journey map and further ideation. In our retail example, once signage was improved, perhaps the next bottleneck became check-out speed, leading the team to focus on that part of the journey next (maybe prototyping self-checkout stations or mobile payment). Thus, visualisation, ethnography, and journey mapping create a continuous feedback loop central to design thinking's iterative nature. Each tool informs the others: ethnography provides content for journey maps; journey maps highlight what needs to be visualised (prototyped); prototypes tested in context lead to new ethnographic insights.

For designers and organisations, integrating these tools means embedding them into their processes and culture. It requires encouraging teams to regularly get out of the office (ethnography), regularly convene to synthesise what they've learned (journey mapping workshops), and regularly make ideas tangible (visual prototyping sessions). When all three are in play, the outcome is a design process that remains grounded in reality and user-centric from start to finish. Problems are identified based on real user journeys, and solutions are evaluated by how well they improve them. The result is often a better product or service and a more empathetic and agile organisation. Designers, product managers, engineers, and business stakeholders start to speak a common language of "user journeys", "pain points", and "prototypes," breaking silos in the process. In the next section, we discuss how organisations can foster this integration, what challenges might arise, and strategies to overcome them to truly improve user-centred design outcomes.

6.6 USING THESE TOOLS TO IMPROVE USER-CENTERED DESIGN

Organisations must embed tools like visualisation, ethnography, and journey mapping into their design thinking process and culture to consistently deliver products and services that delight users. Doing so ensures that focusing on the end-user isn't just a one-time exercise but a persistent habit. However, adopting these practices can come with challenges. In this section, we discuss strategies for effectively using these tools within an organisation and how to overcome common obstacles in implementation.

Embedding visualisation, ethnography, and journey mapping into the process starts with recognising at which stages of a project each tool is most beneficial and then institutionalising their use. For example, a team might establish that at the start of every project, they will conduct ethnographic research (a full field study or even just a few days of user observation) before defining requirements. It could be formalised as an "Empathise phase" in the project plan. Management can support this by allocating time and budget specifically for field research, signalling that it's a valued step, not an extra. Next, teams might set a checkpoint after research to create journey maps and user personas that synthesise findings. Making journey mapping a standard workshop that cross-functional team members participate in can be very effective. It brings designers, developers, marketers, etc., together to digest user research and visually map the user's experience. It creates empathy across the team and aligns everyone on key pain points. Organisations like IBM and Google have internal playbooks that encourage teams to map user journeys and empathy maps before solutions; these practices are often internally facilitated by a UX strategist or design thinking coach.

When it comes to visualisation and prototyping, a strategy is to create a *culture of rapid prototyping*. It might involve setting up a dedicated innovation lab or encouraging low-fi prototypes in regular meetings. Teams can adopt rules like "no meeting about a new feature without a sketch or prototype on the table." Some companies hold internal hackathons or "design sprints" where a team will generate multiple prototypes to test in a week. The idea is to normalise sketching on whiteboards, building quick mock-ups, and even role-playing experiences (acting out a service interaction) as standard practice. Leaders can foster this by celebrating prototypes and learning. Even if a prototype "fails" in testing, it's applauded because it saved the company from investing in a larger failure. This mentality to try it, show it, test it, and learn must be ingrained. For example, fintech startup teams might institute a weekly demo day: every Friday, the team shares something visual, like a wireframe, a click-through demo, etc., based on that week's work or discoveries. It keeps progress tangible and user-focused.

Leadership buy-in and modelling are critical. It sets a tone if executives and managers participate in user research sessions or personally review journey maps and ask questions like "What are our users' biggest pain points right now and how are we solving them?". Conversely, a common challenge is the *surface-level adoption* of design thinking tools, doing them as a checkbox exercise without the underlying empathy. For instance, a team might create a journey map because it's required but then shelve it and proceed to make decisions that contradict what the map revealed. The journey map should be a living document referenced throughout the project to avoid this. One technique is to put the journey map (or user persona posters) literally on the wall of the team's workspace as a constant reminder. When debates occur about features, team members can point to the map: "Remember, the user felt frustrated here—will this feature help with that or not?" This keeps discussions anchored in user-centred evidence rather than opinions or HIPPO (Highest Paid Person's Opinion) syndrome.

Challenges in implementing these tools often include time and resource constraints, organisational resistance, and lack of training. Ethnography, for instance, can be seen as too time-consuming or "fuzzy" by stakeholders who want fast results and hard numbers. A solution is to practice "rapid ethnography", shorter, more focused field engagements, or piggyback on existing opportunities (for example, if customer support staff are already talking to users, designers can listen in or follow up with those users in context). Another tactic is quantifying qualitative findings where possible to speak the language of business. For example, "5 out of 6 customers we observed had trouble finding this feature, that's ~83%, which likely contributes to drop-offs in our analytics funnel." It ties ethnography to metrics.

There can also be resistance to change in organisations that are used to traditional processes. Some engineers or business analysts might be sceptical of sketching and storyboards, feeling it's not their domain. Overcoming this involves building multidisciplinary teams and emphasising that design thinking is *everyone's* job. Running training workshops or bringing in success stories can help. For example, showing the team a case where journey mapping led to a breakthrough product in another company can create buy-in ("Look, this is industry best practice now"). Small pilot projects can demonstrate the value.

One significant challenge is ensuring these tools deliver actionable outcomes without getting lost in translation. It's possible to have great research and maps, but it fails to turn them into design changes. To prevent this, teams should link findings to design requirements explicitly. A good habit is maintaining a backlog of "user needs/ pain points" derived from ethnography and journey maps and regularly prioritising them in sprint planning or product roadmaps. One or more proposed solutions (visualised concepts) should be tested or developed for each pain point. It creates traceability from insight to implementation.

Another challenge can be maintaining a user-centred approach under tight deadlines or conflicting objectives. Often, in group settings, there are conflicting objectives. For example, marketing wants a feature that pushes promotions, while UX is concerned it may annoy users. Here, journey mapping can serve as a neutral ground: bring everyone to look at the user journey and ask how each objective fits in. If a promotional popup is being debated, map where in the user journey it would occur and examine the user's emotional state at that moment. Is it right after purchase (maybe okay) or right when they open the app (maybe intrusive)? It can resolve conflicts by referencing the agreed-upon user experience flow. In essence, use the *user's voice as the arbitrator*.

Solutions to overcome challenges also include investing in the right tools and training. Providing teams with tools like remote research platforms, journey mapping software, or prototyping kits can ease adoption. For example, equipping field researchers with GoPro cameras or voice recorders can make ethnography more efficient (and shareable with the whole team afterwards). Using journey mapping templates or digital boards (like Miro or Lucidchart with journey map frameworks) can speed up the mapping process and allow easy editing as insights evolve. For visualisation, having software like Sketch/ Figma for interface prototypes or simple craft materials for physical mock-ups readily available lowers the barrier to prototyping.

Another solution is to create internal feedback loops and knowledge sharing. Successful teams using these methods in one project should share their experience and results with other teams (perhaps in an internal blog or lunch-and-learn). Hearing peers talk about how ethnography or prototyping saved the day can be more convincing than top-down directives. Many companies develop internal case studies of design thinking success that highlight the role of these tools. For instance, in its Enterprise Design Thinking initiative, IBM often cites how a multidisciplinary team observed healthcare clinicians (ethnography), mapped their workflow, and then rapidly prototyped a new interface that drastically reduced time spent on charting. Such stories underscore the practicality and ROI of the approach, helping overcome lingering scepticism.

In using these tools to improve user-centred design, one should also be mindful of measuring impact. Over time, sustaining support helps to show results: perhaps track customer satisfaction or engagement metrics before and after a design thinking revamp or count how many user issues were discovered and resolved through these methods. When business leaders see that, for example, *ethnographic research identified three major usability problems that, once fixed, led to a 20% drop in support calls,* the value becomes concrete. It encourages further investment in user research and iterative design.

In conclusion, the best strategy is making user-centred design a continuous cycle rather than a one-time phase. Ethnography should happen at the project start and post-launch (to see how users adapt or where new pain points emerge). Journey maps should be updated as services evolve or the team learns more (they can even map *future state* journeys to guide long-term vision). Visualisation and prototyping should continue throughout a product's life, even after launch. Teams can prototype improvements or new features and test them. An organisation essentially hardwires empathy and experimentation by embedding these practices into its DNA. The result is a steady improvement in user experience, which often correlates with improved business outcomes: more satisfied customers, greater loyalty, and a stronger brand reputation for being in tune with user needs. The next section will provide some exercises that can help practitioners (such as MBA students or innovation teams) build skills in these areas and some thought-provoking questions to spur further reflection on applying these tools in various business contexts.

1. Ethnography involves observing users in their natural environments to understand the reasons behind their behaviours. This exposes the latent needs, explaining the "show, don't tell" concept.
2. A journey presents the user's experience at every interaction point. It is essential to pinpoint pain points and "moments of truth," which enable the identification of opportunities for innovation.
3. Visualisation in the form of sketches, storyboards, and prototypes converts abstract ideas into tangible representations. This enhances the clarity of communication and seeks early-stage feedback thereby de-risking development and innovation processes.
4. Storyboards and journey maps capture user interactions and contextualise them. This fosters empathy, clarifies the context of a solution, and ensures functional and emotional satisfaction of the user.
5. Successfully using these tools requires more than just technique; it requires cultural change. Leaders must champion user-centricity, and teams must overcome resistance by demonstrating value through small wins and making these practices a routine part of their workflow.

KEY LEARNINGS

In this chapter, we explored how visualisation, ethnography, and journey mapping serve as foundational tools in design thinking, each contributing to a richer understanding of users and more innovative solutions:

- **Understanding Users is Paramount—Empathy is the Entry Point:** Effective design thinking begins with deeply understanding users' needs, contexts, and emotions. Ethnography immerses designers in the user's world, uncovering authentic behaviours and pain points that surveys or analytics alone might miss. Journey mapping then translates those findings into a clear storyline of the user experience, highlighting critical moments that matter most. Visualisation, through sketches and prototypes, ensures that ideas are always evaluated and developed about the user because visualising forces clarity and invites user feedback early. Together, these tools keep the design process human-centred at every step, from problem definition to solution iteration.
- **Visualisation Accelerates Innovation:** We learned that visualisation is far more than making pretty drawings; a thinking tool. Techniques like sketching, wireframing, and storyboarding help teams externalise ideas and collaborate. By getting ideas out of heads and onto paper (or screen), visualisation prevents misunderstandings and aligns stakeholders around a common vision. The IDEO case demonstrated how rapid prototyping (a form of visualisation) can lead to breakthrough products in a short time by facilitating quick user testing and iteration. A key lesson is "fail fast to succeed sooner". Early sketches and prototypes are expected to be rough but allow cheap failures that inform eventual success. Moreover, storyboards put a face on the user and context to the use case, helping communicate a solution and *why* it matters in a user's life.
- **Ethnography Uncovers the 'Why' Behind the 'What':** Through ethnographic case studies, we saw the power of observation and open-ended inquiry. Ford's ethnographic research unearthed why drivers felt the Mustang lacked power (a sensory expectation mismatch), an insight that pure performance data didn't reveal. Ethnography often reveals latent needs (e.g., Audi learning about horn usage in India) and workarounds users devise, indicating design opportunities. The key learning is that being present in the user's context (physically or via contextual interviews) yields rich qualitative data that can inspire design features and strategies that truly resonate. It reinforces that designers should be humble. Real users often do unexpected things with products; only by observing without bias can we learn those truths.
- **Journey Mapping Connects Dots and Exposes Gaps:** Journey maps taught us to look at the user experience holistically. Instead of optimising one touchpoint in isolation, journey thinking asks: what was the user doing *before* this, and what will they do *after*? By charting the full journey, organisations can avoid simply moving a problem from one stage to another and instead solve it in a way that improves

the flow for the user overall. Airbnb's mapping of guest and host journeys revealed "offline" moments where the company could do more (like the moment of arriving at a listing), leading to solutions beyond the app itself. A key takeaway is the importance of emotional peaks and valleys: they guide where to focus innovation (fix the lows, build on the highs). Journey mapping also serves as a communication tool to rally cross-departmental efforts around the customer's experience. It creates a shared empathy and language (e.g., talking about the "onboarding stage" or "post-purchase stage" with a common understanding of user feelings there).

- **Integrated Use Amplifies Impact:** Visualisation, ethnography, and journey mapping, combined, create a robust user-centered design loop. Ethnography informs journey maps (grounding them in reality), journey maps highlight areas to prototype, and visualisation brings those prototypes to life for testing, which can involve further ethnographic observation. The retail case study illustrated how all three led to tangible store improvements and business gains in tandem. The integrated approach ensures that insights are not lost: research findings directly influence design through journey maps, and design concepts are immediately validated in context with users. This integration leads to solutions that are not only creative but also viable and desired.
- **Challenges and Solutions in Implementation:** We also learned that implementing these tools requires cultural and organisational support. Potential challenges include stakeholder scepticism, time constraints, and superficial adoption (e.g., doing a journey map but not acting on it). Leadership involvement, continuous reference to user data in decision-making, and iterative cycles of prototyping and testing are key to embedding these practices. It's clear that simply having the tools isn't enough, as the team must cultivate empathy, curiosity, and willingness to experiment. When they do, the payoff is significant in terms of products and services that truly meet user needs and, often, innovative leaps that set companies apart from competitors stuck in inside-out thinking.

In essence, this chapter bridged theory and industry application. From academic concepts like empathy maps and user research methods to real company stories, it demonstrated that tools like visualisation, ethnography, and journey mapping are not just buzzwords but are practical techniques that drive better outcomes. By applying these tools, organisations large and small have improved customer satisfaction, uncovered new market opportunities, and de-risked product launches. For MBA students, understanding these approaches is crucial not just for design or innovation roles but for any leadership role that benefits from a deep understanding of customers (which is to say, nearly all). When approaching problems with a design thinker's toolkit, you essentially enforce a discipline: "Let's observe and listen first; let's map it out; let's try something and see if it works." This human-centred, iterative mindset can complement the analytical and strategic skills traditionally emphasised in business education.

EXERCISES

MBA students can engage in various hands-on exercises to solidify their understanding of visualisation, ethnography, and journey mapping and practice the collaboration and empathy these tools require. Individual and group activities are designed to simulate real-world scenarios and challenges. These exercises build skills in using the tools and highlight typical conflicts or constraints that arise in teams, requiring resolution through a design thinking mindset.

1. **Balancing Conflicting Objectives (Group)**—*"Designing a Customer Experience with Trade-offs."* Students are divided into small teams of 4–5. Each member secretly draws a card that assigns them a specific stakeholder perspective with a unique objective (e.g., one card says, *"You are the Marketing Manager—your goal is to maximise opportunities to upsell the customer."* Another says, *"You are the User Experience Lead—your goal is to minimise any friction for the customer."* Yet another: *"You represent Operations—your goal is to reduce service delivery costs."*). The group is told to design the journey map for a new coffee shop mobile ordering app together. Each member will advocate for their objective as they map the user journey (from ordering to pickup). Inevitably, some objectives will conflict (marketing might want a popup offer in the app, UX might argue that it could annoy users, etc.). The task for the team is to openly resolve these conflicts by referring to the user's perspective and finding creative compromises. For example, they might decide to include an upsell offer but only at a point in the journey that doesn't interrupt the flow (perhaps after the order is placed rather than before). By the end, the team produced a journey map poster with annotated notes of how they addressed each stakeholder's concerns in a user-centred way. A debrief discussion follows: How did the journey mapping exercise help balance the conflicting objectives? What was the negotiation like, and what principles guided the resolution?
2. **Role-Playing Ethnographic Research (Pairs or Triads)**—*"Customer Interview and Observation Simulation."* Students pair up (or form triads) and simulate an ethnographic field interview. One student plays the role of a user, and the other plays the role of a design researcher (if triads, one can be an observer/ note-taker). They are given a scenario such as *the user being a busy parent trying to manage their finances (paying bills, budgeting) using whatever tools or methods they currently use.* The "researcher" student must conduct a 15-minute ethnographic interview, preferably in a setting that represents the scenario (if in a classroom, maybe by imagining a home setting or looking at the user's laptop/cellphone as they would at home). The researcher should practice ethnographic techniques: asking open-ended questions ("Can you walk me through how you usually pay your bills each month?"), encouraging the user to demonstrate actions ("Could you show me how you log into your banking app?"), and probing for feelings ("What part of this process do you find most frustrating or time-consuming?"). The user (student playing that role) improvises answers based on common experiences or their

real habits. The researcher must take notes on the user's behaviours and quotes. After the role-play, the researcher summarises the key insights they gleaned. For instance, *"The user keeps a notebook with due dates and finds it annoying to sync that with digital reminders,"* or *"The user expressed anxiety about credit card debt but doesn't have an easy way to visualise payoff progress."* Then, they swap roles so that each student practices interviewing and being interviewed. This exercise builds empathy (as a researcher, you learn to listen and observe; as a user, you realise what it's like to be asked about your life) and skills in ethnographic inquiry. In a class debrief, students can reflect on what surprised them during interviews and how this method differs from a simple Q&A survey, highlighting the value of context and observation.

3. **Hands-on Visualization and Prototyping (Individual or Duo)**— *"Redesign a Service Touchpoint."* Each student (or duo) is given a brief to redesign a specific product or service interface visually. For example, *Redesign the ATM experience, Design a better grocery store check-out lane,* or *Sketch a mobile app for carpool coordination.* With a mix of individual creativity and, if paired, collaboration, students have to produce two forms of visualisation: (a) a sketch or wireframe of the improved design and (b) a storyboard of a user using it. For instance, if the task is ATM redesign, a student might sketch a new ATM screen flow with clearer prompts and maybe a contactless card reader. Then, they draw a 3-panel storyboard: Panel 1 shows a user arriving frustrated because there was a line, Panel 2 shows the user pleasantly surprised by the new ATM's quick one-tap withdrawal feature, and Panel 3 shows the user leaving happy in half the time. The purpose is visualisation to illustrate the solution and the user context. Students should do this within a limited time (say 20–30 minutes), emphasising quick visualisation over polished art. Afterwards, everyone can do a "gallery walk" of the sketches and storyboards and give feedback or ask questions. This exercise drives home how visualisation helps communicate an idea rapidly. Students often find that questions arise from looking at the sketch ("Where would the card slot be?" or "How does the carpool app handle last-minute cancellations?"), leading them to refine their thinking. In discussing the outcomes, the facilitator can highlight how some solutions might solve user pain points (did the storyboard clearly show an improved emotion or outcome for the user?) and how sketching made abstract ideas more concrete for critique.
4. **Journey Mapping with Real-World Personas (Group)**— *"Map the Customer Journey for X"* (with X being a familiar service). Break the class into groups of 4–5 and assign each group a different real-world user persona and scenario. For example, Group A gets *"Persona: young professional renting an apartment; Scenario: finding and moving into a new apartment."* Group B gets *"Persona: patient with a chronic condition; Scenario: monthly process of refilling a prescription."* Group C gets *"Persona: frequent business traveller; Scenario: door-to-door journey of a flight trip."* Each group's task is to create a detailed customer journey map for their persona's scenario. They should draw from their collective experiences or secondary research to outline stages, touchpoints, and emotions. For instance, the renting journey might include stages like searching online → Schedule Visits → Apartment Viewing, → Application →

Lease Signing → Move-in. The team would discuss what the person does and feels at each stage (excitement seeing a new listing, frustration with paperwork, stress on moving day, etc.). They then sketch the journey on a poster or whiteboard, using icons or brief notes, and mark pain points (maybe difficulty scheduling apartment viewings or anxiety waiting for application approval). Finally, each team presents their journey map to the class, speaking in first-person as the persona ("At this point, I'm nervous because I haven't heard back..." etc.). The rest of the class can ask questions or point out additional aspects ("Did you consider what happens if the moving truck is late? Maybe another pain point."). This group exercise reinforces the ability to think from a persona's viewpoint and map an experience from start to finish. It's an integrative practice because teams have to empathise (some light ethnography by recalling or gathering stories), synthesise into a journey (mapping), and communicate it visually. By comparing the different journey maps, students also see common patterns: most journeys have a "waiting" phase, a decision point, an information gap, etc., which often coincide with emotional lows, offering useful insights for any design endeavour.

5. **Conflict and Resolution Role-play (Group)**—*"Stakeholder Meeting: Implementing a Design Change."* This exercise simulates a scenario where a team has a clear user insight from ethnography and a journey map highlighting a needed change but faces internal resistance. Imagine a company that has journey-mapped its e-commerce check-out and found a major pain point: account creation is required before purchase, causing many drop-offs. The design team wants to implement a guest check-out. Now assign roles to a group of students: one is the UX designer advocating for guest check-out (user champion), one is the head of IT worried about data security, one is the marketing manager concerned about losing the ability to follow up if no account is created, one is the CFO thinking about impacts on customer lifetime value, etc. In a mock meeting, the UX designer presents the journey map snippet showing the drop-off at the "Create Account" step and shares a user quote from ethnographic research ("I closed the site when it forced me to register—I was in a hurry"). Then, each stakeholder weighs in with their concerns or support. The group must debate and reach a decision. This role-play often surfaces the classic tension between short-term business goals and long-term user satisfaction. The expected outcome is that the group finds a solution by referencing the user journey data and possibly visualising projected improvements (e.g., the designer might show a quick chart of how conversion could improve with guest check-out). Maybe a compromise like allowing guest check-out but prompting account creation after purchase, satisfying marketing's need for data without hurting the immediate user experience. The debrief highlights strategies to handle such conflicts: using evidence (the journey map, user quotes), visualising outcomes, and finding win-win via design (meeting user and business needs). It prepares MBA students for real corporate settings where they may need to advocate for user-centric changes in cross-functional teams.

These exercises underscore the practical use of visualisation, ethnography, and journey mapping while simulating real-world dynamics like conflicting objectives and team collaboration. By engaging in them, MBA students can better internalise the mindset of always considering the user's perspective, learn techniques to gather and analyse user insights and practice communication skills to convey design ideas and insights compellingly.

THOUGHT-PROVOKING QUESTIONS

To further internalise and apply the concepts from this chapter, consider the following questions. These are meant to stimulate critical thinking and encourage you to apply the tools to diverse business scenarios and strategic decisions:

1. **Beyond Products—Applying Journey Mapping to Systems:** How might you apply journey mapping to a *non-customer-facing* context, such as improving an employee experience or an internal process in an organisation? For example, if you were the HR director trying to improve the employee onboarding process at a large firm, what stages and touchpoints would you map, and what types of ethnographic research might you conduct to feed into that journey map? What emotional highs and lows might a new employee have, and how could visualisation help communicate and solve those?
2. **Ethnography in the Boardroom:** Imagine you are a management consultant hired by a bank that is losing millennial customers. The bank's executives are sceptical about investing in ethnographic research. They prefer Big Data and surveys. What argument would you make to convince them of ethnography's value, and how would you design an ethnographic study to complement the data they already have? Can you think of insights that numbers might miss but observations might catch (for instance, behaviours in a branch or how young customers use fintech apps alongside their bank accounts)? How would you tie those qualitative findings to strategic recommendations?
3. **Rapid vs. Rigorous:** The Time Investment Dilemma: There's often pressure to skip research and get straight to building in fast-paced industries. How can teams balance the need for speed with the need for empathy? Can you imagine a scenario where doing minimal ethnography or a quick-and-dirty journey map might save time by preventing rework or feature creep later? Conversely, are there situations where deep ethnography might not be worth the effort (for example, extremely time-sensitive projects or when prior research exists)? Discuss how you would decide the depth of research appropriate for a project and ensure user feedback is incorporated even under tight timelines.
4. **Global Challenges and Cultural Context:** Many businesses operate globally. How do visualisation, ethnography, and journey mapping help (or need to be adapted) to design for different cultures and markets? For example, consider designing a ride-sharing app in dense cities like New York and more rural regions in India. Ethnographically, what different behaviours or needs might you find? How would you map a user journey for booking a ride in these two contexts, and what differences might emerge? What role could visualisation play in aligning a

global team around these differences to develop a locally relevant product? How do these tools aid in a service's glocalisation (global + localisation)?

5. **Measuring Success of Design Thinking Initiatives:** A CFO might ask, "We invested in all this user research and prototyping; how do we know it's paying off?" What metrics or indicators would you use to measure the impact of ethnography, journey mapping, and rapid prototyping in a project? For instance, would you look at product success rates, development cycle time improvements, customer satisfaction scores, innovation count (number of new ideas implemented), or something else? Can you design a simple framework to attribute improved performance to these practices (recognising it's sometimes hard to isolate cause and effect)? This question asks you to connect the soft tools of design to hard business outcomes, a critical skill in advocating for human-centred design in traditional business environments.
6. **Ethical Considerations in Ethnography:** When conducting ethnographic research, especially in healthcare or public sectors, what ethical considerations should a design thinker be mindful of? (Think about privacy, consent, and impact.) For example, if you're mapping patients' experiences in a hospital ER, ethnography might involve observing people at vulnerable moments. How would you approach that ethically? How can visualisation and mapping be done in a way that respects the dignity and anonymity of participants? This question urges reflection on the responsibility of deeply researching people's lives and representing them in design artefacts.
7. **From Insight to Ideation—Bridging the Gap:** Have you ever used a product or service and thought, "Didn't they realise users would experience X problem?" Describe that scenario and assume the role of a design consultant brought in to fix it. What ethnographic method might you employ to validate the problem's existence and uncover why it was missed? Sketch a quick journey map of that user experience to pinpoint where the breakdown occurs. Then, propose at least one visualisation (prototype) of a solution to address it. Essentially, perform a mini design-thinking analysis on that real-world pain point. This question is personal and practical as it asks you to apply the chapter's tools to something tangible in your experience, closing the loop from theory to practice.

By grappling with these questions, you will deepen your appreciation for how visualisation, ethnography, and journey mapping can be leveraged in various business contexts ranging from high-level strategy to on-the-ground product tweaks. They challenge you to consider implementation in different domains and articulate the value of design thinking tools in business terms. Ultimately, the goal is to train you to think like a design thinker: always observing, always mapping the human side of the equation, and always prototyping improvements, even in domains that aren't traditionally seen as "design." This integration of empathic research and iterative development with business acumen is what many companies are now looking for in management roles, as it has proven to drive innovation and customer-centric transformation.

In conclusion, remember the core lesson: keeping the user at the centre through these tools is not just about doing good design; it's good business. Companies that deeply understand and continuously improve their customer journeys (think Apple, Amazon, and Starbucks, to name a few) tend to outperform those that do not. As you progress, consider how you will champion user-centred approaches in your projects and organisations. What will your next journey map reveal? What surprising user story will your next field observation uncover? And how quickly will you sketch the next idea to make someone's experience better? The tools are now in your hands, and their power lies in how creatively and earnestly you use them to bridge the gap between theory and real-world impact.

REFERENCES

Bell, A. (2021, May 3). Why Ford Thinks Human-Centric Design Is the Future. The Next Web. Retrieved January 10, 2025, from https://thenextweb.com/news/why-ford-thinks-human-centric-design-is-future

CliffsNotes. (2004). Design Thinking Study Notes. CliffsNotes. Retrieved January 10, 2025, from https://www.cliffsnotes.com/study-notes/22363138

Insight7. (n.d.). Real-World Ethnographic Research Examples in Business. Insight7 Blog. Retrieved January 10, 2025, from https://insight7.io/real-world-ethnographic-research-examples-in-business/

Jaafari, S. (2016, July 31). India Inc: Audi makes extra-durable horns for cars sold in India. The World (PRI). Retrieved January 10, 2025, from https://theworld.org/stories/2016/07/31/indiainc-audi-makes-extra-durable-horns-cars-sold-india

Sequoia Capital. (2023, February 10). Visualizing Customer Experience. Sequoia Articles. Retrieved January 10, 2025, from https://articles.sequoiacap.com/visualizing-customer-experience

Smith, J., & Davis, L. (2022, July 15). Stories That Deliver Business Insights. MIT Sloan Management Review. Retrieved January 10, 2025, from https://sloanreview.mit.edu/article/stories-that-deliver-business-insights/

Sprout Social. (2020, June 22). Customer Journey Mapping: A Step-by-Step Guide. Sprout Social Insights. Retrieved January 10, 2025, from https://sproutsocial.com/insights/customer-journey-mapping/

CHAPTER

7 Ten Essential Tools for Design Thinking

LEARNING OBJECTIVES

After reading this Chapter, the readers will be able to:

- Identify ten fundamental design thinking tools—Gain knowledge of ten essential tools used in design thinking and innovation. By the end of the chapter, readers will be able to list and describe each tool, such as empathy maps, personas, brainstorming techniques, mind maps, prototyping, storyboards, customer journey maps, etc., including the purpose of each tool and which stage of the design thinking process it supports.
- Understand the purpose and use of each tool—Explain how each tool facilitates user-centric problem-solving. For example, articulate how empathy mapping and personas help in the Empathise/Define stages by capturing user needs, how techniques like "How Might We" questions or brainstorming spur creative Ideation, and how prototyping and testing tools (like paper prototypes or user feedback sessions) help in quickly validating ideas.
- Learn through real-world examples—Understand how these tools are applied in practice by businesses and teams. The chapter will highlight case studies (e.g., how IBM uses empathy maps to redesign workflows, how Airbnb used storyboarding to improve its service, or how Google employs rapid prototyping in product development). By studying these examples, readers will appreciate the tangible impact of each tool and learn when and why organisations choose a particular tool to drive innovation.
- Select and apply the right tool for the job—Develop the ability to choose appropriate design thinking tools for different challenges. Readers will be able to decide which tool(s) to use in a given scenario—for instance, knowing to use an affinity diagram to organize research findings or a stakeholder map to understand influences in a project. They will also learn how to apply these tools step-by-step, ensuring they can put the chapter's methods into practice during team projects or problem-solving workshops.

- Recognise challenges and best practices: Acknowledge common challenges in using design thinking tools and learn strategies to overcome them. For example, understand how to avoid groupthink during brainstorming, how to ensure unbiased user research when creating empathy maps, or how to iterate a prototype based on feedback without getting discouraged. By the end, readers will master best practices for each tool—like facilitating effective brainstorm sessions, crafting useful user personas, or conducting low-cost experiments—thereby building confidence in their design thinking toolkit.

7.1 INTRODUCTION TO DESIGN THINKING TOOLS

Design thinking is a human-centred approach to innovation, widely adopted to solve complex problems in business and society. It involves a creative, iterative process (often summarized as *Empathize—Define—Ideate—Prototype—Test*) that puts users at the centre of solution development. In practice, design thinking is empowered by tools that help teams apply this approach effectively. These tools matter because they translate abstract design principles into actionable methods. They allow teams to visualize insights, organize ideas, and test assumptions in tangible ways, thus fostering user-centred innovation and collaborative problem-solving.

Leading companies attribute much of their innovative edge to applying design thinking tools. For example, global tech firms like Google and Apple integrate design thinking exercises into product development to refocus on user needs continually. IBM reportedly trained thousands of employees in design thinking methods, using empathy mapping and prototyping tools to reimagine workflows and improve customer experiences. Airbnb famously used storyboards (a design tool discussed later) to overhaul its service experience, leading to a breakthrough in growth. Amazon employs a "working backwards" approach, essentially a design thinking mindset that involves drafting press releases and FAQs from the customer's perspective before development, ensuring empathy for the end-user is built in from the start. These examples underscore that design thinking tools are not academic exercises but practical instruments that drive real-world innovation.

In this chapter, we will explore ten essential design thinking tools, including what they are, how they facilitate user-centric design and concrete examples of their use in business. Each section will introduce the tool, explain its purpose in the design thinking process, and provide case studies from industries like fintech, e-commerce, tech, and entertainment. We'll also consider challenges in using each tool and strategies to overcome them, ensuring you understand the what and how and the when and why for each method. By the end, you should have a well-stocked toolkit for approaching problems with a designer's mindset, a key skill for any MBA aiming to lead innovation.

7.2 EMPATHY MAPS

One of the first steps in design thinking is empathy, understanding the user's feelings, thoughts, and context. An empathy map is a visual tool that captures these insights. Typically divided into four quadrants: *Says, Thinks, Does,* and *Feels,* an empathy map externalizes what we know about a user or persona. By charting direct quotes (Says), observations of behaviour (Does), inferred thoughts (Thinks), and emotional states (Feels), design teams can create a holistic picture of the user's experience. This process helps teams align on a deep understanding of the end user; *"visualizing user attitudes and behaviours in an empathy map helps UX teams align on a deep understanding of end users."*. Empathy maps ensure the team "steps into the user's shoes," going beyond demographics to see the world from the user's perspective.

How empathy maps help: They distil qualitative user research into an easily digestible diagram. By filling out an empathy map, teams uncover user needs and pain points that might not be immediately obvious from raw data. The shared visual reference guides discussions and prevents team members from relying on their assumptions. As design leader Indi Young notes, empathy mapping forces us to focus on *the users' reality,* not our own. The tool is handy early in a project when defining the problem space because it highlights gaps in our knowledge (e.g., an empty quadrant might indicate we need more user interviews in that area). It also lays the groundwork for other tools: empathy maps often feed into creating personas and inform journey maps by revealing what the user is thinking or feeling at each interaction.

CASE STUDY: Empathy Mapping in a Fintech Startup

Imagine a fintech startup designing a new mobile banking app. The product team conducts user interviews and surveys to learn about potential customers, young professionals and older, less tech-savvy retirees. The team creates empathy maps for two archetypal users to synthesise this research. For the retiree persona "Ray," they populate the map with observations: Ray *SAYS* he feels nervous about online security, *THINKS* he might make a mistake and lose money, *DOES* things like writing down his PIN on paper, and *FEELS* embarrassed that he has to ask his daughter for help with mobile apps. This empathy map vividly highlights Ray's pain points (e.g. fear of app complexity) and goals (confidence and security in managing his money).

In contrast, the young professional persona "Aria" *SAYS* she's frustrated by how long traditional bank transfers take. *THINKS* banking should be as easy as texting, *DOES* multitask on several finance applications and *FEELS* anxious about hitting her savings targets. By visualizing these side by side, the designers identify common needs (both users desire more clarity and control) and unique concerns (Ray needs extra reassurance on security, while Aria craves speed and analytics). The empathy maps prevent the team from designing for an "average user" that might miss both targets. Instead, the team empathizes with very specific users when brainstorming features, perhaps leading to a simplified interface mode for Ray and an AI budgeting coach for Aria.

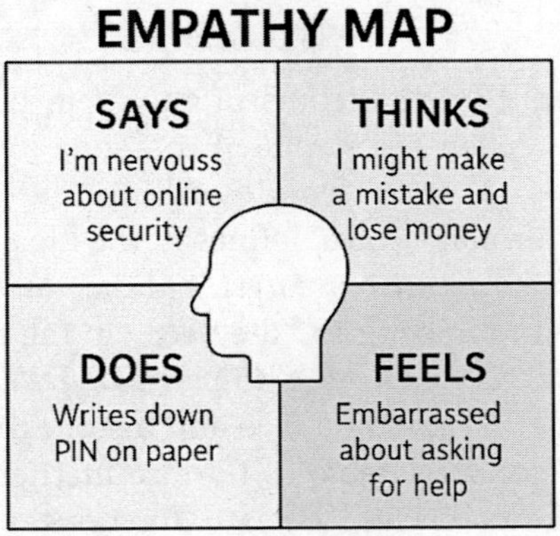

FIGURE 7.1 Empathy Map.

Notably, a real fintech UX case echoes this process. In a UX redesign for a banking app, designers built empathy maps that revealed many pain points and emotional frustrations users had with existing banking services. For example, one finding was that users felt *confused* and *intimidated* by the outdated designs of current banking apps, which hindered them from understanding their finances. Insights like these, drawn from empathy maps, drove the team to prioritize a cleaner visual design and on-screen guidance in the new app. The result was a mobile banking experience that test users described as "enjoyable and fun", a far cry from the typical sentiment toward banking apps.

Challenges and tips: Empathy maps are powerful but have limitations and potential pitfalls. One common challenge is the lack of real data. If the map is based on team assumptions rather than user research, it can become a work of fiction. Jeanne Liedtka, a professor and design thinking expert, cautions that teams must avoid projecting their biases onto the map. Ensuring the map is grounded in *research* (interviews, observations, etc.) is key. Another issue can be creating too many personas or maps, which dilutes focus. It's usually better to start with a few primary user types. Teams also sometimes struggle with how much detail to include, as an overly vague map isn't actionable, but an overly detailed one can be overwhelming. Strive for balance by capturing memorable quotes and striking insights rather than every data point. There's also the challenge of keeping the empathy map up to date. It's a snapshot in time; the map should be updated as user attitudes evolve. Otherwise, it risks becoming a static artefact that doesn't reflect current realities.

Lastly, be aware of the scope. An empathy map usually focuses on a specific context or scenario (e.g., "Using the mobile banking app to deposit a check"). It may become too generic if you try to map everything about a user. Teams should define a clear scope or goal for the empathy mapping session (what insight are we seeking?) and possibly do multiple maps for different scenarios or segments.

In summary, empathy maps are a foundational design thinking tool to build user understanding and empathy. Visualizing what users say, think, do, and feel helps ensure the design process begins with genuine insight. As a result, solutions are more likely to resonate with user needs and overcome user frustrations. Many practitioners consider empathy mapping the first step in design thinking, setting the tone for user-centred innovation.

7.3 PERSONAS

After empathizing with users broadly, teams often create personas, fictional yet realistic characters representing key user segments. A persona typically includes a name, a demographic summary, and a narrative describing the person's goals, needs, and behaviours. As the Nielsen Norman Group defines it, the idea is that *"personas are personified representations of real information about our target audience that enable us to design with real customers in mind."* Rather than referring to "the user" in the abstract, the team can discuss design decisions in terms of *"Would Jim, a 45-year-old freelance accountant and our target persona, find this feature useful?"* By giving a face and a story to user research data, personas make users more memorable and relatable to the product team.

How personas bridge research and design: Personas are created based on patterns observed in user research. Teams aggregate individual data points into a composite character that exemplifies a group of users. For instance, suppose a research phase for a new e-commerce website finds two dominant shopper types: "Bargain Hunter" (price-sensitive, compares many sites, needs trust signals) and "Time-Pressed Professional" (willing to pay more for convenience, values quick checkout). From this, the team might flesh out two personas: *Barry, the Bargain Hunter* and *Priya, the Busy Professional*. Barry's persona would detail his tight budget, how he scours coupon sites, his frustration with unexpected shipping fees (a pain point), and his delight when finding a great deal (a motivator). Priya's persona would highlight her lack of time, preference for reliable brands, irritation with lengthy forms, and relief when a purchase is swift and easy. By articulating these, designers can continually check that design choices serve one or both persona's priorities. For example, Barry's presence will remind the team to make discounts and prices prominent, whereas Priya's needs will push them to offer features like saved payment info for one-click purchases. In this way, personas bridge raw research and design decisions and translate observations into design directives by providing an archetype to design *for*.

Importantly, personas encapsulate functional needs and emotional and social contexts. They often include a quote or tagline (e.g., Priya might say, "I shop on my phone between meetings—speed is everything to me"). It helps the team internalize what matters most to that user. Personas also list specific pain points and motivations. These elements ensure that when trade-offs occur in development, the discussion can reference user impact: *"We can't remove the guest checkout—Priya would abandon the cart if forced to register, as indicated by her persona."*

CASE STUDY: How Amazon uses Personas

Amazon is known for its customer-centric approach, often saying they work backwards from the customer. Amazon's design teams maintain this focus by using detailed personas in the product design process. For example, Amazon has many customer personas, varying from a busy suburban mom shopping for household items to a tech-savvy urban millennial looking for the latest gadgets. In one account, a designer described a persona called "Jane, the Amazon Prime Queen," representing a busy working mother who values convenience. Jane's persona is described as tech-savvy but time-strapped; she values quick delivery and a hassle-free experience. This persona *guides every design decision, from the intuitive search bar to curated product recommendations*. When Amazon was refining its mobile app and website, the team continuously asked, "Does this feature help Jane?" They knew, for instance, that *Jane hates lengthy searches and comparison hassle*, so Amazon invested heavily in search algorithms and filters to surface relevant products quickly and features like "Frequently Bought Together" to assist decision-making. They also knew *Jane appreciated personalized recommendations (as she had* little time to browse), which drove Amazon's well-known recommendation engine. By designing for a persona like Jane, Amazon ensures its customer experience caters to real user needs (millions of "Janes"). The persona gives a human face to piles of user data as it's easier to rally a team around delighting "Jane" than to a nebulous idea of "target user segment A."

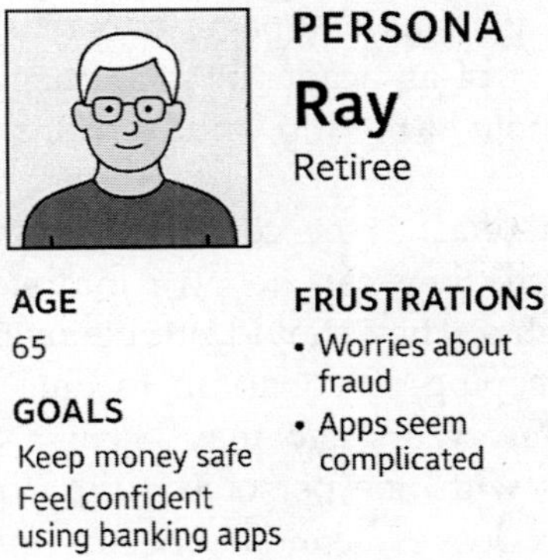

FIGURE 7.2 Personas.

Personas vs. Empathy Maps—when to use each: Personas and empathy maps are complementary tools, and sometimes they can be used together. One recommended practice is to create a quick empathy map for each persona to deepen that persona's profile. However, there are distinctions. An empathy map is typically grounded in a specific user (or an aggregate of a few real users). It focuses on their mindset in a particular context (often early in the research to gather raw understanding). A persona is a more polished artefact, a composite model answering *who* the user is generally and summarizing patterns across many individuals. One key difference: *Personas are fictional (but representative) constructs, while empathy maps are often directly based on real data from real people.* One source notes that *"the main difference between an empathy map and a persona is that personas are based on fictional users, whereas empathy maps are based on real people. User personas tell you who your customers are, while empathy maps tell you what those customers' attitudes and behaviours are."*.

Use empathy maps to immerse the team in the users' mindset or when you have fresh research data to synthesize, especially in the early *Empathize* stage of design thinking. Use personas as you move from research to ideation, as they serve as a reference throughout design and development. Personas are also great for communicating research insights to stakeholders in a storytelling format (stakeholders can often remember "Alice the Entrepreneur" better than a list of demographic stats). If time is short or the project scope is small, teams might skip formal personas and use empathy maps or simple user profiles.

Conversely, personas become part of the product's documentation in long-term product development and help onboard new team members to identify the users.

Illustration: Example of a persona template. A typical persona template includes a name and possibly a photo (to humanize the character), demographic info (age, occupation, and location to ground the context), a brief biography or narrative ("Alice is a 32-year-old marketing manager who commutes to the city..."), goals and needs ("wants to stay fit despite a busy schedule"), frustrations/ pain points ("finds it hard to meal-plan healthy options"), and behaviours ("uses apps like Fitbit, orders groceries online"). It might also list the technologies or channels the persona uses (mostly mobile vs. desktop, for instance) and a quote that sums up their attitude ("I'll try anything that makes my daily routine easier"). Good persona templates use visual cues to make information scannable: icons for goals, perhaps a thermometer icon to indicate tech-savviness level, etc. The aim is for any team member to glance at the persona one-pager and recall the key points when making design decisions. (In the context of an academic text, imagine a figure showing a persona card with name, photo, and quote at the top, split sections for goals, frustrations, bio, and environment.)

Challenges in using personas: One common criticism of personas is that if they are not based on solid research, they can devolve into stereotyping or fiction. Personas must stem from real user insights. They should not be invented by the team's imagination alone. Another challenge is keeping personas up to date. Markets and user behaviours change; a persona created a few years ago may become obsolete if not revisited. Also, teams sometimes over-identify with one persona at the expense of others. Focusing only on the primary persona might leave secondary needs unmet if a product has multiple segments. To mitigate this, keep personas grounded in core needs validated across multiple individuals and use data (analytics or ongoing user feedback) to validate that your personas are still representative continuously. Lastly, ensure the team embraces personas. Sometimes, documentation can be created and ignored. Integrate persona review into design critiques ("Which persona is this feature for? Does it solve their story?") so that they remain living tools rather than wallpaper. When used thoughtfully, personas become "stand-ins" for the customer at every meeting, ensuring the real customer's voice is never lost during design and development.

7.4 CUSTOMER JOURNEY MAPS

A customer journey map is a visual narrative of the end-to-end experience a user (or customer) has when trying to accomplish a goal with a product or service. It typically plots the user's journey as a sequence of steps or stages (often from initial awareness, exploration, purchase, or use to post-use feedback). It highlights the user's actions, thoughts, and emotions at each stage. In essence, a journey map answers the question: *What is the story of the user's experience from their point of view?*

Journey maps usually take the form of a diagram or infographic. Along the top, you might see stages such as *"Discover"* → *"Sign Up"* → *"Onboard"* → *"Use"* → *"Support"*. Under each stage, the map will detail what the user is doing, feeling or thinking and any pain points or delights encountered. Some maps also layer in the touchpoints (e.g., website, phone support, in-store) and the responsible internal departments for each part (marketing, sales, UX, customer service), which can illuminate gaps or handoff issues in the experience. The power of a journey map is that it combines storytelling and visualization. It forces an organization to view the experience holistically, beyond internal silos. By doing so, teams can spot friction points and opportunities that might be missed when looking at individual interactions in isolation.

Steps in creating an effective journey map: While journey maps come in many formats, the creation process generally involves: (1) Define the Persona and Scenario. Decide whose journey you are mapping and for what goal. For example, "the journey of a first-time user ordering food through our app." Ground this in a persona (e.g., Persona: college student Jake, Scenario: ordering late-night pizza delivery). (2) Map the Stages. Outline the key phases of this journey. For ordering food, stages might be *Hunger/ Need → Search → Order → Wait → Receive → Eat → Post-meal.* (3) Research and Data Collection. Use user interviews, surveys, support call logs, etc., to gather information on what users do and feel at each stage. If possible, include direct quotes: e.g., at the "Wait" stage, Jake might think, "Why is it taking so long?" and feel anxious or impatient. (4) Chart User Actions, Emotions, and Pain Points. For each stage, please describe what the user is doing (actions), their questions or thoughts, and their emotional state. Use symbols or colour coding to denote positive or negative emotions (a smile/ frown icon or green/ red shading). (5) Identify Touchpoints and Opportunities. Note where the interactions occur (mobile app, SMS notification, door delivery, etc.) and how smooth or problematic each touchpoint is. It often reveals *moments of truth,* key moments significantly influencing overall satisfaction. (6) Brainstorm Improvements. Once the current-state journey is mapped and pain points are clear, the team can ideate on a future-state journey with a better experience (this might be done as a separate mapping exercise or annotated on the current map).

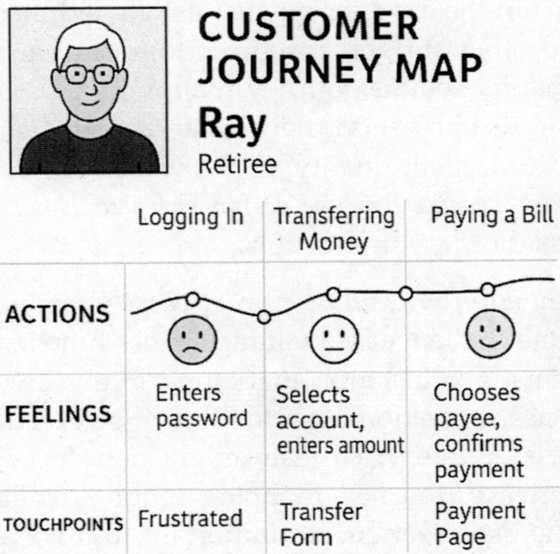

FIGURE 7.3 Customer Journey Map.

To illustrate, consider a journey map for a hotel booking website. Stages: *Dreaming → Research → Booking → Pre-stay → Stay → Post-stay*. In the *research stage, a user's action is browsing photos and reading reviews; a thought might be, "Will this hotel look as nice as the pictures?"* Emotion could be uncertainty. A pain point could be if the site lacks reviews or price comparisons that require extra effort. Later, in the *Stay* stage, the journey map might capture whether the check-in process was smooth, if the room met expectations, etc. By laying this out, the hotel's team sees that even though their website UX might be great up to the booking, the journey falters if the front-desk check-in (a touchpoint) is slow, something a purely digital analysis wouldn't catch. This comprehensive view helps allocate resources to the most impactful parts of the experience, whether digital or physical.

CASE STUDY: How Airbnb used Journey Mapping to Improve Experiences

One famous example of journey mapping comes from Airbnb. Around 2012, struggling to gain traction, Airbnb's founders decided to map out their guests' and hosts' entire end-to-end journey, drawing inspiration from Disney's approach to storyboarding films. They code-named this effort "Project Snow White." The team storyboarded the experience: they *"created a list of the emotional moments that comprise an Airbnb stay"* and then illustrated the most critical moments as frames in a movie. For guests, these moments included things like the excitement of browsing listings, the trepidation before arrival ("Will the place match the photos?"), and the relief of a warm welcome by the host. For hosts, moments included the decision to list their home, preparing for guests, and receiving feedback after the stay. By visualizing each stage and the emotions tied to it, Airbnb identified critical pain points. For example, one *"gap"* in the journey was that new hosts didn't know how to be good hosts, leading to inconsistent guest experiences. In response, Airbnb introduced host education materials and a Superhost program (to incentivize great hospitality), directly addressing that stage of the host journey. They also realized the importance of the first night's stay for guests; any hiccup could ruin the experience. That insight led them to implement a 24-hour customer service line and other support resources to ensure any issues on day one were immediately resolved. This meticulous journey mapping (and storyboarding) approach is credited with transforming Airbnb's service design and is often cited as a turning point that helped Airbnb scale with consistent quality. In the words of Airbnb's Joe Gebbia, journey mapping with storyboards *"became how we design every touchpoint"*, ensuring they deliver magical travel experiences, not just transactions.

Challenges in journey mapping and best practices: Creating a thorough journey map can be time-consuming. One challenge is obtaining a cross-functional view, the journey often spans multiple departments. For instance, marketing might own the "awareness" phase, UX the "website use" phase, operations the "delivery" or execution phase, and customer support the "post-purchase" phase. Each team might only focus on their slice, leading to a disjointed overall experience. Journey mapping requires collaboration and sometimes breaking down silos in the organization. It's important to involve representatives from all relevant departments in the mapping workshops. Another challenge is data, ensuring the map reflects reality. It should be backed by user research and analytics. If you lack direct input for certain stages (e.g., what customers think during shipping), consider methods like surveys or user diaries to fill those gaps.

Once created, a journey map should be used, not just filed away. A common pitfall is treating the map as the end goal; the real goal is to drive improvements. To avoid the journey map becoming "another document gathering dust," assign owners to follow up on the key pain points identified and brainstorm solutions. Also, maintain the journey map as a living document. Customer journeys can change with new technologies or market trends. Reviewing and updating the map (say, every 6-12 months or when introducing significant new features) will keep it relevant. Finally, if your product serves very distinct personas, you may need multiple journey maps, one for each persona's experience, because their journeys could differ significantly. For example, if mapping an e-commerce journey, a tech-savvy millennial's path (mobile app heavy, social media influenced) might vary from a senior citizen's path (desktop site, maybe telephone support included). It's better to have separate maps than to generalize so much that the map loses specificity.

In conclusion, journey mapping is a powerful tool to visualize the *user's holistic experience,* often revealing the "weak links" that need strengthening. It combines the empathy of looking from the user's viewpoint with the analytical process design approach. When done well, a journey map serves as a blueprint for delivering a seamless and positive user experience across all touchpoints. Firms from Airbnb to Starbucks have used journey maps to step up their customer experience game, making this tool a staple in the design thinking arsenal for services and omnichannel products.

7.5 BRAINSTORMING

Once a problem is defined and user insights are gathered, teams move into ideation, generating creative solutions. Brainstorming is the classic tool for this phase. Coined by Alex Osborn in the 1940s, brainstorming is a group idea-generation technique that encourages quantity over quality in its initial stage: the philosophy is that by suspending criticism and letting ideas flow freely, teams can unlock more innovative and out-of-the-box concepts. The core rules of traditional brainstorming are: *defer judgment, aim for a large number of ideas, encourage wild ideas,* and *build on the ideas of others*. The method usually involves a group of people in a room (or virtual space), a facilitator to guide, a time limit, and lots of sticky notes or whiteboard space to capture ideas. Brainstorming is valued in design thinking because it leverages diverse perspectives and creative thinking to explore the solution space without immediate constraints.

Generating a wide range of creative ideas: The strength of brainstorming lies in its ability to tap into collective creativity. Team members might have latent ideas or half-formed notions that only surface in a brainstorming session's energetic, permissive environment. Often, one person's offbeat suggestion will spark a related thought in another participant, leading to a chain reaction of ideas that wouldn't emerge in isolation. For example, one designer might say, "What if our food delivery drone could also play music when it arrives?" which prompts an engineer to add, "Maybe it could have a voice that gives a personalized greeting." Another team member then suggests, "Actually, what if it also projected a light show on your door?", now these might not all be feasible or practical, but within those wild ideas might be a nugget that is useful (perhaps the concept of a delightful, multi-sensory delivery experience). Brainstorming allows the team to explore far-fetched concepts safely, which can later be toned down or combined into viable solutions.

Techniques to enhance brainstorming: Over the years, many variants and methods have been developed to improve the effectiveness of brainstorming sessions:

- **Crazy 8s:** This is a fast-paced ideation exercise often used in design sprints. Each person takes a sheet of paper, folds it to create 8 panels, and then has 8 minutes to sketch 8 distinct ideas (rough drawings), one per panel. The purpose is to push participants beyond their first idea (often the obvious one) and encourage quick divergent thinking. The tight time limit forces people not to overthink and to illustrate concepts rapidly. Crazy 8s is beneficial for UI/ UX design, where participants sketch interface ideas that can be adapted to any visual ideation. After 8 minutes, everyone shares their sketches. Even if some squares are "crazy," the exercise guarantees a minimum of 8 × N ideas (if N participants) to discuss.
- **Brainwriting:** A twist on brainstorming, brainwriting involves individuals writing down ideas on paper or notes *quietly* before any discussion happens. In one common format, each person writes three ideas in 5 minutes, then passes their paper to the next person, who reads those ideas and adds 3 more, and so on for a few rounds. This method addresses a challenge in traditional brainstorming: often, louder or more assertive voices dominate the conversation, and social pressure or groupthink can stifle independent ideas. Brainwriting ensures everyone contributes, including more introverted team members, resulting in a richer pool of ideas. It also allows building on others' ideas in written form. Studies have found brainwriting can produce more ideas than verbal brainstorming in many cases. After the writing rounds, the group can discuss the collected ideas.
- **SCAMPER:** This is an acronym-based prompt list to spur idea generation by systematically modifying existing ideas. SCAMPER stands for Substitute, Combine, Adapt, Modify (or Magnify/ Minify), Put to another use, Eliminate, Reverse. Using SCAMPER, the team takes a current product or process and asks questions like: *"What can we Substitute here?"* (e.g., substitute material or a step), *"What can we Combine?"* (e.g., combine two features into one), *"Can we Adapt something from another industry?", "What if we Magnify this element or Minify it?", "Could this be used for a different purpose?", "What if we Eliminated this step?"*, and *"What if we Reversed the process or did it backwards?"*. Each prompt often yields several ideas. SCAMPER is a structured way to break out of conventional thinking by systematically exploring transformations of an idea.

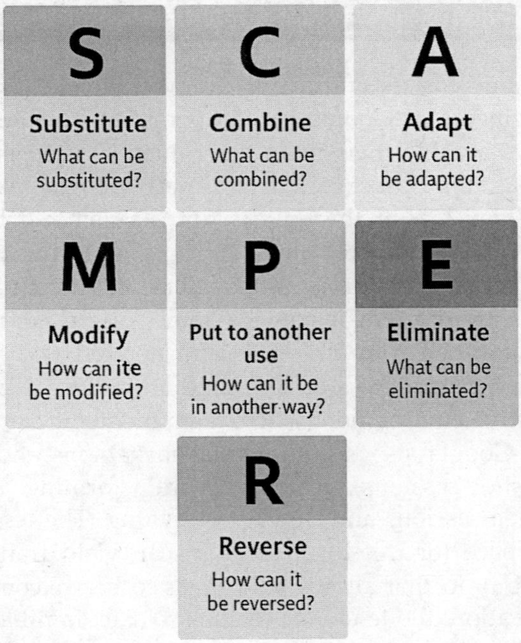

Additionally, there are other ideation techniques like role-storming (brainstorming as if you are someone else, e.g., "What would Elon Musk suggest?"), worst possible idea (imagine terrible solutions to inspire good ones by inversion paradoxically), and mind mapping (which we cover in the next section but can be used during brainstorming to expand on themes). Using a mix of techniques keeps sessions fresh and can overcome creative blocks.

Readers are encouraged to watch the lecture on SCAMPER by visiting—https://youtu.be/_qgSZikOPB4.

Alternatively, one could scan below presented QR code to watch the lecture.

SCAN ME

Scan to watch the lecture—SCAMPER.

CASE STUDY: Google's 20% Time Fosters Innovation through Brainstorming

Google has become iconic for its culture of innovation, one aspect of which was the "20% time" policy. Engineers at Google could spend 20% of their time (essentially one day a week) on projects outside their main assignments, often effectively brainstorming and pursuing their ideas. This practice led to Gmail, Google Maps, AdSense and other significant products. While 20% of the time is not a structured brainstorming *session*, it institutionalized the spirit of brainstorming, giving people unstructured time to ideate and experiment. Within those 20% projects, Googlers often team up (mini brainstorming groups) to bounce ideas around. For instance, Gmail's origin is attributed to an engineer, Paul Buchheit, who prototyped it in 20% time and iterated with peer feedback before it became an official project. The success of 20% time underlines a key principle of effective brainstorming: a supportive environment where team members can explore and share ideas without fear of failure. Google also hosts internal hackathons and innovation workshops (like Google X's moonshot sessions), essentially brainstorming at scale, often applying techniques like crazy idea sessions and rapid prototyping. The lesson from Google is that carving out time and space for free-form ideation can yield transformative innovations, but it requires cultural buy-in that allows wild ideas to be welcomed. It addresses one of the biases hamper innovation: the tendency to stick to safe, familiar solutions. By formally allocating time to "think outside the box," Google counteracted that bias and empowered employees to take creative risks.

When brainstorming fails—pitfalls and solutions: Despite its popularity, brainstorming doesn't always work perfectly. Some common pitfalls include:

- **Groupthink:** In traditional brainstorming, once a few ideas are spoken, the group may subconsciously converge around those ideas' themes, limiting originality. People might hesitate to voice ideas that are too different from what's already been said.

  Solution: Encourage independent idea generation first (as in brainwriting or silent brainstorming) before group discussion. Also, having a diverse group helps; if participants come from different backgrounds, they are less likely to all think alike.
- **Dominating personalities:** Strong or senior voices may overshadow others. Others might self-censor if the boss is in the room enthusiastically suggesting ideas.

  Solution: Set ground rules like *"all ideas have equal weight"*. A facilitator can actively ensure everyone gets to speak. Techniques like going around in a round-robin fashion or giving everyone equal post-it notes to contribute can prevent one-person dominance. Brainwriting, again, is a great equalizer.
- **Evaluating too soon:** If critique or evaluation creeps in (even via body language or a sceptical tone), it can shut down the free flow of ideas.

  Solution: The facilitator should remind everyone that *no idea is criticized* during the idea generation phase. Separate the phases of *ideation* and *evaluation*. You might even physically separate them. For example, use one sticky note colour in a brainstorm, then move to another colour for comments/votes on those ideas.

- **Too abstract or unfocused questions:** A brainstorming session can flounder if the prompt is unclear or too broad. Ideas will be scattered or superficial if people are unsure what problem they're solving.

  Solution: To focus the brainstorm, define a clear problem statement or "How Might We...?" question. For example, "How might we reduce wait time in our support chat without sacrificing quality?" is better than "Improve customer service." The former gives a specific angle to explore.
- **Lack of closure or follow-up:** Sometimes teams generate a wall full of ideas, but then no next steps are taken, leading to cynicism about the value of brainstorming.

  Solution: Always allocate time to *converge* after diverging. Use a tool like dot voting (see section 11) or a quick discussion to highlight promising ideas. Then, assign owners to evaluate further or prototype those ideas. It shows the team that their creative input leads somewhere, increasing engagement in future sessions.

By preparing for these pitfalls, a facilitator can turn a mediocre brainstorming session into a productive one. For instance, a study in *Harvard Business Review* pointed out that allowing individuals to brainstorm alone before a group session (combining brainwriting with group brainstorming) yields more and better ideas. It addresses both groupthink and dominance issues. Also, in distributed teams or remote settings, using digital whiteboard tools (like Miro or Mural) for silent brainstorming can level the field and capture input simultaneously from many people.

Illustration: Facilitating a practical brainstorming session. Picture a conference room with a small cross-functional team—perhaps six people: a designer, a product manager, an engineer, a marketer, a customer support rep, and an operations specialist. On the wall is a whiteboard titled "How Might We Improve the onboarding experience for new users?" The facilitator begins by reviewing the HMW (How Might We) question, ensuring everyone understands the focus. For the first 10 minutes, the facilitator gives each person a pad of sticky notes and asks them to write down as many ideas as possible (one per note) silently (brainwriting combined with individual brainstorming). Soft music plays to ease nerves. After 10 minutes, each person has a pile of notes. The group then posts their ideas on the board, briefly explaining each. The facilitator clusters similar ideas as they go (forming affinity groups like "Tutorial ideas", "Incentives", "UI improvements", etc.). Now, the group moves into a free-form discussion to piggyback and generate new ideas ("I see we have many ideas about tutorials—what if instead of a tutorial, we had a chatbot that guides you? Could that be more interactive?"). The energy is high; people laugh at a few outrageous suggestions, but no one says, "That wouldn't work." The whiteboard is filling up.

After about 30 minutes, the facilitator senses diminishing returns, it's time to converge. They hand out dot stickers to each person (say three each) and ask them to dot-vote on the ideas they find most promising or intriguing (more on dot-voting later). The team steps back and places their dots. It quickly becomes clear which ideas have group appeal. For example, an interactive chatbot guide has four dots, a gamified tutorial has three dots, and most others have 0–1. The facilitator and team discuss the top few: Are they feasible? Do they address the problem well? They decide on one idea to pursue immediately (maybe to storyboard it or prototype it in the next sprint) and two runner-ups to investigate (perhaps assign someone to do a quick research on them). The session ends with clear next steps. Everyone contributed and saw their influence in at least one of the ideas chosen. Such a well-facilitated session can produce a bounty of ideas, team alignment, and enthusiasm for solving the problem.

In summary, brainstorming remains a fundamental design thinking tool for ideation. Executing with structure and an open mind helps teams break free of analytical mindsets and venture into creative territory. By combining techniques like Crazy 8s, brainwriting, and SCAMPER and avoiding pitfalls like groupthink, organizations can substantially increase the innovation potential of their brainstorming sessions. As the Google example shows, giving people freedom and encouragement to brainstorm (whether in dedicated sessions or a portion of their work time) can lead to breakthrough products and solutions.

7.6 MIND MAPPING

While brainstorming often produces a flurry of disconnected ideas, mind mapping is a tool that helps organize and connect ideas visually. A mind map is essentially a diagram that represents thoughts, information, or concepts branching off from a central theme or problem. It typically starts with a single word or concept at the centre, and then related ideas radiate as branches. Each branch can further subdivide into sub-branches, capturing hierarchical relationships or associations. The resulting structure often resembles a tree or a neuron, hence the term *"mind map,"* as it mirrors how our brain might connect ideas through association. As one source succinctly put it, *"A mind map is a visual representation of a system or process… it leverages our mind's tendency to understand a subject by making associations."* (Shopify, 2021).

Organizing and connecting ideas visually: The main benefit of mind maps is that they externalize the mental model of a problem or topic. For instance, if you are designing a new smartphone app, you might write the app's name in the centre. Then, create branches for each major component or consideration: *User Needs, Features, Technology, Content, Marketing,* etc. Under *User Needs,* you might branch out into *Convenience, Privacy, Entertainment,* etc., and further branch *Convenience* into *quick login, saved preferences, offline access,* etc. Under *Features,* branches might list *Social Sharing, Notifications, Search,* etc. As you draw this, you'll naturally start linking some branches: maybe *Privacy* (a user need) connects to *Data encryption* (a technology) or *Privacy settings UI* (a feature). You can draw lines or arrows to denote these connections in a mind map. Mind mapping forces you to consider the relationships and groupings of ideas. It's a form of structured brainstorming that brings order to chaos.

Mind maps are handy for problem-solving because they allow you to break a problem into components and see the whole landscape. They provide a "bird's eye view," which can prevent the team from getting lost in details too soon. By looking at a mind map, you might notice imbalances (e.g., one branch is extremely detailed while another is sparse, prompting you to research or think more about the sparse branch). It also helps in identifying missing elements. For example, if you have a branch for *user needs* and only listed functional needs, you might realize missing emotional needs and add another sub-branch. Thus, mind maps help ensure a more comprehensive exploration of a space.

Another way to use mind maps in design is to map out user flows or experiences. For instance, consider Tesla's approach to rethinking battery and energy management in their vehicles. While not publicly confirmed as a "mind map" exercise, one could imagine Tesla engineers mapping out all aspects of battery usage: starting from *Raw Materials* → *Battery Manufacturing* → *In-Car Battery Management* → *Charging Infrastructure* → *Recycling*. Each might branch further (e.g., *In-Car Battery Management* branches into *Cooling Systems, Software Algorithms, User Usage Patterns*). By visually connecting these, Tesla could identify opportunities for improvement at each node, which is essentially what they did, resulting in innovations like the Gigafactory for production and breakthroughs in battery range through software updates. In spirit, this resembles a mind map connecting supply chain, engineering, and user experience considerations in one visual network. (Elon Musk has remarked on learning a new subject by building a "tree of knowledge," ensuring he understands fundamental principles (trunk) before details (leaves), which is analogous to mind mapping a knowledge domain).

Readers can watch the lecture on mind mapping by visiting the link—https://youtu.be/0v0JrjNqGTY.

Alternatively, below presented the QR code can be scanned to watch the same.

SCAN ME

Scan to watch the lecture—Mind Mapping.

CASE STUDY: How Tesla used Mind Mapping to Rethink Battery Efficiency and Supply Chains

While we don't have documentation of Tesla engineers pinning a mind map on a wall, we can infer from Tesla's method of first-principles thinking that a mind-map-like breakdown occurred. For example, Tesla approached the electric car as an isolated product and an ecosystem. If one were to mind map "Electric Vehicle Success," Tesla addressed branches like *Battery Technology, Charging Network, Software Integration*, and *Supply Chain*. Under *Battery Technology*, Tesla dug deep (branching into *cell chemistry, module design*, and *thermal management*). Under the *Supply Chain*, they considered *raw material sourcing (lithium, nickel, etc.)*, which branched further into *mining, partnerships*, and *recycling*. In the process, Tesla realized a significant threat (or node) was battery supply, leading them to combine and innovate on that front (building Gigafactories to produce batteries at scale, a strategy that combined manufacturing innovation with supply chain control). In essence, Tesla's groundbreaking decision to become as much a battery company as a car company can be seen as mapping out all factors impacting EVs and identifying which ones they needed to tackle themselves. Similarly, Tesla's development of features like regenerative braking or over-the-air software updates may have come from mapping out the energy usage and user experience branches and finding connections (e.g., *Software* branch connecting to *Energy Efficiency* branch leading to an idea: "manage acceleration curves via software to extend range").

Whether or not Tesla drew literal mind maps, many companies use mind mapping in their product strategy sessions. IBM has used mind mapping in design thinking workshops to let multidisciplinary teams collectively draw out a problem space, say, mapping everything that influences "employee engagement" for an HR app, which surfaced issues like corporate culture and recognition programs that needed addressing alongside app features. IDEO designers often use mind maps when starting projects to organize their research findings or to map stakeholders in a service system.

Mind Mapping vs. Brainstorming—when to use which: Brainstorming and mind mapping are not mutually exclusive; they can complement each other. *Brainstorming* is best when you need lots of divergent ideas quickly. It excels at breaking free of constraints and generating raw material. *Mind mapping* is great for structuring ideas, exploring a topic more systematically, and drawing connections. One way to integrate them is: after an initial brainstorm, take the heap of ideas and mind-map them to find clusters and relationships. Alternatively, use mind mapping first to outline sub-problems, then brainstorm solutions for each. For example, if the problem is "improve the online learning experience," a mind map might reveal sub-areas like *content, interaction, feedback,* and *motivation*. The team can then brainstorm ideas specifically for each branch (targeted brainstorming sessions), which can be more productive than a broad brainstorm.

Another difference is that brainstorming is often a group verbal activity, whereas mind mapping can be done individually or collectively but usually in a more quiet, reflective mode. It engages analytical and spatial thinking alongside creative association. Individuals who are visual thinkers might prefer mind mapping to sketch out their thoughts rather than generating long lists from scratch.

Illustration: A mind map example applied to product design. Let's say we are designing a new smart home device. We put "Smart Home Device X" in the centre of a canvas. The first level branches could be user needs, features, hardware, software/ AI, connectivity, user interface, competitive products, and revenue m*odel*. Now, we expand each. Under *User Needs*, through user research findings, we add branches: *Security, Ease of use, Energy saving,* and *Entertainment*. Under *Features,* we branch out to *Voice Control, Mobile App, Automation Routines,* and *appliance integration*. We draw a line linking *Voice Control* (feature) to *Ease of Use* (need), noting a connection that voice control addresses ease of use for non-tech-savvy users. Under *Hardware,* branches: *Sensors, Camera, Speakers, Processor, Design (aesthetics)*. Maybe we draw an arrow from *Camera* to a branch under *User Needs* like *Security,* indicating the camera is mainly for security needs. Under *Software/AI,* branches: *Machine Learning for user behavior, Voice Recognition, Data Privacy. Data privacy under software connects strongly to security under user needs, which marks* a crucial point.

Connectivity branches: *Wi-Fi, Bluetooth, and SmartHome Standards (e.g. Zigbee)* connect to *Integration* under Features (because using common standards ensures integration with other appliances). Under *Competitive Products,* we list competing brands and note their unique features (this can highlight opportunities or required parity features). Finally, *revenue model branches include one-time device sales, subscription service, data monetization, etc., which might link back to features (e.g., subscription might be tied* to offering premium cloud storage for camera footage).

Once this mind map is complete, the team can visually scan it to ensure all key aspects are considered in the design. It becomes apparent which areas are heavily developed and which are sparse. Perhaps the *entertainment branch under user needs had no corresponding features or hardware. Still, it may* be an opportunity to add something fun to the device (like it doubles as a smart speaker for music). Or one sees that *Integration* is critical (lots of lines connecting to it), so they decide to prioritize that in the product roadmap. The mind map is a one-page *knowledge map* of the product space, useful for making decisions and communicating the complexity to stakeholders.

Benefits of mind mapping in problem-solving: Studies in cognitive psychology suggest that visual representations can enhance memory and creativity. Mind maps engage the left brain (logical, orderly) and right brain (creative, associative) by combining words with spatial layout and sometimes images or colours. In practical terms, teams using mind maps often report better recall of discussions and a clearer mental model of the project. It's also a flexible tool with no rigid format, so teams can adapt it to their needs (some add numeric priorities on branches or use colour coding to denote risk levels, etc.).

Challenges: One must be cautious that mind maps, if too large or detailed, can become unwieldy and hard to read. It's important to balance detail with clarity. Sometimes, making multiple mind maps (one per sub-topic) is wiser than one giant map. Additionally, mind mapping software exists (like MindMeister, XMind, etc.), which can be helpful, especially for remote teams and keeping a tidy digital version. However, a simple hand-drawn map on paper or whiteboard can often be more spontaneous and collaborative. There's no one "right" mind map for a given topic, and it's a subjective representation. So, teams should not overanalyze the structure; its purpose is to serve the team's understanding.

Mind mapping is a valuable design thinking tool for organizing information, seeing relationships, and ensuring a comprehensive exploration of a design challenge. It is particularly effective after initial research or ideation phases when the team needs to synthesize information or converge ideas into a structured concept. As Nick Babich noted in a discussion on product design, a well-crafted mind map provides *"an overview of the experience…helping designers keep track of the most critical aspects of the interaction."* (Shopify, 2021). It focuses on user goals and the big picture, preventing the team from getting lost in minutiae too early.

An example of a mind map for a user's "My Account" experience shows high-level sections (Profile, Preferences, Order Status, etc.) and sub-features branching out. This visual organizes key elements and their relationships at a glance.

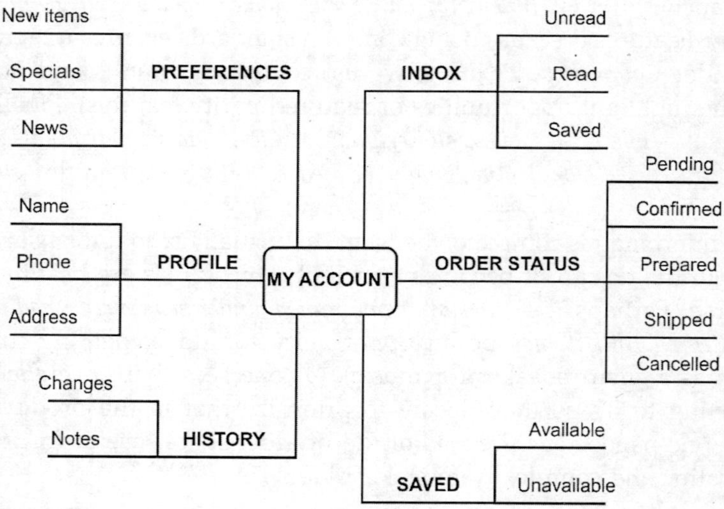

7.7 STORYBOARDING

Design is ultimately about *users' interactions over time*. Storyboarding is a tool that visualizes a sequence of events, much like a comic strip, to illustrate how a user would interact with a product or service step by step. A storyboard is a series of frames or sketches, each representing a key moment in a scenario. Storyboards often feature a character (representing the user or persona) and incorporate context (where they are and what's around them) along with the product interfaces or touchpoints they use. This tool was borrowed from filmmaking and animation, where storyboards are used to plan the narrative, and it has found powerful applications in UX and service design to prototype experiences and communicate design concepts.

How storyboards bring concepts to life: A storyboard forces the design team to think about the *flow* of an experience, not just static touchpoints. Drawing out each step, you consider What triggers the user to engage. What is their first action? What do they see or feel? What happens next? For example, say we are designing a new onboarding process for a fitness app. A storyboard might start with Frame 1: *John (the persona) hears about the app from a friend and decides to download it*. Frame 2: *John opens the app, and the welcome screen greets him*. Frame 3: *John is guided to create a profile and input fitness goals*. Frame 4: *John struggles with a form and maybe looks confused*. Frame 5: *The app offers to import data from his Facebook to ease the process. John looks relieved*. Frame 6: *John completes onboarding and sees a dashboard with his daily step count; he smiles, feeling accomplished*. In these simple sketches, we've outlined a user journey. Storyboards convey context (maybe in Frame 1, John is at a café when his friend tells him about the application by showing the environment), user emotion (smile, confusion), and progression. It helps the design team and stakeholders imagine the *entire experience* rather than focusing only on individual screens or features.

Storyboards can expose gaps or impractical aspects of a concept by visualising interactions. Perhaps while storyboarding, you realize there's no frame covering how John

FIGURE 7.4 Storyboard.

finds the app in the first place, which might prompt marketing considerations or referral features. You might notice John had confusion in frame 4, which indicates a UX issue to address in the design (maybe simplifying the form or providing better guidance). In this way, storyboards act as a low-fidelity prototype of the user experience. They're cheap and quick to create (just sketches). Still, they can validate a design concept's logic and emotional journey.

CASE STUDY: How Pixar and Apple use Storyboarding to Refine user Experiences

In the realm of animation, Pixar is renowned for its storyboarding process. They create thousands of storyboard drawings for each movie, allowing them to iterate on story and timing long before expensive animation work begins. Pixar's Andrew Stanton (director of *Finding Nemo, WALL-E*) has said, "We'll storyboard the sequence, and it won't work, and we'll redo it, and we'll redo it. It's like sketching in the filmmaking process." The analogous approach in design is to storyboard user interactions early and often. Pixar's influence has spilt into tech and product design: Apple, known for its meticulous focus on user experience, has reportedly used storyboarding techniques, especially when designing narrative interactions. For instance, when designing the iPhone's onboarding tutorial or the Apple Watch's activity animations, Apple designers storyboarded the sequence of screens and transitions to craft a smooth, engaging flow (this isn't publicly documented in detail, but one can infer this practice as Apple often hires talent from creative industries and emphasizes storytelling in marketing).

A more concrete example: The Airbnb Snow White project we discussed earlier in journey mapping (Section 4) was fundamentally a storyboarding exercise applied to service design. Airbnb had a Pixar artist, Nick Sung, draw storyboards of a host's and guest's journey frame by frame (Bennett, 2020; Metropolis Magazine, 2019). They treated the service experience as a story, with a beginning (the trip planning), middle (the stay), and end (after checkout), and depicted key scenes. This storytelling approach uncovered emotional highs and lows that might not surface in a purely analytical process. For example, one storyboard frame showed a traveller arriving late at night at a dark apartment, highlighting a moment of anxiety. That insight led Airbnb to implement better host instructions for late check-ins or even something simple like hosts leaving a light on or a friendly note to make that critical first moment warmer. The result of storyboarding was a more empathetic design of the service.

In their marketing of new features, Apple often uses storyboards in ad form to show how a user's day flows with the product. However, internally, one can imagine storyboard interactions. Take the FaceID unlock sequence on the iPhone: Apple would have designed and storyboarded the interaction mentioning that the user raises the phone (frame 1), infrared dots scan the face (could be a conceptual frame if explaining to the team), the phone unlocks with a subtle animation (frame 2), the user goes to the home screen (frame 3). By detailing it, they refine the *timing* and *feedback*: how quickly does the padlock icon animate to an unlocked state? Do we show a visual cue of the scan? These "story" decisions of the interaction can significantly affect the perceived magic and trustworthiness of the feature. Only through a narrative lens (what is the mini-story of unlocking one's phone) can they perfect these details.

Another small but illustrative example: when designing the Apple Watch's fitness rings (the animated rings that close upon achieving goals), Apple likely storyboarded the daily story of a user glancing at their watch in the morning (rings empty), during lunch (rings partially filled), in the evening after a workout (rings closing and celebrating). Sketching out those frames would help them decide how the ring animation should behave to be glanceable and motivating at each point. It's a story of motivation told through a simple graphic over time.

Techniques: Sequential vs. Non-sequential storyboarding. In design, most storyboards are sequential: step 1, step 2, etc., in chronological order of how a user would encounter an experience. It is great for linear tasks (e.g., booking a ride in a rideshare app from start to finish). However, sometimes, experiences are not strictly linear or have conditional flows. Here, non-sequential storyboarding can be useful. It might mean illustrating key moments or touchpoints in no particular order to capture all scenarios. For instance, if designing a museum visit experience, one might storyboard a visitor's journey sequentially (buy a ticket, enter an exhibit, interact with the display, and leave feedback). But one could also create a set of vignette storyboards: one showing the visitor struggling to find the entrance (highlighting a signage issue), another showing them delighted by an interactive exhibit, and another showing frustration at a crowded gallery. These are out-of-sequence, but each storyboard frame tells a piece of the experience puzzle that the design needs to address. This non-linear approach is more like a collection of user *stories* rather than one narrative, and it's useful when an experience can start or end at different points or when trying to improve specific moments in an existing journey.

Additionally, storyboards can be low-fidelity or high-fidelity. Low-fi are sketchy stick figures or simple cartoons, great for early ideation and team discussions (everyone feels comfortable contributing because it's not polished). High-fi storyboards (sometimes called "story sequences" or "UX comics") can be more artistic and detailed. These are often used in final presentations to stakeholders or as part of the documentation to convey the envisioned user experience with clarity and emotional impact. Some companies employ illustrators to create beautiful storyboard narratives when pitching new product concepts precisely because a picture is worth a thousand words to get buy-in.

Illustration: A sample storyboard for a mobile app onboarding experience. Imagine we are designing an onboarding for a language-learning app. We draw a six-panel storyboard:

- *Panel 1:* A character (Ana) sees an ad or friend using the app and decides, "I want to learn Spanish", she has a thought bubble, "I really should learn Spanish for my trip."
- *Panel 2:* Ana downloads the app and opens it. She is prompted with a friendly welcome and a question, "Why do you want to learn Spanish?" In the sketch, Ana taps "For travel". (This indicates personalization is starting).
- *Panel 3:* The app now shows a quick lesson preview. Ana's face looks determined as she tries a simple quiz in the onboarding. (We're showing that onboarding is interactive, not just static).
- *Panel 4:* Ana struggles with one question. A helpful tooltip in the app UI says, "Don't worry, you can review this later!" She looks relieved. (This frame captures the app's supportive tone to prevent drop-off).
- *Panel 5:* Onboarding complete. The app shows "You're all set, Ana!" and maybe a celebratory graphic. Ana smiles, feeling accomplished. (This depicts the reward moment).
- *Panel 6:* Ana is now on the app's main screen, beginning her first real lesson, feeling confident. Perhaps in this frame, she will also receive a welcome email or notification (reinforcing the experience across channels).

After reviewing these panels, the team can check if the onboarding tells a coherent story. Are we addressing the user's potential anxieties (like Panel 4 did)? Is the value proposition clear by the end (Panel 5's celebration shows success)? This storyboard becomes a reference when designing onboarding screens. It is possible as the UI designers and copywriters strive to create the same feelings in users that the storyboard portrays.

Why storyboarding is useful: It engages our empathetic and narrative faculties. Humans naturally think in stories, so when you frame a user interaction as a story, it's easier to identify with the user and notice if something doesn't make sense. It also helps communicate designs to others. A product manager can show a storyboard to executives to illustrate how a customer will use the new feature in context, much more tangible than describing it abstractly. Storyboards also consider context: physical environment, time of day, etc. A wireframe of a mobile app won't tell you that the user might be driving or cooking while using it. Still, a storyboard might explicitly draw the user into a kitchen trying to use a cooking app with wet hands, which might lead to designing larger touch targets or voice controls.

Sequential vs. non-sequential usage: Usually, you will use sequential storyboards to design new flows (like the onboarding example). Non-sequential storyboards (or multiple sequence sketches) are useful during research synthesis. For example, sketching key moments observed in user research to discuss pain points. In practice, many design teams storyboard the current state (how users experience something, including pain points) and the future state (how they *will* experience it with the new design). It is akin to mapping the current and desired journeys in visual storytelling.

In sum, storyboarding is about *bringing time and emotion into design*. It pushes the team to think beyond static interfaces and consider how interactions play out as narratives in users' lives. Whether improving an existing service or creating a new product, storyboards can illuminate the human experience you aim to create and ensure that each step of that story is intentionally designed.

7.8 RAPID PROTOTYPING

Ideas are cheap; in the testing and iteration, good ideas are turned into great solutions. Rapid prototyping is the practice of quickly building a tangible (though often simplified and rough) version of a product or feature so that it can be tested and improved. In design thinking, rapid prototyping is vital in the later stages of the process (Prototype and Test) as it embodies the fail-fast, learn-fast mantra. A prototype can be anything from a paper sketch of a user interface to a clickable digital mockup to a physical model made of cardboard, whatever form allows the team to experience and evaluate the idea. The key is that it's created *rapidly* (hours or days, not weeks) and is just detailed enough to elicit useful feedback but not so precious that the team is reluctant to throw it away if it doesn't work.

7.8.1 Types of Prototypes

- **Low-Fidelity (Lo-fi) Prototypes:** These are very rough product approximations. In software or UX, a common lo-fi prototype is a paper prototype, such as hand-drawn screens or elements that a tester can manipulate (sometimes called "Wizard of Oz" testing if a facilitator manually changes screens). Paper prototyping is extremely fast, as one can sketch many variations of a screen in minutes, and it's great for early-stage testing of layouts or concepts. Testers might tap on the paper, and a human "computer" swaps the paper to simulate navigation. In physical product design, a lo-fi prototype might be a foam, cardboard model, or even Lego. For example, when designing a new coffee machine, a team might cut foam core pieces to represent the size and shape and use that to discuss ergonomics or the placement of buttons. Lo-fi prototypes are cheap and encourage experimentation; because they look unfinished, testers are more likely to give honest feedback ("It's not final, so I can critique it freely").
- **Digital Prototypes (Medium to High Fidelity):** Teams often create interactive digital prototypes as ideas mature. Tools like Figma, InVision, or Adobe XD allow designers to build clickable mockups of apps or websites without coding, ranging

from medium fidelity (basic grayscale wireframes with clickable hotspots) to high fidelity (fully designed screens that look real, with some interactive behaviour). A high-fi digital prototype can simulate the user experience so well that users may not realize it's not a fully coded product in testing. However, it might have limitations (for instance, maybe only a few "happy path" flows are prototyped, and if the user strays outside them, the prototype might not respond). The advantage of high-fi prototypes is testing visual design, content, and more nuanced interactions. However, they take more time to build, so they are usually used once the team has confidence in the flow from low-fi testing.

- **Physical Prototypes:** Prototypes can involve physical fabrication for hardware or tangible services. Techniques like 3D printing have revolutionized rapid prototyping for products. For example, IKEA designers 3D-print furniture components to test assembly and look. They might even build full-scale mockups with cheaper materials. *Service prototyping* might involve role-playing in a mocked-up environment. For instance, prototyping a new airport check-in process by setting up a fake counter and having team members act as passengers and staff to run through the scenario.

The fidelity chosen depends on whether you're still figuring out if the concept solves the right problem; low-fi might suffice. Suppose you're refining the details of the solution. Higher fidelity might be needed to get accurate feedback on those details (e.g., testing a gesture interface likely needs a reasonably interactive prototype).

Quickly building models for testing and iteration: The mantra is "build to think." By creating a prototype, the team often uncovers practical considerations that weren't obvious on paper. For example, a team designing a new remote control could prototype it with a 3D printer and then realize it's uncomfortable to hold in one hand, leading to immediate design adjustments. The speed is crucial: the faster a prototype is built, the sooner it can be tested, and thus, the sooner the team learns what works or doesn't. An iterative loop forms: prototype, test, learn, refine, repeat.

Agile and Lean methodologies also emphasise rolling out a Minimum Viable Product (MVP) quickly. In design thinking terms, a prototype is an MVP of an idea to test internally or with a small user sample.

CASE STUDY: How IKEA Rapidly Prototypes Furniture Designs

IKEA is known for its affordable, flat-pack furniture. One might not immediately think of them in a software-like prototyping context, but they heavily use prototyping in product development. An IKEA designer, Sarah Fager, described how the design process involves *quick hand sketches to understand the project*, then moves to 3D modelling and 3D printing, "sending prototypes back and forth with suppliers". It means that rather than spending months setting up a production line for a chair to see if it works, they'll model it and maybe print a scale or full-scale model in days to check proportions and ergonomics. Do they also create prototypes to test assembly to answer instances like, "Can a user put this together easily with the given screws and instructions?". If not, they iterate. In one instance, IKEA built a very high-fidelity prototype of a new sofa using actual production materials, realized it was too costly to manufacture, and ended up scrapping that design after testing (the prototype was built, evaluated for comfort and cost, and provided the insight that it wouldn't meet IKEA's price points). While that might seem like a "failure," learning that via a prototype was much better than after mass production. IKEA also uses *virtual prototyping*. They have a large research lab that simulates living spaces and uses VR to prototype how furniture fits in homes. Rapid prototyping for them might mean mocking up an entire bedroom with prototype furniture to see how it all works together as a system.

In the digital domain, consider how a company like Facebook might prototype a new feature like "Reactions" (the emojis you can react with besides just liking). Before writing complex code to animate emoji reactions, Facebook designers and engineers prototyped the interactions (likely with simple software demos or hacked-together versions in a test app) and internally dogfooded it. They would test: Do people understand these new icons? Does pressing and holding to get the reaction palette feel natural? Those prototypes (some possibly in Keynote or simple HTML/ CSS, as many Silicon Valley teams use lightweight prototyping for interactions) allowed quick iteration on the design of the icons and animations.

The role of rapid prototyping in agile development: Rapid prototyping aligns perfectly with agile principles of iterative development. In agile, you aim to have shippable increments frequently. If we broaden "prototype" to mean any early version tested, one could say each agile sprint outputs a prototype of new functionality, which is tested (either by QA, beta users, or A/B tests). Agile teams use techniques like spike solutions (throwaway code to explore feasibility), essentially technical prototypes, to reduce risk. For example, an agile team at a startup might allocate one sprint to prototyping a machine learning algorithm with a small dataset to see if it's viable before committing to it. That's rapid prototyping in code.

Design thinking often feeds into agile: designers may create rapid prototypes in parallel to development sprints to validate user experience assumptions, and then, once validated, those become requirements for the development team. The concept of *"failing fast"* is key: it's much cheaper to discover a design or concept failure through a quick prototype than after full implementation. Rapid prototypes encourage an experimental mindset, and teams are more willing to try bold ideas if they can test them in a day or two.

Illustration: Examples of low-fidelity vs. high-fidelity prototypes. Consider a new e-commerce checkout page design. A low-fi prototype could be a series of paper sketches or wireframes representing each step: shipping info, payment, and review. You could even simulate the checkout by putting these papers before a user and asking, "What would you do next?" The user says, "I'd click Next", you swap the paper to the payment form, etc., and you observe where they hesitate or get confused. After a couple of iterations, you might move to a medium-fi digital prototype using a tool to create a greyscale clickable version that the user can click through on a phone or laptop. It looks more like a real interface so that you can test more nuanced things like the labels' wording or the buttons' placement. After refining that, a high-fi prototype might connect to a test database, maybe a semi-functional front end where the user can input real text, see error messages, if any, and go through the whole flow and at the end maybe it doesn't charge a card, but everything else feels real. That high-fi prototype (sometimes called a "pilot" or "beta") could be given to a small set of users in a live environment (like an A/B test on a website) to gauge drop-off rates vs. the old checkout. At each fidelity stage, the prototypes gather feedback appropriate to their level: paper to catch big UX issues, medium-fi to catch interaction and content issues, and high-fi to catch integration issues and measure actual behaviour.

From a business standpoint, rapid prototyping de-risks innovation. As an MBA, you might be interested in how prototyping can save costs. GE's FastWorks program (inspired by Lean Startup) had engineers 3D print parts to test in industrial machines rather than machining them, saving weeks and lots of money in development. Similarly, software companies that prototype and user-test early UI can avoid costly rework after development.

Challenges of prototyping: One must be careful to prototype the *right* aspect. Sometimes, teams prototype something peripheral and get a false sense of security about the core idea. Ensure your prototype is aligned with what you need to learn. Also, stakeholders might sometimes mistake a high-fidelity prototype for the final product ("It looks done; why do we need to spend more time?"). Communicating what's real and what isn't in a prototype is important. Another challenge is knowing when to go from prototyping to building for real. Analysis paralysis can happen if you iterate prototypes forever. Typically, you set criteria, for example, "once 5 out of 5 users complete the flow without major issue, we'll move to implementation" or time-box the prototyping phase.

In essence, rapid prototyping is the engine of iterative design. It gives form to ideas so they can be tested and accelerates the learning loop that drives a design toward success. As the saying goes in the design world, *"If a picture is worth a thousand words, a prototype is worth a thousand meetings."* Building something people can interact with often cuts through debates and reveals truths that slide decks and discussions cannot.

One can watch the lecture on rapid prototyping by visiting the link—https://youtu.be/6d3KP0mxNy0 .

Alternatively, the below presented QR code can be scanned to watch the lecture.

SCAN ME

Scan to watch the lecture—Rapid Prototyping.

7.9 SWOT ANALYSIS

As design thinking projects move toward implementation, it's crucial to evaluate solutions in the context of the real world, including business viability and external factors. SWOT analysis is one tool widely used in business strategy and can complement design thinking. SWOT stands for Strengths, Weaknesses, Opportunities, and Threats. It provides a simple yet structured way to assess an idea, product, or business venture by listing its internal strengths, weaknesses, external opportunities, and threats. In the context of design thinking, a SWOT analysis can be used to evaluate a set of solution concepts or a prototype's potential, ensuring that the chosen solution is desirable for users and feasible and viable in the market.

SWOT in design thinking—aiding decision-making: After rounds of ideation and prototyping, teams (especially in an MBA or corporate setting) need to decide which concept to invest in. A SWOT analysis can synthesize a lot of considerations in one framework:

- **Strengths:** These are internal positives of the solution or organization. In a design context, strengths could be unique features, patents, superior user experience, or team expertise. For example, if you've prototyped a new e-commerce checkout, a strength might be *"Our design reduces steps compared to competitors (5 clicks vs. 8), which user tests show leads to a higher completion rate."* Another strength could be *"leverages our existing payment infrastructure, so easy to implement."* In product terms, strengths often highlight what gives your solution an advantage (perhaps it's more affordable, faster, more intuitive, etc., based on what you discovered).
- **Weaknesses:** These are internal negatives or limitations. Continuing the example, a weakness might be *"Requires users to have a smartphone for two-factor auth—might exclude some older users"* or *"The new system is dependent on a stable internet connection; in low-bandwidth scenarios, it may perform poorly."* Being honest about weaknesses is important; identifying them doesn't mean the idea is doomed, but it might indicate areas to improve or things to monitor. Sometimes, weaknesses in a design thinking project can include *limited validation* (e.g., only tested with tech-savvy users) or reliance on a partner or technology that is not yet confirmed.
- **Opportunities:** These external factors could be exploited to benefit the solution. Market trends, regulatory changes, gaps in competitors' offerings, or evolving user behaviours can all be opportunities. For the e-commerce example, an opportunity might be *"Growing trend of voice-assisted shopping—we can be first to integrate voice checkout"* or *"Competitors have higher cart abandonment—an optimized checkout is a marketable differentiator."* Opportunities often align with the *Desirability* and *Viability* lenses, for example, an untapped customer segment that our solution could attract or a new technology (AI, AR, etc.) we could incorporate to leapfrog others.
- **Threats:** External factors that could hinder success. Common threats include *competition* (if others can easily copy your improvements, or a big player is working on a similar solution), *market shifts* (maybe a downturn in the economy reducing consumer spending, etc.), *technological changes* (the API you rely on might get deprecated), or *regulatory issues* (new privacy laws could complicate your personalized features). For our checkout example, a threat might be *"Payment regulations (PSD2 in Europe, for instance) will require two-factor authentication, potentially adding friction"* or *"Major competitor is rumoured to be investing in one-*

click checkout too." Another threat can be internal organizational factors like *"lack of engineering capacity to implement this quickly—the risk of delay."* (Though internal, that threat plays out externally as losing market window.)

By laying these out, the team (and stakeholders) can have a more holistic view of the concept's landscape beyond user desirability. It ensures considerations of *feasibility (strengths & weaknesses often relate to technical or organizational feasibility)* and *viability (opportunities & threats relate to market and financial viability)*.

CASE STUDY: How Netflix used SWOT Analysis to Transition from DVDs to Streaming

Netflix in the early 2000s was a DVD-by-mail service. By 2007, they began moving into streaming. A simplified retrospective SWOT around that pivot might look like this:

- **Strengths:** Netflix's strengths at the time included a vast library of content (via DVDs), an established subscriber base, and a strong brand for easy, no-late-fee rental. They also had a recommendation algorithm (Cinematch), which gave them a tech edge. As streaming took off, a strength was that they were early entrants with a usable platform.
- **Weaknesses:** In the DVD model, weaknesses included reliance on USPS (postal service) for deliveries, not instant; physical discs could be damaged or lost. When thinking of streaming, weaknesses were that initially, the content available for streaming was limited (due to licensing) compared to DVDs, and some customers had slow internet access or were not tech-savvy with computers/Smart TVs at that time. Another internal weakness was the cost structure of mailing DVDs (postage, handling), which streaming could reduce if done right, but the streaming infrastructure itself was a new competency to build.
- **Opportunities:** Externally, the rise of broadband internet was a huge opportunity. By the mid-2000s, more households were becoming capable of video streaming. Also, an opportunity was the inefficiency of physical retail (Blockbuster's inconvenience and fees), and Netflix could further differentiate itself by offering instant gratification via streaming. Globally, streaming could allow Netflix to expand without shipping logistics. They likely saw the opportunity in data to personalize viewing, etc., much easier via a digital platform. The *long tail* opportunity: streaming could eventually carry a wider selection of content without the cost of stocking physical DVDs (inventory optimization).
- **Threats:** At the time, threats included *competition*—Blockbuster started its mail service and eventually streaming, Amazon began renting videos online, and new streaming competitors could emerge (which indeed they did: Hulu, etc.). *Studios* could threaten to withhold content or charge high licensing fees once they saw Netflix's model succeeding (which later happened, leading Netflix to invest in originals). Technologically, there was the threat that internet infrastructure or user adoption might not be as fast (some analysts thought the streaming quality wouldn't satisfy customers used to DVD quality—a threat of customer backlash). Another threat is cannibalization, which is transitioning users from a profitable

DVD subscription model to an uncertain streaming model (indeed, Netflix faced user confusion and anger in 2011 when they attempted to split the services). Also, piracy was (and is) a threat, as easy digital content could mean more unauthorized distribution.

Netflix did, in essence, weigh these factors. In 2011, they did a notorious (and eventually reversed) split of the DVD and streaming businesses (remember "Qwikster"). One can read that as an internal SWOT decision: DVD had the strength of profitability but the threat of decline; streaming was the future opportunity but a short-term weakness in profit. Their solution was to separate them (which was poorly received, so they backtracked). Eventually, of course, Netflix focused on streaming and wound down the DVD service. A SWOT analysis would have aided those strategic moves by clearly delineating the scenario.

In a design thinking project, one wouldn't necessarily do a full SWOT early on. Still, as you narrow to a solution that will be implemented, a SWOT is a great checkpoint to ensure alignment with business strategy. For example, if your design thinking team at Netflix had brainstormed streaming features, a SWOT would remind you of "Weakness: limited content rights for streaming", which might push you to propose in your plan: "We should invest in licensing or creating original content", which Netflix famously did, turning a threat (losing licensed content) into a strength (original shows).

Illustration: A sample SWOT analysis for a new product launch. Imagine a startup that has developed a smart home energy device that optimizes electricity usage. Before launch, the team does a SWOT:

- **Strengths:** Innovative machine learning that adapts to user habits (patent pending), the device is easy to install (plug-and-play), and the companion app has a highly-rated UI from beta testers. The team is small but highly skilled in AI and UX. Also, the device can integrate with popular smart assistants (Alexa, Google Home), which is a strength in compatibility.
- **Weaknesses:** The hardware is currently a bit expensive to produce, which might push the retail price higher than ideal. The startup has a limited marketing budget/experience, so reaching customers is a weakness. The brand is new and unknown (no trust yet). Also, the device currently only supports single-phase power (a weakness for some international markets). Customer service capability is unproven (small team). These are internal issues to address.
- **Opportunities:** Growing consumer interest in energy savings and sustainability is a market opportunity, as people are actively looking for such solutions. Potential partnerships with energy companies or home builders could also accelerate adoption (opportunity for channels). Perhaps government incentives for energy-efficient homes could subsidize devices like this. There's also an opportunity to expand services: the data collected could allow an energy consultancy service (future revenue stream). There is no dominant competitor in the smart energy device showcases the chance to be a market leader.
- **Threats:** Big smart home players (like Nest/Google) might enter this space with their energy optimization features. Economic threat: if electricity prices fall or

people are less cost-conscious, demand might drop (or conversely, if privacy concerns surge, people might not want an AI monitoring their usage—social threat). Another threat is supply chain issues for electronic components (especially during chip shortages). Also, new regulations or standards in electrical systems could make the device outdated or non-compliant.

After listing these, the team can formulate strategies, e.g., strengths to leverage, such as highlighting the ML innovation in marketing (to counter being unknown and build thought leadership). A weakness to shore up could be to find a manufacturing partner to reduce cost (address pricing weakness). Opportunities to seize may be to approach a green energy rebate program to piggyback on incentives. Threats to mitigate are securing IP, developing a quick roadmap for a cheaper version if a big competitor undercuts the price, etc. Essentially, the SWOT analysis informs a robust go-to-market plan, and it ensures the product as designed (from a design thinking perspective) aligns with business realities.

Using SWOT during design iterations: Doing a mini-SWOT on different design concepts is possible before finalizing one. For instance, if a team has two prototypes for a service (one high-tech, one low-tech), a SWOT comparison might reveal that the high-tech one has great user appeal (strength) but relies on a technology that's not reliable yet (weakness, threat). In contrast, the low-tech one is easier to implement (strength) but might not stand out in the market (weakness, threat from competitors). Such analysis can guide whether to pursue a simpler or more ambitious solution.

Combining SWOT with design thinking in an MBA context connects creative solution development with strategic assessment. Design thinking ensures the solution is desirable and user-centric; SWOT (along with perhaps a business model canvas or other tools) checks that it's viable and sustainable in the big picture. It's interesting to note that some design thinking practitioners include a "pseudo-SWOT" in the form of Feasibility/Viability analysis as part of later stages (e.g., IDEO's approach looks at Desirability, Feasibility, and Viability, which maps to user, technical, business lenses). SWOT is a more formal way to tackle the viability and feasibility checkpoints.

To conclude, SWOT analysis provides a balanced view of a solution's potential by forcing consideration of both positive and negative factors, internal capabilities and external environment. The design thinking journey can be the bridge to strategic planning, ensuring that the innovative solutions developed are grounded in an understanding of business realities and a plan to navigate challenges. Whether you're pivoting a business model like Netflix or launching a new product line, SWOT helps make informed, holistic decisions.

The chart outlines internal Strengths & Weaknesses (e.g., unique technology but high cost) and external Opportunities & Threats (e.g., growing market demand vs. strong competitors). Such a matrix helps teams evaluate

TABLE 7.1 SWOT Analysis of a Product Concept

Strength	*Weaknesses*	*Opportunities*	*Threats*
Favorable brand positioning Rapid growth The company offers its service to a wide range of customers Their ability to offer exclusive Netflix original content Their capability for rapid customer-centric adaptation The company has a strong influence on consumer culture	Restricted copyright policies Worrying relationship with debt The company has lost its price competitiveness Recent subscriber loss Over-reliance on their North American market	Strategic re-branding There is still further room for expansion New innovative customer-centric services Offering more local content	Rising competition from other streaming services Rampant content piracy Password sharing Failure to invest in a greener future Slowing growth in the North American market Rising operational costs

7.10 AFFINITY DIAGRAMS

Throughout a design thinking project, teams collect a lot of qualitative data: user interview quotes, observations, ideas from brainstorming, feedback from testing, etc. Making sense of all that information can be challenging. The affinity diagram (affinity mapping or the K-J method) comes in handy. An affinity diagram organises a large set of unstructured data or ideas into meaningful groups based on natural relationships or themes. Typically, it involves writing down individual data points or ideas on sticky notes and then collaboratively arranging them on a wall, clustering similar notes together. The goal is to identify patterns or categories (the "affinity" between items) that might not be obvious when looking at raw data in a list or transcript form.

How affinity diagrams help teams organize qualitative data: Imagine you have 100 post-it notes, each with a key insight from user research (e.g., "User struggles to find the save button," "User wishes there was a dark mode," "User concerned about the privacy of data," etc.). By spreading and grouping them, you might form clusters such as *Navigation Issues, Feature Requests, Visual Preferences,* and *Trust Concerns*. Within each cluster, you see sub-themes. Under Navigation Issues, half the notes are about search functionality, and the other half are about menu labels. This grouping reduces the cognitive load (you can think of 5 categories instead of 100 separate points) and often reveals relationships. For instance, you might realize that many "feature requests" are trying to solve "trust concerns" (users request a feature to download their data—the underlying concern is privacy). It can inform your problem definition or solution prioritization. Affinity diagrams enable a bottom-up synthesis, letting patterns emerge from data rather than imposing preconceived categories.

Creating an affinity diagram in team settings is a great way to achieve shared understanding. Each team member might have read different interviews or have their takeaways; when everyone puts the notes up and moves them into groups collaboratively, it democratically incorporates everyone's perspective and often leads to *"aha!"* moments collectively ("We're hearing the same pain point from many different customers, that's a priority to address."). It ensures that design decisions or next steps are grounded in evidence-based insights, not just gut feeling.

For example, a communication platform can use affinity diagramming when redesigning the user experience by sorting hundreds of customer feedback into themes. By doing so, they identified four key areas (as earlier referenced: Communication & Collaboration, Privacy & Security, UI Application, Support & Maintenance) that structured their design efforts. The affinity process distilled a mass of input into clear focus areas. Similarly, IDEO and other design firms routinely use affinity mapping after field research to make sense of ethnographic observations and find insights that lead to design opportunities.

CASE STUDY: How did a Well-established Corporation Employ Affinity Diagrams to Redesign their Communication Platform based on Feedback

In developing the platform (the collaboration software), the team collected extensive customer feedback from various channels: user interviews, support tickets, user forum posts, etc. Let's say they had 200 feedback items after a major release. The UX research and design team creates an affinity diagram to improve the product systematically. They write each feedback point on a sticky note (virtual or physical). Then they start grouping: they notice clusters like *"Notifications"* (users complaining about too many or missed notifications), *"Meetings"* (issues with scheduling or joining calls), *"Chat interface"* (desires for better threading or search in chat), *"Permissions/ Security"* (confusion about guest access, etc.), and *"Performance"* (app slow or heavy on memory). By labelling these groups and counting notes, they see, for instance, that the Notifications cluster has 50 notes, clearly a hotspot of user frustration, while *Performance* has 15 notes, and *Meetings* has 40, etc. They may further sub-cluster; e.g., within Notifications, 20 notes are "want more granular control of notifications," 15 are "notifications not syncing across devices," etc. These become actionable insights: perhaps they realize a need for a *revamp of Notification Settings* and an *improved notification syncing mechanism*. Indeed, in a published insight, platform noted that affinity diagram analysis of Teams feedback highlighted *notification overload and lack of prioritization* as a key issue, which drove design changes in how the platform shows activity.

The affinity mapping guided what problems to tackle and likely informed *how to tackle them*. For example, seeing a cluster around "Quiet hours feature request" in notifications may lead them to implement a Do Not Disturb mode. Their designers have shared that organizing user feedback into themes via affinity diagrams helps ensure the design roadmap addresses the most pressing user needs first, rather than reacting ad-hoc to individual comments.

How to create an affinity diagram (step-by-step): First, gather all qualitative data points (notes, quotes, observations). Second, ensure each point is concise, usually one idea per sticky note. Third, as a team, start grouping notes that seem related. It is usually done silently at first, where team members move notes around without speaking to avoid bias or debates too early. The pattern recognition part is somewhat intuitive; if one person groups something and another disagrees, they might move it elsewhere. After an initial grouping, the team discusses the emerging clusters: *"Do these two groups belong together, or are they different issues?"* They can split or merge clusters as needed. They then create header notes or labels for each cluster (often in a different colour). Finally, they discuss implications: *What insights do these clusters reveal? What might we name each insight?* Sometimes, the team will write a short insight statement per cluster, e.g., "Users have trouble discovering advanced settings" or "Managers need a better overview of team progress", which become design directives or problem statements for ideation. In some cases, a cluster might be very large; that might warrant breaking it down into another affinity sort (affinity diagrams can be multi-level: clusters within clusters).

Illustration: Creating an affinity diagram from user research. Suppose an MBA class project is to improve the campus library experience. The team interviewed 15 students and five librarians, gathering lots of comments. They put all the individual thoughts on the wall: *"I can never find a quiet space after 7 pm"*, *"Wish we could book study rooms in advance"*, *"The library website search is frustrating"*, *"I love the café, but it's always crowded"*, *"As a librarian, I see students struggle with research databases"*, etc., maybe 100 notes total. As they cluster, themes emerge: one around *Space & Noise* (quiet vs. social spaces), one around *Resource Discovery* (finding books, articles, databases), one around *Amenities* (café, lockers, etc.), and one around *Booking & Availability* (study rooms, computer availability). Within *Resource Discovery*, notes are separated into *Physical books* vs. *Digital resources*. The cluster of *Digital resources* has many librarian notes about students not knowing how to use databases and student notes like "I just use Google; the library database is too hard." That signals an insight: *The library's digital research tools have a usability/education problem.*

Meanwhile, the *Space & Noise* cluster might show a tension between students wanting quiet vs. collaborative environments. From this affinity sort, the project team could derive key opportunity areas:

1. Redesign digital resource access or instruction,
2. Improve space management (maybe zoning or soundproofing?),
3. Implement a room booking system. They gained these from seeing the forest (themes) rather than the trees (individual quotes).

Why it's called "affinity": because you group ideas by their natural affinity to each other, it's bottom-up, so categories are not pre-decided but rather emerge. It helps avoid forcing data into presumptive buckets that might mask what users are truly saying.

Common uses in design thinking: Affinity diagrams are often used right after the Empathize phase (to analyze research findings) and after brainstorming (to organize a bunch of brainstormed ideas into categories). The brainstorming post-its can be affinity-grouped to combine similar ideas and then dot-voted (combining tools). It's also used to evaluate open-ended survey responses. Sort features into must-have vs. nice-to-have via clustering or whenever a team is overwhelmed with information.

Challenges: If not facilitated well, teams might argue over where a note goes. Emphasize that there's no single correct grouping; it's about what's useful. Sometimes, a note could logically belong to two clusters; in that case, either duplicate the note or place it where it was primarily meant. Another challenge is when clusters are too broad (e.g., a "Miscellaneous" cluster with many items indicates the team might need to break it down further or re-think categories). It's also important to note frequency vs. importance: a big cluster might indicate frequency of mention but not always importance (though often there's a correlation). The team should still use judgment, maybe a small but critical cluster (e.g., "security concerns" might have few mentions but a high impact). Affinity diagrams are a tool to reveal patterns, not to dictate priorities blindly.

In conclusion, affinity diagrams are a foundational tool for sense-making in design thinking. They *"help teams cluster and make sense of qualitative research findings or idea lists, highlighting patterns and priorities"*. By using affinity mapping, teams move from data to insights, the bridge between Empathize and Define stages (making insights) or between Ideation and Prototyping (choosing concepts to develop). It encourages collaboration, ensures everyone's data is heard, and often builds consensus on what problems to solve or ideas to pursue. As an MBA student or manager, facilitating an affinity mapping session can greatly enhance group analysis of complex information, leading to well-informed, user-centred strategic decisions.

7.11 DOT VOTING

When a team has generated ideas or identified several options to pursue, how do they decide which ones to prioritize? One simple and popular method is dot voting (also known as "multi-voting" or "sticker voting"). In dot voting, each team member is given a set number of votes (often represented by dot stickers or by marking with a pen) to distribute among the ideas they find most promising or important. After everyone places their dots, the clustering of votes reveals which ideas have the most support within the group. It's a quick, democratic way to gauge the collective preference and converge on options worth further discussion or prototyping.

Collaborative decision-making through voting: Dot voting is typically used after a divergence phase. For example, post-brainstorming or when reviewing a list of product features or initiatives. Suppose a team brainstorms 50 ideas for improving a mobile app. They can't pursue all 50, so dot voting helps surface which ideas resonate most. Each team member might get five dot stickers to place next to their favourite ideas (they can put multiple dots on one idea if they feel strongly or spread them out). The result might show that Idea #7 got eight votes, Idea #12 got seven votes, a bunch got 1–3, etc. The facilitator then typically focuses the conversation on the top-voted items. It's important to note this doesn't have to be the final decision; rather, it's a tool to identify where there is energy or agreement in the group. It reduces a large set to a smaller set for more analysis.

Dot voting is popular in workshops and design sprints because it gives everyone a voice, including quieter members (they vote even if they don't speak up). It also helps avoid endless debate; instead of arguing which idea is better, vote and see the group's pulse. For example, at IDEO, after brainstorming, it's common for designers to dot-vote ideas to decide which ones to prototype first. In Agile ceremonies, teams might vote on which customer story or pain point to tackle next.

Another scenario: Suppose you're mapping a user journey and identify 10 pain points along the way. The team shall dot vote on which pain points seem most critical to solve. If "checkout process confusing" gets the majority of votes, that's where you focus first. It is more objective (based on collective input) than a HIPPO (highest paid person's opinion) picking randomly, and it *feels* fair, which increases team buy-in for the outcome.

How dot voting helps prioritize ideas: Dot voting's power is in its simplicity. Visualizing votes quickly highlights consensus. It's a tool for convergence, narrowing down options. For instance, in a design sprint at Google, the team might have sketched various solutions (Crazy 8s) and then dot vote on the sketches to decide which concept to prototype on Day 3 of the sprint. In the book "Sprint" Jake Knapp calls a refined version of this the "heat map". All team members quietly place dots on interesting parts of solution sketches, and the decider makes the final calls. Even if you ultimately have a decision-maker who isn't bound by the vote, the dot patterns inform their decision by showing the team's perspective.

Dot voting is especially useful to prevent analysis paralysis. In design thinking, teams might be overwhelmed by options after a rich ideation. Voting injects a quick structure to move forward. It's also time-efficient: a dot voting exercise might take 5 minutes in a meeting instead of a lengthy discussion on each item.

CASE STUDY: How IDEO uses Dot Voting in Rapid Idea Evaluation

IDEO is known for its brainstorm sessions, during which hundreds of Post-its might be generated. They often give participants dot stickers (sometimes playful ones, like star stickers) and have them vote on the ideas they find most intriguing or aligned with the design challenge. For example, the team might brainstorm features in designing a new medical device. After dot voting, they see that ideas related to "real-time feedback to patients" have lots of votes, whereas "gamification for doctors" got few. This collective signal steers the project: focus on the patient feedback feature. In a video of an IDEO workshop, you might see boards covered in coloured dots, where each dot physically represents one person's support (Harrison, 2018; Tufts University, n.d.). Sometimes, they differentiate by colour (e.g., blue dots from engineers' perspective or red from designers, if they want to see cross-discipline alignment).

IDEO also uses dot voting in design research synthesis. For example, after identifying various user needs, dot voting can let a multidisciplinary team indicate the most important needs to address. It blends well with affinity diagrams: first cluster insights, then vote on which insight group should be the top priority.

In a client context, dot voting is a great facilitation tool because it actively involves stakeholders. As a consultant, if you present five concepts to a client team, instead of asking, "So which do you like?" you can run a dot voting exercise with them. It makes the decision process transparent and inclusive. At the end, you might say, "Concepts B and D have the most votes. Let us discuss those further." It is less contentious than someone championing an idea through persuasion alone.

Mechanics and variations: Each person gets a finite number of votes (often around 3-5, depending on the number of options). They can place only one per idea or multiple (we call that dot voting vs. dotmocracy; some allow stacking votes on one idea). Allowing multiple per idea lets someone signal strong preference, but you risk vote stacking by assertive members. A way to mitigate that is by giving two colours of dots: one colour means "first choice", and another means "second choice" if you want to weigh votes. But typically, keeping it simple with one colour and equal weight works.

It is important to clarify what the voting criteria are: Is it "vote for the idea you like best", "vote for what you think is most feasible", or "most innovative"? Usually, brainstorming involves a balance of interest and perceived value. Some workshops have done separate votes, for example, one round for the *most innovative* and *easiest to implement*, to highlight quick wins vs. moonshots.

Example: In a city planning workshop, architects, citizens, and officials brainstorm 20 ideas for improving public parks. The facilitator gives everyone five red dot stickers and says, "Place your dots on the ideas you feel would have the biggest positive impact on the community." After voting, the idea "Community Garden Space" has 10 dots, "Free Wi-Fi in Park" has 8, and "Skate Park" has 2, etc. They concluded that they should focus on community gardens and Wi-Fi since those clearly resonated as having a high impact among the stakeholders.

When brainstorming fails: pitfalls and solutions related to voting. We should note some caution: dot voting can sometimes become a popularity contest disconnected from criteria or end-user perspective. To counter that, ensure that everyone understands the design criteria or user needs well before voting. Also, dot voting works best with a manageable set of options (if there are too many, people can't evaluate each well). If you have 100 ideas, maybe do an initial cluster or pre-filter to get to, say, 20, then vote. Another pitfall is groupthink; some might wait and then follow where others put the dots. To reduce this, you can vote simultaneously and somewhat privately (everyone goes up at once or cover your dots until all have been placed). In digital whiteboards (e.g., during remote workshops using Mural or Miro), you can have an anonymous voting mode so people aren't influenced by seeing results live.

Illustration: Dot voting in action. Picture a team standing around a wall of sticky notes. Each sticky has an idea from their ideation session on improving customer onboarding. Team members have small coloured dot stickers in their hands, studying the wall. One by one (or together), they walk up and stick their dots on the notes. A pattern emerges in a minute or two: one note might have a little cluster of 4 dots, a couple others have 2 or 3, and many have none. The note with four dots, saying "Personalized welcome email with tutorial", clearly stands out. The facilitator might circle those dots or rewrite that idea on a separate "shortlist" area. Perhaps the top 3 ideas by votes will now be considered in detail. The team might then discuss, "Do we agree these three are the ones to prototype? Anyone wants to champion an outlier idea that didn't get votes, but do you believe in it strongly?" Dot voting is not binding if strong arguments exist for an underdog idea, but it provides a baseline of group preference.

Why dot voting is valued: It's democratic and engages all participants equally. It externalizes what might otherwise be a murky conversation about which idea is "best"; the visuals of the dots make it clear. It also speeds up decision-making, crucial in time-boxed processes like design sprints or workshops. For MBA students, this technique can be used in design tasks and in any context for team decision-making. For example, prioritizing strategic initiatives in a business plan or deciding which job candidate attributes to focus on in hiring (list attributes, dot vote on what the team values most).

In summary, dot voting is a straightforward but powerful tool to help teams collectively prioritize and make decisions in the design thinking process. It complements the creative phases by adding a structure for evaluation that is quick and inclusive. When used appropriately, with clarity on voting criteria and openness in post-vote discussion, it can effectively harness the crowd's wisdom while maintaining progress and momentum toward implementation.

7.12 COMPARING THE TOOLS: WHEN AND WHY TO USE EACH

We have explored various design thinking tools, including empathy maps, personas, journey maps, brainstorming, mind mapping, storyboarding, prototyping, SWOT, affinity diagrams, and dot voting. Each tool has a distinct purpose, but there is overlap, and they often complement each other. It's useful to summarize and compare these tools across a few dimensions: stage in design thinking, complexity, and collaboration needed. A comparison matrix can help determine *when and why to use each tool.*

Let us outline a matrix (conceptually) with rows as the tools and columns as characteristics such as the primary design thinking stage, key benefits, typical outputs, team involvement, and maybe use case *examples.*

- **Empathy Maps vs. Personas:** Both are used in the Empathize/Define stage to understand users. An Empathy Map is quick, done right after user research, focusing on one experience scenario at a time. It's highly collaborative, often made in a group based on raw data, and the output is a one-page visual that captures the user mindset. Personas, in contrast, might be created once a broader research analysis is done (often after empathy maps or other synthesis). Personas compile patterns across many users into a fictional archetype. Creating personas can take more time, and validation and results in a profile document can take longer. Use *empathy maps* when you need to quickly put the team "in the user's shoes" for a specific context, and use personas when you need a reference character to design for the entire project. Empathy maps are situational (could even do multiple per persona for different tasks), whereas each persona represents a segment in a more holistic way. Many projects use both: empathy maps feed persona creation.
- **Customer Journey Maps vs. Storyboards:** Both visualize the sequence of user interaction steps. A customer journey map is a structured diagram (often like a table) highlighting stages, user actions, thoughts, pain points, and opportunities at each stage. It's used in Define to identify problems or in Ideate to identify where to innovate (and later to communicate improvements). A storyboard is a narrative,

comic-strip depiction used either in Define (to illustrate current experience) or Prototype/Test (to simulate and communicate a new concept's experience). Journey maps are great for aligning cross-functional understanding of an entire service experience and spotting gaps (used often in service design and UX strategy). Storyboards excel at *communicating* a concept and empathizing with the user's emotional journey in a visceral way. Storyboards typically require some drawing skill (though stick figures suffice in the early stages) and are often collaborative in brainstorming the story, so one person might refine the sketches. Journey maps tend to be compiled using research and sometimes require cross-department input (making them collaborative).

- **Brainstorming vs. Mind Mapping:** Both are ideation tools in the ideation phase. Brainstorming is a divergent idea generation focusing on volume and creativity. It's highly collaborative, often done in groups with facilitation. Output is usually a list or pile of ideas (which then need filtering). Mind Mapping is more about *organizing thoughts and exploring connections* in a problem or solution space. It can be used in Define (to map out problem factors) or Ideate (to systematically expand solution aspects). Brainstorming is free-form and thrives on group energy. Mind mapping can be done solo or in a group; it's slightly more analytical even though it links concepts creatively. Use *brainstorming* when you need breakthrough ideas and lots of them, especially for specific "How might we" questions. Use *mind mapping* to ensure you've thought of all problem elements or to structure a brainstorming outcome (e.g., mind map your ideas into categories). For example, brainstorming might give 100 feature ideas; mind mapping those features against user needs might show which needs have many solutions and which have few, guiding focus.
- **Rapid Prototyping vs. SWOT Analysis:** These are quite different and usually come in different phases. Rapid Prototyping is in Prototype/Test; it's about *making tangible models to learn and iterate*. It's hands-on, requires design and engineering collaboration, and yields interactive or tangible artefacts for user testing. SWOT Analysis is more of a strategy tool often applied around Define (if assessing current product) or after ideation in the Decide phase (to evaluate concepts). It's more analytical and business-focused, often done by a smaller team or leadership to check strategic fit. Prototyping answers, "Can we make it, and will users like it?" SWOT addresses "Does it play to our strengths, is there a market opportunity, what could go wrong?". Both are crucial: a design could test great with users (prototyped well), but if SWOT reveals major threats (e.g., regulatory issues or cost problems), you might pivot strategy. Conversely, SWOT might identify an opportunity, but you need prototyping to seize it with a good design. Regarding collaboration, prototyping engages designers, engineers, and maybe end-users; SWOT often engages stakeholders like product managers, marketers, or execs besides the design team to weigh in on business/environmental factors.
- **Affinity Diagrams vs. Dot Voting:** These are facilitation tools to process information and make decisions collaboratively. Affinity Diagrams are best in Define (after research) and sometimes post-ideation (to organize ideas). They involve the whole team, especially in research synthesis. Dot Voting typically occurs

in Decide moments, after ideation or affinity grouping, to prioritize where to move forward. Affinity mapping is more time-consuming (it could take an hour or more for lots of data) and is about sense-making and generating insights from qualitative data. Dot voting is quick (a few minutes) and is about gauging preferences or importance among options already on the table. They often work sequentially by using affinity mapping to go from chaos to categorized info, then dot vote to highlight which categories or items to tackle first. In terms of complexity, affinity diagramming can handle complex, ambiguous data. Dot voting is simple and works well when choices are clearly defined. Industry uses: affinity diagrams are heavily used in UX research and product planning (e.g., grouping user feedback into themes), dot voting is common in agile sprint planning (selecting user stories or retrospective ideas), and any workshop-like scenario to drive group decisions.

To summarize in a simplified matrix form:

- **Empathy Map:** *Stage:* Empathize/Define. *Purpose:* Understand user mindset in a specific context. *Collaboration:* Team activity using research data. *Use when:* Start the design to ground the team from the user's perspective.
- **Persona:** *Stage:* Define. *Purpose:* Summarize key user segments as fictional profiles. *Collaboration:* UX researchers & stakeholders need a research basis. *Use when:* Need a reference user to design for, but keep the focus on the target audience.
- **Journey Map:** *Stage:* Define (current state) and Ideate (to identify opportunities). *Purpose:* Visualize the entire end-to-end user experience. *Collaboration:* Cross-functional (shows touchpoints across departments). *Use when:* Designing complex services or multi-step processes to pinpoint pain points and moments of truth.
- **Storyboarding:** *Stage:* Define (current story) / Ideate-Prototyping (future story). *Purpose:* Illustrate user interaction sequence with context and emotion. *Collaboration:* Team brainstorming, one or two draws; great for communicating with others. *Use when:* Needing to convey or test a scenario in narrative form, bringing a concept to life.
- **Brainstorming:** *Stage:* Ideate. *Purpose:* Generate many ideas creatively. *Collaboration:* Group (divergent thinking). *Use when:* You have a well-framed question or challenge and want a broad idea pool.
- **Mind Mapping:** *Stage:* Can be Defined or Early Ideate. *Purpose:* Explore and organize related ideas around a central concept. *Collaboration:* Individual or group; good for systems thinking. *Use when:* You must understand the scope, connect the dots between different aspects, or systematically ideate (ensuring no area is overlooked).
- **Rapid Prototyping:** *Stage:* Prototype/ Test (and sometimes late Ideate to evaluate concepts). *Purpose:* Tangibly try ideas, get feedback, and iterate. *Collaboration:* Design & development team, plus user testers. *Use when:* You have an idea worth testing or comparing; you need to learn by doing and from user reactions.
- **SWOT Analysis:** *Stage:* Define (context analysis) and Decide (concept evaluation). *Purpose:* Strategic assessment of internal/external positives and negatives.

Collaboration: Team with business stakeholders to do an analytical exercise. *Use when:* Ensuring solution aligns with business reality, prioritizing strategies, often prelude to making go/no-go decisions or crafting business cases.

- **Affinity Diagram:** *Stage:* Define (synthesizing research) & sometimes Post-Ideation (organize ideas). *Purpose:* Find patterns in lots of qualitative data. *Collaboration:* The Team, including researchers and designers, is often a hands-on workshop. *Use when:* After research or brainstorming to cluster information and derive insights or themes.
- **Dot Voting:** *Stage:* Decide (after ideation or whenever choices need narrowing). *Purpose:* Prioritize options democratically. *Collaboration:* Whole team (each member votes). *Use when:* There is a need to gauge the group's top interests quickly or break a stalemate among many ideas, especially in workshops and sprints.

Additionally, we could mention complexity: Some tools are quick and low-effort (dot voting, empathy mapping, basic brainstorming), whereas others take more time or expertise (journey mapping may require research mapping skills; prototyping might need coding or craft; SWOT might need market analysis). So, depending on project scope and resources, one chooses appropriately. For instance, on a very tight timeline, you might do empathy maps, quick personas, a rudimentary journey map, brainstorming, dot vote, and a paper prototype tested with five users—skipping heavier tools. In a large project, you might do all plus thorough personas, high-fi prototypes, etc.

Industry and context considerations: Some industries emphasize certain tools. Empathy maps, personas, journey maps, wireframe prototypes, and usability testing are common in software UX, with affinity diagrams to analyze user research, dot voting in design studios, etc. In product innovation (physical products), personas and scenarios, brainstorming, and rapid prototyping (from foam models to working alphas) are key, and SWOT is used for product strategy. In service design (e.g., healthcare, retail experiences), journey maps and storyboards are heavily used to orchestrate multi-channel experiences, affinity mapping to synthesize patient or customer journey research, etc. MBA contexts might see SWOT and personas often in marketing strategy, brainstorming in innovation workshops, and journey mapping in customer experience projects.

The overarching point is that design thinking isn't a rigid sequence of all these tools but rather a toolbox. Depending on the project stage and need, you pick the right tool. For example, you might use empathy maps and journey maps to define the problem early on. In ideation, brainstorming, mind maps, and maybe storyboards are used to explore solutions. In evaluation, use prototyping, dot voting, and perhaps SWOT to decide what moves forward. They often feed one another (the output of the empathy map informs the persona, the output of brainstorming is input to dot voting, etc.).

7.13 CHALLENGES IN IMPLEMENTING THESE TOOLS IN BUSINESS

While the value of these design thinking tools is clear in theory, practitioners often encounter challenges when integrating them into real business processes. Common challenges include organizational culture, time constraints, siloed departments, lack of training, and misalignment with traditional processes.

Cultural resistance: In some organizations, especially those with a long history of analytical or top-down decision-making, methods like brainstorming or empathy mapping might be met with scepticism. Employees might be unaccustomed to the freewheeling nature of creative workshops or feel that spending time on "post-it exercises" is more frivolous than immediately jumping into solutions or spreadsheets. Leadership might also be hesitant to let decisions be guided by group voting or user stories instead of their intuition or extensive quantitative data. For example, an engineering-driven company might undervalue empathy maps because they seem too fuzzy or "soft". To overcome this, it often helps to show results, perhaps run a small pilot design sprint to tackle a minor problem and demonstrate how tools led to a well-received solution. Also, educating stakeholders on the purpose of each tool is critical: explaining that empathy maps lead to a better understanding of customer needs, which can reduce product failures, or that prototyping and testing early saves money by catching issues before full rollout. Over time, as people see success stories (like "Remember when journey mapping that service uncovered the bottleneck that we fixed and customer satisfaction improved?"), cultural buy-in grows. Another tactic is blending design thinking tools with existing processes. For example, incorporate a quick dot vote at the end of a strategy meeting to prioritize initiatives; this sneaks into the practice non-threateningly.

Time and resource constraints: Teams often feel they "don't have time" to do additional workshops or user research needed for these tools. In fast-paced environments, taking time to create personas or journey maps may be skipped, leading to solutions that miss the mark. Design thinking proponents often counter this by highlighting how these upfront investments save time by preventing costly backtracking (the classic *"pay now or pay more later"* argument). However, to make it feasible, tools can be right-sized: maybe you don't have time for a full research study to build perfect personas, but you can gather internal people who interact with customers (sales, support) for a 1-hour persona creation workshop using their knowledge, not perfect, but better than nothing. Or use existing survey data to inform an empathy map. Another approach is to integrate tools into meetings you already have. For instance, a weekly team meeting can be turned into a mini-brainstorm on a current problem for 15 minutes. The key is to avoid making them feel like add-on tasks; rather, show that using the tools can replace or streamline some current activities. A journey map might replace a lengthy PowerPoint report by succinctly summarizing customer issues on one page.

Siloed thinking: Many tools require cross-functional collaboration (like journey maps needing input from marketing, ops, etc.). In organizations with silos, getting the right people in a room can be challenging politically or logistically. Sometimes, one department might not see the relevance of participating in a "design" exercise. For example, IT might say, "Why must we be in a customer journey workshop? That's for the UX team." Overcoming this requires stakeholder management: convincing each silo of the benefits for them. Possibly present a case where lack of cross-functional insight caused a failure. For example, a new product launch might have flopped because marketing promised something the product didn't deliver. A journey mapping exercise with marketing and product could have caught that mismatch. Another solution is obtaining executive sponsorship for design thinking initiatives so that top management encourages all departments to engage. Some companies institutionalize it: for instance, IBM developed an Enterprise Design Thinking framework and made design thinking a part of everyone's objectives; this helps break silos by common methodology.

Lack of training or facilitation skills: Tools like affinity diagrams or storyboarding don't yield great results without some know-how. If team members have never done them, they might do them incorrectly or inefficiently (e.g., cluster data by preconceived categories rather than emerging themes, missing the insight). Or poorly run brainstorming can lead to groupthink or one person dominating, leaving others disenchanted (like "we tried brainstorming, but it was just the loudest person's ideas"). Overcoming this involves building some *design thinking capability,* such as training certain team members (like an "innovation catalyst" or "design thinking facilitator" program). Many companies, like SAP and Intuit, trained internal facilitators to lead design thinking sessions. MBA programs (like this one, presumably) are equipping future managers with these skills, which is great. If you don't have an expert, use resources such as templates and online guides or hire a consultant for initial workshops to model the process. Another practical approach starts with simpler tools: dot voting and SWOT are straightforward and familiar to many business folks. Success with those can open minds to trying the more "designy" tools. Also, incorporate fun but structure: if brainstorming sessions in the past failed, introduce a specific technique like *brainwriting* or *Crazy 8s* with strict time boxes as these impose methods that can mitigate common failures (like one person talking too much). Having even a one-page cheat sheet for a technique can help a new facilitator keep things on track.

Integration into business processes: Design thinking tools might seem separate from "real work." People often ask, *"Who will do the work after the sticky notes?"* It's crucial to connect the outputs of these tools to the next steps in the business process. For example, after an affinity diagram yields insights, ensure those insights translate into requirements documents, KPIs or user stories so that they are implemented. If a brainstorming session yields ideas, assign someone to prototype the top idea or do market research on it. If dot voting picks a concept, that concept should enter the project plan. Often, the challenge is the handoff: a UX team might do personas and journey maps, but product development or marketing might not use them. Overcoming this requires involving those downstream teams in the creation (so they trust and understand it) and framing the results in their language. For instance, turn journey map pain points into specific "user requirements" that the product backlog can consume. Or link SWOT findings to the business strategy documentation or OKRs (Objectives and Key Results). Essentially, translate the artefact into actionable next steps. Some companies embed designers or design researchers in product squads to ensure continuity.

Measuring impact and ROI: Business stakeholders might ask, *"What is the ROI of empathy mapping or prototyping?"* They might prefer investing in coding features or marketing campaigns directly. It's challenging to quantify directly because it's about risk reduction and user satisfaction improvements, leading to ROI. However, one can use proxies: for instance, prototype usability testing might show that success rates improved from 40% to 90% after redesign, implying fewer support calls (cost savings) and happier customers (potentially improved retention). Or cite well-known industry cases: e.g., Intuit's CEO said their Design for Delight (design thinking) program helped increase market share and innovation pipeline (anecdotal but persuasive). Also, track internal metrics: number of ideas generated vs. implemented, time from concept to launch (often faster with prototyping to iron out specs early). Another way is to start with a critical project where the design thinking approach leads to market success and then publicize that internally.

In summary, implementing these tools effectively is not just about knowing the tool but about change management: changing mindsets, workflows, and skills in an organization. Strategies to integrate these tools effectively include starting small with pilot projects (demonstrate value), getting leadership buy-in, providing training and perhaps external facilitation at first, integrating with existing processes (don't make it feel like extra work), tailoring the tool usage to company context (maybe rebranding some tools in terminology that suits company culture), and importantly, emphasize a *user-centred, collaborative mindset* as the foundation—the tools then follow naturally.

Many companies have navigated this journey. For instance, in the late 2000s, Ford started using journey mapping and personas to revamp their showroom and digital experiences and had to bring entrenched engineering and sales teams. They reportedly created cross-functional "experience teams". They did internal workshops to gradually shift perspective to customer-first (a challenge in a company long driven by engineering and finance). Banks adopting design thinking also face compliance and hierarchical cultures; one approach they took was hybridizing, for example, doing rapid prototyping (normally at odds with risk-averse culture) but in a contained environment like a "digital innovation lab" separate from core operations, which then proved concepts before scaling.

Finally, there may be domain-specific challenges: e.g., in healthcare, storyboarding patient experiences might clash with strict privacy rules, or dot voting might undervalue clinical viewpoints if not carefully considered. Customizing tools can navigate these (maybe have patients and providers brainstorm in separate groups, then merge outputs to avoid power distance issues, etc.).

Implementing design thinking tools is a transformation that involves human factors as much as the methods themselves. Persistence and showing quick wins are key. The reward, as many firms have found, is a more innovative, user-aligned organization.

KEY POINTS TO REMEMBER

1. The foundational tools help designers step into the user's shoes. Empathy maps capture a user's mindset in a specific context, and personas create realistic archetypes of key user segments for making design decisions throughout a project.
2. To understand the user's experience over time, use journey maps to chart the end-to-end process and identify pain points. Storyboarding can be employed to create

a visual narrative of a specific interaction, which helps communicate the context and emotional arc of a solution.

3. Brainstorming techniques can be used to generate several ideas without judgment. Use mind mapping to organize those ideas, explore relationships between concepts, and ensure a comprehensive look at the problem space.
4. The core of iteration is rapid prototyping. Low-fidelity models (paper sketches, cardboard mockups) shall help to test concepts quickly and cheaply. This "build to think" approach allows teams to seek user feedback at an early stage, thereby de-risking the innovation process before development.
5. Affinity diagrams can be used to cluster qualitative information into meaningful themes. Once ideas or priorities are clear, use dot voting as a quick, democratic method for a team to converge on which concepts to pursue next.
6. SWOT analysis provides user-centric and business-viable solutions. This strategic lens helps teams assess a concept's market fit and potential challenges.
7. The ten tools are a flexible toolkit, not a rigid checklist. Successful design thinkers know when to use each tool—empathy tools for understanding, ideation tools for creating, prototyping for testing, and prioritization tools for deciding. They are often used in combination to move from insight to implementation.

KEY LEARNINGS

Throughout this chapter, we explored how design thinking tools provide structured yet creative ways to approach problem-solving. Some overarching learnings include:

- **Empathy is the foundation:** Tools like empathy maps and personas centre our focus on the user's perspective. By walking in the user's shoes (empathising), we uncover latent needs and emotional drivers that purely analytical methods might miss. A key lesson is that understanding users deeply leads to solutions that truly resonate. For example, Netflix's pivot to streaming succeeded because it empathized with customers' desire for instant access, not just because of technology.
- **Visualization aids understanding:** Whether journey journey maps, storyboards, or mind maps, visual tools help teams see the big picture and the relationships between parts. They make intangible concepts (like an experience or a system of ideas) tangible. It often leads to team alignment, and a journey map on the wall becomes a single source of truth about customer pain points to which everyone can refer. The phrase "make it visible" is a recurring theme; when problems and ideas are visualized, they're easier to tackle collaboratively.
- **Iteration and experimentation are crucial:** Rapid prototyping and brainstorming teach us that the first idea is rarely the best, and early failure is acceptable and desirable. By testing prototypes, we iterate towards better solutions in cycles, embodying a growth mindset. This iterative approach is far more effective than designing the perfect solution in one go. In business terms, it reduces risk and can shorten development cycles (failing fast to succeed sooner). Students saw in

our prototyping exercise how initial concepts changed after feedback—a mini demonstration of iterative improvement.

- **Collaboration harnesses diverse thinking:** Many tools (affinity diagrams, dot voting, brainstorming) explicitly engage a group to contribute and decide. This inclusivity yields a richer set of ideas (because people from different backgrounds will contribute different perspectives) and builds shared ownership of the outcomes. One learning is that structure helps here. For example, brainstorming rules or brainwriting methods overcame typical teamwork pitfalls to let quieter voices be heard and prevent groupthink. When teams genuinely collaborate, the solutions tend to be more robust (e.g., a journey map created with input from customer service, sales, and operations will address more facets than one made by marketing alone).
- **Design thinking and business strategy go hand in hand:** Tools like SWOT analysis remind us that innovation must be viable and feasible, not just desirable. Conversely, the creative tools ensure that business strategy remains grounded in human needs and innovation. The balanced approach yields solutions that are desirable, feasible, and viable (the sweet spot of design thinking as per IDEO's framework). A takeaway is that an MBA can use these tools to connect customer-centric design with strategic decision-making; they are not at odds. For instance, using a persona can make a marketing strategy more targeted and effective (customer segmentation with empathy), and prototyping a new service concept can save a firm from investing in the wrong solution.
- **Process matters as much as a product:** A meta-level insight is that the methodology, following empathize, define, ideate, prototype, and test, improves the problem-solving process. Students likely felt how starting with research (instead of assumptions) opened up better questions, how diverging before converging yielded more thoughtful outcomes, and how testing prevented overconfidence in an unproven idea. The process is non-linear and iterative, and that's okay. We learned to embrace ambiguity initially, then add structure through these tools to navigate it. It is a valuable skill in any business context where problems are often "wicked" and not predefined.

EXERCISES

A mix of individual and group activities can be very effective in solidifying understanding of these tools and encouraging practical skill-building. Here are some exercises tailored for MBA students who often work on interdisciplinary team projects and case studies. These exercises will help students apply design thinking tools to business problems in a hands-on way:

1. **Role-playing exercise on persona development:** Break the class into small groups. Give each group a brief description of a product or service (could be an existing one or a new concept—e.g., a meal delivery service, a fintech app,

etc.) and some basic market research data about its customers. Each group's task: develop 1–2 personas for that product. To do this, one or two members of the group take on the role of "user research participants" (perhaps using provided data or imagined details), and the others interview them to gather insights (this can be playful role-play). Then, the group synthesizes what they learned into persona profiles. For example, for the meal delivery, one persona might be "Busy Brittany, 29, a young professional who values healthy options but has no time to cook", and another might be "Family Dad Frank, 45, uses it for convenience on busy soccer practice nights." The groups then share their personas with the class, explaining how they arrived at those and what key needs and pain points each persona has. This exercise trains interviewing, empathy, and synthesis. It shows how personas bridge raw info and design decisions (the group should mention "we'd design feature X because Brittany needs…"), connecting to the earlier chapter content. It also surfaces the importance of not designing for oneself but for target users.

2. **Customer journey mapping challenge:** Each group is tasked to create a customer journey map using a business scenario (maybe a case study or a known brand's customer experience). For instance, consider a retail bank's loan application process or an e-commerce purchase journey. Provide some fictionalized customer feedback or a touchpoint list if needed. Have groups map stages (e.g., Awareness, Consideration, Purchase, Usage, Support) to identify customer actions, feelings, and pain points at each stage. Then, crucially, ask them to brainstorm at least one improvement idea for each pain point (thus linking journey maps to ideation). After mapping, groups can present: walk through their journey ("Meet our customer persona going through taking out a car loan... at first he feels intimidated, then research, etc.—here he hits a snag... we propose the bank could do X to fix that."). For an extra twist, assign each group a different industry (one does travel booking, one does hospital patient journey, one B2B software onboarding, etc.) to get a range of examples discussed. This exercise underscores the holistic view and highlights interdepartmental issues (for instance, marketing promises vs. service delivery in the journey). It also practices identifying opportunities from the user's perspective.

3. **Brainstorming and dot voting session:** Pick a generic problem relevant to MBA life or a small business case. For example, "How might we improve the experience of using public transportation in our city?" or "Design a better on-campus recruiting process for students." First, have everyone individually do a quick Crazy 8s sketch or list five ideas (individual ideation to avoid groupthink). Then, in groups, compile the ideas onto a board or virtual board. Encourage classic brainstorming rules (defer judgment, etc.) and allow a short round of adding/building more ideas in groups now that they see each other (maybe 5–10 more minutes to discuss and add). Then, give each student 3 dot votes to stick to the ideas they think are best under whatever criteria (could be most innovative or easiest to implement, but likely "which ideas do you want to pursue further"). Identify the top-voted ideas, then assign task groups to pick one and do a quick storyboard or concept description of how it would work. They then share these top concepts. This combined exercise gives experience in divergent

thinking and converging with dot voting. It shows pitfalls, too (maybe someone complains their favourite idea got no votes, then the class can discuss if the voting missed something, touching on the facilitator's role or need for criteria). Rotating facilitators is important so each student may try leading the rules or time-keeping (builds facilitation confidence).

4. **Hands-on affinity diagramming:** Using qualitative data (perhaps a short list of feedback comments from customers of a service or reviews of a product, the instructor can provide a set of 20-30 raw feedback statements gleaned from online reviews or a simulated survey), have the groups perform an affinity sort. Provide each statement on a separate slip of paper (or use an online board if virtual). Instruct groups to silently group them into clusters of related themes. After grouping, have them label each cluster with a theme name (insight) and discuss what that theme means for the business (e.g., "many customers find installation difficult, which is a weakness to address" or "lots of love for our customer service—that's a strength to maintain"). Then, tie it to SWOT: have them take the identified themes and do a mini SWOT for the product: maybe the clusters revealed 1–2 strengths, weaknesses, etc. Each group can then present one insight and suggestion—e.g., "We found a cluster of 'long wait times' comments—a major Weakness/ Threat, our suggestion is the company should implement a callback system or better communication in queue." It connects the dots from raw data to strategic action, using affinity and SWOT. It reinforces how to digest qualitative input that MBAs often see in customer surveys, focus groups, etc., and turn it into strategy.
5. **Prototyping competition:** For a fun group activity, give a simple design challenge and basic materials (cardboard, markers, tape—or digital prototyping tool or presentation software). For instance, "Design the ideal backpack for an MBA student." Each group has to create a low-fi prototype of their backpack concept in 30 minutes using materials. They must also prepare a short "user testing" script. Then, groups pair up to test each other's prototypes: one group acts as testers (with one playing the student using the new backpack), the other observes and notes feedback, and then they swap. After this, each group will have feedback; give them another 15 minutes to iterate, maybe they will sketch version 2 or modify their prototype. Then, have a brief show-and-tell to see how ideas evolved. It simulates the rapid prototyping and iteration cycle. If physical prototyping is tough in class, alternatively, do a paper prototype of an app, for example, design an app for scheduling MBA group meetings. The key is to go through build-test-refine quickly. Students experience how early feedback can dramatically improve a concept (maybe one group discovered via testing that their backpack was too heavy or missed an essential feature, so they changed it—better to learn with a mockup than after manufacturing!). It drives home prototyping's value and testing techniques with users, even if in a role-play format.

These exercises incorporate individual work (so each student reflects and contributes), group collaboration, role-play, and real-world simulation, aligning with the interactive nature of design thinking. They cover empathy (role-play interviews), definition (affinity and personas), ideation (brainstorming), prototyping (making backpacks or paper UIs), and testing (peer feedback and dot voting preferences). As MBA students, reflecting on these after execution is important: e.g., discuss "What was challenging about prioritizing ideas?" or "How did having a persona in mind change your brainstorming versus if you hadn't had one?"—to cement the connection between tool and outcome.

THOUGHT-PROVOKING QUESTIONS

1. **User vs. Business Trade-offs:** *How should a team handle user-centred findings (e.g., empathy map insights) conflict with business constraints (like cost or technical feasibility)?*
   This question asks students to consider desirability, feasibility, and viability. For example, if users want an expensive feature to implement, how do you decide? It provokes discussion of prioritization techniques, SWOT's role in bringing in those perspectives, or iterative solutions (maybe scaling down the feature to an MVP). It highlights that design thinking doesn't ignore business reality but how to reconcile them (often through iterative prototyping and stakeholder engagement).
2. **Scalability of Solutions:** *Once a successful prototype is tested with a small group of users, what steps would you take to scale that solution for a global launch? How might tools like journey mapping or SWOT come back into play at that stage?*
   It prompts thinking about how initial design outputs transition to implementation. Perhaps journey mapping a scaled deployment (including new stages like "Localization" or "Data privacy compliance in each region" as part of the journey for internal teams) or doing a SWOT for each new market. It pushes students to consider that design is iterative, even post-launch (continuous improvement) and planning for scale may require revisiting design tools at a macro level.
3. **Design Thinking in Non-Product Contexts:** *Can these tools be applied to internal business challenges (like improving team collaboration or redesigning an organizational process)? Choose a tool and describe how you would use it for an internal problem.*
   This question broadens application beyond product/service design. For instance, affinity diagrams could be used to sort employee feedback about company culture, or storyboarding could map the "employee onboarding journey" in HR. It makes students translate these skills to management problems: maybe a persona for "the new hire" to empathize in HR policy making, etc. It underlines the versatility of design thinking.
4. **Evaluating Brainstorming Outcomes:** *In a brainstorming session, suppose your team generated a lot of "wild" innovative ideas and a few conservative, incremental ones. Dot voting shows the team gravitating toward the safer options. How would you ensure that potentially disruptive ideas aren't prematurely dismissed?*
   It deals with group dynamics and innovation culture. It encourages thinking about facilitation tweaks (maybe separate voting for "most innovative" and "easiest" and then discussing a portfolio approach). Or maybe have a principle that at least one risky idea gets prototyped along with an incremental one (a dual-track

approach). It's provoking thoughts on avoiding complacency and balancing risk in innovation. It also touches on how dot voting could inadvertently favour familiar ideas and how a leader might counter that bias by strategy (maybe the HIPPO or product manager can save a high-risk idea intentionally, even if not top-voted, acknowledging the team's bias).

5. **Measuring Design Thinking Success:** *What metrics or indicators would you use to convince executives that investing time in empathy mapping and prototyping yields results?*

   It pushes students to connect design thinking to business outcomes. Ideas might include decreased development rework (thus cost savings), improved customer satisfaction/NPS after implementing a design thinking-informed change, faster time-to-market due to clearer initial requirements, or several new ideas that turned into new revenue streams. It makes them think of bridging qualitative and quantitative. Maybe "customer complaints about X issue dropped 40% after we journey-mapped and fixed that part of service, demonstrating ROI." It's an open question with no single answer, but it gets them to strategize the value demonstration, which is key for managing up.

These thought questions aim to deepen understanding, ensure students can adapt these tools flexibly, and prepare them to articulate the value of design thinking in a business context. They require applying chapter concepts to hypothetical but realistic scenarios, which tests comprehension at a higher Bloom's taxonomy level (application/ analysis/ synthesis).

In conclusion, design thinking tools equip MBA students (and future managers) to tackle problems with a user-centric, innovative lens. By practising empathy, visual thinking, open ideation, and iterative testing, they build solutions and more agile and collaborative team processes. The chapter's journey from introduction to deep-dive tools and exercises should empower students to lead design thinking initiatives in whatever field they enter, continually asking the empathetic question: "Are we solving the right problem, and is our solution truly meaningful for the people it's meant for?"

REFERENCES

Bennett, R. (2020). Storyboard Art with Nick Sung. Rain Bennett Blog. Retrieved February 18, 2025, from https://www.rainbennett.com/post/storyboard-art-with-nick-sung

Harrison, T. (2018, February 5). How to perfect the facilitation tool "sticky dot" voting. Michigan State University Extension. Retrieved February 18, 2025, from https://www.canr.msu.edu/news/how_to_perfect_the_facilitation_tool_sticky_dot_voting

Metropolis Magazine. (2019, June 11). Rooms with a View. MetropolisMag.com. Retrieved February 18, 2025, from https://metropolismag.com/projects/rooms-with-a-view/

Shopify. (2021, April 5). Mind Mapping (with Examples). Shopify Partners Blog. Retrieved February 18, 2025, from https://www.shopify.com/partners/blog/mind-map

Tufts University. (n.d.). Dot Voting. Tufts Design Thinking Toolkit. Retrieved February 18, 2025, from https://designthinking.it.tufts.edu/framework/ideate/dot-voting

CHAPTER 8

Strategic Planning and Implementation Management

LEARNING OBJECTIVES

After reading this Chapter, the readers will be able to:

- Understand scenario analysis in strategic planning—Grasp what scenario analysis is and how it helps organisations anticipate multiple future environments for better strategy formulation.
- Strategic planning in uncertainty—Appreciate the importance of strategic planning in volatile, uncertain, complex, and ambiguous (VUCA) environments and learn approaches to remain agile and proactive.
- Conduct stakeholder analysis—Identify and map stakeholders and understand their influence on strategic decision-making using stakeholder analysis and engagement tools.
- Apply change management frameworks—Learn key change management frameworks (Kotter's 8-Step Model, ADKAR) and how they facilitate successful strategy implementation amid organisational change.
- Leverage design thinking for problem-solving—Recognise how design thinking offers a human-centred approach to solving strategic problems and how it differs from traditional problem-solving methods.
- Integrate concepts in practice—Synthesise scenario planning, stakeholder engagement, change management, and design thinking into cohesive implementation plans for real-world strategic challenges.

8.1 SCENARIO ANALYSIS

Scenario analysis is a strategic planning technique used to imagine and prepare for multiple possible future states of the business environment. Rather than trying to predict a single outcome, scenario analysis involves developing a set of diverse scenarios and stories about how the future could unfold based on varying assumptions about key uncertainties and trends. It helps organisations "think about future changes systematically" and understand how different factors might affect their plans. The goal is not to get the future right but to broaden strategic thinking and "modify the mental model of decision-makers faced with an uncertain future". By challenging executives to consider best-case, worst-case, and alternative scenarios in between, scenario analysis encourages proactive planning and flexibility.

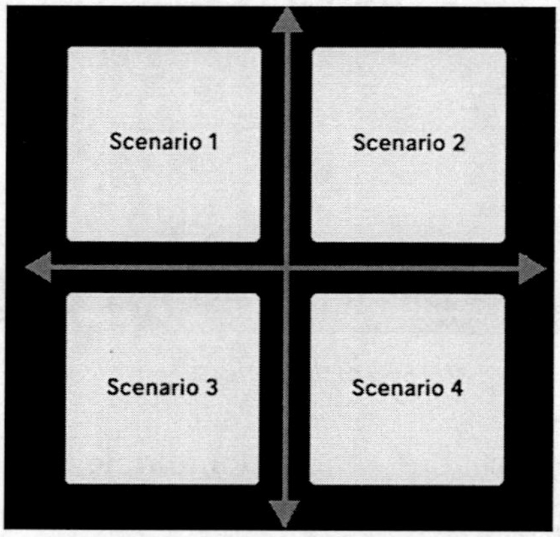

FIGURE 8.1 2 × 2 scenario planning matrix.

Figure 8.1 shows a 2 × 2 scenario planning matrix where each quadrant represents a distinct future scenario defined by two critical uncertainties. In practice, strategists identify key drivers of change (for example, regulatory environment and technology adoption rate) and plot scenarios that explore different combinations of extreme outcomes for those drivers (e.g. Scenario 1: high regulation + rapid tech adoption, Scenario 2: high regulation + slow tech adoption, etc.). This visual framework helps teams consider a range of plausible futures rather than just the most expected ones.

Real-World Examples of Scenario Planning: One of the most famous examples of scenario planning comes from Royal Dutch Shell. In the late 1960s and early 1970s, Shell's strategists developed multiple global oil market scenarios, including one in which Middle Eastern oil exports were sharply curtailed. When the 1973 oil crisis hit, Shell had anticipated the possibility of an oil shock and was able to respond more swiftly than competitors. Shell's use of scenario planning (pioneered by Herman Kahn of RAND) helped it weather that turbulent period, illustrating the value of preparing for unlikely but high-impact futures. At Shell, the aim was explicitly "not to predict the future but to modify the mental model of decision-makers" so they would be better prepared. The success of Shell's scenarios also depended on integrating them into routine strategy and risk discussions, not treating them as one-off thought experiments.

Many other companies have since adopted scenario analysis. In the technology industry, firms like Microsoft and Google use scenario planning to explore how emerging technologies or shifts in consumer behaviour could create new markets or render current products obsolete. For example, a tech company might develop scenarios around the future of artificial intelligence. One scenario is where AI advances rapidly, and competitors leverage it thoroughly, and another is where progress is slower due to regulatory or ethical constraints. Independent themed scenarios focused on specific drivers (like technological breakthroughs) are common in tech. Scenario planning is almost routine in the energy sector: energy companies model futures with different oil price levels, from optimistic to pessimistic, to guide long-term investments. Likewise, financial institutions employ scenario analysis for stress testing, imagining recession, interest rate spikes, or other economic scenarios to ensure adequate capital and risk controls for each case. The practice is widespread: industries as diverse as pharmaceuticals (considering scenarios for drug approvals or pandemics), consumer goods (scenarios for changing consumer preferences or supply chain disruptions), and government agencies (urban planning scenarios for population growth or climate change) all use scenario analysis to inform strategy.

Comparing Use Across Industries: While the core method of scenario analysis, envisaging multiple futures, is consistent, its application varies by industry based on the types of uncertainty each faces. For instance, energy companies often focus on macroeconomic and geopolitical uncertainties (oil supply, global policy changes), whereas software companies might focus on technological and market adoption uncertainties. An energy firm might create quantitative "arrayed scenarios" examining slight, moderate, or severe fluctuations in commodity prices. In contrast, a technology firm might craft more qualitative narratives about how a breakthrough (or lack thereof) in AI or quantum computing changes the competitive landscape. Similarly, manufacturing companies may develop scenarios around supply chain dynamics or raw material costs, and retail companies might scenario-plan for shifts in consumer behaviour (e.g. a scenario where e-commerce dominates versus one where in-store experience makes a resurgence). The level of uncertainty also differs: stable industries (like utilities in regulated markets) might use scenario analysis in a limited way (planning around regulatory or demand scenarios). In contrast, highly volatile industries (like tech or startups) embrace it more fully to navigate rapid changes.

Regardless of industry, scenario planning broadens the view of what is possible. It pushes companies to consider optimistic and pessimistic cases, not just the "most likely" forecast. In doing so, it yields several benefits. First, it forces an in-depth analysis of how different factors interact so that complex, non-linear events do not blindside strategists. Second, it is a form of proactive problem-solving. Organisations can devise contingency plans in advance by identifying potential problems before they happen. Third, it encourages diverse thinking and debate. In scenario workshops, participants from different functions bring unique perspectives, which helps avoid groupthink and fosters innovative solutions. And importantly, scenario analysis can act as an early warning system. If you have imagined a scenario (a new competitor or a supply shock) and see early indicators of it coming true, you can respond faster.

Best Practices in Scenario Planning: Effective scenario analysis is as much an art as a science. Some best practices have emerged to guide managers in doing it well. These are summarised in Table 8.1.

TABLE 8.1 Best Practices in Scenario Planning

Best Practice	*Key Idea/Why It Matters*
Use diverse questions and perspectives	Encourages strategic focus and open exploration; balances internal goals with external unpredictability.
Categorise scenario types	Ensures decision-makers consider a range of futures: base, worst-case, and best-case, not just "business as usual."
Balance scope (avoid extremes)	It avoids scenarios that are too vague or too far-fetched. Keeps focus on credible, actionable narratives.
Be imaginative and realistic	Promotes creativity within logical bounds; supports bold thinking without becoming detached from reality.
Engage cross-functional teams	Enhances richness and diversity in scenario development while improving buy-in and implementation feasibility.

Each practice helps ensure the scenarios developed are insightful, credible, and useful for informing strategy. For example, classifying scenarios (realistic, pessimistic, aspirational) prevents the analysis from clustering around a single vision of the future and prompts thinking about contingency plans for downturns or opportunities for breakthroughs.

Another recommended practice is to leverage tools or software for scenario modelling. Modern planning software can help teams model financial outcomes under each scenario and quickly adjust variables. However, tools are only an aid. The quality of scenarios still depends on human creativity and judgment.

Finally, scenario planning should be ongoing, not a one-time exercise. As time passes, some scenarios will start looking more likely while others will look less likely. Organisations should periodically revisit and update scenarios based on the latest information and use them to "adjust their strategies accordingly". The true value of scenario analysis is in making an organisation more agile and prepared. It instils a mindset that since the future is uncertain, strategy must be flexible. Companies that excel in scenario planning have a culture that embraces uncertainty rather than fearing it. They treat strategy not as a static plan but as a portfolio of possible plans that can be activated as the world changes.

In summary, scenario analysis expands a company's peripheral vision. It encourages leaders to ask, "What would we do if X happened?" for a range of Xs. By doing so, it builds strategic resilience. One consultancy noted, "The hallmark of companies that chart the right course through turbulence is that they embrace uncertainty...lay out the possible scenarios… and identify trigger points. Planning becomes a cycle of 'execute, monitor, and adapt'." (McDowell & Sneader, 2021). Rather than being caught off-guard by change, scenario-savvy organisations have playbooks ready for many eventualities. This proactive approach can distinguish between merely reacting to external events and confidently navigating them.

8.2 STRATEGIC PLANNING IN UNCERTAIN ENVIRONMENTS

Today's business landscape is often described as a VUCA world of Volatility, Uncertainty, Complexity, and Ambiguity. In such an environment, strategic planning cannot be a rigid, once-a-year exercise. Traditional planning methods that assume a stable future and rely on linear forecasts tend to break down when the ground shifts continuously. Instead, organisations need strategic planning approaches tailored for volatility, i.e., approaches that are flexible, iterative, and responsive to change.

Why plan at all in uncertainty? At first glance, planning amid high uncertainty might seem futile because if the future is unpredictable, what good is a plan? However, uncertainty *increases* the need for strategic planning, but it doesn't eliminate it. As McKinsey experts said, "Lack of certainty about the future is the very reason you need a strategy" (Dye & Sibony, 2020). The key is to change how we plan. In unstable environments, strategic planning aims not to produce a perfect prediction but to prepare the organisation to pivot effectively as new information arrives. It's about creating a directional roadmap and a set of options rather than a fixed destination.

Characteristics of Uncertain Environments: Uncertain or volatile business environments are marked by rapid change (e.g. technological disruption, sudden shifts in consumer preferences), unpredictable external shocks (economic crises, pandemics, political upheaval), and complex interdependencies (global supply chains, ecosystems). For example, consider the environment during the COVID-19 pandemic or the 2008 financial crisis. Companies faced sudden and drastic changes to demand, supply, and operating conditions. Sticking rigidly to an annual plan made months earlier can be disastrous in such cases. What's needed is an *adaptive* strategy.

Effective strategic planning in uncertainty starts with acknowledging the unpredictability. Leaders must be vigilant, continuously scanning the horizon for weak signals of change. Many companies formalise this through dynamic planning cycles by revisiting strategic assumptions quarterly or more frequently than annually. Some employ real-time dashboards of key risk indicators linked to their strategic plans, so they know when a scenario envisaged in their planning (like a drop in consumer confidence or a raw material shortage) is beginning to materialise.

One useful concept is identifying "trigger points" or signposts in advance. For instance, a global retailer might decide: *"If currency exchange rates move by more than X%, or if a trade war tariff is enacted, we will activate Plan B, which we developed for that scenario."* In Bain & Company's words, companies thriving in turbulence "focus on the vital few uncertainties that matter, lay out possible scenarios that could develop, and identify critical trigger points or signposts that signal swings in direction" (Dye & Sibony, 2020). It means predefining what actions to take under certain conditions so the organisation isn't caught flat-footed. Planning becomes an ongoing cycle of "execute, monitor, and adapt" rather than a set-and-forget plan.

CASE STUDY: Global Company in Uncertainty

Company X's Agile Strategy during a Crisis: A real-world example of strategic planning in an uncertain environment is the response of many global companies to the COVID-19 crisis around 2020. Let us consider Unilever, the consumer goods giant, as a case. During the pandemic, Unilever faced wildly volatile demand in different product categories (e.g., surges for cleaning products and drops for out-of-home food). Instead of sticking to its pre-2020 strategic plan, Unilever rapidly convened a cross-functional strategic team to run scenario analyses (pandemic lasts 6 months vs. 18 months, etc.) and to re-prioritise resources accordingly (Futures Platform, 2022). They created short-term "sprints" focusing on supply chain continuity and digital commerce, essentially re-writing parts of their strategy on the fly. Unilever's leadership communicated new strategic priorities (like increasing the production of hygiene products, shifting marketing to emphasise health/ safety, and scaling direct-to-consumer channels) and empowered country managers to make quick decisions aligned with those priorities. This agile re-planning each quarter helped Unilever weather the uncertainty and prepare for emerging opportunities (such as consumer preference for sustainable, hygienic products post-pandemic).

Another illustrative case is Microsoft's strategic shift under Satya Nadella in the mid-2010s, which can be seen as planning for an uncertain tech future. When Nadella became CEO in 2014, the technology landscape was changing fast with the rise of cloud computing and mobile platforms, areas where Microsoft was lagging. Nadella treated this as a volatile environment requiring a strategic pivot. He articulated a new strategic vision ("mobile-first, cloud-first") and reallocated investments, such as heavily investing in Microsoft Azure cloud services. Microsoft also adopted continuous planning for its product groups, embracing agile development so that product strategies could adjust to customer feedback and competitive moves in real-time. Culturally, Nadella encouraged a "growth mindset" among employees, meaning the company should always be learning and iterating. This cultural change supported a more flexible strategic approach. As a result, Microsoft was able to reinvent itself from a Windows-centric strategy to a cloud-centric strategy in a few short years, demonstrating how embracing uncertainty (rather than sticking to the old, certain PC-centric world) led to long-term success (Knolskape, 2023).

The contrast between stable vs. uncertain environments in strategic planning can be stark. In stable, predictable markets (say, a utility company in a region with steady regulation and demand), strategic planning often involves multi-year plans with incremental improvements and efficiency gains. These plans might be revisited annually but generally remain constant, and success comes from the disciplined execution of a well-defined strategy. In such environments, companies can afford to make detailed forecasts and stick to them; there is little need for frequent course correction. By contrast, strategic plans in highly uncertain environments or emerging markets must be more like "adaptive roadmaps". They set a direction and key priorities but also include conditional strategies ("if X happens, we will shift to Y"). In emerging markets, for example, political or economic instability might force companies to have contingency plans for sudden inflation or policy changes. A company operating in both a stable geography (like Western Europe) and an uncertain one (like Sub-Saharan Africa) will often have two different planning styles: a traditional strategic plan for the former and a flexible, scenario-based plan for the latter. Additionally, in uncertain environments, the planning horizon may be shorter. Companies might focus on 1–3 year strategic initiatives with a vision toward a longer-term direction rather than committing to very long-term detailed plans that unforeseen changes could upend.

Geography can play a role as well. For instance, Japanese companies traditionally engage in long-term planning and consensus-building, but they have also had to become more agile in recent volatile decades. In Silicon Valley (a very uncertain, fast-paced context), startups often use "pivoting" as part of their strategy, acknowledging that their initial strategy might change multiple times based on market feedback. The need for speed is greater in such contexts, so planning processes are often faster and involve more real-time data.

One effective framework for planning under uncertainty, proposed by strategy researchers, is to identify the level of uncertainty your business faces and tailor your strategy process to that. Hugh Courtney of McKinsey outlined levels: clear enough future (Level 1), alternate futures (Level 2), a range of futures (Level 3), or true ambiguity (Level 4). Suppose you're at Level 3 or 4 (high uncertainty). In that case, the recommendation is to develop strategic options and keep them open as long as possible. For example, make small investments in multiple potential opportunities (real options strategy) until uncertainty resolves somewhat (Dye & Sibony, 2020). Many companies did exactly this during the early internet era: they invested in multiple digital initiatives, unsure which would pan out but ready to scale up the winners.

Strategic Agility as a Mindset: A recurring theme for managing uncertainty is building a culture of agility. Companies that handle uncertainty well tend to "embrace uncertainty—they don't try to fight it". It means managers are rewarded for adaptability and rapid learning, not just for executing a fixed plan. For example, Netflix famously evolved its strategy from mail-order DVDs to streaming to content production by continuously learning and adapting to technological and consumer changes. It treated each strategic plan as provisional, subject to change when the data or environment indicated a new direction was needed. Such companies often have mechanisms like internal innovation labs or budgeting for experimentation to explore new strategic directions if needed swiftly.

Strategic planning in an uncertain environment often merges with risk management. The strategic plan will explicitly list major uncertainties (market, technology, geopolitical, etc.), and for each, the plan will outline risk mitigation or opportunity capture strategies. It could be in the form of maintaining strategic options, for example, securing a partnership or licensing agreement that can be exercised if a new technology takes off but that doesn't cost much if it doesn't. An oil company, for example, might "buy an option to establish a beachhead" in a new market like China, as one McKinsey piece noted (Dye & Sibony, 2020), meaning they set up a small presence that can be expanded rapidly if conditions turn favorable, but isn't a huge loss if the bet doesn't pay off.

To summarise, volatile and uncertain business climates demand a shift from linear planning to adaptive strategy management. Key practices include continuous monitoring of the environment, scenario planning (as covered earlier), predefined trigger points for action, shorter planning review cycles, and fostering an organisational culture that is comfortable with change. As one Bain report highlighted, the companies that navigate turbulence best are those that prepare a "clear and practical set of strategic playbooks that bring both commitment and flexibility to the planning process" (McDowell & Sneader, 2021). They commit to a direction but remain ready to adjust tactics and even core strategies as new information emerges.

In uncertain times, strategy becomes not a rigid map but a compass and a toolkit. The compass gives direction based on the company's vision and values, and the toolkit (scenarios, options, triggers, contingency plans) equips the company to travel through whatever terrain lies ahead. The overarching need is to remain proactive. Companies cannot control external volatility, but they can maintain their preparedness and response through diligent strategic planning. Thus, rather than being paralysed by uncertainty, an organisation with strong strategic agility can thrive by quickly seizing opportunities that others stuck in old plans might miss.

8.3 STAKEHOLDER ANALYSIS

No strategy can be effectively planned or implemented without considering the stakeholders involved. Stakeholder analysis is the systematic process of identifying all parties that have an interest in or can influence a strategic decision and assessing their impact, needs, and perspectives. Stakeholder analysis is critical in strategic decision-making because strategies often succeed or fail based on stakeholder support. A brilliant strategy on paper can be derailed if key stakeholders (for example, a regulatory body, a community, or employees) oppose it or are not engaged. Thus, understanding stakeholders, who they are, what they want, and how to manage their expectations is foundational to implementation management.

Definition of Stakeholder Analysis: An organisation's actions can affect or affect a stakeholder. It includes internal stakeholders (employees, management, owners) and external stakeholders (customers, suppliers, investors, regulators, community members, etc.). Stakeholder analysis involves creating a detailed list of these groups and evaluating their level of interest in the project/strategy and their power or influence over it. According to one strategic guide, *"Stakeholder Analysis is a process used to identify all parties who may be affected by or interested in the success of an organisation's project or strategy. It includes internal (employees) and external (customers, vendors, suppliers) stakeholders"*. The analysis doesn't stop at identification; it also examines how each stakeholder could impact the decision (positively or negatively) and their motivations.

The importance of stakeholder analysis in strategic decision-making cannot be overstated. First, it provides insight into the "critical stakeholders" and how they might influence outcomes. By mapping out stakeholders, leaders can anticipate where support or resistance will come from. Second, it helps craft communication and engagement strategies tailored to each stakeholder group, improving buy-in. One source notes that by *"understanding the needs and expectations of stakeholders, organisations can better engage with them to create an environment where everyone is working towards a common goal. This engagement increases buy-in, essential for successful strategic decision-making"*. In short, stakeholder analysis is about aligning your strategy with those who have a stake in it to ensure smoother execution.

Steps in Stakeholder Analysis: Typically, stakeholder analysis follows a few key steps:

1. **Identify Stakeholders:** Brainstorm or list all individuals, groups, or organisations affected by the decision or who can influence it. Depending on the context, it should be exhaustive, including obvious stakeholders like customers and less obvious ones like local communities or media (2F-STX, n.d.).

2. **Assess their Interests and Influence:** For each stakeholder, evaluate what their interest is (what do they stand to gain or lose? What are their objectives?) and how much power or influence they have over the decision (can they block it? Do they have resources or authority the project needs?). A common method is categorising stakeholders on a power/interest grid, plotting them in a high/ low-interest matrix vs. high/low power.
3. **Prioritise Stakeholders:** Not all stakeholders are equal. Identify key players that require close management, which ones need to be kept satisfied or informed, etc. This prioritisation helps focus the effort where it matters most.
4. **Develop Engagement Strategies:** Plan how to engage with each key stakeholder or category of stakeholders. It could include communication plans (how to keep them informed or involved), negotiation or influence tactics, addressing their concerns, and assigning relationship owners (someone responsible for managing the relationship with that stakeholder).
5. **Execute and Monitor:** Engage stakeholders as planned and monitor their feedback or any change in their stance. Stakeholder attitudes can change, so this is an ongoing process.

One of the popular tools to aid stakeholder analysis is the stakeholder mapping matrix, often using Mendelow's power-interest grid. This visual tool helps strategists categorise stakeholders into four groups: generally labelled as: (1) High Power/High Interest (key players to manage closely), (2) High Power/Low Interest (keep satisfied), (3) Low Power/High Interest (keep informed), and (4) Low Power/Low Interest (monitor with minimal effort). For example, a government regulator might be high power (they can approve or shut down a project) but low interest (not deeply concerned unless something goes wrong)—strategy: keep them satisfied by meeting all compliance requirements and proactively communicating major changes. On the other hand, a project's end-users might have high interest (the outcome matters a lot to them) but low formal power—strategy: keep them informed and involved through feedback sessions because their support can still be influential indirectly (especially if negative feedback could sway public opinion or employee morale). Managers can develop appropriate engagement plans by plotting stakeholders on such a grid. Figure 8.2 illustrates a generic stakeholder power-interest matrix and typical management strategies for each quadrant.

Figure 8.2 shows a stakeholder Power/Interest grid (Mendelow's Matrix). Stakeholders are categorised into four quadrants, namely "Keep Informed" (low power, high interest), "Actively Consult" (high interest, high power—manage closely), "Regularly Engage" (high power, high interest, key players), and "Maintain Interest" (high power, low interest—keep satisfied). This tool helps strategists tailor how they manage each stakeholder group. For instance, stakeholders in the top right (high power, high interest) must be actively engaged and consulted at every stage, possibly even brought into decision-making forums. Those in the bottom-right (high power, low interest) should be kept satisfied. They may not want frequent updates, but they should be assured that their interests are not harmed (for example, a major investor might only need quarterly briefings focusing on ROI). The top left (low power, high interest) should be kept informed and given opportunities to voice

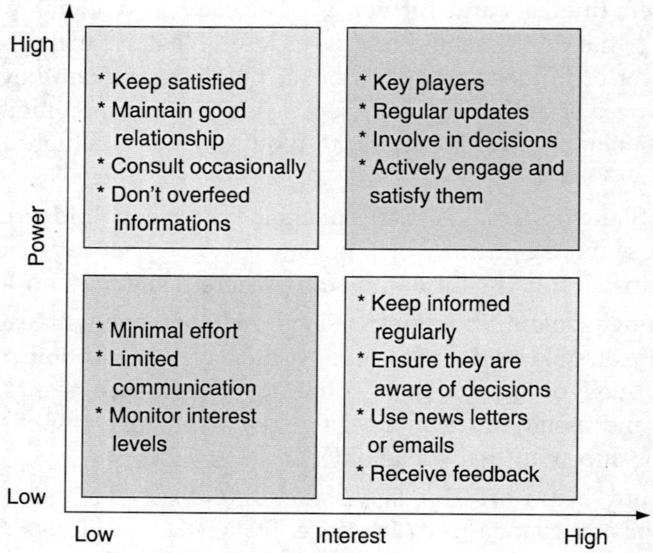

FIGURE 8.2 Power/Interest grid (Mendelow's Matrix).

concerns. They can become champions or critics despite lacking formal power (e.g., a highly engaged community group). Finally, bottom-left (low power, low interest) stakeholders require minimal effort and a light communication touch to ensure they don't feel ignored if circumstances change. Still, otherwise, they're not heavily involved.

(In the above figure, note that different sources use varying labels for the quadrants; the core idea is consistently to adjust the engagement level based on stakeholder power and interest.)

Real-World Examples of Stakeholder Engagement: Consider a company planning to build a new manufacturing facility in a town. The strategic decision (where and how to build) involves numerous stakeholders: the company's executives and shareholders, local government, the town's residents, environmental groups, employees/unions, and perhaps customers (interested in the company's capacity and community image). A stakeholder analysis might reveal, for example, that:

- The local community residents have high interest (it affects their environment and jobs) but individually low power. However, collectively, they could gain power by forming a coalition or influencing local elections. So, the company might hold town hall meetings (engagement strategy: inform and consult) to address their concerns (pollution, traffic, job creation).
- The environmental regulatory agency has high power (they can approve or deny permits) but maybe moderate interest (one of many projects they oversee). The company would keep regulators satisfied with rigorous environmental impact studies and compliance measures, submitting regular reports (engagement: satisfy and comply).
- The company's employees have high interest (their jobs or conditions may change) and some power (especially if unionised or their expertise is critical). The company

might involve employee representatives early in planning (engagement: actively consult) to design shift schedules or training programs for the new plant, thereby securing their support.

- Shareholders/investors have high power (funding approval) and high interest in the project's return. They would be managed closely through board meetings and transparent financial projections (engagement: actively engage and seek approval).

Another example: In software development strategy (like launching a new platform feature), key stakeholders include the end-users, the development team, customer support, and possibly partners (like third-party developers). Engaging end-users through beta testing (keep informed and involved) can provide valuable feedback and build buy-in. The internal development team must be fully on board (high interest and power to succeed or fail the project). So, leadership should ensure the team understands the strategic vision and feels heard regarding timelines or technical challenges (engagement: internal stakeholder workshops, agile ceremonies for feedback). If the feature impacts partners (say, API changes for third-party apps), those partners need proactive communication to adapt their systems (engagement: keep satisfied/informed).

Stakeholder Engagement Benefits: When done well, stakeholder analysis and engagement bring several advantages:

- *Better Risk Management:* By identifying potential sources of resistance early (e.g., a stakeholder who may be negatively impacted), the organisation can address issues proactively. *"It allows organisations to anticipate any potential issues better before they arise… identify potential sources of resistance and adjust strategies accordingly"*. For instance, if a stakeholder analysis in a project shows that a particular department might resist because the change increases its workload, the strategy can include additional support or incentives for that department.
- *Increased Support and Buy-In:* People are more likely to support what they had a chance to influence. Organisations build trust and create a sense of shared purpose by engaging stakeholders. It often leads to smoother implementation because stakeholders help push the strategy rather than block it. A study of project success factors found that active stakeholder participation correlates strongly with better outcomes (stakeholders feel "heard and accounted for in the decision-making process, which increases the likelihood of success").
- *More Robust Decisions:* Stakeholders bring diverse knowledge. Engaging them can surface insights management might miss. For example, front-line employees (stakeholders) might highlight customer pain points that a new strategy should address, or suppliers might advise how to reduce costs or avoid logistical pitfalls. Including these insights leads to a more well-rounded strategy that is practically feasible.
- *Enhanced Reputation and Goodwill:* Particularly with external stakeholders (like the community, customers, and NGOs), genuine engagement can enhance the organisation's reputation. Even if not everyone gets what they want, transparency and responsiveness earn goodwill. This social capital can be crucial, for example,

when companies need public support for an initiative (think of how Tesla often engages its customer community for feedback, building a loyal fan base who advocate for the brand).

Tools for Stakeholder Analysis: Other tools exist besides the power-interest matrix. One is the stakeholder mapping table, which lists each stakeholder along with their interests, potential impact, current level of support or opposition, and strategy to engage them. Another is the RACI matrix (Responsible, Accountable, Consulted, Informed) used in project management to define each stakeholder's role in tasks, ensuring clarity on who needs to be consulted or informed for each part of the plan. Visualisation tools like influence diagrams or social network maps can also illustrate how stakeholders relate to each other (sometimes, influencing one key stakeholder can have a cascading effect on others).

Case Example—Stakeholder Mapping in Action: As part of its sustainability strategy, a global beverage company wanted to switch to biodegradable packaging. Stakeholder analysis revealed a complex web: consumers (demanding eco-friendly products), municipal recycling facilities (needing to handle new materials), shareholders (concerned about costs), suppliers (for new packaging materials), environmental advocacy groups, and government regulators setting recycling targets. By mapping these out, the company identified that environmental NGOs and certain customers were potential allies (they would strongly support and amplify the initiative—high interest and some influence via public opinion). In contrast, the suppliers had concerns about costs and technology (high power because if they couldn't deliver affordable materials, the project would fail). Therefore, the company engaged the suppliers early, even offering to co-invest in R&D for the new packaging material (a strategy addressing supplier concerns) while partnering with NGOs to publicly endorse the move (turning them into champions for the strategy). Simultaneously, they worked with regulators to ensure the new packaging met standards (keeping regulators satisfied) and launched consumer awareness campaigns (keeping consumers informed about how to dispose of the new packaging). Ultimately, this careful stakeholder orchestration led to a successful rollout of biodegradable packaging with broad support, minimal backlash and positive publicity, which boosted sales. Without stakeholder analysis, the company might have faced supplier pushback or consumer confusion, jeopardising the strategic initiative.

Stakeholder analysis and engagement are about building a coalition for your strategy. As the famous management thinker Peter Drucker noted, "Culture eats strategy for breakfast," part of culture is the people and groups who have a stake in the business. If you neglect them, even the soundest strategy can stall. Conversely, if you actively manage stakeholder relationships, you turn potential hurdles into partners. The stakeholder analysis process brings strategic rigour to what might be handled ad hoc, ensuring no key player is overlooked, and their needs are considered in the strategy implementation plan.

One final point: Stakeholder analysis is not a one-time activity. Stakeholders' positions can evolve. New stakeholders can emerge. Therefore, companies often maintain a stakeholder register and update their analysis periodically or whenever a new strategic initiative is launched. Especially in projects that run over the years, stakeholder sentiment should be monitored. For example, public opinion (a collective stakeholder) might shift due to external events, prompting a change in engagement approach. Effective strategy managers remain in tune with the stakeholder landscape throughout execution.

To conclude, successful strategic implementation is rarely a solo endeavour by top management; it is a team sport involving the entire ecosystem of interested parties. Stakeholder analysis provides the playbook for that sport, identifying who is on the field, their position, and how to get them on your side or at least keep them from blocking progress. It brings a human dimension to strategic planning, ensuring that the strategy is theoretically sound and practically achievable given the people and organisations it touches.

8.4 CHANGE MANAGEMENT

Even the best strategic plan will fail if an organisation cannot implement it effectively. Change management is the discipline that focuses on the people's side when implementing strategies or transformations. It provides structured approaches to transition individuals, teams, and the whole organisation from the current state to a desired future state. In the context of strategic implementation, change management frameworks offer roadmaps to help leaders introduce new strategies, processes, or behaviours in a way that gains acceptance and minimises resistance. This section will explain key change management frameworks, notably Kotter's 8-Step model and the ADKAR model, and discuss how they are applied, including a case study of successful change implementation. We will also examine common challenges in change initiatives and how different regions or cultures might approach change.

Why Change Management Matters: Research consistently shows that many organisational change efforts (some studies say ~70%) fail to meet their objectives, often due to people-related issues (resistance, lack of buy-in, poor communication). A new strategy might require employees to work in new ways, managers to adopt different leadership styles, or processes to be overhauled. These changes can provoke anxiety, confusion, or pushback. Change management provides tools to prepare, equip, and support individuals through the change process to achieve strategic outcomes. A structured change management approach has been identified as one of the strongest predictors of successful change. In other words, change management bridges the gap between a great idea on paper and making it a reality in practice.

8.4.1 Kotter's 8-Step Change Model

One of the most widely known frameworks is Dr. John Kotter's 8-Step Process for Leading Change, introduced in his 1995 book and HBR article "Leading Change". Kotter's model provides a comprehensive checklist of phases an organisation should go through to implement change successfully. The steps are as follows:

1. **Create a Sense of Urgency:** Build and communicate a strong business case for why change is needed. Kotter observed that change efforts often fail when people don't see why they can't keep doing what they've always done. Thus, step 1 is about lighting a fire, for example, sharing data about a looming threat or a big

opportunity to mobilise initial motivation. It might involve exposing complacency ("If we don't change, we will fall behind competitors or face serious loss") or highlighting great prospects ("If we act now, we could lead the market"). The urgency needs to be felt organisation-wide.

2. **Build a Guiding Coalition:** Assemble a group with enough power and influence to lead the change and encourage them to work as a team. This coalition often includes senior executives, but Kotter stresses it should involve key influencers at various levels, not just title authority but also people with informal influence. The coalition's role is to drive the change forward, resolve obstacles, and demonstrate commitment. For example, in a digital transformation strategy, the coalition might include the CIO, a few respected tech-savvy managers, and an enthusiastic business unit leader collectively championing the effort.
3. **Form a Strategic Vision and Initiatives:** Clarify the change and craft a clear vision to direct the effort. Along with the vision, identify the strategic initiatives (projects) that will realise that vision. The vision gives a picture of the future (e.g., "We will be a customer-centric, data-driven organisation"), which helps align everyone's efforts and decisions. Kotter emphasises that a good vision is imaginable, desirable, feasible, focused, and clear. This step ensures everyone knows what the end goal looks like.
4. **Communicate the Vision (Kotter's original) or Enlist a Volunteer Army (as updated in Kotter's later revision):** This step is about widespread communication and buy-in. The guiding coalition should communicate the vision and strategy "at every opportunity" and "embed it in everything": meetings, emails, and town halls. It's not one memo but repeated, varied communication. The updated idea of a "volunteer army" means getting many employees on board willingly rather than mandating compliance from a few. It involves addressing people's concerns, answering questions, and generally winning hearts and minds so that many individuals become change agents.
5. **Enable Action by Removing Barriers:** Identify what obstacles (processes, structures, or mindsets) impede change and work to remove them. This step is about empowerment, giving people the freedom and tools to implement the change. Barriers could be formal (e.g., outdated workflows, hierarchical approvals that slow things) or informal (a manager who opposes the change or employees lacking certain skills). For instance, if the strategy requires faster product development, a barrier might be a bureaucratic approval process, and the solution could be streamlining or delegating authority. If people fear punishment for taking the initiative, leadership must change that climate (perhaps by encouraging experimentation and tolerating mistakes).
6. **Generate Short-Term Wins:** As change is often a long journey, Kotter advises creating visible, unambiguous successes as early as possible. These "wins" (e.g., a pilot project success, hitting a milestone, a first major customer victory under the new strategy) provide proof that the change is working and help to build momentum. They also reward the team's effort and can convert sceptics. Kotter

says these wins should be obvious and linked to the change effort, not random or minor. Managers should actively plan for and celebrate these wins. For example, if a company implements a new sales strategy, a short-term win could be securing a certain number of new client contracts within 3 months of rollout, broadcasting that success energises everyone.

7. **Sustain Acceleration (Build on Change):** Don't declare victory too soon. Use the credibility from early wins to tackle bigger or more stubborn change projects. In this stage, the organisation refines and expands the change. For example, after a few wins, you might introduce more challenging changes in processes that couldn't have been tackled initially. It's about maintaining urgency and pushing, bringing in new projects, resources, and leaders to keep the momentum. Kotter observed that many transformations fail because leaders relax after the first achievements; instead, he argues to press harder for full deployment. Treat the initial wins as the first inning of a longer game.
8. **Institute Change:** The new approaches should be anchored in the organisational culture. The change becomes "the way we do things around here." Leadership ensures that new behaviours are tied to success (e.g., through promotions or appraisal criteria reflecting the new values), and stories about the change effort's benefits are shared. For instance, if a company's strategy is to become more customer-centric and achieve it through certain changes, it must continue reinforcing customer-centric behaviour in hiring, training, and reward systems. Over time, the memory of "how we used to do it" fades, and the new state is simply normal. Only when the culture has been internalised, the change can leaders step back and consider the change effort truly completed.

Kotter's 8-step model is often visualised and taught as a guiding framework for organisational change. Many practitioners appreciate its emphasis on *creating buy-in* (the early steps about urgency, coalition, vision, and communication) before diving into the technical aspects of change and its emphasis on *reinforcement* at the end. The model aligns well with the major phases: preparing for change (steps 1–3), engaging and enabling the whole organisation (steps 4-6), and implementing and sustaining (7–8).

One can see how this model would directly apply to implementing a new strategy: Suppose a company wants to shift from a product-centric to a customer-centric strategy. Using Kotter:

- They might start by sharing competitive data that shows if they don't become more customer-focused, they will lose market share (urgency).
- They form a team of influential marketing, sales, and product managers passionate about customer experience (coalition).
- Together, they craft a vision like "Delight Every Customer" and strategy initiatives like new customer feedback systems and revamped service protocols (vision & initiatives).
- They communicate this in all-hands meetings, internal newsletters, and through managers modelling the behaviour (communicate/enlist).

- They remove barriers such as siloed data (enabling cross-department data sharing so customer info is accessible to all service reps).
- They shoot for a short-term win: e.g., in 3 months, improve customer satisfaction scores by 15% in one pilot region, and indeed, they do and celebrate it (short-term win).
- Building on that, they roll out the changes to all regions and tackle harder issues like re-aligning the incentive structure for salespeople to encourage long-term customer relationship building (sustain acceleration).
- Finally, a year later, they integrate "customer first" into their core values and onboarding and have senior leaders exemplify it consistently, ensuring it sticks (anchor culture).

By following Kotter's steps, the company increases the chances that the strategic shift will take hold across the organisation.

8.4.2 ADKAR Model

Another popular framework, especially for managing individual change, is the ADKAR model developed by Jeff Hiatt and popularised by Prosci (a change management consultancy). ADKAR is an acronym representing five outcomes each needs to transition through for a change to be successful: Awareness, Desire, Knowledge, Ability, Reinforcement (Prosci, n.d.).

In context:

- *Awareness of the need for change*—Do people understand why this change is happening? (This is similar to Kotter's urgency but on an individual level.)
- *Desire to participate and support the change*—Are people motivated to change? It touches on their choice. Even if they know why, do they want it?
- *Knowledge of how to change*—Do they know what to do differently? It often involves training or education on new skills, processes, or behaviours.
- *Ability to implement the change*—Can they actually do it? It is about translating knowledge into action, overcoming obstacles, practising new skills, and performing in a new way.
- *Reinforcement to sustain the change*—Are there mechanisms to keep the change in place? It could be recognition, rewards, feedback, or other support so people don't revert to old habits.

The ADKAR model is useful because it pinpoints where a change may fail. For example, if a strategy implementation isn't progressing, ADKAR helps diagnose: Do employees *know* what to do (Knowledge)? If yes, do they *want* to do it (Desire)? If they want to, are obstacles still preventing them (Ability)? And so on. It reminds managers that all five elements are needed for each person. You might achieve awareness and even provide Knowledge (training programs, etc.). Still, the implementation can stall if you haven't secured genuine desire (maybe people fear the change or see no incentive). Likewise, one might assume that people can do the new process (Ability) after training, but maybe they need more hands-on practice or better tools. If not, their ability is lacking, and performance will suffer.

For instance, imagine implementing a new software system as part of a strategy to improve data analytics. Using ADKAR:

- ✦ You would first communicate broadly to create awareness ("Our current system is too slow; the new system will allow us to respond to customers in real-time, which is critical for our strategy.").
- ✦ Next, build desire: maybe highlight WIIFM ("what's in it for me") for employees—the new system will make their jobs easier, or involve them in the selection process so they feel ownership. Also, address fears (ensure no jobs are lost, etc.). Perhaps share success stories or involve influential employees as change champions to generate buy-in.
- ✦ Then, ensure knowledge by providing training on how to use the new system, documentation, help desks, etc.
- ✦ Ensure ability: give people time to practice in a sandbox environment, maybe phased rollout so they can build confidence or one-on-one coaching sessions. Remove obstacles like old system dependencies or adjust workload so they have the bandwidth to learn.
- ✦ Finally, reinforcement: after going live, celebrate teams that fully adopt the system, gather feedback and show improvements achieved, maybe tie part of performance evaluations to effective system use (to reinforce that this is now expected). Continue monitoring usage and addressing any relapses or issues.

The ADKAR model aligns well with change management and complements project management. Prosci often integrates ADKAR into a larger methodology (prepare change, manage change, sustain change), but ADKAR is straightforward and focuses on the human aspect.

One advantage of ADKAR is that it's outcome-oriented. You need all five outcomes for each individual. Line managers can use it as a checklist: if an employee isn't embracing the new strategy, have I created awareness?, have I helped them have the desire?, etc. It's also sequential: Awareness comes first, then desire, etc., often mapping how people experience change. First, they hear about it, then react emotionally (support or resistance), learn how to do it, try it, and incorporate it.

CASE STUDY: Successful Change Management Implementation

Let us look at a well-known example: Satya Nadella's cultural transformation at Microsoft (which we touched on earlier). When Nadella took over, Microsoft was known for a competitive, siloed culture (the old "know-it-all" culture, internal rivalries). To execute a new strategy (cloud, cross-platform software), Nadella believed the culture had to shift to one of collaboration and learning ("learn-it-all" instead of "know-it-all").

He effectively applied many change management principles:

- He created Awareness and Desire by articulating the need for cultural change at all levels, saying that past success had made employees complacent and that a new mindset was needed to innovate in a fast-changing tech world. He often told employees, *"Our industry does not respect tradition—it only respects innovation."* This urgency was the burning platform.

- He role-modelled the desired behaviour (humility, learning, collaboration) to build desire and credibility. People saw the CEO himself changing the tone.
- Microsoft brought in knowledge and ability elements by launching training programs with a growth mindset, encouraging teams to adopt new collaboration tools (like Teams instead of just email) and new ways of working (agile projects). Managers were trained in coaching and empathy to support the new culture.
- They celebrated short-term wins, for example, early collaborative efforts that led to product successes (like different divisions coming together to create integrated solutions, which previously hadn't happened). Each win reinforced that the new way worked.
- Importantly, Nadella embedded reinforcement by changing performance review criteria. Microsoft shifted away from stack-ranking employees (which had fostered internal competition) to evaluating people on how well they collaborated and contributed to others' success. This structural change cemented the new cultural behaviours.

Over a few years, Microsoft's culture shifted, evidenced by higher employee satisfaction scores and the company's resurgence with more innovative and customer-focused products. This transformation is widely cited as a change management success, enabling Microsoft's broader strategic pivot. It shows how combining vision (Kotter's steps like urgency and coalition) and systematic reinforcement (ADKAR's reinforcement, structural changes) can yield real organisational change.

Another case: Kotter's 8-Step in a Merger Integration. Mergers are classic situations requiring careful change management. When two large companies merged in the pharmaceutical industry, leadership used Kotter's framework to guide the integration of cultures and processes. They started with a clear, urgent message: the merger was needed to innovate and survive against larger competitors (urgency). They formed an integration team (coalition) with leaders from both original companies. This team developed a vision for the new combined company ("OneTeam to cure disease X") and key initiatives (integrating R&D pipelines and combining sales forces). They communicated relentlessly, including roadshows to every major office explaining what would happen and why. To remove barriers, they harmonised IT systems quickly (so people could communicate) and proactively addressed legal/regulatory hurdles. They set 6-month post-merger targets as short-term wins (e.g., launch one joint product using the strengths of both firms—and succeeded, touting that as proof the merger yielded results). Over the next year, they continued merging departments and practices, keeping the momentum. Two years later, they worked on institutionalising new cultural norms (like a new company identity and values). While not every merger goes smoothly, this one achieved its cost savings and innovation goals largely because the change was managed in a structured way, not left to chance or purely dictated top-down without support.

Challenges in Change Management: Despite frameworks, change is hard. Common challenges include:

- *Resistance to Change:* Humans are creatures of habit, and fear of the unknown or losing control can cause pushback. Resistance can be overt (employees protesting, negative feedback) or covert (foot-dragging, "malicious compliance", or simply not adopting new behaviours). Causes range from fear of losing jobs/status to disagreement with the change or change fatigue (too many changes). Managing resistance often requires empathy, listening to concerns, involving people in solutions, finding quick wins to prove value, and sometimes negotiating (e.g., offering early retirement or new roles to those who feel threatened).
- *Poor Communication:* Rumours fill the void if the change's vision or "why" isn't communicated well. Miscommunication can lead to misunderstandings (e.g., employees thinking a new strategy means something it doesn't, causing unnecessary alarm) or lack of alignment. Many change efforts falter because leaders under-communicate. Kotter suggested that leaders must communicate the change vision 10x more than they think necessary. Clear, honest, and two-way communication (allowing feedback) is vital.
- *Insufficient Leadership Commitment:* Middle and front-line employees watch their leaders. Change efforts lose credibility if managers are not genuinely committed or are inconsistent (saying one thing, doing another). Also, if leaders do not allocate adequate resources (time, money, staff) to the change initiative, people see that it's not truly a priority.
- *Cultural Inertia:* Sometimes, the existing culture strongly resists change (the "way we do things" is deeply ingrained). It is especially true in older companies or certain regional cultures. Overcoming this requires symbolic and substantive actions. Leadership behaviour changes, aligning systems and incentives to the new way and often bringing in fresh talent or ideas to break old norms.
- *Change Collision and Fatigue:* In large organisations, multiple changes may happen simultaneously (new strategy, IT system, reorganisation, etc.). If not coordinated, employees can feel overwhelmed. There's a capacity for change, and exceeding it leads to burnout or apathy. Prioritising and sequencing changes and demonstrating how they connect to a cohesive vision can mitigate this.
- *Lack of Adaptability in the Plan:* Ironically, change programs may need to change mid-course. It can fail if a change management approach is too rigid (not listening to feedback and adjusting tactics). For example, maybe the initial approach to training isn't working—a flexible change leader might switch to a different method. Being too dogmatic about a framework without sensing the organisation's pulse is a risk.

Regional and Cultural Approaches to Change: Approaches to change management can differ across cultures and regions. Culture influences how people view authority, uncertainty, communication, and individual vs. group priorities. For example:

- In cultures with high power distance (where hierarchy is respected), top-down directives might be accepted more readily. Still, it could also mean lower-level employees are less candid about problems. A change leader in such a culture might rely more on formal authority and need to engage the hierarchy (e.g., get endorsements from respected figures) to legitimise the change. Conversely, in low power distance cultures (more egalitarian), involving employees in decision-making is critical, or they'll resent being told what to do without input.

- *Individualistic vs. Collectivistic cultures:* In a collectivist culture (many Asian and Latin cultures), framing the change regarding group benefit and harmony is effective, and utilising group forums or consensus-building (like the Japanese ring-sho decision process) can be important. People may not voice open dissent in meetings (to preserve harmony), so change agents must read the air or get feedback indirectly. Individuals in individualistic cultures (like the U.S. and Western Europe) might be more vocal, and change strategies might focus on personal incentives and opportunities.
- *Uncertainty Avoidance:* Some cultures (e.g., some in Southern Europe and Latin America) have higher discomfort with uncertainty and change. In such places, change management might need to move more slowly, providing detailed plans, clear rules, and reassurance. In contrast, cultures that are more comfortable with ambiguity (perhaps Anglo cultures) might embrace change more readily and even get excited if it promises innovation.
- *Communication Style:* Direct vs. indirect communication differences mean that a "burning platform" message that's very direct might galvanise an American audience but could be seen as too confrontational in Japan, for instance. Adjusting the tone, maybe using more implicit messaging or finding culturally appropriate metaphors can help. Similarly, celebrating individual achievements (common in the U.S.) vs. team achievements (more common in Japan or China) affects how you reinforce change (whom do you publicly reward? one person or the whole team?).
- *Approach to Conflict:* In some cultures, open conflict or debate is normal (e.g., in many Western contexts, employees might openly challenge a new idea in a meeting). In others, people might quietly resist and never say anything to the boss. To truly gauge sentiment, a savvy change manager will use different techniques: perhaps anonymous surveys or one-on-one check-ins in cultures where public confrontation is avoided.

What is nearly universal is the need to show respect for local norms when managing change in a multinational context. For example, a global company rolling out the same strategic change in the U.S., France, and India will likely have a core change plan. Still, local change leaders will adapt the messaging and engagement to fit local employees' mindsets and values. In France, involving the workers' council or unions formally in the change is crucial (given labour traditions), whereas in the U.S., that might not apply. Still, you'd focus on individual buy-in and perhaps emphasise career development aspects of the change.

Prosci published insights from their global partners on cultural differences in change management, noting things like: in Japan, successful change often emphasises consensus (Nemawashi—laying groundwork privately before formal proposals) and senior leader presence is taken as a strong signal (if the CEO personally speaks about the change, it is powerful). In Brazil, personal relationships and trust might be prerequisites for getting candid feedback, so change managers spend more time in informal conversations. In Germany, employees might expect very thorough plans and expertise from change leaders (a more formal approach), whereas in Sweden, involving everyone in dialogues (true to their egalitarian culture) works better.

Despite differences, the core principles of change management, namely, communicate, participate, support, and reinforce, are quite universally applicable; they just get executed in culturally nuanced ways. Change managers benefit from being culturally intelligent, adapting their style to match how local stakeholders will best receive and engage with the change. In global projects, it's wise to have local change champions who understand the culture and can translate (literally and figuratively) the change vision into terms that resonate locally.

Key Frameworks Recap: To tie Kotter and ADKAR together, note that Kotter's model is often considered at the organisational level (steps a leadership team takes). At the same time, ADKAR focuses on the individual level (what each person needs). They are complementary: Kotter might tell you to "communicate vision" and "remove barriers" at a broad level, while ADKAR reminds you "Is each person aware? Do they have the desire? If not, maybe our communication didn't hit personal motivation. Fix that." Using both, one can design a robust change plan. Additionally, other frameworks exist (e.g., Lewin's Unfreeze-Change-Refreeze model, which is simpler: prepare people by unfreezing current habits, then change, then refreeze to lock in new habits; or the ADKAR-inspired ADKAR for each phase of Prosci's 3-phase process). Some organisations develop their change playbooks, mixing elements of these.

Different Regions Approach Example: One interesting observation is that in some regions like Western Europe, there is more legal or formal involvement in changes (e.g., informing and consulting labour councils is often a legal requirement in EU countries for major changes—something a change manager must account for). In contrast, in the U.S., employment is more at-will, so formal consultation isn't required, but you risk disengagement if you don't involve people voluntarily. So, "how different regions approach it" can also refer to regulatory environments, not just culture. A savvy change plan for a global strategy rollout will address these, doing a more formal process in regions where needed.

In conclusion, change management is the linchpin connecting strategy formulation and execution. Frameworks like Kotter's 8 Steps provide a roadmap for leading large-scale change, ensuring that aspects like vision, communication, and consolidation of gains are not overlooked. The ADKAR model zooms into the individual journey, reminding us that each person needs to be guided through their change curve. By applying these frameworks, organisations can systematically tackle change challenges like reducing resistance, increasing engagement, and improving the odds that their strategic initiatives will deliver results. By remaining mindful of human factors and cultural nuances, leaders can cultivate an environment where change is not something to dread but rather a natural, even positive, part of the organisation's evolution.

Readers are encouraged to watch the lecture on change management by visiting the link—**https://youtu.be/OWo5sckh_-M**

Alternatively, one can scan the QR code presented below to watch the lecture.

SCAN ME

Scan here to watch—Change Management.

8.5 DESIGN THINKING APPROACH TO PROBLEM-SOLVING

In recent years, Design Thinking has gained prominence beyond product design and has been embraced as a powerful approach to strategic problem-solving. Design thinking is a human-centred, iterative process for solving problems and discovering innovative solutions. In the context of strategy, it offers a way to tackle complex business challenges by starting from user or customer needs, encouraging creativity, and iterating through prototyping and feedback. This section will define design thinking in a strategy context, present a case study of a business using design thinking for strategic problem-solving, and compare traditional problem-solving approaches with design thinking.

What is Design Thinking (in strategy)? Design thinking originated in the design field (as used by designers to create products that truly meet user needs), but its principles are broadly applicable. The core principles include empathy (profoundly understanding the people affected by the problem), ideation (generating a wide range of creative solutions), Prototyping (building rough versions of solutions), and Testing (getting feedback and iterating). In strategy, these translate to an approach where instead of just analysing data and making a top-down plan, you involve stakeholders, brainstorm boldly, test strategic ideas on a small scale, and refine them. It's beneficial for "wicked problems", ambiguous, multi-faceted challenges where purely analytical approaches might not yield breakthrough solutions.

A succinct description: *"Design Thinking is a non-linear, iterative process that seeks to understand the user, challenge assumptions, and redefine problems to identify innovative solutions... emphasising empathy, ideation, prototyping, and user-centric design."* (Kumar, 2021). It contrasts with traditional problem-solving, which often is linear and heavily analytical (define problem ◎ analyse ◎ solve). Design thinking is more exploratory: you might reframe the problem itself after empathising (perhaps discovering the initial problem statement wasn't what users needed to be solved), and you allow for creative techniques (like brainstorming wild ideas, storyboarding future scenarios, etc.).

CASE STUDY: Design Thinking in Practice—A Business

A celebrated example of design thinking in strategy is PepsiCo's transformation under CEO Indra Nooyi, who explicitly championed design thinking to drive innovation (Ignatius, 2021; Randall, 2020). Around 2012, PepsiCo was a traditional consumer products company facing stagnation in some core product lines. Indra Nooyi brought in a Chief Design Officer, Mauro Porcini, and together, they set a vision to embed design thinking into PepsiCo's culture and strategy.

What did this mean in practice? They did not limit design to packaging; they applied design thinking to product development, brand strategy, and even internal processes:

- *Teams began with empathy:* They studied consumers in their homes, observing how people snack or hydrate to uncover unmet needs or pain points (for example, noticing that busy parents wanted healthier snack options that still felt fun for kids). These insights sometimes reframed PepsiCo's strategic opportunities.
- *They engaged in deep ideation:* Rather than rely only on market research data and traditional R&D, they ran innovation workshops where cross-functional teams brainstormed new product concepts or experiences (with designers facilitating to push beyond the obvious). It led to ideas like the drink dispenser "Spire" or new healthy product lines that integrated into lifestyle trends, things that might not surface from spreadsheet analysis alone.
- *Prototyping and testing became commonplace:* For instance, before a global launch of a new product concept, they'd test it in a limited market with experimental branding and gather feedback, then iterate on everything from flavour to marketing strategy. One story involved Pepsi's redesign of the Tropicana orange juice packaging, which initially failed (sales dropped due to consumer backlash). PepsiCo learned from that by prototyping and testing packaging changes more carefully with customers before the full rollout.

According to research by Politecnico di Milano, PepsiCo identified nine design thinking practices that drove organisational innovation, centred on aligning personal aspirations to corporate vision and nurturing "co-conspirators" (internal champions). One quote from Mauro Porcini encapsulates their approach: *"Design thinking permeated the entire organisation not only as a tool for managing innovation projects but also as the set of mindsets... In PepsiCo, design thinking is not just about doing. It is also the thinking, absorbing, and reflecting."* (Randall, 2020). Essentially, design thinking became part of PepsiCo's strategic DNA: they weren't just using it for one-off design projects but to inform strategy at the highest level (like envisioning the future of food and beverage consumption and how PepsiCo should respond).

The outcomes? PepsiCo launched several successful new products (like Bubly sparkling water, which was developed with a keen sense of user persona and branding design) and improved the design and experience of existing products (the Drinkfinity pod-based beverage system was a result of looking at user convenience and sustainability). Also, internally, the design thinking approach broke silos. Marketing, R&D, design, and insights teams started collaborating much more, which is a strategic win. PepsiCo became recognised as a more innovative company; Nooyi credited design thinking with driving business results and helping the company adapt to changing consumer preferences (like the shift to healthier lifestyles). This case shows design thinking driving strategic innovation and cultural change in a large organisation.

Another example is Airbnb's turnaround through design thinking. In its early days (around 2009), Airbnb struggled to gain traction. The founders applied design thinking and realised through empathy (literally meeting users) that the quality of listing photos was poor and hindering bookings. They went to New York, met hosts, and even took high-quality photos of apartments. This user-focused insight (renters need to see appealing places) and quick prototyping (better photography) led to a significant uptick in engagement on the platform. It is often cited as Airbnb's design-thinking-fueled insight that helped it find product-market fit. More broadly, Airbnb's culture emphasises user experience and journey mapping as central to creating trust between strangers. The result was that they solved a strategic trust problem (people were wary of staying in strangers' homes) with design thinking approaches. For example, developing the review system and crafting the website/app flows to feel safe and welcoming, as much as with pure business strategy.

8.6 TRADITIONAL VS. DESIGN THINKING APPROACHES IN STRATEGY

It's useful to contrast the two mindsets:

- **Focus:** Traditional problem-solving is often problem-focused and solution-driven. Define the problem clearly and apply logical analysis to solve it. Design thinking is user-focused and problem-*oriented*, meaning it spends a lot of time ensuring we're solving the right problem (via empathy) and may redefine the problem in the process. It emphasises understanding human needs and experiences at the centre of the problem.
- **Process:** Traditional approaches are typically linear: state problem → gather data → analyse → decide → implement. It's heavy on analysis and planning upfront, with a precise sequence of steps, and often assumes the problem is well-understood and stable. In contrast, design thinking is iterative and non-linear. You might start with research (empathise), then define the problem, then ideate, but you could go back to research after prototyping if you learn something new. It accepts that one might need to cycle through understanding and solving multiple times.
- **Certainty vs. Exploration:** Traditional strategy often works with forecasts, historical data, and expertise to come to a singular "best" solution and is more comfortable when problems are quantifiable and structured. Design thinking thrives in ambiguity and explores multiple possible solutions through experimentation. Not knowing the answer initially is okay; you discover it through iteration. Whereas traditional thinking might say, "Let's analyse until we pick the right path," design thinking says, "Let's prototype these three ideas and see which shows more promise through testing."

- **Creativity vs. Analysis:** Traditional problem-solving appreciates rigorous analysis, logic, and often compartmentalised expertise (the finance team does financial analysis, etc.). It might use tools like spreadsheets, ROI calculations, and so forth. Design thinking values creativity and insight, using methods like brainstorming (quantity over quality in ideation) and storytelling, which can lead to more innovative, outside-the-box solutions. That's not to say design thinking ignores analysis. Eventually, any idea must be viable, but it invites more generative thinking first.
- **Failure and Risk:** Traditional approaches sometimes avoid failure at all costs. You plan thoroughly to avoid making mistakes in implementation (sometimes leading to analysis paralysis). By promoting early prototyping and testing, design thinking *encourages small failures* as learning opportunities. "Fail fast to succeed sooner" encapsulates that a prototype that doesn't work is seen as valuable feedback, not as a disaster because it happens initially when adjustments are cheap.
- **Engagement:** Design thinking tends to be more collaborative and interdisciplinary. A department might devise a traditional strategy, or executives might hand it down. A design thinking approach often involves a broader set of stakeholders in workshopping ideas (maybe including customers and front-line employees), which can increase buy-in and surface tacit knowledge. It combines more bottom-up information flow with top-down guidance, whereas traditional can be more top-down.

Let us illustrate with a scenario: A bank faces declining engagement among millennial customers—a strategic problem. A traditional approach might analyse transaction data and segment the market, and then executives decide to launch a new credit card product with certain features they believe will attract millennials and roll it out with a marketing campaign. A design thinking approach would start by talking to millennial customers (and maybe non-customers), empathising to see why they are not engaging: maybe they distrust financial institutions or prefer fintech apps. The team might redefine the problem as "How might we improve young customers' financial well-being using our bank's capabilities?" Then, ideate many solutions: maybe a budgeting app, community financial education events, or an entirely new type of account. They would prototype some of these ideas (perhaps a mock-up of the app or a pilot event) and test with a small user group. Suppose they find the budgeting app idea resonates while the event does not. They iterate on the app, adding feedback-based features, and eventually scale it. The end solution might be very different (maybe it's not a credit card, but a mobile platform with integrated rewards), something more innovative than the traditional approach might have yielded. Also, by the time they launch broadly, they have evidence and refinement from testing, increasing their chance of success.

It does not imply that traditional problem-solving has no place, but a straightforward analytical approach is efficient for certain types of well-bounded technical problems. For example, reducing errors in a manufacturing process might be solved by Six Sigma methods (measure, analyse, improve) rather than a design sprint. However, design thinking can lead to more user-aligned and creative solutions for strategic issues that are as much about human behaviour or novel opportunities (like entering new markets, creating new experiences, and transforming culture).

There's also a complementary relationship: After design thinking generates a great concept, traditional analysis can kick in to optimise it, calculate business cases, etc. Many companies blend the approaches—using design thinking in early exploratory phases of strategy (to identify what to do) and traditional planning in later phases (to implement at scale efficiently).

Benefits of Design Thinking in Strategy: It often leads to more innovative strategies because it breaks out of the status quo assumptions. It keeps the end-user or customer squarely in focus, which increases the likelihood that the strategy will meet market needs (versus strategies that are too internally driven or technology-for-technology-sake). It also encourages rapid learning, where strategies can be refined before huge resources are committed. Moreover, it can improve team morale and engagement, as people find it energising to be part of a creative process and see their input matter. Design thinking brings strategy to life through tangible prototypes and stories, whereas traditional strategic plans can remain abstract or paper-bound for too long.

Challenges of Design Thinking: Traditionalists can see it as too "fuzzy" or time-consuming. Senior executives used to hard data might question the reliability of insights from a handful of empathy interviews. There's also a risk of focusing too much on desirability (what users want) and forgetting feasibility and viability. Classic design thinking emphasises balancing these three, but inexperienced teams might generate lovable ideas that aren't financially or technically feasible. Thus, a mix of design thinking and rigorous analysis is ideal. Another challenge: company culture might resist the iterative trial-and-error approach (some see it as a lack of planning). It requires a tolerance for ambiguity and a mindset shift, which not everyone finds easy, especially in very conservative industries.

Design Thinking vs. Traditional: A Comparative Summary:

- Traditional = "Plan then execute"; Design thinking = "Prototype and experiment then implement what works".
- Traditional = Linear, analytical; Design = Iterative, creative.
- Traditional = Expert-driven; Design = User-informed, multidisciplinary.
- Traditional measures success by adherence to plan and ROI; Design thinking measures success by user satisfaction and solving the right problem (with ROI considered after concept validation).
- They ultimately can be blended: Use traditional problem-solving to evaluate and scale the solutions that design thinking discovers.

In strategic management education, students are now often taught to use both toolkits. For instance, a student might do Porter's Five Forces analysis (traditional strategy tool) to understand an industry but then use design thinking to figure out how to address an industry challenge in a novel way that the five forces alone wouldn't reveal.

CASE STUDY: Design Thinking vs. Traditional in Action

A global logistics company wanted to improve its delivery operations in congested cities. A traditional approach gave them ideas like "optimise routes with better algorithms" and "adjust delivery windows." They then ran a design thinking workshop that included managers, couriers, and customers. Through empathy mapping, one insight emerged: couriers struggled to find legal parking, and customers sometimes weren't home, causing re-deliveries (frustrating both sides). The team devised solutions, and one radical idea was a network of smart lockers in convenience stores where packages could be dropped off for customers to pick up later (solving parking and missed delivery issues). They prototyped it in one city, and it worked well. Then, the company rolled it out widely as a new service. The traditional analysis helped in optimising routes (an incremental efficiency gain). At the same time, the design thinking concept of alternate delivery points was a more transformative solution that improved customer experience and cut costs of failed delivery attempts. Together, these made a robust strategy. The design thinking piece might not have surfaced through numbers alone because it required empathising with the courier's daily pain and the customer's schedule.

In summary, design thinking brings a fresh lens to strategic problem-solving. It complements analytical rigour with creativity and empathy. Traditional approaches ensure feasibility and thoroughness, while design thinking ensures relevance and innovation. Combining both strengths can significantly enhance how organisations identify and tackle strategic challenges, leading to solutions that are not only clever on paper but also deeply resonant with stakeholders in practice.

KEY POINTS TO REMEMBER

1. Scenario analysis helps to compare multiple feasible future strategies that can produce various outcomes. This builds organisational agility and readiness for unexpected shifts.
2. Traditional, static strategic plans can become obsolete quickly. Uncertain environments need iterative planning, flexibility, continuous monitoring, pre-defined trigger points for action, and a willingness to change.
3. Stakeholder support is crucial to success. Segmenting can help us understand different needs and power to help in development of targeted interventions.
4. Implementing a strategy often meets resistance to change. Kotter's 8-Step Model (for organisational change) and ADKAR (for individual transition) provide guidance throughout the change process to ensure proper adoption.
5. Effective development of strategies require analysing future scenarios, aligning stakeholders, managing change, and finding innovative solutions to problems. This requires consideration of external environment, internal culture, and human needs is required.

KEY LEARNINGS

- **Scenario Planning as a Strategic Tool:** Organisations should plan for multiple future scenarios, not just a single forecast. Scenario analysis enhances preparedness by forcing strategists to imagine diverse outcomes (best case, worst case, and alternatives) and develop contingent strategies. This practice is especially vital in volatile environments, as seen in Shell's successful anticipation of the 1970s oil shock through scenario planning. Key takeaway: Embrace uncertainty by planning for it. Use scenario thinking to become agile and "execute, monitor, and adapt" as the future unfolds.
- **Strategic Planning in Uncertainty Requires Agility:** In VUCA environments, traditional static strategic plans are less effective. Companies must adopt agile planning cycles, continuously scanning the environment and ready to pivot. Embracing uncertainty (rather than denying it) is a hallmark of successful firms. They create flexible roadmaps, define trigger points for action, and cultivate a culture responsive to change. The contrast between stable vs. unstable contexts underscores that strategy formation and execution must be tailored to the level of uncertainty, with more frequent updates and scenario contingencies in high-volatility markets. A key lesson is that lack of certainty is the reason to plan but plan differently, dynamically, and with options.
- **Stakeholder Analysis is Crucial for Strategy Execution:** No strategic initiative exists in a vacuum; stakeholder support can make or break a project. Through stakeholder analysis, leaders identify who will be impacted or can influence the outcome and devise engagement strategies to gain buy-in or mitigate opposition. Tools like the power-interest matrix help prioritise stakeholders (manage those with high power/interest closely and keep others satisfied or informed accordingly). The main point is that early and proactive stakeholder engagement leads to better decisions and smoother implementation. By understanding stakeholders' interests and addressing their concerns, organisations increase the likelihood of success, turning potential resisters into partners and ensuring the alignment of all parties with the strategic objectives.
- **Change Management Frameworks Enable Successful Implementation:** Implementing strategic change is as important as formulating strategy, and frameworks like Kotter's 8 Steps and ADKAR provide proven roadmaps. Kotter's model emphasises building urgency, a guiding coalition, and a clear vision for change, then communicating relentlessly, empowering employees by removing obstacles, celebrating short-term wins, and anchoring the culture change. ADKAR zooms in on individual change, insisting people need Awareness, Desire, Knowledge, Ability, and Reinforcement to fully adopt new ways. The key learning is that change must be managed systematically: create a compelling case for change, equip and enable people, and reinforce new behaviours until they become the norm. This structured approach reduces resistance and builds momentum, as illustrated by real cases (e.g., Microsoft's cultural change) where leadership applied these principles to drive successful transformation.

- **Design Thinking Enhances Strategic Problem-Solving:** Human-centered design thinking can lead to more innovative and user-aligned strategies than traditional analytic approaches. By deeply understanding user or customer needs (empathy), encouraging creative ideation, prototyping solutions, and iterating based on feedback, organisations can solve the *right* problems and often discover breakthrough ideas. We saw how companies like PepsiCo used design thinking to reimagine products and experiences, fueling growth and innovation. The lesson is that blending design thinking into strategy can break habitual thinking, focus strategy on what truly matters to stakeholders, and reduce risk through early testing. In contrast to purely linear problem-solving, design thinking accepts ambiguity and failure in early stages as pathways to better solutions. This approach can produce more robust and creative outcomes for complex strategic challenges.
- **Integration of Concepts:** The chapter's topics are interrelated in practice. For example, scenario planning can inform change management (each scenario may require a different change plan and stakeholder approach), stakeholder input can feed into design thinking (empathise with stakeholders to generate ideas), and agile planning in uncertainty aligns with the iterative mindset of design thinking. An overarching takeaway is that strategic management today is a holistic exercise: one must anticipate external changes (scenarios, uncertainty), mobilise and align people (stakeholders, change management), and foster innovation in solutions (design thinking). The best strategic leaders can navigate uncertainty with agility, engage people with empathy and clarity, and continuously learn and adapt their strategies.

Each of these learnings reinforces the notion that successful strategy is not just about deciding what to do but also about how you plan for diverse futures, who you involve and affect, and how you carry out the needed changes in mindset and operations. Strategic planning and implementation management is thus a multi-faceted discipline. Part analytics, part psychology, part creativity, and mastery of these tools and approaches can significantly improve an organisation's ability to achieve its long-term objectives in a complex world.

EXERCISES

1. **Scenario Planning Exercise—Envisioning Futures:** Imagine you are part of the strategy team at a retail company entering the e-commerce space. The future business environment is uncertain. Develop two contrasting scenarios for the next 5 years: one in which online consumer demand grows explosively, and another in which demand grows slowly due to a return to in-store shopping. For each scenario, list 2–3 key assumptions (e.g. technology adoption, customer behavior, competition) and outline strategic actions your company should take under that scenario. Finally, identify one "no-regret move"—an action that would benefit the company in *any* scenario (for example, investing in a robust customer data platform). This exercise practices scenario analysis by preparing multiple plans for different possible futures.

2. **Stakeholder Analysis—New Strategy Rollout:** Your company is implementing a major change in operations (for example, introducing an AI-based system to streamline workflows). Perform a stakeholder analysis for this initiative:
   (a) *Identify Stakeholders:* List at least five key stakeholder groups affected by this change (e.g., front-line employees, managers, IT support, customers, regulators, etc.).
   (b) *Assess Interests and Concerns:* For each stakeholder group, briefly note what they most care about or might fear regarding this change (e.g., employees might worry about job security or needing new skills; customers might care about service quality).
   (c) *Plan Engagement:* For each group, suggest one strategy to engage or communicate with them to gain their support or mitigate resistance. (For instance, *training workshops* for employees to feel confident with the new system, or an *announcement campaign* to customers highlighting improved service features.) This exercise helps you map out the human element of implementation—ensuring that all parties impacted by a strategic decision are considered and managed.
3. **Change Management Plan—Applying a Framework:** Consider a scenario where a mid-size company decides to shift to a fully remote work strategy to stay competitive and cut costs. Outline a brief change management plan using Kotter's 8-Step model (or alternatively, the ADKAR model) to implement this change. For each step of Kotter's framework, write 1–2 sentences about what actions you would take:
   (a) How will you *create a sense of urgency* among employees about the move to remote work?
   (b) What is your *vision for change* (how do you explain the future state and its benefits)?
   (c) How will you *empower broad action* (e.g., providing necessary tools and training for remote work)?
   (d) What short-term *wins* could you achieve to show progress (perhaps a successful one-month pilot with improved productivity)?
   (e) etc., through all 8 steps (ending with anchoring the change in the culture). This exercise requires you to think through a structured approach to change, ensuring that the strategy (going remote) is implemented smoothly by addressing the people side of change at every stage.
4. **Design Thinking in Strategy—Reflection:** Write a short essay or outline addressing the following question: *"How can design thinking complement traditional strategic planning and implementation?"* In your answer, describe at least one benefit of incorporating design thinking into strategy work—for example, using empathy to better understand customer needs before formulating strategy, or prototyping strategic initiatives on a small scale to gather feedback before full rollout. Provide a concrete example or hypothetical scenario (such as designing a new service or policy) where blending design thinking with strategic planning leads to a better outcome. This exercise encourages you to connect the user-centred, iterative

mindset of design thinking with the formal processes of strategy execution, highlighting that strategic decisions can often be improved by considering the human experience and testing ideas iteratively before wide implementation.

THOUGHT-PROVOKING QUESTIONS

1. **Scenario Planning Application:** Your company manufactures electric vehicles and is expanding internationally. Outline two very different future scenarios (e.g., one of booming EV adoption and one of regulatory hurdles and slow adoption) and describe how your strategic plan might differ in each. What triggers alert you to which scenario is unfolding, and how would you prepare the organisation to pivot accordingly?
2. **Stable vs. Uncertain Strategy:** Compare how you would approach strategic planning for a family-owned hotel in a well-established tourist destination (stable environment) versus a tech startup offering AI-driven services (highly uncertain environment). What planning horizon, flexibility, and review mechanisms would you implement in each case, and why?
3. **Stakeholder Engagement Strategy:** Imagine you are leading a project to implement a new data analytics system in a multinational corporation. Identify four key stakeholder groups (top executives, IT staff, end-user employees, and data privacy regulators). For each group, discuss their likely concerns or interests and propose specific engagement actions to address those (such as workshops, training, and policy assurances). How will your approach ensure each stakeholder group supports the project?
4. **Leading Change with Frameworks:** You have been tasked with improving customer service quality in a large retail chain, which requires significant changes in employee behaviour and processes. How would you apply Kotter's 8 Steps to lead this change? Provide brief examples of actions you would take at each step (from creating urgency around customer complaints to anchoring customer-centric values in the company culture). Additionally, anticipate one major source of resistance and how you would address it to maintain momentum.
5. **Design Thinking for Strategic Innovation:** Your company is facing a strategic problem: declining usage of its mobile app among young users. Using a design thinking approach, describe how you would tackle this problem. Who would you involve in the empathy stage, and what techniques would you use? What kinds of ideas might you brainstorm (ideation), and how would you prototype and test them on a small scale? Finally, compare this to how a purely traditional problem-solving approach might address the issue and the pros/cons of each in this scenario.
6. **Integrating Approaches:** Consider a scenario where a healthcare provider wants to improve patient experience through a new strategic initiative. How could scenario planning, stakeholder analysis, change management, and design thinking

collectively be used to ensure the initiative is successful? (Hint: Consider using design thinking to develop the initiative, scenario planning to anticipate future healthcare trends, stakeholder analysis to get doctors and patients on board, and change management to implement new clinic processes).

These questions are designed to encourage you to apply the chapter's concepts to realistic situations. In formulating your answers, draw on the frameworks and examples discussed. For instance, use stakeholder mapping or Kotter's steps explicitly and tailor them to the specifics of the scenario. The goal is to practice a holistic, thoughtful approach to strategic planning and implementation, considering uncertainty, human factors, and innovative problem-solving.

REFERENCES

2F-STX. (n.d.). Leveraging Stakeholder Analysis. 2F-STX Insights. Retrieved March 12, 2025, from https://www.2fstx.com/leveraging-stakeholder-analysis

Dye, R., & Sibony, O. (2020, May 15). How to Confront Uncertainty in Your Strategy. McKinsey & Company. Retrieved March 12, 2025, from https://www.mckinsey.com/capabilities/strategy-and-corporate-finance/our-insights/how-to-confront-uncertainty-in-your-strategy

Futures Platform. (2022, September 8). 2x2 Scenario Planning Matrix Guideline. Futures Platform Blog. Retrieved March 12, 2025, from https://www.futuresplatform.com/blog/2x2-scenario-planning-matrix-guideline

Ignatius, A. (2015, September). How Indra Nooyi Turned Design Thinking Into Strategy: An Interview with PepsiCo's CEO. Harvard Business Review. Retrieved March 12, 2025, from https://hbr.org/2015/09/how-indra-nooyi-turned-design-thinking-into-strategy

Knolskape. (2023, July 14). Top 10 Change Management Examples and the Companies That Implemented Them. Knolskape Blog. Retrieved March 12, 2025, from https://knolskape.com/blog/top-10-change-management-examples-and-the-companies-that-implemented-them/

Kumar, V. (2021, May 10). Design Thinking vs. Traditional Problem Solving: A Comparative Analysis. Medium (Personal Blog). Retrieved March 12, 2025, from https://vadimcan.medium.com/design-thinking-vs-traditional-problem-solving-a-comparative-analysis-f144e210fdd6

McDowell, M., & Sneader, K. (2021, October 5). A Strategy for Embracing Uncertainty. Bain & Company Insights. Retrieved March 12, 2025, from https://www.bain.com/insights/a-strategy-for-embracing-uncertainty/

Prosci. (n.d.). ADKAR: A Model for Change. Prosci Methodology. Retrieved March 12, 2025, from https://www.prosci.com/methodology/adkar

Randall, K. (2020, June 8). PepsiCo's Design Thinking Approach to Organizational Innovation. R&D Today. Retrieved March 12, 2025, from https://www.rndtoday.co.uk/design-thinking/pepsicos-design-thinking-approach-to-organizational-innovation/

CHAPTER 9

The Trends and Future

LEARNING OBJECTIVES

After reading this Chapter, the readers will be able to:

- Recognize evolving trends in design thinking across global and regional contexts, including how different industries (healthcare, technology, manufacturing, financial services, etc.) are shaping and being shaped by design thinking practices.
- Compare design thinking applications in large corporations versus startups and developed markets versus emerging markets, understanding each context's unique drivers, challenges, and opportunities.
- Understand the role of advanced technologies, such as artificial intelligence (AI), machine learning, digital twins, and automation, in enhancing each stage of the design thinking process (from empathy and ideation to prototyping and testing).
- Learn from case studies illustrating AI and design thinking integration (e.g. at Google, in healthcare diagnostics and logistics) to see practical examples of technology-augmented human-centred design.
- Appreciate what it means to cultivate a design-driven mindset at both organizational and individual levels, including strategies for building a design-centric culture, as exemplified by companies like IBM and PepsiCo and newer design-mature enterprises.
- Plan the next steps for personal and professional growth in design thinking with practical tools, recommended resources for further learning, potential career paths (and certifications), and activities to continue the journey beyond this chapter.

9.1 TRENDS SHAPING THE FUTURE OF DESIGN THINKING

Design thinking has evolved from a niche approach in product design to a mainstream strategy for innovation across industries and regions. As organizations worldwide grapple with complex challenges, design thinking's human-centred ethos is applied in novel ways to meet emerging trends. This section explores several key trends shaping the future of design thinking, looking at global vs. local dynamics and comparing how large corporations versus startups and developed versus emerging markets embrace design thinking. The analysis is supported by recent industry reports, academic insights, and real-world examples to ground these trends in evidence.

9.1.1 Global and Cross-Industry Trends

One clear trend is that design thinking is gaining broader traction across industries and functions. No longer confined to product development teams, its principles are being used to redesign services, customer experiences, and even internal processes in domains as diverse as healthcare, finance, manufacturing, and education. For example, in healthcare, providers use design thinking to improve patient journeys and hospital workflows; in financial services, banks employ it to craft intuitive digital banking experiences; in manufacturing, human-centred design informs the development of safer, more efficient equipment interfaces. A recent industry analysis highlights that design thinking is increasingly crucial for strategic foresight—going beyond solving today's problems to anticipating tomorrow's needs. Companies use tools like trend mapping and scenario planning with design thinking, effectively combining human-centred design with strategic future casting to innovate proactively. One report notes, "The future of the industry will be about using the concepts of strategic foresight and design thinking to embrace uncertainty, identify opportunities, and make headway on future needs". It indicates that design thinking is maturing into not just a problem-solving toolkit but a forward-looking innovation approach.

Another global trend emphasises building trust and social value through design. Organizations are facing an environment of sceptical consumers and rapid information flows. Traditional metrics like revenue are balanced with customer trust, ethical impact, and inclusivity. Design thinking is seen as a way to rebuild trust by genuinely empathizing with users and being transparent. A projection in one industry outlook suggests companies will shift to "designing for trust instead of revenue," using design thinking to make more empowered, user-respecting decisions. For instance, rather than just pushing products, firms might co-create with customers to ensure offerings align with users' values, thereby earning loyalty. It ties into a broader social trend: increased focus on social impact and sustainability. Design thinking's human-centred focus naturally lends itself to tackling social and environmental challenges. Across industries, teams apply it to issues like accessibility, sustainability, and well-being. We see more design thinking initiatives aimed at social innovation (e.g., improving public services, designing for underserved communities, creating eco-friendly products). It reflects a recognition that future innovation must be responsible and inclusive, considering a wide array of stakeholders.

Data-driven empathy is another trend, seemingly a paradox, but an important development. With the explosion of digital data and analytics, design teams can now access unprecedented insights into user behaviour. It has led to what we might call "quantitative empathy," where big data and ethnographic research converge. Companies are building communities and insight platforms to involve customers early. For example, businesses increasingly use online community forums and insight platforms (such as Vision Critical's Sparq) to gather continuous user feedback. By blending these data-driven insights with traditional empathetic techniques (like interviews and observation), designers can form a more holistic understanding of user needs. While analytics can reveal patterns, teams still use classic design thinking to interpret the "why" behind the numbers. This synergy between data science and design is tightening; as noted in one trends report, "the relationship between design and data science grows tighter", and leveraging consent-based, insightful customer data will give companies an edge. We will explore the role of AI and data further in Section 9.2, but suffice it to say that technology is amplifying design thinking, enabling deeper empathy at scale and rapid iteration.

Finally, the human-centred design mindset is more important than ever in the face of advancing technology. Paradoxically, the need for empathy and human insight grows as automation and digital tools proliferate. Competitive advantage is shifting to those who keep a genuine user focus amid the tech frenzy. As one forecast put it, "In this technological age…it's easy to get swept up in creating the latest product, but the ability to empathize will see a huge increase in importance". Several high-profile companies saw major improvements only after refocusing on human-centric design: Airbnb, for example, experienced a breakthrough once it deeply empathized with customers' end-to-end experience. We see a renewed emphasis on deep qualitative research (psychographics, ethnography, sociology) to complement tech-driven. The more digital our world becomes, the more design thinking is needed to humanize products and services, ensuring they truly resonate with people across different ages and cultures.

9.1.2 Regional Perspectives: Developed vs. Emerging Markets

While many trends are global, there are distinctive regional dynamics in how design thinking is applied. In developed markets (such as North America, Western Europe, Japan, etc.), design thinking often focuses on enhancing sophisticated user experiences, personalizing services, and differentiating brands in crowded markets. Consumers in these markets usually have high expectations for convenience, integration, and aesthetics. Think of how a smartphone's success can hinge on subtle user interface design or how an automobile's appeal can depend on the experience of interaction, not just performance. Thus, companies in developed economies frequently use design thinking to push the envelope on delight: making products more intuitive, services more seamless, and interactions more engaging. For example, a smartphone maker in a developed market might use design thinking to reimagine the customer journey of buying and setting up a device, ensuring every touchpoint (from store layout to unboxing to user tutorial) is optimized for delight. Developed market companies also incorporate design thinking into digital transformation efforts, merging it with agile methodologies to modernize legacy systems with a user-first perspective. The availability of resources dedicated to design teams, innovation labs, and advanced tools in many large firms in developed countries helps embed design thinking at scale.

In emerging markets (such as parts of Asia, Africa, and Latin America), the context for design thinking can be quite different. Here, innovation is often driven by the need for affordable, sustainable solutions for large, underserved populations. Design thinking in emerging markets frequently intertwines with frugal innovation, an approach of "doing more with less" to meet essential needs within severe resource constraints. Many of these markets face infrastructure challenges (like intermittent electricity, limited internet access in rural areas, and lower-income consumers) that shape user needs. For instance, consider what features a mobile phone must prioritize in an emerging market: one study highlighted that users in India, China, or Bangladesh value battery life, durable hardware, dual SIM functionality, and even built-in flashlights far more than cutting-edge display resolution, reflecting practical needs given unreliable power and unique use patterns. Such insights underscore that value perception differs greatly by context: a product considered "good design" in a developed country might be impractical in an emerging economy if it's not affordable or rugged enough.

Emerging markets have embraced design thinking to co-create solutions with local communities and ensure relevance. There is a growing movement of grassroots design thinking where NGOs, social enterprises, and local startups work closely with communities to design products and services. For example, developing low-cost medical devices, water purification systems, or educational tools that fit the local context. Researchers Patnaik and Tarei (2024) observe that design thinking is "increasingly gaining traction as a human-centred approach to innovation" in emerging markets, particularly when paired with sustainable business models to yield frugal innovations for disadvantaged. The goal is often to transform an undesirable current state (e.g., lack of healthcare access) into a desired one (affordable clinics or mobile health services), focusing on understanding the people for whom these solutions are intended. When successful, this fusion of design thinking with frugality can create solutions that are not only low-cost and accessible but also socially and environmentally impactful in the long run.

A hallmark of emerging-market design thinking is extreme constraint-driven creativity. Companies and innovators must solve problems under tight limits, which leads to inventive outcomes. As one report described, frugal innovation means adopting a "more with less, for more" strategy, delivering more value using fewer resources for more people. It often involves stripping away non-essentials and focusing on core needs. For example, India's $2,000 Tata Nano car and a $35 tablet computer were born from asking, "What can we remove or radically simplify to cut costs dramatically while still meeting the fundamental need?" (Soni, 2019). These solutions required rethinking standards: engineers had to challenge assumptions from developed-market design (which can lead to over-engineering). A European CEO noted that Western engineers might "set excessively high standards" that overshoot emerging market needs, resulting in too expensive products. By contrast, emerging-market innovators work backwards from the basic outcomes required, even if the end product looks nothing like traditional designs. It is design thinking: empathize with local users, define the core problem (e.g., need for affordable mobility), ideate around unconventional approaches, prototype lean versions, and test them in context. The trend is so strong that frugal innovation is described as growing, with media spotlighting examples like ultra-low-cost healthcare and energy solutions from India and Africa.

It is important to note that emerging markets are not monolithic. Urban middle-class consumers in China's megacities have different needs from those of rural villagers in sub-

Saharan Africa. Design thinking in emerging contexts thus requires a nuanced, segment-specific approach. One must consider local culture, literacy levels, and infrastructure. For instance, in parts of Africa, mobile banking (like Kenya's M-Pesa) succeeded in designing a text-based money transfer service via basic cell phones, fitting the context of low banking access but high mobile penetration. That success came from empathizing with users who had no formal bank accounts but did have mobile phones and prototyping a service they could use without needing a smartphone or internet. Such examples illustrate how emerging market design often leapfrogs. Innovating new solutions outright rather than incrementally improving old ones precisely because legacy systems were absent.

Interestingly, the flow of innovation is increasingly bidirectional. The term "reverse innovation" has been used to describe innovations born in emerging markets that later inform products in developed markets. Large multinationals have learned that solutions crafted via frugal, human-centred design in places like India or Kenya can find applications elsewhere. For example, GE Healthcare's portable ultrasound machine, originally designed for rural clinics in China and India, used design thinking to make it compact and affordable. However, it later found a market for mobile medical care in the West. This cross-pollination is a trend: global companies are adopting emerging-market design principles of simplicity and affordability to serve cost-conscious segments everywhere. In summary, developed markets drive design thinking toward refinement and personalization, while emerging markets drive it toward inclusivity and resourceful innovation, and both are learning from each other.

Below is a comparative framework highlighting some differences in design thinking applications between developed and emerging markets:

TABLE 9.1 Comparison: Developed vs. Emerging Markets in Design Thinking

Factor	*Developed Markets*	*Emerging Markets*
Primary Innovation Drivers	Differentiation, convenience, and superior user experience (often solving wants). Example: new features to delight users or seamless omnichannel services.	Accessibility, affordability, and solving fundamental needs (often solving needs). Example: low-cost medical devices and basic banking via mobile phones.
Resource Environment	*Generally high-resource:* Large design teams, advanced tools, ample user data. Can invest in extensive research and testing cycles.	*Resource-constrained:* Limited budgets, infrastructure challenges. Solutions require frugality and creative use of available tech (e.g., widespread mobile but limited internet).
Design Approach	Tends toward formalized processes, specialized roles (UX researcher, service designer, etc.), and integration with corporate innovation frameworks. Human-centered design used to refine sophisticated products and services.	Tends toward grassroots, improvisational approaches. Multi-role innovators (one team does it all) work closely with communities. Design thinking often merged with frugal innovation and Jugaad (improvisation) to create robust, essential solutions.

Factor	*Developed Markets*	*Emerging Markets*
Cultural Context in Design	Must account for diverse, often global user bases with high expectations for polished experiences. Also addresses issues like ageing populations or differently-abled users (accessibility as a quality marker).	Must account for local languages, cultures, and varying literacy/education levels. Solutions may need to function in low-literacy environments (using visuals over text, etc.) and leverage local cultural norms for adoption.
Examples of Outcomes	*High-end innovation:* e.g., a financial app using AI to provide personalized investment advice to tech-savvy users; a car with an AI assistant enhancing the driving experience.	*Inclusive innovation:* e.g., a solar-powered fridge for vaccines in rural clinics; an app that uses voice prompts in local dialect to guide low-literacy users through telehealth steps. These often prioritize function and cost over form.

Both contexts leverage the core of design thinking, namely, empathy, ideation, and experimentation, but tailor it to their realities. The trend is that practitioners in each context increasingly learn from the other. Emerging-market innovators are adopting more structured methods and measuring impact, while developed-market designers are embracing constraint-based creativity and social focus. Ultimately, the future of design thinking is pluralistic: it will be moulded by many contexts yet unified by the principle of designing for real human needs.

9.1.3 Large Corporations vs. Startups in Design Thinking

Another important lens on design thinking trends is the difference between how large, established corporations versus startups and small enterprises adopt and implement the approach. Both have embraced design thinking, but their motivations and constraints differ significantly. Understanding these differences provides insight into the evolving innovation landscape and why a one-size-fits-all approach to design thinking does not work.

Large corporations often turn to design thinking as part of a broader strategy to rekindle innovation, break down silos, and stay competitive in fast-changing markets. Many companies have decades of history, complex structures, and established processes. A common challenge they face is overcoming inertia; traditional "business as usual" mindsets and bureaucratic procedures can stifle creativity. For corporations, design thinking injects agility and customer focus by empowering cross-functional teams to collaborate and think like agile startups. Numerous Fortune 500 firms (banks, consumer goods giants, automotive companies, etc.) have launched internal design thinking initiatives or innovation labs in recent years. For example, IBM famously invested heavily in design thinking (detailed in Section 9.3), training tens of thousands of employees in a user-centric approach to problem-solving. The trend is that corporate design thinking is scaled enterprise-wide, not just isolated in design departments. Companies are establishing frameworks and governance for design thinking (like appointing Chief Design Officers, creating physical innovation spaces, and integrating design milestones into project management). The expected payoff is better alignment and more creativity. Indeed, a study of large firms practising design thinking found that over 80% reported more aligned and focused teams, a significant boost to employee productivity and collaboration.

However, implementing design thinking in a big company comes with challenges. Cultural resistance is one: employees accustomed to risk-averse cultures may be wary of the "fail-fast" ethos of design thinking. Large firms also have longer decision cycles, approvals, budgeting, and compliance, which can slow down the rapid experimentation that design thinking encourages. A notable analysis by innovation expert Steve Blank points out that "startups are not smaller versions of large companies, and interestingly, companies are not larger versions of startups." Each has a different DNA (Blank, 2014). In large companies, even enthusiastic innovation teams can hit systemic barriers. Blank describes that corporations are optimized for executing a proven business model with structures that value efficiency, predictability, and risk mitigation. As a result, even innovative projects aren't usually life-or-death for the company, which can breed a certain complacency: "In large companies…the culture is dominated by process, procedures and incentives. Killing a project may frustrate the team, but everyone still has their jobs, and the company does not collapse; it adds up to a 'complacency culture' rather than an 'urgency culture.'". It contrasts sharply with startups (we'll discuss it momentarily). The trend among forward-thinking corporates is to consciously combat this complacency by creating pockets of urgency and freedom. For instance, giving innovation teams more autonomy, setting ambitious "moonshot" goals, or even co-locating teams offsite to break them from daily bureaucracy.

Another corporate trend is integrating design thinking with other methodologies. Corporations blend design thinking with Lean Six Sigma, Agile, and other process improvement methods to fit their operating style. For example, some use design thinking for early problem framing and customer research, switch to Agile sprints for development and go back to design thinking for user testing in a hybrid cycle. There's also a rise in corporate partnerships. Big firms create incubators or venture arms to work with startups, effectively outsourcing some risk-taking. It is driven by the recognition that startups often excel at radical innovation and speed, so corporations want to learn from them. Design thinking is a common language in such partnerships: corporate teams and startups can collaborate on human-centred experiments. The Mack Institute at Wharton noted that corporations increasingly engage in these collaborations for financial investment and strategic alignment and learningmackinstitute.wharton.upenn.edu. In summary, large companies trend toward institutionalizing design thinking, making it a repeatable, scalable part of how they operate while trying to keep it from being smothered by corporate processes.

Now, turning to startups and small enterprises, design thinking is almost second nature to many of them, even if they don't always call it that. Startups, especially tech startups, live and die by understanding users and iterating quickly, essentially design thinking in practice. Techniques like rapid prototyping, A/B testing, and pivoting based on user feedback are common startup behaviours that mirror the ideate-prototype-test cycle of design thinking. The Lean Startup methodology (popularized by Eric Ries) is closely aligned with design thinking principles, emphasizing quick experiments with real users (via MVPs—Minimum Viable Products) and learning through iteration. It's been said that "Lean Startup is about building and measuring, whereas design thinking adds the front-end of empathizing and defining the problem" They form a robust innovation approach netmind.netnetmind.net. Many startups practice this combo intuitively: they start with a hypothesis about a customer problem, quickly build a simple solution, get it in front of users, gather feedback, and refine or pivot as needednetmind.netnetmind.net. The urgency factor in startups cannot be overstated—unlike a big corporation, a startup usually has a limited cash runway. It imposes a "gun-to-the-head" mentality where experimentation and learning must happen at breakneck speed. As Steve Blank notes, a startup CEO constantly knows how many days of cash are left; this survival pressure drives a bias toward action: getting prototypes in front of customers now because otherwise, the company might not exist tomorrow. It creates a culture of extreme urgency and focus that propels design thinking activities swiftly. There's little patience for over-analysis or internal turf wars when the priority is finding product-market fit before the money runs out.

Startups thus exemplify the fast-cycle iteration ideal of design thinking. They often have the advantage of starting with a clean slate, no entrenched departments to convince, no rigid protocols. A two-person or ten-person startup can easily gather around a whiteboard, brainstorm wild ideas, build a prototype in a day, and put it in front of users the next. Decision-making is flat and fast. Many rising startups explicitly credit user-centric design for their success. For instance, Airbnb's early breakthrough came when the founders applied empathy: they went to stay with hosts and discovered trust issues in the experience. That led them to implement features like host/ guest profiles and reviews, dramatically improving user confidence. They even storyboarded their user's journey in a project nicknamed "Snow White," mapping out every emotional moment of an Airbnb stay, an exercise straight out of design thinking. By visualizing the end-to-end experience with Disney-like storyboards, Airbnb's team identified pain points and opportunities to delight, which became a product. This story has become legendary as an example of a startup embracing design thinking (storytelling and empathy) to shape strategy. Many startups similarly build their brands on superior user experience: consider how Uber revolutionized taxi service by focusing on user pain points (uncertainty of when the car will arrive, payment hassle) and solving them with a user-centred app.

That said, startups face their challenges in adopting design thinking thoroughly. One challenge is the lack of resources and expertise: a tiny startup might not have a dedicated designer or researcher on staff. The founding team may understand the value of user feedback, but they might not be versed in formal design methods (like conducting ethnographic research or advanced prototyping). Time pressure can also cause startups to cut corners on the empathy stage; they might rush to build something on a hunch without fully researching user needs, especially if investors push for quick growth. In recent times, however, even among startups, there's a trend of increased design literacy. Accelerator programs and incubators often include design thinking workshops, and many startups now have at least one co-founder with a design or user experience background. It's not uncommon to see job titles like "Design Strategist" or "UX Lead" among the first 10 hires of a tech startup, reflecting the importance of crafting a good user experience from the ground up.

Interestingly, as startups grow into larger companies (scale-ups and eventually mature firms), they often struggle with the "loss of the garage spirit." The agility and user focus that drove early success can be diluted as the organization adds layers. A trend among successful scale-ups is to institutionalize design thinking early, almost in anticipation of this growth challenge. For example, some companies implement processes like regular user testing sessions that every engineer must attend or maintain small, cross-functional product squads (as Spotify famously does) to keep the team user-focused and nimble. It blends the startup culture with the needed structure.

To summarize the comparison, we provide a consolidated table of how design thinking tends to manifest in large corporations versus startups:

TABLE 9.2 Comparison: Design Thinking in Large Corporations vs. Startups

Dimension	*Large Corporations*	*Startups*
Speed and Urgency	Typically slower moving. Innovation projects run in parallel to core business, often without life-or-death urgency. Need deliberate efforts to create urgency (e.g., innovation tournaments, executive mandates). Culture risk: complacency, with lengthy approval cycles.	Extremely fast-paced. Driven by survival instinct, a limited cash runway means rapid iteration is necessary. Constant bias to action, deploying prototypes quickly to learn before funds deplete. Culture risk: chaos, but urgency keeps the team focused.
Resources and Talent	Large pools of resources (funding, personnel, labs). Can afford specialist roles (UX researchers, prototype engineers) and extensive user research. Often train many employees in design thinking at scale (e.g., IBM's 100k+ trained design thinkers). *Challenge:* Resources can lead to over-analysis or "innovation theatre" if not channelled properly.	Limited resources require wearing multiple hats. Team members do research, design, and coding themselves. Reliance on creative, low-cost solutions (e.g., using free tools, quick-and-dirty experiments). *Challenge:* Skill gaps may lack formal design training, making it harder to conduct structured research (but this is improving as design education permeates the startup world).
Risk Attitude	Generally risk-averse institutionally. Stakeholders (shareholders and boards) expect steady performance, so radical ideas face scrutiny. Design thinking initiatives often need executive champions to protect them. Tolerance for failure is growing but still moderate. Failures are ideally small and contained.	The embrace of risk is part of the DNA. Investors in startups accept that many experiments will fail on the path to finding a viable product. "Fail fast" is a mantra. As long as learning is gained, failure is seen as a step forward. High tolerance for pivoting entirely, if the initial idea does not pan out.

Dimension	*Large Corporations*	*Startups*
Process Integration	Design thinking might be a structured program, workshops, formal "innovation sprints," and stages that align with existing phase-gate processes. Often integrated with Six Sigma, Agile, etc., to fit company workflows. There may be playbooks and metrics (e.g., the number of empathy interviews conducted) to institutionalize it.	Design thinking is informally embedded. The process is fluid and may not be labelled as such. A startup may not say, "Empathize phase now," but they will talk to users, feel their pain, and brain-storm solutions in a single day. The process is more organic and less documented. However, many startups adopt frameworks like Lean Canvas or Design Sprints (from Google Ventures) to structure their rapid cycles.
Focus of Design Efforts	Often applied to both incremental and transformative innovation. Corporations use design thinking to improve existing product lines (incremental enhancements based on customer feedback) and explore new offerings (like entering a new market with a human-centred research project). Also applied to internal processes (e.g., redesigning an HR onboarding experience via design thinking).	Usually applied to finding a viable product and business model. Early-stage startups use design thinking to achieve product-market fit, deeply understand an unmet need, and craft a solution that users love. The emphasis is on disruption, solving a problem in a new way. Once product-market fit is achieved, a startup might use design thinking to refine features or expand to new user segments, but the first critical use is often to discover what the product should be.
Examples	A global bank might use design thinking to revamp its mortgage application process, involving stakeholders from IT, legal, and branch offices to co-create a simpler customer experience (a typically slow process, but with a big impact on customer satisfaction once done). A manufacturing giant might run a design thinking workshop to envision the factory of the future, bringing engineers and floor workers together to ideate on safety and efficiency improvements.	A fintech startup uses design sprints to iterate a budgeting app interface weekly based on user test feedback, quickly improving usability. A healthcare startup developing an AI diagnostic tool works closely with doctors and patients from day one, using their input to pivot from an initial concept to one that truly fits clinical workflows—all within a few months.

In essence, both large corporations and startups benefit from design thinking, but they execute it differently. Large companies are learning to be more like startups in their agility, and startups (as they grow) are learning from big companies how to add just enough structure to sustain innovation. The future likely holds a middle ground: agile enterprises that maintain user-centred agility at scale and disciplined startups that leverage design best practices from day one. Both will continue to drive design thinking forward, ensuring it remains a cornerstone of innovation regardless of an organization's size or age.

9.1.4 Industry-Specific Trends

Beyond the broad strokes of global, regional, and company-size differences, there are specific trends within industries worth noting, as these domains add unique flavours to design thinking practice:

- **Healthcare:** Healthcare organizations are increasingly adopting design thinking to improve patient experiences, whether in hospitals, clinics, or digital health apps. A major trend is patient-centric care design, involving patients (and clinicians) in co-designing solutions for everything from hospital layouts to medication management apps. The empathy stage in healthcare often uncovers emotional and personal factors (anxiety, trust in providers, privacy concerns) that are as important as functional needs. Telehealth and digital health services have boomed recently, and design thinking helped tailor these services to be user-friendly for non-tech-savvy patients (e.g., simplifying app interfaces and adding human touches to remote consultations). We see hospitals establishing innovation labs to prototype new service delivery models. For example, a hospital might use a design thinking approach to redesign the chemotherapy experience, consulting patients on what would make them more comfortable and then prototyping changes (like clinic room layouts, informational materials, and scheduling systems) to reduce stress. With the rise of healthcare AI (like diagnostic tools, which we discuss in Section 9.2), design thinking ensures these technologies are implemented human-centred—complementing doctors and comforting patients rather than causing confusion or fear. The COVID-19 pandemic also accelerated design thinking in healthcare by forcing a rapid rethinking of systems (drive-through testing, vaccine clinics, etc.) with constant prototyping under urgent conditions.
- **Technology (Software and Hardware):** The tech industry was an early adopter of design thinking (even if it used different names like user-centered design). Current trends include AI-driven design (tools that assist designers in generating ideas or interface layouts) and the integration of design thinking in agile product development. Tech firms like Google and Apple have long championed design thinking. Google's popularization of the design sprint (a five-day process for answering critical product questions) is a testament to merging design thinking with startup speed. Now, tech companies are exploring how design thinking can guide responsible technology development, particularly AI ethics and privacy. There's a trend of "design ethics", ensuring empathy extends to considering the broader societal impact of tech products (for example, a social media platform using design thinking to mitigate negative behaviours and promote user well-being). Also, as products become more connected (IoT devices, smart home ecosystems), tech

companies use design thinking to orchestrate seamless experiences across devices. It often means prototyping a single product and the whole service ecosystem (e.g., how a smart thermostat app, the thermostat device, and customer support all work together as one user journey).

- **Manufacturing and Industrial Design:** Design thinking influences Industry 4.0 initiatives (the drive towards smart, connected factories). Traditionally, manufacturing focused on efficiency and lean operations. Now, there's recognition that understanding the needs of all stakeholders (from machine operators on the factory floor to maintenance technicians) can lead to better solutions. Human-centred design for operators is a trend. For instance, factory control systems or safety procedures should be designed with direct input from workers (empathizing with how a worker interacts with a machine or what might cause fatigue or error). Prototyping in this context might involve simulations or digital twins of production lines to test improvements in a user-centric way. Another trend is manufacturers applying design thinking outwardly to innovate their business models and customer engagement. For example, automotive companies use design thinking to re-imagine the car buying experience (shifting from showrooms to more interactive, online and experience-driven models) because customers now demand a more engaging journey. In product design, sustainable and circular design is rising, using design thinking to create products that are easier to recycle and repair or minimize environmental impact, reflecting global sustainability trends.
- **Financial Services:** Banks, insurers, and fintech startups are heavily adopting design thinking to transform previously viewed as staid or user-unfriendly services. A clear trend is digitization with empathy, ensuring that moving services to mobile apps or ATMs don't lose the human touch. Many banks now involve customers in designing their mobile banking apps, simplifying workflows (like opening an account or applying for a loan) that used to be paperwork nightmares. The empathy phase often reveals pain points like customers' anxiety in financial planning or confusion in insurance policies. As a result, companies are prototyping solutions like financial coaching chatbots or clearer policy explanation interfaces. A specific trend in financial design thinking is tackling financial inclusion, e.g., designing services for the unbanked or underbanked populations (in both developed and emerging markets). It might involve brainstorming new credit evaluation methods or community-based banking aided by tech, always focusing on why people may be left out of the financial system. We also see large banks establishing customer experience labs where multi-disciplinary teams (including compliance officers, who traditionally are seen as "blockers") engage in design sprints to find ways to meet regulations while still delighting customers, a challenging balancing act, but one that design thinking is uniquely suited for by reframing problems creatively.
- **Startups and Entrepreneurship:** Finally, within the startup ecosystem, beyond the general differences discussed earlier, a trend is the formalization of design thinking in entrepreneurship education. Many accelerators and business schools teach design thinking as a core approach to starting a company. "Design-led

startups" are becoming a genre. These ventures were founded with design and user experience as the primary differentiator. For instance, a startup might enter a crowded market (say, project management software) but win by delivering a vastly superior, design-driven user experience identified through user research. Investors are also looking at design as a marker of potential success; venture capital firms have started including design experts in their teams to coach startups, indicating that good design (and the thinking behind it) is critical to commercial success.

In all industries, the common thread is that design thinking moves from the periphery to the core of strategy. It's not just a buzzword; companies integrate it with serious investment and expect measurable outcomes (customer satisfaction scores, Net Promoter Scores, innovation ROI, etc.). The Design Thinking Market, as one report estimates, is growing rapidly. One market research projection estimates the global market for design thinking (including training, consulting, and tools) will grow from about $7.3 billion in 2025 to over $12.5 billion by 2034, reflecting a CAGR of over 6%. While such figures should be taken with a grain of salt, they underscore the optimism around design thinking's continued expansion. As we progress, design thinking will likely become as standard in business as disciplines like finance or marketing, a ubiquitous part of how organizations, big and small, approach problems. The following section explores one of the most significant trends influencing design thinking's future: the rise of AI and advanced technologies and how these tools challenge and supercharge the human-centred design process.

9.2 ROLE OF AI AND TECHNOLOGY IN ENHANCING DESIGN THINKING PRACTICES

Technology and design thinking have always been intertwined; many case studies of design thinking involve creating or improving technological products. But in recent years, a wave of advanced technologies (especially artificial intelligence, machine learning, digital twin simulations, and automation tools) has begun to transform the practice of design thinking itself. In this section, we examine how these technologies enhance (and sometimes reshape) each stage of the design thinking process, from how we empathize and gather insights to how we ideate and generate concepts to how we prototype and test solutions. To illustrate these concepts in action, we will also delve into 2–3 case studies from different sectors, including Google's approach to AI in design, an example from healthcare diagnostics, and a logistics case. We consider the benefits of tech integration and the importance of keeping a human-centred focus so that AI becomes a partner in design rather than a distraction.

9.2.1 AI in the Empathy and Define Stages

One of the earliest and most impactful ways AI influences design thinking is in the Empathize stage, the phase where designers seek to deeply understand users' needs, motivations, and pain points. Empathy is traditionally built through interviews, observations, and immersion. These remain invaluable, but AI can augment them by handling large-scale data that would be impossible to synthesize manually. For example, machine learning algorithms can analyze millions of social media posts or customer reviews to detect user sentiment and behaviour patterns. AI-driven text analysis might reveal hidden themes in what users are complaining about or wishing for, thereby uncovering needs that weren't obvious. AI can help "uncover hidden insights in user data, enabling a better understanding of user needs and preferences," one practitioner noted. It does not replace human observation but complements it. A designer might use AI to crunch big data and follow up with targeted ethnographic research on the insights discovered.

Another emerging concept is "behavioural data empathy." For instance, a digital product team can use AI analytics to watch how users navigate an app in real-time; the AI may spot that users consistently get stuck at a certain step. It is a signal to empathize with their frustration and investigate why. In the past, we relied on user testing with a few dozen participants for such insights; now, AI can parse thousands or millions of users through behaviour to flag pain points quickly. AI-powered tools like facial recognition or voice sentiment analysis (used with consent in research settings) can also gauge emotional responses. Imagine showing a prototype to users while a camera (with AI) gauges their facial expressions to note moments of confusion or delight. Such technology provides a richer empathy map of user emotions throughout an experience.

In the Define stage, where insights are synthesized into a clear problem statement, AI can assist by clustering and categorizing large amounts of qualitative data. Tools now exist that use natural language processing to group interview transcripts by themes, helping teams see the forest for the trees. For example, if a team interviewed 100 customers, an AI summarization tool might identify that 30% mentioned "difficulty in setup," 50% mentioned "cost concerns," etc. It aids designers in prioritizing which problem is most pressing for users. AI can also feed into creating personas: by analyzing user data, AI might help identify distinct user segments, which designers flesh out into persona archetypes. AI can rapidly crunch data to support the definition of the right problem, which is critical; as the saying goes, "a problem well-defined is half-solved."

However, it's worth noting that while AI brings scale and speed, human judgment is still crucial in Empathize and Define. AI might tell us "what" users do and even hint at "what" they feel through sentiment, but the "why" often requires human interpretation. Design teams, therefore, treat AI as an assistant or a sensing tool. Google's People + AI Research (PAIR) group emphasizes this—they've developed a "People + AI Guidebook" to help designers effectively integrate AI insights while keeping humans at the centre. Google's approach underscores that AI should address real human needs effectively, enhancing rather than detracting from a user experience. For example, PAIR's guidelines remind designers to prioritize people over technology: just because an AI model finds a pattern does not mean it's a meaningful problem to solve. Designers must validate AI-derived insights with real user context. Google's design teams have learned to manage AI's sometimes unpredictable results and explain AI findings in clear, non-technical terms so that the whole team (and stakeholders) understands the user implications. This blend of AI and human empathy leads to more robust problem definitions—you get the breadth of big data and the depth of human understanding.

A hypothetical example in empathy: consider a public transit agency trying to improve ridership experience. Traditional design thinking would involve riding buses, interviewing passengers, etc. With AI, they can also analyze thousands of tweets about daily commutes. Suppose AI finds that uncertainty about bus arrival times is a major source of frustration. Combined with field observations, that insight might lead to a clear definition: "Commuters need a more reliable way to know when the bus will arrive to reduce anxiety during waits." The team can ideate solutions like improved real-time tracking apps or better station signage.

9.2.2 AI in Ideation and Brainstorming

Moving to the Ideation stage, AI and automation are becoming surprisingly useful creative partners. It might sound counter-intuitive; ideation is often seen as a deeply human, imaginative process, but AI can stimulate creativity by generating novel combinations or challenging assumptions. One way AI aids ideation is through generative design. Generative design tools, powered by AI algorithms, can take a set of constraints and rapidly produce dozens or hundreds of design alternatives. It has been used in architecture and engineering (for instance, to generate many structural designs that meet certain strength requirements). Still, it's increasingly being applied in product and UI/UX design. For example, an AI might generate numerous layout options for a webpage given goals like "maximize clarity and user engagement", and designers use these as fodder for discussion, perhaps mixing and matching ideas. It does not remove the designer's role. Rather, it's like having a tireless brainstorming assistant who says, "How about this? Or this? Or this?" repeatedly. The designer still applies critical thinking to select and refine the ideas that best address the defined user needs.

AI can also help teams ideate based on patterns of what has worked before. Machine learning systems trained on successful design solutions (say, apps with high usability ratings) might identify certain common features or flows, suggesting them as starting points for new ideas. Additionally, AI can act as a provocation tool. Consider a natural language AI (like GPT-style chatbots): a team could prompt an AI with "Brainstorm ideas for how to make grocery shopping more enjoyable for elderly customers," the AI will list suggestions. Some suggestions might be obvious or impractical, but some could spark a genuinely useful direction the team hadn't considered. The key advantage is speed and breadth. AI can spitball far-fetched ideas without judgment, which can free human designers to explore paths they might have prematurely dismissed. It's worth noting that using AI in brainstorming requires curation; the team must filter and build upon the AI's ideas, ensuring they remain grounded in empathy findings and feasibility.

There is a case to be made that AI encourages divergent thinking. In design thinking, we often emphasize diverging (coming up with many possibilities) before converging (narrowing down). AI is excellent at divergence. It can generate in one minute what a human team might take hours to dream up. For example, in the video game design industry, AI tools can generate many character designs or story plot variations, which designers then review for the most promising or intriguing ones. This trend gives designers a new skill: prompt engineering, knowing how to ask the AI the right questions or set the right parameters to yield useful generative output. Designers who can effectively direct AI (e.g., telling a generative model the constraints and style guidelines to respect) can get more relevant and inspiring results.

However, there is a balance to maintain. One risk is over-reliance on AI for creativity, which could lead to homogenization (especially if everyone uses the same AI trained on the same data) or solutions lacking human touch. To mitigate this, teams often use AI to broaden ideation but then switch back to human-driven critique and refinement. Also, some ideas need human sense-making. AI might suggest something novel, but human insight is needed to evaluate its appropriateness or ethical implications. For example, an AI brainstorming for "elderly shopping enjoyment" might suggest installing AR goggles in supermarkets to gamify shopping. Interesting idea, but the team's human perspective might catch that many elderly users won't be comfortable with AR goggles. They might still salvage the core idea (gamification) but adapt it to something simpler, like a bingo-like game that works via a smartphone or even a paper booklet, thus making it truly user-centric for that demographic.

Google's design teams have reportedly experimented with using their own AI (like large language models) during ideation for certain products. In one internal case, designers working on an AI-based photo app used a generative model to propose fun features by analyzing what users do with photos. The AI suggested a feature that would automatically create storybooks out of a set of photos. The team hadn't listed that in their initial brainstorm, but seeing it appear in the AI output, they considered it and realized through user feedback that it had appeal (e.g., parents loved the idea of a storybook of their kid's birthday party). It shows AI can surface latent user desires indirectly by cross-referencing patterns (in this case, noticing that many people manually arrange their photos into albums and write captions, essentially creating narratives).

In summary, the trend is that AI is becoming a co-creator. As one design article put it, at the intersection of AI and design thinking lies "a synergistic fusion of human creativity and technological innovation", where AI's analytical and generative capabilities complement designers' empathetic and critical thinking. The combination can foster enhanced innovation and user-centric solutions that neither could achieve alone. Designers are learning to "co-create with AI," treating it as a teammate. It means embracing some level of unpredictability. AI might output something completely unexpected, which can be good for breaking cognitive fixedness. The next step after ideation is prototyping, and technology is leaving its mark here, too.

9.2.3 AI, Digital Twins, and Automation in Prototyping and Testing

The prototype and test stages of design thinking have also been significantly enhanced by technology, such as digital twins, simulation, and automation. Prototyping is about making ideas tangible; the faster and more realistically you can do that, the quicker you learn. Digital prototyping tools have been around (from simple mockup software to interactive app prototyping platforms), but AI is taking it further with automation. For instance, AI tools can now convert a hand-drawn sketch of an interface into code or a functional app in seconds. It means a designer can sketch an idea on paper and let AI instantly generate a working prototype for testing. Such speed was unimaginable a few years ago. It compresses the iteration cycle dramatically.

Digital twins deserve special mention. A digital twin is a high-fidelity virtual model of a real-world system that can simulate how that system behaves under various conditions.

This concept, originally from engineering and IoT, is applied to design thinking in urban planning, logistics, and even service design. By creating a digital twin of, say, a city transportation network or a supply chain, designers and engineers can prototype changes in the virtual model and observe outcomes without risking real-world disruption. It is incredibly useful in testing ideas that are too costly or risky to pilot physically. For example, a logistics company might have a digital twin of its warehouse operations and use it to prototype a new workflow for order picking using autonomous robots. They can simulate the throughput and identify bottlenecks in the twin before purchasing robots or rearranging the warehouse. In terms of design thinking, it allows rapid iterative prototyping at a systems level. The trend is that such simulations are becoming more user-friendly and integrated with the design process, not just a back-end engineering activity. Teams can tweak variables in a digital twin via a simple dashboard (no coding required in some modern tools), which democratizes the experimentation.

AI also aids in the usability testing of prototypes. For digital products, analytics can measure how users interact with a prototype (where they click and hesitate), and AI can quickly analyze these interactions to suggest improvements. Even in physical prototypes, such as devices, sensors and AI can monitor user actions, how they hold a device and where their gaze goes, providing rich feedback. Automation can further facilitate testing by handling repetitive tasks. For instance, a conversational AI (chatbot) prototype can be tested with thousands of automated test queries to see where it fails to answer well, which would be tedious manually.

Let's dive into the promised case studies to illustrate these ideas:

CASE STUDY: Google's AI in Design—Enhancing User Experience with Human-Centered AI

As a tech leader, Google integrates AI into many of its product design processes. One notable example is the development of Google Assistant (the AI voice assistant). The design challenge was to create an AI that could genuinely help users in daily tasks via natural conversation. Google's team employed design thinking heavily: empathizing with users by studying how people give instructions or ask questions in real life, ideating around various personas and contexts (busy moms, driving scenarios, etc.), prototyping voices and dialogue flows, and testing with users. AI played multiple roles here. First, the product was AI, but in developing it, Google used machine learning on its troves of search query data to understand the myriad ways people phrase questions, an empathy aid. They also used Wizard-of-Oz prototyping, where early on, a human behind the curtain would simulate the AI's responses to test how users reacted; later, they phased in actual AI algorithms. Google's PAIR guidebook (aforementioned) provided principles so that the Assistant's design remained user-first. For example, they discovered through testing that users felt awkward if the Assistant responded with overly long answers, so they trained the AI to give more concise answers, a tweak informed by human emotional response. In essence, Google treated the AI's behaviour as part of the design to be iterated. Key learning: AI can be prototyped like any other feature. You can start with a simple rule-based version as a prototype, gather user feedback, and gradually increase the AI's complexity. Today, Google Assistant uses advanced neural networks, but its core interactions were shaped by design thinking methods supported by AI usage analysis. The result is an AI product that millions find intuitive; it's technology-powered but user experience-designed.

Another Google-related example is how Google Maps continuously improves via AI and design thinking. Empathy research showed commuters valued real-time information like traffic congestion and ETAs. Google uses AI to predict traffic and suggest routes. Still, the design team ensures that information is presented in a user-friendly way (clear colour coding of traffic simple route options). They prototype changes (like a new way to display delays) via A/B testing to millions of users, an automated form of testing design variants in the wild. Those results feed back into the design cycle. This kind of large-scale prototype testing is unique to software: release an update as a "beta" to a subset, let AI analyze the engagement and success metrics, and then refine.

CASE STUDY: AI in Healthcare Diagnostics—Human-Centered AI for Medical Imaging

Imagine a healthcare startup that designs an AI-powered diagnostic tool for radiologists to detect lung cancer from X-rays. The team is multidisciplinary: data scientists, software engineers, and, importantly, design thinkers and clinicians. They used design thinking from the get-go, interviewing radiologists and observing their workflow (Empathize) to understand needs. They found that radiologists don't just want a blunt "AI result;" they want to know why AI flags an X-ray as cancerous (because, ultimately, the human doctor is responsible for the diagnosis). So, the defined problem became how to integrate an AI tool into radiologists' workflow in a trustworthy and interpretable way that saves them time. With this user-centred requirement, the team ideated solutions such as an interface where the AI highlights areas of the X-ray it finds suspicious and provides a confidence score, along with an explanation (e.g., "lesion with irregular border detected").

They prototyped this by creating a digital mock interface overlay on real X-ray images and manually simulating the AI output (doctors didn't know, but early tests had a human in the loop picking the same spots an AI model would). Feedback from those tests guided refinements; for example, Radiologists said they'd like the ability to give feedback to the AI ("mark this suggestion as incorrect") so it could learn. The engineers then implemented an AI model and indeed included a feedback feature. AI helped in prototyping by enabling a digital twin of the diagnostic workflow: they could simulate how many cancers would be caught or missed under different settings of the AI's sensitivity before deploying.

One year into use at a pilot hospital, they gathered data: the AI was very accurate, but initially, some doctors ignored it. Using design thinking, they conducted follow-up empathy work. Interviews revealed that doctors felt the AI sometimes pointed out obvious things. Occasionally, it highlighted normal anomalies that were not cancer, so they were getting "alert fatigue." In response, the team adjusted the AI's threshold (making it less trigger-happy). It redesigned the interface to make alerts more nuanced (perhaps colour-coding by confidence and adding a snooze feature for alerts). This case illustrates a crucial point: design thinking ensures AI tools in healthcare augment rather than frustrate the human user. The outcome was a tool that indeed improved diagnostic rates and saved time, but only because the team iterated with human feedback. In fact, a LinkedIn case study from a UK hospital found that implementing AI (for operations tracking) led to both efficiency gains and unexpected human benefits like improved staff psychological safety and reduced stress, as the system made their work environment feel more predictable and connected. It underscores how a well-designed AI (in this hospital's case, a digital twin presence system) can support human needs beyond the obvious. It was a "paradox: tech for efficiency strengthened human emotional well-being," highlighting that AI can create space for meaningful human interactions by handling the routine stuff.

CASE STUDY: Logistics—IBM's Cognitive Supply Chain

In logistics, IBM applied AI and design thinking internally to reinvent its supply chain management. Faced with a complex global network and legacy systems, IBM set out to build a "cognitive supply chain", essentially an AI-driven, highly responsive supply chain nervous system. But this was not just an IT upgrade; IBM used a user-centred approach focusing on the experience of their supply chain planners and managers (the internal "users" of the system). They empathized with these employees across different regions to understand pain points, like how hard it was to get information quickly or to predict supply disruptions. They defined the goal as an integrated platform that could provide real-time visibility and answer users' questions in natural language.

During ideation and prototyping, IBM's team (with IBM Consulting) leveraged AI by incorporating their Watson AI as an interface. They created prototypes of a dashboard where a planner could ask, for example, "Which shipments might be delayed due to the China port closure?" the system would analyze data and respond. Early prototypes might have been Wizard-of-Oz (with a human analyst behind the scenes fetching answers), then progressively automated as the AI models trained. Using hybrid testing (human + AI) ensured that the responses aligned with what users needed by the time it was fully AI. The result was IBM Supply Chain Advisor 360, running on a cloud and AI platform. It gave IBM's supply chain team immediate access to information and the ability to respond to changes in demand as they happen (VKTR, 2023). One manager noted that they could now manage both "guaranteed supply" and "predictability of supply" more effectively, balancing customer expectations. In practice, during disruptions like a hurricane or pandemic, the cognitive system helped reroute shipments and find alternative sources quickly. This AI-driven design fulfilled functional needs and improved the experience for IBM employees who could get answers in seconds rather than hours. By focusing on the humans in the loop and designing the AI around their workflows (rather than forcing them to adapt to a complex system), IBM achieved impressive outcomes, fulfilling 100% of orders during disruptions by fast re-routing and drastically cutting the time to answer supply chain queries (VKTR, 2023).

This case shows that design thinking with AI is not just for end-user consumer products; it is equally powerful for internal systems and B2B contexts. The key trend is making advanced technology like AI accessible through good design. Natural language interfaces (like IBM's use of Watson to let employees query in plain English) are one-way designs that make AI usable. Another trend is the automation of routine decisions. IBM's system can automate certain supply decisions, freeing humans to focus on exceptions and strategy, which employees appreciate since it takes grunt work off their plate. However, automation was introduced gradually, with trust-building measures (like letting users review AI suggestions initially) reflecting human-centred change management.

9.2.4 Balancing Technology and Human-Centered Design

As our case studies illustrate, technology amplifies what design thinking can achieve. AI and machine learning lend data-driven rigour and speed, digital twins and simulations allow risk-free experimentation, and automation executes repetitive tasks so humans can focus on creative and empathetic aspects. The combined result can be smarter and faster innovation cycles. Teams can iterate more quickly and base decisions on richer evidence. One article stated that combining AI's analytical power with design thinking's creativity leads to "enhanced innovation, improved user experience through personalization, and greater efficiency and scalability in the design process." AI can help generate and test many ideas, while design thinking ensures the ideas are meaningful and user-centric. This convergence is giving rise to what some call "AI Thinking" as a complement to design thinking. AI Thinking means integrating AI capabilities (data analysis, predictions) into the problem-solving approach alongside human insight. By leveraging this, designers can create adaptive solutions (learning and improving in real time) and scalable ones (handling millions of personalized interactions) in ways that purely human-centred design might struggle to achieve.

However, with great power comes great responsibility. A crucial part of this trend is maintaining ethical and human-centred guardrails. Design teams must be vigilant so that when using AI, they do not inadvertently introduce bias or reduce transparency in the user experience. For example, suppose an AI is used to personalize a service. In that case, the design needs to ensure users feel in control and understand why certain recommendations are made, otherwise, trust can erode. AI can also over-complicate things; part of human-centred design is sometimes choosing a simpler, perhaps less "smart" solution if it fits users better. The motto "just because we can, does not mean we should" applies. A well-known instance is when some companies tried using AI chatbots for all customer service queries, only to find that many customers grew frustrated and just wanted a human for complex issues. A design thinking approach would iterate on that feedback, perhaps designing a hybrid system where AI handles basic questions but seamlessly hands off a human agent when it detects confusion or emotional distress, thus leveraging technology strengths and human empathy.

In practice, successful tech-enhanced design thinking requires cross-disciplinary collaboration. It's no longer just designers and end-users; data scientists, AI engineers, and ethicists might also be present in the ideation room. It ensures feasibility and ethics are considered early. One emerging practice is to include an "AI ethics checklist" in the design process: questions like "Could our AI recommendations inadvertently discriminate or exclude someone?" or "How do we explain the AI's decision to the user?" become part of the design criteria. It keeps the technology in service of the user.

To conclude this section, the role of AI and technology in design thinking is a story of synergy. AI's strengths in data, speed, and scale are enriching the design thinking process, enabling what we might call "design at scale" (personalizing solutions for millions of users) and "design at speed" (rapidly iterating through possibilities). The case studies from Google, healthcare, and IBM logistics demonstrate that AI can augment human creativity and empathy when done right. Designers are not being replaced; rather, they are gaining powerful tools, akin to how the advent of computer-aided design (CAD) gave architects and engineers new capabilities. Now, AI is giving all designers a new superpower. It remains critical, though, that we keep the mindset of a designer: curiosity, empathy, and ethical responsibility. If we do, then AI and related technologies will undoubtedly help us tackle more complex problems, test bolder ideas, and ultimately arrive at solutions that are not only innovative but deeply attuned to human needs.

With technology reshaping how we practice design thinking, the next section focuses on the human factor: the mindset and culture needed to sustain design thinking in organizations. After all, tools and trends are only as practical as the people wielding them. Cultivating a design-driven mindset ensures that all these trends, whether global shifts or AI enhancements, truly take root and lead to meaningful innovation.

9.3 FINAL THOUGHTS ON CULTIVATING A DESIGN-DRIVEN MINDSET

As we look to the future of design thinking, one of the most critical factors is mindset. Trends, tools, and case studies show what's possible, but realizing the potential of design thinking in any context ultimately depends on people, individuals and organizations embracing a design-centric way of thinking and working. This section will explore how organizations and individuals can cultivate a design-driven mindset and build a sustaining culture of human-centred innovation. We will draw examples from companies renowned for their design maturity, such as IBM and PepsiCo, and mention newer enterprises that have initially put design at their core. The goal is to distil lessons on what makes a culture "design-centric" and how readers (as future practitioners or leaders) might foster these qualities in their environments.

9.3.1 Building a Design-Centric Culture in Organizations

Creating a design-driven culture in an organization is not an overnight task—it is a journey of change management, education, and practice. A true design-centric culture is one where empathy, experimentation, and collaboration are ingrained values, not just one-off project tactics. People at all levels think about the end-user or customer in decision-making, and cross-functional teamwork is encouraged to tackle problems holistically.

One of the hallmark examples of a traditional company transforming into a design-driven organization is IBM. By the early 2010s, IBM recognized that it needed to radically change how its teams approached problem-solving to stay innovative. The company invested over $100 million in a program to embed design thinking throughout its global workforce. IBM hired experienced design leaders and more than 1,600 formally trained designers, creating the largest corporate design team in the world (Renganathan, 2020). But just hiring designers was not enough. They also trained over 110,000 employees in design thinking methodologies, from engineers to product managers to salespeople, giving each a baseline understanding of the human-centred approach. This combination of skilled designers collaborating with newly trained "design thinkers" across the company became a "difference-maker" in IBM's workflow. The results, as analyzed by Forrester Research, were powerful: teams aligned faster, product development cycles shortened, and outcomes improved, yielding a significant return on investment for IBM. In essence, IBM shifted from an engineering-driven culture to a user-driven culture. They institutionalized certain practices. For example, "Hills" (statements that define what outcome a user should achieve, used to guide projects), "Playbacks" (regular sessions where teams present work in progress to stakeholders, focusing on user stories), and "Sponsor Users" (IBM invites real users to be part of the design team on projects). These practices ensured that empathy and user feedback loop were constant, not occasional. Equally important, IBM's leadership actively supported this culture change; their CEO and senior VPs communicated the importance of design thinking, making it clear it was not a fad but a new way of working. The IBM case shows that with commitment and comprehensive strategy (hiring, training, new processes, leadership buy-in), even a 100-year-old, 380,000-employee company can truly pivot to embrace design at scale.

Another shining example is PepsiCo, the global food and beverage company. PepsiCo's journey illustrates transforming a culture through leadership vision and persistent advocacy. In 2012, then-CEO Indra Nooyi declared a new vision: for PepsiCo to become "a pioneer in organizational innovation through design thinking". To realize this, she hired the company's first Chief Design Officer (CDO), Mauro Porcini. At that time, PepsiCo had essentially no internal design capability. Porcini was the first designer to infuse design thinking across a huge marketing- and sales-driven organization. Over the next decade, Porcini built a design empire within PepsiCo: by 2022, PepsiCo had 160 designers and 15 design centres globally. More important than the numbers was how design thinking spreads in mindset. Porcini insisted that "design thinking permeates the entire organization not only as a tool for managing innovation projects but also as a set of mindsets that organize our teams… It's not just the doing. It's the thinking, absorbing, reflecting.". In other words, it was not just about having a design department making shiny new products; it was about every function, from R&D to marketing to strategy, adopting a human-centric, holistic way of thinking.

How did PepsiCo achieve this cultural shift? Researchers who studied PepsiCo's transformation identified nine design thinking practices the company implemented to drive organizational innovation. The core of these was aligning people's passion with the corporate vision and nurturing "co-conspirators", internal champions who advocate and spread the new mindset. Porcini started by building empathy internally: he spent time one-on-one with key stakeholders, sharing his passions and listening to theirs (often outside of the work context), effectively building human connections and trust. It addresses a subtle but important aspect: to change a culture, you must touch hearts, not just processes. Porcini created moments of genuine personal connection (like inviting colleagues to his favourite Italian restaurants, using food and storytelling as a medium to share perspectives). Through these interactions, he conveyed what design thinking could do and ignited excitement, an effort to empathize with his internal audience! Two initial principles he applied were: (1) empathy with people (talk about values and vision, not just business metrics) and (2) placing people in a comfort zone where they can be open and creative.

From those foundations, PepsiCo's nine practices included things like leveraging one-to-one connections (as mentioned), engaging external stakeholders as partners (they started involving customers, like major retailers, early in innovation to co-create), adopting cultural change by redefining design's role (taking design beyond packaging into strategy), encouraging abductive reasoning (to imagine future opportunities beyond current data by creating physical spaces that inspired creativity, empowering visualization through prototypes and storytelling to make ideas concrete, and celebrating successes to create positive reinforcement for the new way of working. For example, when PepsiCo launched a new successful product (like a healthier snack or a new SodaStream platform feature), they would internally publicize it as a proof point of design thinking's value. Over time, these practices snowballed: more people got on board ("co-conspirators" increased), and the culture reached a tipping point where design-led innovation became the norm rather than the exception. Indra Nooyi noted that design now has a voice in almost every important decision at PepsiCo—from product development to how the company approaches brand and even internal processes. Performance-wise, PepsiCo introduced several successful innovations during this era (like the award-winning Drinkfinity beverage system, new healthier snack lines, and a redesign of the Pepsi vending and fountain experience) and saw tangible business growth in segments where design was heavily involved. They also significantly elevated their brands' consumer perception by focusing on delightful packaging and brand experiences, proving that design thinking can drive differentiation even for a food and beverage company.

Aside from IBM and PepsiCo, numerous other enterprises have pursued design-centric culture building:

- SAP, the enterprise software giant, embraced design thinking in the 2000s under the influence of Hasso Plattner (one of its founders, who co-founded the Stanford d.school). SAP created internal networks of design thinking coaches and made it a key part of how they develop software, with notable success in moving from a purely engineering-driven mentality to one that better satisfies users (which is critical in software UX).
- Capital One, a financial services company, acquired design agencies and embedded design teams, leading to banking apps and services that customers highly rate. They infuse design thinking in developing new financial products, emphasising empathy for customer financial stress and prototyping new service concepts (like café-style bank branches).
- Airbnb (a "newer" company relative to those above) was founded by designers and scaled up without losing its design culture. They famously have core values around creativity and belonging, and even as they grew, they set up an internal program called "Snow White" (as mentioned earlier) to ensure every employee understands the customer journey story. Airbnb's design-driven mindset means departments beyond design (like customer service engineering) also think about user experience. For example, engineers have been known to join research trips to hosts' homes to understand user context better.

- Apple is often cited as a design-led company (with the late Steve Jobs and former Chief Designer Jony Ive setting a tone where design decisions held paramount importance, and every employee was expected to sweat user experience details). Apple's culture of secrecy is unique, but internally, it has long fostered a reverence for design, evidenced by how teams work meticulously on prototypes and how cross-functional integration (hardware, software, retail) is oriented around delivering a signature user experience.

From these examples, we can distil some common elements of a design-centric culture:

- **Leadership Advocacy:** In every case, top leadership endorsed and pushed the design thinking agenda (e.g., IBM's executives, PepsiCo's Indra Nooyi, and Capital One's CEO, who invested in design). Leadership sets priorities, and if they show that "user experience matters as much as quarterly numbers," the organization listens.
- **Empowerment and Training:** Spreading skills through training programs or workshops helps demystify design thinking. When non-designers are trained and invited to participate, they feel ownership. IBM trains 100k employees, and PepsiCo teaches brand managers to use ethnographic research tools. These efforts embed capabilities across the organization.
- **Cross-Functional Teams:** Breaking silos is crucial. Many companies create dedicated innovation teams with members from different departments or encourage more collaborative workflows. When diverse perspectives meet in a design thinking workshop, it yields better ideas and builds respect and understanding among departments, which is the cultural glue.
- **Physical and Virtual Space for Innovation:** A small but symbolic factor, companies often create innovation labs, studios, or creativity-friendly spaces (e.g., with whiteboards, Post-its, and comfortable areas for informal meetings), signalling that brainstorming and prototyping are welcome anytime, not just off-site. Even virtually, enabling collaboration tools (Miro boards, etc.) and allocating time for creative exploration sends a message.
- **Rewarding Experimentation:** Culturally, people must feel safe trying new ideas. Design-centric organizations celebrate attempts and lessons learned, not just successful outcomes. Some implement systems to fund small experiments or have "innovation awards" to recognize teams that took bold approaches, even if those projects didn't ultimately ship. It encourages the mindset of continual experimentation (which is the engine of design thinking).
- **User Connection as Part of Jobs:** A cultural shift happens when each person in their role starts considering the end-user. Companies have done things like inviting customers to speak at internal meetings, sharing customer feedback company-wide, or briefly rotating employees into customer-facing roles to build empathy. At design-mature companies, even a finance analyst or a legal counsel is aware of how their work impacts the customer or end-user experience, which influences their decisions (for instance, a legal team might simplify terms & conditions language as a result of a design thinking initiative focusing on clear communication).

A design-driven mindset at the individual level means approaching problems with curiosity, willingness to understand others' perspectives, and comfort with ambiguity and failure. Organizations that foster this provide training and also model behaviours from the top. As David Kelley of IDEO often emphasizes, it's about developing "creative confidence", the belief that you can develop innovative solutions and have permission to act on them. The GE MRI Adventure case from Chapter 1 is a great example of creative confidence: one engineer, Doug Dietz, shifted his mindset to reimagine an MRI machine as a kids' adventure, and because GE had begun valuing such human-centric innovation, he was supported. When that story (improving pediatric MRI experience) circulated inside GE, it inspired others, showing that even in a very technical company, empathy and imagination can solve tough problems and be celebrated.

9.3.2 Design-Driven Individuals: Everyone as a Designer

Building a design-driven mindset is not just an organizational endeavour; it's also personal. The future of work suggests that skills like empathy, creativity, and collaborative problem-solving (all nurtured by design thinking) will be highly prized across roles. Thus, a "design-driven individual" does not have to have "designer" in their title. It could be a project manager who always starts projects by deeply understanding stakeholder needs, a sales professional who uses empathy to grasp a client's pain points and tailor solutions truly, or an engineer who insists on prototyping and testing her code with real users rather than assuming specs alone are enough.

For individuals, cultivating a design mindset involves habits such as:

- **Continuous Curiosity:** Asking questions and seeking to learn directly from users or data rather than taking assumptions for granted. For instance, if you work in product development, regularly engage with actual users, not just when officially scheduled. It might mean reading user forums, watching usability test recordings, or spending a day in customer support to hear issues firsthand.
- **Embracing Empathy Beyond Work:** Many design thinkers practice empathy in daily life, listening intently to people's stories, observing interactions in public, etc., to keep the empathy muscle strong. This openness and lack of judgment help in professional contexts when dealing with users or colleagues.
- **Comfort with Iteration:** Personally adopting the mindset that drafts and prototypes are part of progress, not signs of imperfection. For example, when writing a report or preparing a presentation, a design-minded person might seek feedback early, treating it like a prototype to be improved rather than polishing it in isolation and being afraid to show rough versions.
- **Storytelling and Visualization:** Individuals can champion a design mindset by communicating ideas via stories and visuals, which engage others and clarify direction. Whether using a quick sketch in a meeting to illustrate an idea or narrating a user's journey to explain a point, these techniques spread the impact of design thinking. Storytelling is powerful culturally. One well-told success story is how listening to users solve a problem can convert more people to a design

mindset than hours of lecture. We saw that internally at PepsiCo, Porcini's sharing of stories (like how a new package design came from an insight about customers wanting sustainability) helped convince others.

- **Lifelong Learning:** The best design thinkers always learn about new tools, psychology, domain knowledge, and anything that helps them better understand contexts and generate ideas. Someone with a design-driven mindset might take courses on topics outside their immediate expertise, read widely, and cross-pollinate ideas from different fields. This intellectual flexibility is a hallmark of design leaders (e.g., a design thinker in a bank might read up on behavioural economics to better design how people make financial decisions).

A design-driven individual also helps spread the culture by example. If you demonstrate empathy in meetings (e.g., "Have we thought about how this change will affect our elderly customers?"), others pick up on that. You normalise that behaviour if you handle failures gracefully ("Our first prototype failed, but we learned X and Y, so let's iterate"). Culture is often a sum of small actions at all levels. So, each individual with a design mindset contributes to the overall culture shifting in that direction.

9.3.3 Examples of Design Maturity and Mindset

It's worth highlighting a couple more contemporary examples of companies known for a design-driven mindset:

- We discussed IBM and PepsiCo, which show transformation in big firms.
- One of Airbnb's early internal mottos was "Be a cereal entrepreneur." This quirky phrase comes from the founders selling cereal boxes ("Obama O's" and "Cap'n McCain's" during the 2008 U.S. election) to fund the startup. Still, metaphorically, it means being scrappy and creative. They also embraced storytelling with the Snow White project, as mentioned. Airbnb's design culture emphasizes empathy so much that designers and researchers will stay in Airbnb and host guests themselves to walk in customers' shoes. The company also encourages employees to use their travel stipend to stay at Airbnbs and then share stories of their experiences with the team, keeping everyone connected to the user's perspective. This constant user immersion is a practice any organization can emulate in its domain (Core77, 2013).
- Spotify, is known for both agile and human-centric practices. Spotify's squads and tribes model encourages small, autonomous teams that include design, tech, and product roles working together. They have a strong user focus, continually testing new features (like new playlist formats or social features) with segments of their users. Spotify's design mindset is evident in how they create user delight (e.g., the yearly "Spotify Wrapped" feature that compiles a user's listening data into a fun, sharable story, a data-heavy feature made delightful by design and storytelling). Internally, Spotify fosters a culture of innovation by hackathons and by giving teams the freedom to pursue ideas that improve user experience, even if they're not directly tied to short-term revenue.

- Atlassian (an enterprise software company) has built a culture around openness and continuous improvement that is aligned with design thinking. They use an exercise called "Heart" (Happiness, Engagement, Adoption, Retention, Task success) to measure user experience, which guides teams to empathize with users beyond just functional needs. The Atlassian team also practices blameless post-mortems, when something fails, instead of blame, they focus on learning, which correlates with the fail-forward attitude of design thinking.

One concept in cultivating a design-driven organization is achieving design maturity. Design consultancies like McKinsey and InVision have created models to assess how mature an organization's design culture is, ranging from nascent (design used ad hoc) to advanced (design is a core strategic driver, measured at the C-suite). Many companies are on the journey upward. For instance, a business might start by hiring a few designers (formative stage) and involve them in projects (adaptation stage). Leadership sees results and starts investing more in design (integration stage), and eventually, design sits at the table for strategy (mature stage). Not every company will reach the likes of IBM or PepsiCo levels, but moving up even one level in maturity can have a notable impact. A Forrester study (commissioned by IBM) found that organizations that deeply integrate design thinking experienced faster product cycles and ROI; another study by McKinsey found that top design-mature companies outperformed industry benchmark growth by as much as 2:1. These kinds of evidence further encourage organizations to invest in a design mindset not just as a "nice-to-have" but as a competitive advantage.

9.3.4 Key Takeaways for Cultivating the Mindset

From the above, the final thoughts on mindset can be summarized:

- *Design thinking is as much a culture as a process.* To sustain it, cultivate an environment where empathy, experimentation, and user focus are default behaviours. It involves leadership commitment, widespread training, and integration into everyday workflows.
- *Lead with stories and champions.* Successful cultural shifts used storytelling (the power of narrative to illustrate why design matters) and developed internal champions at various levels who lead by example and bring peers along.
- *Encourage cross-pollination.* Break down silos so that diverse expertise informs design. When engineering, design, business, and users are in dialogue, a design-driven culture flourishes because people see the value of perspectives beyond their discipline.
- *Institutionalize but don't bureaucratize.* It's a fine line: provide enough structure (methods, playbooks, spaces) to help people practice design thinking confidently, but not so much red tape that it loses its agile, creative spirit. Companies like IBM found a balance by introducing common methods (like Hills Playbacks) but still allowing teams flexibility in execution.
- *Long-term perspective.* Cultivating a mindset is an ongoing journey. There will be initial wins, perhaps some setbacks (like projects that fail or old habits that

resurface). Persistence and continuous reinforcement are key. Over the years, hiring practices, performance evaluations, and reward systems can be aligned to support the design mindset (e.g., including user satisfaction as a KPI for teams).

- *Inclusivity in design.* A modern design mindset also means inclusive design—ensuring diversity in design teams and considering a broad range of user backgrounds. A culture that values empathy naturally values inclusivity because to empathize, you must consider perspectives unlike your own. Companies building design culture now are increasingly mindful of inclusion, accessibility, and global perspectives as integral to design thinking (not afterthoughts).

In closing this section, a design-driven mindset is arguably the most important legacy of design thinking's rise. Tools and fads come and go, but an organization (or person) that has learned to keep the user at the centre, iterate towards solutions, and break out of conventional thinking patterns will stay resilient and innovative no matter what the future brings. It is the mindset that allows one to navigate new trends (like the AI wave or whatever comes next) responsibly and creatively. As readers, whether you aim to lead a team or just be an effective practitioner, focusing on mindset and culture is crucial. Think about how you can be an ambassador of design thinking values in your environment. That might mean starting small, running a brief empathy exercise in your next team meeting or sharing an article about a design success in another company to inspire colleagues. Over time, these small acts can catalyze bigger changes.

Having explored trends, tech, and mindset, our final content section looks outward to you, the reader, and the path forward. How can you take what you've learned in this book and continue to grow? What practical steps and resources can you leverage to further your design thinking journey? We address these in the next section, ensuring you leave this chapter with insights and a clear sense of the next steps.

9.4 MOVING FORWARD WITH DESIGN THINKING—NEXT STEPS FOR READERS

Design thinking is often called a journey, not a destination. As this book reaches its final chapter, your journey with design thinking is likely just beginning. This section provides practical guidance on how to continue applying and learning design thinking beyond these pages. We will outline actionable steps, useful tools, recommended resources for further reading, and avenues for professional development (including career paths and certifications) to help you move forward. Whether you are a student, a professional in another field, or an aspiring designer or innovator, these next steps are meant to solidify your skills and keep your momentum going. Consider this a launchpad for integrating design thinking into your daily work and long-term career.

9.4.1 Putting Design Thinking into Practice Immediately

One of the best ways to cement what you've learned is to apply design thinking to a real problem as soon as possible. Look around your current academic, professional, or personal environment for an opportunity to practice. It does not have to be a grand innovation project; it can be a small but meaningful challenge. For example:

- If you're working in an organization, identify a process that frustrates people (perhaps onboarding new employees, how meetings are run, or a customer complaint handling process). Form a small team or even go solo through the design thinking steps: interview those involved to empathize and gather perspectives, define the core issue, ideate possible improvements, prototype a tweak or new tool (even if just a checklist or a mock-up of a form), and test it out on a small scale. Not only could you make a positive change, but you'll also refine your skills.
- If you're a student, you might apply design thinking to a group project or campus life (like improving a study space or a service at the college). Propose to your group that you spend some time upfront understanding user needs (could be fellow students, faculty, etc.) and follow the process. It may lead your project to a more impactful result and teach your peers the methodology, too.
- On a personal level, consider using design thinking for something in everyday life—say, planning a family event or improving your daily routine. It might sound funny, but you can empathize with your family members' needs for that event, ideate ways to accommodate everyone, prototype (maybe try a rough agenda or arrangement), and get feedback. This informal use reinforces that design thinking is fundamentally about structured creative problem-solving, applicable anywhere.

In doing these, make use of some foundational tools and templates:

- Empathy maps (a simple quadrant to jot down what a user says, thinks, does, and feels) are excellent in the empathize phase to summarize insights about user emotions and behaviours.
- Journey maps can plot out the user's steps in the current process and highlight pain points and opportunities, a great way to define problems and see them holistically.
- How Might We… statements help frame ideation questions from insights (e.g., "How might we reduce the anxiety customers feel during checkout?" derived from empathy findings).
- Remember that prototypes can be low-fidelity in prototyping: sketches, paper interfaces, and role-playing scenarios. Don't over-invest time initially; the point is to learn cheaply. Use sticky notes, slide decks, or basic craft supplies. If it's a digital idea, you can use tools like Marvel, Figma, or Adobe XD, which have learning curves, but many offer templates or drag-and-drop ease for beginners to create clickable mockups.
- Prepare a simple feedback form or discussion guide for testing to capture what works and what does not. If testing in person, observe and take notes diligently, focusing on where the user seems confused or delighted.

By actively using these tools, they will move from concepts in a book to practical skills in your toolkit.

9.4.2 Tools and Technologies to Aid Your Design Thinking Work

We have talked about high-level trends like AI. Still, on a day-to-day level, many software tools and resources facilitate design thinking activities, especially in an era where teams may be remote or distributed. Here's a brief toolbox you might consider adopting, along with their purposes:

- **Collaboration and Whiteboarding Tools:** Mural, Miro, and FigJam are popular digital whiteboard platforms. They come with templates for empathy maps, journey maps, brainstorming, etc., which can guide you step by step. If your team is remote, these are invaluable for running virtual design thinking workshops (you can all stick digital notes on a board simultaneously, for example). They often have free tiers or educational licenses.
- **User Research and Empathy Tools:** Dovetail and UserZoom help organize user research, from transcription of interviews to tagging insights. Even something as simple as Otter.ai (for transcribing interviews and allowing you to highlight key quotes) can save time. If you need to conduct surveys as part of empathy, tools like Google Forms or Typeform can quickly gather input (considering surveys are less deep than interviews but good for reaching many people). Also, consider the wealth of publicly available user research: for many industries, there are whitepapers or forums where users voice opinions (e.g., Reddit communities, product review sites). Mining these can supplement your empathy work.
- **Ideation Tools:** Besides classic methods (post-its and brainstorming rules), some apps can spark creativity. For instance, there are random word or image generators that you can use in a mash-up ideation technique (combining a random prompt with your problem to think of new angles). There's an app called Brainstormer, which provides random constraints to provoke ideas. Even using AI chatbots (like ChatGPT) to generate a list of ideas or analogies can be a tool, so just remember to filter AI suggestions critically.
- **Prototyping Tools:** For digital prototypes (apps, websites), tools like Figma, Sketch, Adobe XD, or InVision Studio are standard. Figma is particularly popular for its collaboration features. Multiple team members can work on a design simultaneously, similar to Google Docs for design. It also has many community-created UI kits (pre-made elements) that can help you quickly assemble a realistic prototype without designing from scratch. For non-digital prototyping, sometimes the best tool is cardboard! Many teams have a prototyping cart filled with cardboard, foam core, markers, tape, Lego blocks, etc., to quickly build physical models. Consider setting up a small prototyping corner with such materials if you're in an office. For service experiences, you might use role-play; in that case, storyboarding templates (to sketch scenes of an experience) are useful, or just plain paper and pen.
- **Testing and Feedback Tools:** If you have a prototype ready to test with a wider audience and can't be there in person, consider using tools like UsabilityHub or Maze for quick remote usability tests or surveys on your design. They let you

show designs, ask questions, and gather user clicks and responses. Something like Hotjar can record user sessions for analysis if it is a live website prototype. But for many cases, especially early on, a simple approach works: share a prototype link (if digital) with a few target users, ask them to think aloud and record the session on Zoom or similar, and then review the recording for insights. Always combine quantitative feedback (e.g., "3 out of 5 users clicked the wrong button first") with qualitative (the why behind their actions).

- **Project Management for Iteration:** As you continue beyond one iteration, it helps to have a place to track insights, decisions, and next steps, whether that is a section in your collaboration board or a dedicated project space in tools like Notion or Trello. Some teams like to maintain a "design log", a simple document recording what they learned and what they will do after each test. It shows how the design evolved through user-centred iterations, which is great for keeping stakeholders in the loop and learning.

Remember that tools are aids, not solutions by themselves. The mindset and methods you've learned guide how to use these tools effectively. Try a few and see what fits your style and team's needs.

9.4.3 Further Learning: Books, Courses, and Resources

Design thinking is dynamic, and staying up-to-date or diving deeper is beneficial. Here are some highly recommended resources to continue your learning journey:

- **Books:** There are several seminal books on design thinking and related topics. If you enjoyed the concepts in this book, consider reading:
  - Change by Design by Tim Brown (2009). Written by the CEO of IDEO, this book lays out how design thinking can be applied to solve complex problems and transform organizations. It is filled with case studies from IDEO's work.
  - Creative Confidence by Tom Kelley and David Kelley (2013). A motivating read about unlocking everyone's creativity, with many anecdotes on how people overcame fear to innovate. It's very accessible and inspirational, reinforcing the individual mindset aspect.
  - The Human Side of Innovation by Mauro Porcini (2022). PepsiCo's design chief (whom we discussed) shares his perspective on building a culture of innovation focused on people. It's part memoir, part manifesto, and offers insight into real corporate change, echoing many points we covered in 9.3.
  - Designing for Growth by Jeanne Liedtka and Tim Ogilvie (2011). A more practical guide for managers, with step-by-step techniques and even worksheets. Jeanne Liedtka (a Darden professor) has done extensive research and writing on design thinking in business; any of her books or articles would be valuable, including Design Thinking for the Greater Good (2017), which focuses on social sector applications.
  - Sprint by Jake Knapp (2016). Details the Google Ventures 5-day design sprint process. It's a concrete methodology for a rapid design thinking cycle, which

you can try with your team. Many find it a useful framework for running a time-bound project, and it demonstrates the power of prototyping and testing in just a week.

These books will deepen your understanding and provide new examples and techniques beyond what we could cover here.

- **Online Courses and Certifications:** If you prefer structured learning or want a credential, there are numerous courses available:
  - IDEO U offers online courses in design thinking (Foundations in Design Thinking Certificate) and related topics (e.g., human-centred storytelling and unlocking creativity). Experienced IDEO practitioners teach these and have a mix of videos and assignments. IDEO U even has a newer offering combining AI and design thinking, reflecting cutting-edge practice.
  - Coursera has a popular sequence: Design Thinking for Innovation by Darden School (Univ. of Virginia). Jeanne Liedtka teaches it, and there is a Design Thinking specialization by the University of Virginia. There are also Human-Centered Design courses by UC San Diego on Coursera. These often include hands-on projects and peer feedback.
  - Acumen+ (with IDEO.org) previously offered a free course called Introduction to Human-Centered Design, which was project-based and team-oriented—check if they still offer sessions. It was a great primer, especially for social impact contexts.
  - IBM's Enterprise Design Thinking online course—IBM offers a badged course free on their website. It teaches their approach (which aligns with general design thinking), and you get an "Enterprise Design Thinking Practitioner" badge after passing a quiz. It's recognized and shows you've been through the basics with IBM's rigour.
  - Design Thinking Professional Certification (CDTP) by organizations like the Global Innovation Institute (GInI) is for those who want a formal certification. They typically require some training and an exam. While not universally required, a certification could demonstrate your commitment and knowledge to employers. Similar programs exist from LUMA Institute (they have workshops and certs in their system of design methods) and IDEO U's certificate, as mentioned.

  As with any education, the value comes from applying what you learn. So, if you take a course, try to do it with a real project in mind that you can work on as you go.

- **Communities and Events:** Engage with the vibrant global community of design thinkers. Some avenues:
  - Meetups: Many cities have design thinking or service design meetups where practitioners share experiences or do mini-workshops. It's a great way to network and learn locally. If none in your area, you might find virtual meetups/webinars post-2020 that you can join from anywhere.

- Global Design Thinking Alliance (GDTA) and Interaction Design Foundation (IxDF) communities often host talks and conferences.
- Design sprints or hackathons: Participating in a design sprint event or a hackathon (with a design thinking approach) can be an intense hands-on experience. Look out for innovation challenges in your industry or community; they often welcome people with a design-thinking mindset, and it's a chance to tackle a fresh problem and maybe even win recognition.
- Conferences: If possible, attend design or innovation conferences (e.g., IDEO's events, UX conferences, Service Design Global Conference, etc.). They expose you to the latest trends and success stories. Many conferences now have virtual attendance options or post talks online (for instance, TED talks related to design or talks from SXSW can be found on YouTube).

✦ **Company Resources:** Companies like IBM, IDEO, and Google have publicly available resources. IBM's design thinking site shares their Loop framework and techniques (like their Hills, Playbacks, etc.), which can be downloaded. Google has the Design Sprint Kit, which is available online for free. IDEO has IDEO.org's Design Kit (a free toolkit for social impact design) and IDEO's methods cards (which describe many methods in a handy format). These can serve as references when you plan your workshops or need inspiration for which method to use.

✦ **Journals and Articles:** If you are academically inclined, the Stanford Social Innovation Review often has articles on design thinking in social sectors. The Journal of Product Innovation Management sometimes covers design thinking research. Also, business magazines like Harvard Business Review have featured design thinking pieces (e.g., the famous 2015 HBR article "Design Thinking Comes of Age" by Jon Kolko). Keeping an eye on these can give insight into how thought leaders evaluate and evolve the practice.

Given that the field continues to evolve, I also want to stay curious about adjacent disciplines that complement design thinking: service design, system thinking, business model innovation, behavioural science, etc. Often, the best innovators pull from multiple disciplines.

9.4.4 Career Paths and Opportunities with Design Thinking

Understanding design thinking opens up a variety of career possibilities. Not everyone will become a "Design Thinking facilitator" by title (though that is a role in some consultancies), but the skillset is highly transferable and valued in many positions:

✦ **Design and UX roles:** Obvious paths include UX Designer, Product Designer, Service Designer, or Design Researcher. These roles explicitly involve doing the work we've covered: user research, prototyping, and iterative design. Suppose you enjoy the hands-on, creative aspects. In that case, you might pursue further training in visual design or human-computer interaction to complement your design thinking know-how, making you a strong candidate for such roles. More organizations are hiring design strategists, people who connect design thinking with business strategy, which could be appealing if you have domain expertise plus design thinking (for instance, someone with healthcare experience might become a healthcare design strategist at a consulting firm or large hospital network).

- **Innovation and Product Management roles:** Many companies have innovation teams, labs, or digital transformation groups, and they often seek people proficient in design thinking to lead workshops, manage innovation portfolios, or coach others. Titles might include Innovation Manager, Design Thinking Lead, or Product Innovation Specialist. Alternatively, product management has embraced design thinking, a Product Manager with strong design thinking skills is equipped to champion the user's perspective and drive a product's vision in a customer-centric way. You'd work cross-functionally, translating user insights into product features and prioritizing development based on user value.
- **Consulting and Facilitation:** Professional services firms (like McKinsey, Deloitte, Accenture), as well as specialized design consultancies (IDEO, Frog, Continuum, etc.), hire people to help client organizations solve problems and build capabilities using design thinking. It could be a path if you like working on diverse industry challenges. These roles require not only doing design thinking but teaching it because a big part of consulting now is facilitating design thinking workshops for clients and guiding them through innovation programs. Strong communication and workshop skills are key. Some independent consultants also build a career by facilitating workshops or training sessions for various organizations, effectively becoming design thinking coaches. For example, many ex-IDEO folks offer corporate training. If you want to move in that direction, accumulating experience through smaller workshops and getting certifications (like those from LUMA Institute or IDEO U) can lend credibility.
- **Entrepreneurship and Startups:** If you plan to start your own business or social enterprise, design thinking is almost a must-have approach to ensure you're building something people truly need. Entrepreneurs can use design thinking to iterate their business model, not just products. The Lean Startup method is very aligned. You'll run experiments (prototypes) and pivot based on feedback. Thus, one path is founding or joining a startup team as the design/customer experience champion. Some venture capital firms even seek founders with design backgrounds because they trust they will craft solutions users love. There is also a rise in impact ventures and NGOs using design thinking to address social issues. If your passion is more humanitarian, roles in organizations like Ideo.org, UNICEF Innovation, or various nonprofits applying HCD (human-centred design) could be fulfilling.
- **Other fields:** Even if you stay in your current field, design thinking can propel you. For example, in marketing, a person might leverage design thinking to deeply understand customer journeys and create better campaign experiences, making them stand out as a customer experience expert. In HR, people are using "employee experience design" to improve everything from recruitment to retention (sometimes called "talent experience" or "HR design thinking"). It has led to roles like Employee Experience Manager. If you're in engineering or

IT, you might become the user advocate and help the team adopt more iterative development, possibly moving into a UX Engineer or Product Owner role. Even in the public sector and policy, governments are hiring service designers to redesign public services (for instance, the UK's Government Digital Service famously used design thinking to revamp how citizens interact online with the government). So, whatever your domain, think about how design thinking principles can be applied and seek roles or initiatives that allow you to do so.

Aside from short courses, in terms of certifications or degrees for career, if you're considering further formal education, some universities now offer Master's programs in Design Thinking, Innovation Management, or Human-Centered Design. For example, the Hasso Plattner Institute in Germany (and its partnership with the University of Potsdam) offers a design thinking program. The Royal College of Art (UK) and Parsons (USA) have Transdisciplinary Design or Strategic Design programs. Though they are significant commitments, these can be great for a deep dive and networking.

Finally, keep a portfolio of your work. Document your design thinking projects even if your work is not "design" in the narrow sense. It could be a slide deck or case study write-ups showing the problem you tackled, how you applied the process, the outcome, and reflections. If you facilitated a workshop, note the outcome. If you led an innovation initiative, detail it (sensitive info aside). Employers increasingly ask for evidence of problem-solving ability and teamwork; a design thinking portfolio (with visuals like journey maps, prototypes, etc.) can impress because it shows you cannot only talk but have walked the walk. It sets you apart. You are not just saying, "I'm creative," but showing methodology and results.

9.4.5 Sustaining the Mindset and Spreading the Word

As you apply design thinking, it's important to continuously reflect and refine. A good habit is to do a retrospective for yourself or your team after each project or major use of design thinking: What went well? What could be improved in our approach? Perhaps you will discover you did not involve a certain stakeholder early enough, or you rushed from ideation to prototype without fully converging and, as a result, had to backtrack. These lessons will make you a better practitioner next time.

Also, as a newfound proponent of design thinking, you might face some scepticism in your organization or among peers. Not everyone immediately buys into post-it notes on walls or spends time in fuzzy front-end research. It is where your storytelling and persuasion skills matter. Tie design thinking efforts to outcomes that stakeholders care about. Did it reduce costs by eliminating a feature users didn't need? Did it increase customer satisfaction scores? Or even anecdotal wins like a customer testimonial after a redesign. Communicate these. Sometimes, small pilot wins can convince leadership to support scaling design thinking broadly. Be patient and use both data and narrative to make your case.

To sustain your personal growth, find a mentor or a peer group. Maybe someone more experienced in design thinking who can give feedback or someone at your level at another company to exchange experiences. Mentorship can guide you through political or practical hurdles in implementing design thinking. Meanwhile, mentoring others (once you have some experience) will also deepen your mastery. Teaching forces you to articulate the why and how solidifying your understanding. Perhaps you can volunteer to run a design thinking exercise for a local school or community group, and doing so will contribute to society and hone your facilitation chops.

Finally, the creative confidence and optimism that design thinking embodies should be kept. Not every problem will be solvable easily, real-world constraints can be challenging, and organizational change can be slow. But the mindset you've developed through this journey that problems can be approached creatively and collaboratively and that by understanding people, we can create meaningful change, is powerful. Even small improvements are worth celebrating, as they often pave the way for bigger ones. And sometimes, a string of small, human-centred changes can quietly revolutionize an entire experience.

As you move on, remember that design thinking is a team sport. Bring others along with you on this journey. In the next section, we provide some activities and exercises you can use with teams or for self-practice to reinforce these concepts. They're realistic scenarios that mirror what we discussed throughout this chapter. Engaging with those will prepare you to lead and participate in design thinking initiatives.

The world needs more design-minded leaders and problem solvers. Now you're well-equipped to be one of them. Keep learning, keep empathizing, and keep designing a better future.

KEY POINTS TO REMEMBER

1. Performance improvement can be achieved through strategic foresight, service design, and social innovation. Designing for trust and sustainability, and adapting to different contexts, is the key.
2. AI can enhance every stage of the design, from analysing user data to generating novel concepts and enabling rapid prototyping. Future system design must be such that it augments human creativity to guide AI tools.
3. A design-driven mindset that prioritises empathy, collaboration, and experimentation is more important than any tool. This is fostered by strong leadership, extensive training, and a method for integrating human-centred practices into our daily workflows.
4. Startups apply design thinking for immediate requirements and iteration, while large corporations institutionalise it to overcome resistance and scale innovation. Mutual learning will aid larger organizations to adopt agility, and startups to benefit from structured design practices.
5. Design thinkers are curious, empathetic, comfortable with uncertainty, and can apply multiple tools to solve diverse problems.

6. Mastering design thinking comes through practice and learning. Apply the concepts to common challenges that you observe everyday, explore available tools and resources, and build a portfolio of your problem-solving experiences.

KEY LEARNINGS

The Trends and Future, we traversed the evolving landscape of design thinking and drew several important insights:

- **Global and Cross-Industry Evolution:** Design thinking has become a global movement, now vital in numerous industries beyond design studios. Key trends include an increased focus on strategic foresight (designing for future needs, not just present) and leveraging design for trust and social impact. Companies are shifting from just solving immediate problems to anticipating tomorrow's opportunities using tools like trend mapping and integrating sustainable and inclusive design principles. We learned that as technology races ahead, the human-centric approach of design thinking is "more important than ever" to ensure empathy in innovation. Also, design thinking is being applied holistically, from product interfaces to end-to-end service experiences and even internal processes, marking a shift to viewing it as a mindset for problem-solving.
- **Developed vs. Emerging Markets:** The practice of design thinking varies by context. In developed markets, it often refines high-end user experiences and differentiates brands, whereas, in emerging markets, it converges with frugal innovation to create affordable solutions for basic needs. We saw that understanding cultural and resource differences is crucial. For example, what users value in an emerging market product (battery life, durability) might differ from a developed market. Frugal, human-centric solutions born in emerging contexts increasingly inspire global innovation (reverse innovation). The takeaway is that empathy must account for context: design thinking's core remains the same, but its execution adapts to whether one is addressing a tech-savvy urban consumer or a resource-constrained rural community. Both contexts benefit from design thinking, proving its versatility in solving complex and basic problems.
- **Corporations vs. Startups:** We examined how large enterprises and startups embrace design thinking differently. Large corporations are institutionalizing design thinking to overcome silos and inertia, exemplified by IBM training 100k+ employees and PepsiCo infusing design into its culture. Design thinking is becoming an enterprise capability measured and managed for ROI (Forrester found IBM's approach yielded faster workflows and strong ROI). Startups, conversely, often live design thinking implicitly through lean startup practices, rapid prototyping, iterating with user feedback, driven by urgency and necessity. They show us the pure form of "bias to action" and comfort with failure as learning. The key learning is that speed and user focus are common. Still, scale demands adaptation: big companies must cultivate an "urgency culture" to mimic startup agility, and startups should adopt some structure (like a customer development process)

to systematically harness their creativity. Ultimately, any organization, big or small, thrives by deeply understanding customers and iterating. It's the heart of innovation.

- **The Role of AI and Technology:** A major theme was that emerging technologies, especially AI, are not replacing design thinking but enhancing it. AI can supercharge the Empathize stage by analyzing big data for user insight patterns, augment ideation by generating ideas or variations (e.g., generative design), and accelerate prototyping/testing via simulations and automated feedback. Case studies illustrated this: Google's human-centred approach to AI (ensuring AI like Google Assistant is guided by user needs and feedback, a hospital's AI system that unexpectedly improved staff's emotional well-being by addressing human needs (safety and connection), and IBM's cognitive supply chain that used AI to empower employees with information, not replace them. The core learning is that AI and design thinking can yield smarter, personalized, and scalable solutions. Still, the designer's role is to ensure the technology serves human needs and stays transparent and ethical. We must design the AI's behaviour and integration as carefully as any user interface. In practice, the future designer is part creative and data-savvy, able to co-create with AI while upholding empathy and ethics.
- **Cultivating a Design-Driven Mindset:** We learned that tools and projects succeed in the long run only if backed by a supportive culture and mindset. Through examples like IBM and PepsiCo, it became clear that a design-driven mindset at an organization's top leads to structural changes: hiring or training people in design, altering processes to include user research and iteration, and measuring impact in new ways (like user satisfaction or alignment). Culturally, the traits of a design mindset include empathy (considering the user in every decision), experimentation (willingness to prototype and fail), collaboration across silos, and continuous learning. Final thoughts emphasized that as individuals, nurturing this mindset—being curious, user-focused, and creative, can make one an agent of change even in resistant environments. Building such a culture is an iterative design challenge, requiring empathy with colleagues and leadership to "align personal aspirations to corporate vision" and create champions of change. A big lesson here: design thinking is not just a process you do. It's a way you and your team operate. When that clicks, it sustains innovation beyond one project, becoming part of the organization's DNA.
- **Practical Steps Forward:** The chapter gave concrete advice for continuing the design thinking journey. We highlighted that bridging theory to practice is key: actively applying design thinking on small projects consolidates learning. There is a rich ecosystem of tools (digital whiteboards, prototyping software, user research platforms) and resources (courses, books, communities) to support ongoing development. We identified the importance of portfolio-building and possibly pursuing roles or certifications that solidify one's expertise. The reader is encouraged to see themselves as evolving designers with a roadmap for growth. The underlying message is empowerment: design thinking skills are highly transferable and increasingly sought-after, opening career pathways from

innovation leadership to social impact design. By planning the next training, a pilot project at work, or networking with like-minded practitioners, readers can convert what they have learned into tangible career and personal growth. In essence, the chapter ends by turning the focus to the reader's future, asking them to be proactive in applying design thinking to their own life and organization.

EXERCISES

To solidify the concepts from this chapter and give you hands-on practice, this section presents a set of practical activities and exercises. These are designed to be done either individually or (ideally) in a group, simulating real-world scenarios where you can apply design thinking. You will find a variety of exercise types: some focusing on strategic decision-making, others on empathy and problem definition, some on ideation with technology, and others on team collaboration. Each exercise is tied to a sub-section of this chapter, ensuring you reflect on and practice the ideas discussed. Feel free to adapt these scenarios to your context. You can perform these as role-plays or brainstorming sessions if you have a study group or workshop.

1. **Trend Spotting and Strategy Pitch Scenario:**
   You are part of an innovation strategy team at a large healthcare company. Your task is to brief the executive board on how global trends in design thinking (Section 9.1) could influence the company's next 5-year strategy..
   Step 1 (Research & Identify Trends): Individually, list out at least three major trends shaping the future of design thinking that are relevant to healthcare (e.g., increased focus on telehealth patient experience, frugal innovation for emerging markets, AI in medical diagnosis tools, etc.). Use evidence—a stat or example—for each trend (you may draw from this chapter or any current sources you know).
   Step 2 (Impact on Company): For each trend, discuss with your team how this trend might impact our company. For instance, if a trend is "design for trust," you might say: "Healthcare users increasingly demand transparency and empathy, we should design our services (like billing or informed consent processes) to build trust. It could improve patient retention." Jot down key points.
   Step 3 (Pitch Creation): As a group, create a brief 5-minute pitch to the board summarizing (a) what the trends are (explain each one succinctly) and (b) recommendations for the company (at least one action or initiative per trend). Example recommendation: "Invest in a human-centred design lab in India to capitalize on emerging market innovations, ensuring our product development is globally relevant." Ensure you articulate differences in approach for corporate vs. startup style (maybe your company needs to partner with startups for agility) or developed vs. emerging market focus, as applicable.
   Step 4 (Pitch & Feedback): Present your pitch to another group or mentor acting as an executives. Field their questions, e.g., "Why should we invest in design thinking capabilities? What's the ROI?" and practice using both data (like IBM/

PepsiCo success stories) and narrative (a mini-story of a patient's frustration turned delight through design). This not only practices trend analysis but also persuasion in advocating design thinking.

2. **Activity 9.2: AI-Augmented Design Challenge Scenario:**

   You are on a product team at a logistics startup (tying to Section 9.2's AI and case studies). Your challenge is improving recipients' package delivery experience using AI and design thinking. Deliveries sometimes fail because people aren't home or can't coordinate easily with couriers, causing frustration.

   Step 1 (Empathize with Users): Split roles in your team—some of you are interviewers/designers, others act as users. Role-play short interviews with two user types:

   (a) a busy working adult who often misses deliveries

   (b) a courier with many packages and a tight schedule. As designers, ask about their pain points (e.g., "Can you describe the last time you missed a delivery? What happened? How did you feel?" or ask the courier, "What is most frustrating about attempting a delivery and failing?"). Take notes of key quotes or emotions.

   Step 2 (Define the Problem): Come together and synthesize: write a POV statement like "Working professionals need a more flexible delivery method because they feel frustrated and helpless when they miss packages due to rigid delivery times." Also, consider the courier's perspective: "Couriers need a smarter way to route or reschedule deliveries on the fly because failed delivery attempts waste their time and upset customers." Ensure the problem definition reflects the human needs discovered.

   Step 3 (AI Ideation Storm): As a group, brainstorm how AI and tech could help solve this. Aim for at least five ideas. Use prompts from Section 9.2: Could we use an AI prediction model? (e.g., an app that learns the recipient's schedule patterns to predict the best delivery window) or a digital twin simulation? (e.g., simulate various delivery route changes if someone is not home), or perhaps a chatbot for recipients to communicate in real-time with couriers? Encourage wild ideas (like a smart delivery box with an AI lock that couriers can access securely). Use "How Might We" framing: "How might we leverage AI to make delivery more convenient?" and piggyback off each other's suggestions. If stuck, use a quick generative AI tool: ask ChatGPT or similar "What are innovative ways to improve last-mile delivery using technology?" See what it suggests, and evaluate those suggestions as a team.

   Step 4 (Select & Prototype): Choose one promising and user-centred idea. Say you choose an "AI-driven delivery scheduling system" that sends recipients a notification in the morning with a 1-hour delivery slot based on an AI prediction of when they'll likely be home. It allows them to adjust in an app (with an AI chatbot offering alternative times if needed). Sketch a prototype of the app interface or the service blueprint. One part of your team can sketch the recipient's app screen (notification, options to reschedule or leave instructions), and another can sketch the courier's interface (maybe an optimized route map updating in real-time as schedules change). If time permits, sketch what happens if the user is not home, maybe integrate with a nearby locker or neighbour as a backup. AI triggers those contingencies (e.g., after one failed attempt, the system auto-offers delivery to a locker).

Step 5 (Test via Role-Play): Now, role-play the scenario with your prototype. One member as the recipient: act out receiving the AI-driven notification, talk through using the prototype ("I see the app suggests 6-7 pm, but I would not be back till 7, so I ask the chatbot to reschedule to 7:30."). Another as the courier: simulate how the system updated their route ("My app tells me to skip this stop till 7:30 and fill in with another delivery first"). Have an observer watch and note any confusion or friction in the role-play. After, discuss: Did this solution address the needs? Maybe you find the user still does not trust the AI's prediction or wants manual control. That's an insight to refine. Or maybe the courier worries about user input causing constant changes. Maybe the AI should limit options to maintain efficiency.

Reflection: This exercise combines empathy, AI, prototyping, and testing. Discuss how AI made a difference in the solution (it provided real-time adaptation, which manual systems couldn't), and also what safeguards or design considerations emerged (like needing to keep user trust and not overwhelm courier—balancing AI and human needs). It mirrors real design cycles where tech and design must mesh.

3. **Cultivating Design Culture Simulation Scenario:**

   You have been tasked with introducing design thinking to a division in a conservative corporation (pick an industry like finance or government). The division's employees are used to traditional processes and are sceptical of "trendy" ideas. It relates to Section 9.3 on mindset and culture.

   Step 1 (Assessment Role-Play): Assign one person as the design thinking champion (that is you) and a few others as various stakeholders you'll talk to: e.g., a Senior Manager who cares about efficiency and ROI, an experienced Employee who's comfortable with how things are, and maybe an End-customer representative or junior staff open to new ideas. The champion should "interview" each stakeholder (in the role) to empathize with their perspective on problem-solving and innovation. For example, ask the manager, "What are your main concerns with trying a new approach like design thinking?" and ask the employee, "Have you seen any challenges in our current way of developing solutions?" Let them express reservations ("We have deadlines, we can't just experiment endlessly" or "I'm not sure talking to customers will reveal anything we don't already know"). It gives insight into cultural barriers.

   Step 2 (Define Strategy): Based on those inputs, define the core challenge as a group: "How might we demonstrate the value of a human-centred approach in a low-risk way so that the team feels comfortable and sees benefits?" Write a brief problem/opportunity statement like that. Essentially, treats the culture change as a design problem. Your "users" are your colleagues whose mindsets need shifting, and you need to meet their needs (for safety, for results) while introducing new practices.

Step 3 (Ideate Initiatives): Brainstorm ways to introduce and cultivate a design-driven mindset in this division. Use ideas from 9.3: examples like organizing a small pilot project addressing a known pain point, where you use design thinking and invite sceptics to participate and see outcomes first-hand, or bringing in a customer to share their story at a team meeting to spark empathy; or setting up a wall with user feedback (visualizing customer quotes) in the office as daily reminders; or lunch-and-learn sessions where you do a mini design exercise (like marshmallow challenge or a journey mapping of an internal process) to give them a fun taste. Also, consider how to align with existing values: if efficiency is prized, maybe frame design thinking as reducing rework by getting requirements right via user input; if innovation is in their mission statements, highlight that this method feeds innovation. Be creative, maybe create a friendly competition or "innovation day" where teams try design thinking on small issues. List 3-5 initiative ideas.

Step 4 (Plan & Role-Play the Pitch): Now outline an action plan combining these ideas. For instance: Plan: "Start with a 2-day design thinking workshop focused on improving our employee onboarding process (an internal issue everyone knows needs work). Have volunteer reps from each team join (especially include one of the sceptics). Day 1, we bring in 3 recent hires to share their onboarding experiences (build empathy), map the journey, and identify issues. On day 2, we ideate and prototype a better onboarding approach and present it to management. We measure success by improvements in new hire satisfaction next quarter. Meanwhile, share quick wins through an internal newsletter." Also, plan follow-up: perhaps monthly short sessions to tackle other small problems and gradually build a norm. Now, role-play, pitching this plan to the Senior Manager stakeholder. One of you is the champion explaining the proposal, and another is the manager questioning it ("How does this affect our bottom line? Who will do their regular work if they're in a workshop?"). Practice addressing concerns: e.g., "We've scoped it small to limit time away (only 2 days with a small team). If it's successful, we expect to reduce new hire turnover, which saves considerable cost. I have data that poor onboarding cost us X last year. Plus, the team will learn skills to apply on other projects." Use references: maybe mention IBM or PepsiCo examples to reassure that even big companies benefit. Also, mention intangible benefits like alignment and employee morale, as experienced in those caseson.

Step 5 (Debrief): Discuss what tactics felt persuasive as a group. Did the stakeholder buy-in when hearing about competitor or industry success? Did focusing on a specific pilot (instead of abstract culture talk) help? How did addressing their personal needs (e.g., manager's need for ROI) smooth the way? Reflect on how cultivating a mindset is an exercise in empathy and iterative persuasion. You might need to try a small thing, show value, and expand (iteration!). This exercise prepares you to be a change agent in real life, anticipating resistance and finding empathetic ways to address it, much like Porcini did by connecting personally and IBM by demonstrating measurable wins.

4. **Personal Design Thinking Roadmap Scenario:**

   It is an individual-focused exercise (moving from Section 9.4) where you create a personal action plan to continue your design thinking development and integrate it into your career or studies.

   Step 1 (Self-Reflection Quiz): Answer the following for yourself: (a) Which stage of design thinking do I feel strongest in (Empathize, Define, Ideate, Prototype, Test)? Which do I feel weakest in? (b) How have I applied design thinking so far (in coursework, at work, personal projects)? What was the outcome? (c) What problems am I passionate about solving (tech products, social issues, business strategy, etc.)? And how could design thinking play a role? Jot down answers succinctly. This self-empathy helps identify areas to focus on.

   Step 2 (Learning Goals): Set 2–3 learning or skill goals based on the above. For example: "Improve prototyping skills, specifically learn Figma to create interactive app prototypes," "Gain experience facilitating design thinking with a team," or "Apply design thinking to a community project in sustainability (my passion area) to build domain experience." Make them specific.

   Step 3 (Resource and Action Mapping): List resources or actions for each goal. If the goal is learning a tool, find an online course or set aside 2 hours a week to practice that tool on a pet project. If the goal is facilitation, maybe plan to volunteer to lead a small workshop at work or with friends; also, perhaps paired with a mentor or colleague who can observe and give feedback. If domain project, identify local organizations or competitions around that theme (e.g., join a civic design challenge or propose a project to an NGO you volunteer at). Also, list any readings or communities from 9.4.3 that align with goals (e.g., if interested in social impact, maybe take an Acumen+ HCD course or read "Design Thinking for the Greater Good"). Basically, for each target, what concrete next steps will you take?

   Step 4 (Timeline and Accountability): Sketch a simple 6-12 month timeline. For instance: "By next 3 months, complete IDEO U Foundations course; by 6 months—have one case study of an applied project to put in a portfolio; by 12 months—attain XYZ certification or get a role on an innovation project at work." It can be rough. Also, who can help keep you accountable or be a sounding board? Note a friend, mentor, or online group where you can share progress. Perhaps write an entry on a forum about your plan to make it "public."

   Step 5 (Role-play the future & obstacles): Imagine it's a year from now and you achieved one of your goals—describe briefly what you did and the result (e.g., "I facilitated a 1-day hackathon at my company that produced two prototype ideas for improving customer onboarding, one of which is now being developed. As a result, leadership trusts me to lead more design sessions."). Imagine one obstacle in your way (e.g., "I struggle to convince my manager to let me spend time on this training/project"). Role-play (with a partner or just in writing) how you address it using your design thinking mindset (maybe empathize with the manager's perspective and find a win-win, or iterate on approach by doing something on your own time to show value). By visualizing success and challenges, you prepare yourself.

Step 6 (Execute & Iterate): This is not just a paper exercise. Commit to starting on Step 3's actions within the next week. To keep it dynamic, treat your roadmap as a living prototype: revisit it every couple of months to adjust based on opportunities that arise or new interests that develop.

This personal exercise ensures you don't just leave the learnings in this book but actively weave them into your growth. It's about designing your journey. An ultimate meta-use of design thinking where you are both designer and user! Share your roadmap with a mentor or peer for feedback (test your plan, so to speak) and then refine and follow it.

Each of these activities is designed to encapsulate chapter concepts tangibly. By engaging in them, you're effectively doing what the chapter preaches: combining theory with practice, reflecting on successes and failures, working collaboratively, and focusing on real human needs (whether those are your customers', colleagues', or your own). They should also be enjoyable and eye-opening, reinforcing an important tenet: design thinking is as much about mindset and teamwork as it is about methods.

Feel free to adapt scenarios to better fit your context. The more realistic and relevant you make them, the more you and your peers will gain. Don't hesitate to create additional exercises, maybe a spin-off of Activity 9.2 focusing on another sector, a role-play debating a design ethics dilemma (AI bias, etc.), or a creative ideation game. The possibilities are endless; use design thinking to design learning experiences too!

THOUGHT-PROVOKING QUESTIONS

Reflect on the chapter content with these higher-order thinking questions. They are designed to provoke analysis, synthesis, and application of the concepts, going beyond mere recall. Use them to test your understanding or as discussion prompts in a study group. Each question requires you to draw on multiple sections of the chapter and possibly your own experience:

1. **Trend Application:** Choose one major trend discussed in Section 9.1 (for example, the focus on trust or the rise of design thinking in emerging markets). How would you apply this trend to innovate in a specific industry or sector of your choice? Outline a brief scenario of the industry's current state, the trend's relevance, and a design thinking-led initiative that leverages the trend. For instance, if you pick "designing for trust," you might apply it to social media platforms, describing how a platform could redesign its features and policies through design thinking to rebuild user trust. What challenges might you face, and how would you address them using the principles from this chapter?
2. **AI and Empathy Analysis:** Section 9.2 shows how AI can enhance empathy by analyzing user data. Consider a situation where AI analysis and direct user interviews give conflicting insights (e.g., data shows a feature is used frequently, but interview users say they dislike it). How should a design team reconcile this conflict? Frame your answer in a design thinking approach, perhaps discussing how you would iterate the research (maybe the users who dislike it still use it due

to lack of alternatives, a nuance data alone didn't show). What does this tell you about the importance of combining quantitative and qualitative empathy methods?

3. **Culture Change Evaluation:** Section 9.3 detailed how companies like IBM and PepsiCo transformed their culture. Imagine you are evaluating your own organization's design thinking maturity and culture. What key indicators would you look for to assess how design-driven it is currently? Consider structure (like, is there a head of design or cross-functional teams?), process (do projects include user research and prototyping cycles?), people (are non-designers conversant with design thinking?), and outcomes (any notable innovative successes attributed to design thinking?). Based on your evaluation, propose two concrete steps to advance your organization's design maturity, explaining why you chose those and how you'd measure success.
4. **Ethical Design Scenario:** With the integration of AI (Section 9.2), ethical considerations become critical. Present a scenario where a design team must address a potential ethical issue arising from an AI feature (for example, AI making decisions that lack transparency to users or biases in an algorithm affecting certain user groups). How should the team apply design thinking to resolve or mitigate this ethical issue? Outline the steps: empathy (understanding impacted users' concerns), define (articulate the ethical problem clearly), ideate (possible solutions like explainable AI interfaces or bias mitigation strategies), prototype (perhaps simulate the solution with users), and test (getting feedback specifically on whether the ethical concern is alleviated). What principles from design thinking help ensure the solution is responsible and user-centred?
5. **Startup vs. Corporate Application:** Sections 9.1.3 and 9.1.4 discuss differences between startup and corporate approaches. Suppose you have experience in one environment (say, a startup) and join the other (a large corporation). What elements of the startup design thinking approach would you try to introduce to the corporation, and conversely, what aspects of a mature corporate approach might you bring back to a startup? Formulate your answer as a comparative analysis. For example, you might bring the rapid experimentation and "fail-fast" attitude from startup to corporate (and explain how you'd implement that in a risk-averse setting) and bring a bit more structure or user research rigour from corporate to a freewheeling startup (explaining how that can improve outcomes). This question tests your ability to adapt practices to context and appreciate the value each can learn from the other.
6. **Personal Plan Defense:** Referencing Section 9.4, imagine you're in a job interview or performance review, and you're asked: "How do you plan to develop your design thinking competency further, and how will that benefit our organization?" Formulate a response that outlines a personal development plan (perhaps mentioning a certification you aim for, an initiative you want to lead, etc.) and explicitly link it to organizational value. Essentially, practice articulating the case you compellingly made in Activity 9.4. You should draw on chapter points (e.g., citing how design-led companies outperform others or how cross-functional design

skills can save cost by reducing project failure rates). This question is about applying your knowledge to advocate for yourself and the methodology in a real-world scenario.

7. **Design Thinking Beyond Design:** One chapter's theme is that design thinking spreads beyond traditional design fields (e.g., into HR, strategy, and policy). Propose how design thinking could be applied to a non-traditional domain, such as human resources, education, or government policy-making. Choose one domain and outline a specific problem (for instance, high employee turnover in HR, remote learning engagement in education, or low public uptake of a government program). Describe how you would apply the design thinking stages to tackle that problem. What unique challenges might that domain present (like bureaucracy in government or measurement of success in education), and how could the design thinking mindset help overcome them? It tests your ability to transfer and adapt what you learned to any context.
8. **Critical Reflection:** Critique one potential limitation or challenge of design thinking in the future that was not explicitly discussed in the chapter. Provide a thoughtful analysis of why it's a concern and how practitioners might address it. For instance, you could discuss the risk of diluting design thinking as it becomes a buzzword (everyone says they do it, but not deeply) or the scalability challenge. Can every employee truly be empowered as a "designer"? Or perhaps there is a tension between data-driven approaches and human intuition (as AI grows, will designers lean too much on data and lose sight of empathy?). Use insights from the chapter to inform your critique, but also think beyond it. Then, suggest solutions: e.g., to avoid buzzword fatigue, ensure training is accompanied by real projects and leadership modelling the behaviour, maintain empathy in a data world, set guidelines for "no data without context" in teams, etc. This question encourages you to engage critically and not just champion design thinking unilaterally, recognizing it, like any methodology, has to continuously prove and renew itself.

Discussing and answering these questions will reinforce a deeper understanding of the chapter's content and practical implications. They encourage connecting the dots between trends, tools, mindset, and real outcomes, which is the essence of strategic design thinking. There are often no single "right" answers, especially for scenarios and open-ended challenges. Still, a strong answer will reference chapter learnings (and even specific examples or data points) while demonstrating original thought and foresight.

REFERENCES

Blank, S. (2014, July 30). Driving Corporate Innovation: Design Thinking + Customer Development. Steve Blank Blog. Retrieved April 8, 2025, from https://steveblank.com/2014/07/30/driving-corporate-innovation-design-thinking-customer-development/

Core77. (2013, November 21). How "Snow White" Is Turning Airbnb into a Service Design Company. Core77.com. Retrieved April 8, 2025, from https://www.core77.com/

posts/25743/How-Snow-White-is-Turning-Airbnb-into-a-Service-Design-Company-and-Other-Highlights-from-the-Service-Experience-Conference-2013

Renganathan, V. (2020, January 24). A New Study on Design Thinking is Great News for Designers. IBM Design Blog on Medium. Retrieved April 8, 2025, from https://medium.com/design-ibm/a-new-study-on-design-thinking-is-great-news-for-designers-593f71b40627

Soni, P. (2019, March 15). Frugal Innovation: Creating and Capturing Value in Emerging Markets. IMD Knowledge. Retrieved April 8, 2025, from https://www.imd.org/research-knowledge/articles/frugal-innovation-creating-and-capturing-value-in-emerging-markets/

Tarei, P. K. (2024). Design Thinking for Frugal Innovation: Unleashing Sustainable Business Models in Emerging Markets. Proceedings of the 19th European Conference on Innovation and Entrepreneurship (ECIE). Retrieved April 8, 2025, from https://papers.academic-conferences.org/index.php/ecie/article/view/2417

VKTR. (2023, May 22). 5 AI Case Studies in Logistics. VKTR Insights. Retrieved April 8, 2025, from https://www.vktr.com/ai-disruption/5-ai-case-studies-in-logistics/

Index